THE ART OF
M&A INTEGRATION

THE ART OF M&A INTEGRATION

A Guide to Merging Resources, Processes, and Responsibilities

Second Edition

ALEXANDRA REED LAJOUX

McGraw-Hill

New York   Chicago   San Francisco   Lisbon   London   Madrid
Mexico City   Milan   New Delhi   San Juan   Seoul   Singapore
Sydney   Toronto

The *McGraw·Hill* Companies

1 2 3 4 5 6 7 8 9 0 DOC/DOC 0 9 8 7 6 5

ISBN 0-07-144810-1

McGraw-Hill books are available at special quantity discounts to use as premiums and sales promotions, or for use in corporate training programs. For more information, please write to the Director of Special Sales, McGraw-Hill Professional, Two Penn Plaza, New York, NY 10121-2298. Or contact your local bookstore.

 This book is printed on recycled, acid-free paper containing a minimum of 50% recycled de-inked fiber.

Library of Congress Cataloging-in-Publication Data

Lajoux, Alexandra Reed.
    The art of M&A integration : a guide to merging resources,
processes, and responsibilities / by Alexandra Reed Lajoux.— 2nd ed.
        p. cm.
    Includes bibliographical references and index.
    ISBN 0-07-144810-1 (hardcover : alk. paper)
    1. Consolidation and merger of corporations. I. Title:
Art of M and A integration. II. Title.
HD2746.5.L35 2006
658.1'62—dc22

                                        2005027353

To my son Franklin, a wise entrepreneur in the spirit of Benjamin

CONTENTS

Chapter 3

Integration Planning and Communication   35

PART TWO

Integrating Resources   107

Chapter 4

Retaining and Integrating Human Resources   111

Chapter 8

Integrating Compensation Plans   261

Chapter 9

Integrating and Enhancing Technology and Innovation   293

PART FOUR

Integrating Corporate Responsibilities—Fulfilling Stakeholder Commitments   355

Chapter 10

Fulfilling Commitments to Customers and Suppliers   357

Chapter 11

Fulfilling Commitments to Shareholders, Bondholders, and Lenders   387

Chapter 12

Fulfilling Commitments to Employees and Communities   417

APPENDIXES

To the second edition

Most major companies in the world today have experienced a merger or acquisition at some point in their history. And at any given time, thousands of these companies are adjusting to postmerger reality.

For example, during the past five years (from January 1, 2000, to December 31, 2004), some 300,000 companies around the globe have either made acquisitions or been acquired—and that's just counting acquisitions valued at $10 million and over. In recent years, a significant percentage of the transactions have been large. In 2004, for example, merger partners closed nearly 400 transactions valued at $1 billion or more—compared to fewer than 100 such transactions a decade before. In 2005, the pace and scale has continued, with nearly 5,000 U.S. companies being involved in mergers worth $10 million or more during the first six months of the year, inspiring predictions of a $1 trillion-plus total in merger values for the year. Add to this the merger experience of many smaller companies, as well as that of nonprofit and governmental entities large and small, and the M&A universe becomes large indeed. To be sure, acquisition activity rises and falls based on a number of economic and strategic factors. But even during times of relatively low merger activity, the fact remains that *acquisitions are a permanent strategic option for businesses and organizations around the world.* Thus, as a routine part of strategic planning, every company should prepare for the eventuality of combining with another company.

In recognition of this fact, a "cottage industry" of integration specialists has arisen to provide guidance in postmerger integration. These consultants and other have made a market for a variety of books on postmerger integration—including this one. Ever since its original appearance in December 1997, *The Art of M&A Integration* has gone through 10 printings, showing that readers continue to find its general framework useful. In the past decade, however, the business world has changed, rendering parts of the book obsolete.

Some companies mentioned in the original edition have taken new names—often as a result of a merger. Furthermore, and perhaps more important, new rules and regulations have affected postmerger integration.

Here are some of the changes reflected in this edition.

- The Financial Accounting Standards Board's (FASB's) elimination of "pooling" accounting (July 1999) changed the reporting of postmerger financial results, depressing some acquirers' "bottom lines." (Pooling accounting had been favorable to income statements.) In addition, the FASB has issued several other new standards that affect postmerger accounting.
- The bankruptcies of Enron (December 2001) and WorldCom (May 2002) heightened financial vigilance on the part of directors, managers, and internal and external auditors.
- The passage of the Sarbanes-Oxley Act (July 2002), as well as subsequent rules issued by the Securities and Exchange Commission, raised the bar for internal financial controls and institutional ethics.
- New listing rules on the New York Stock Exchange and the Nasdaq (November 2003) codified high standards for board involvement in the oversight of many corporate areas, including financial performance and senior executive compensation.
- Several major new transactions, such as the $41 billion merger between Cingular and AT&T in 2004, or the $36 billion Sprint-Nextel merger in 2005, have posed new challenges and inspired new solutions.

Like the original edition of *The Art of M&A Integration*, this one uses a question-and-answer format. Every query is a *practical question* that would naturally occur to a competent business executive involved in a merger. And every response is a *straightforward answer* based on interviews with leading experts and supported by extensive research. These experts are acknowledged in the introductions to the four parts of this book. The joint contributions of these M&A experts truly "make" this book—so much so that I, as author, will be using the editorial "we" more than once in the following pages. In the course of the book, readers will be treated to expert views on real cases involving companies large and small. In order to focus on principles rather than personalities, however, these mini-cases name individual executives only when this would make the example easier to understand or recognize.

Most of the principles discussed in this book apply to companies around the world. Although the regulatory information in this book is "made in the U.S.A.," readers from other countries may find it instructive as a model. Also, every chapter contains a brief discussion of issues that arise in cross-border mergers.

We hope to add *your* expertise to future editions of this book. Achieving excellence in the M&A field, like any other, is a collective journey.

If you have questions that this book does not answer, or comments on any of our answers, please e-mail them to *arlajoux@aol.com*.

Alexandra Reed Lajoux
Arlington, Virginia
December 2005

ACKNOWLEDGMENTS

In the first edition of this book, my family and friends received well deserved acknowledgments for their support, which continues to this day. This second edition is dedicated to my long-time employer, the National Association of Corporate Directors, for giving me an opportunity to work with a talented and visionary team to foster and champion the worthy cause of sound corporate governance. I also wish to acknowledge the superb professionals at McGraw-Hill, including senior editor Stephen Isaacs, publisher Jeffrey Krames, editing supervisor Daina Penikas, copy editor Alice Manning, proofreader Valerie Miller, and the other dedicated McGraw-Hill employees and contractors who have contributed their skills and knowledge to the production and marketing of this book.

In closing, sincere thanks to Kelli Christiansen, who made so many sterling editorial contributions to this and other "Art of M&A" series books in her years at McGraw-Hill.

A. M. D. G.

THE ART OF
M&A INTEGRATION

PART ONE

Prerequisites

Great is the art of beginning . . .

Henry Wadsworth Longfellow,
Elegiac Verse

INTRODUCTION AND ACKNOWLEDGMENTS

When two companies come together through a merger or acquisition, they face many changes. This section, "Prerequisites," can be a compass for navigating them.

Chapter 1, "Basic Definitions and Data," provides basic terminology and a review of leading research on the subject of post-merger performance. Scholars quoted here include Robert F. Bruner, Dean, Darden Graduate School of Business, University of Virginia, and John Fred Weston, Cordner Professor of Money and Financial Markets, Graduate School of Management, University of California at Los Angeles. Their research refutes the common assertion that most mergers fail to deliver value.

Chapter 2, "The Path to Integration," traces the strategic decision making that leads to integration. This chapter contains general guidance from Kenneth W. Smith, of Mitchell Madison in Toronto, Canada; Harvey Pitt, former chairman of the Securities and Exchange Commission, now head of Kalorama Partners, Washington, D.C.; and Peter D. Goodson, former principal, Clayton, Dubelier & Rice, Inc., and now adjunct professor at the Haas School of Business, University of California, Berkeley.

Chapter 3, "Integration Planning and Communication," explains how to form and communicate a postmerger integration plan. Our chief planning experts here were George A. Steiner, Kunin Professor of Management emeritus, Graduate School of Management, University of California at Los Angeles, and Manuel Sanches, president and co-founder, E-know, Inc. (eknow.com), in Arlington, Virginia. Their planning checklists (with several M&A-specific additions) should be very useful to managers as they chart their postmerger reality. Jim Jeffries, CEO, M&A Partners, Dallas, Texas, shared his successful experience in recruiting outsourced managers to help plan an integration. Comments on the role of third parties in postmerger planning were provided by William J. Altier, CMC, president, Princeton Associates, Buckingham, Pennsylvania. Mark J. Feldman, senior vice president of strategy at Versa Systems, Inc., in Fremont, California, gave guidance on the importance of position statements in postmerger planning.

Observations on the typical merger agreement and on the legal aspects of communicating the M&A plan came from Gabor Garai and Susan Pravda, partners in Foley & Lardner, LLP, Boston, Massachusetts, who also provided valuable commentary for the chapter as a whole. Experienced guidance on communications came from Michael J. Reilly, president of Hally Enterprises, Inc., Babylon, New York, and William F. Mahoney, an author and investor relations consultant based in West Chester, Pennsylvania. Eugene Grossman, partner, Siegel & Gale, and former chairman, Anspach Grossman Enterprises, New York, provided the "Audience/Media Communications Matrix" at the end of the chapter. Price Pritchett, chairman and CEO of Pritchett, in Plano, Texas, provided remarks on postmerger scenarios.

The tools at the end of Chapter 3 were provided courtesy of the co-founders of E-Know, Inc., Arlington, Virginia Manuel Sanches and Larry Dell.

CHAPTER 1

Basic Definitions and Data

All M&A is local.

Robert F. Bruner,
Deals from Hell

INTRODUCTION

Every year, thousands of companies, large and small, public and private, join forces through merger or acquisition, hoping to accomplish together what they could not accomplish separately. But will they make the grade? Their success depends in part on the effectiveness of their integration. On paper, many corporate marriages have "synergy." That is, they hold out a promise that when it comes to corporate performance, two plus two will equal something more than four. This is one reason that so many sellers can convince so many buyers to pay a generous premium over the stock price or a high multiple of sales. Yet a buyer will meet with disappointment unless he or she can make that "plus factor" happen—and that result often depends on thorough, rapid integration.

A typical acquisition announcement will state that the two companies are merging in order to combine specific aspects of themselves—for example, to gain greater efficiency in buying, selling, and producing. (Consider, for example, the gains in procurement, sales, administration, and manufacturing cited by IMCO Recycling and Commonwealth Industries in their June 2004 merger announcement, creating Aleris International.[1]) But wherever the strongest points of synergy may lie, combining some aspects of two companies (for example, the functions just listed) will almost certainly require combining *all* aspects of these companies. This introductory chapter offers basic definitions and data for use in merger integration.

THE MEANING OF INTEGRATION

What is M&A integration?

The term *M&A integration* refers primarily to the art of combining two or more companies (not just on paper, but in reality) after they have come under common ownership. *M&A* refers to the merger or acquisition transaction that leads to the combination, and *integration* refers to the combining of elements that will enable the two companies to function as one.

M&A integration can involve entities other than companies (for example, nonprofit and governmental organizations) and transactions other than mergers or acquisitions (for example, joint ventures, strategic alliances, and partial acquisitions). This book, however, will emphasize standard mergers and acquisitions involving two companies, with occasional references to these other applications.

M&A integration should be planned well in advance, from the planning phase through the transaction phase. For a diagram of all the phases, see Appendix A in the back of this book.

Is integration following a merger different from integration following an acquisition?

It depends on how you are using the term *merger*.

In the narrow, technical sense, there is no difference. *Acquisition* describes any transfer of ownership, whereas *merger* describes a transfer of ownership in which one entity legally disappears into the other, or both entities disappear into a third entity created for the purpose of the merger. These terms describe the nature of the *transaction* that brings two companies together, not the nature of their subsequent life together.

In the more common, *non*technical sense, however, the term *merger* is used generally for any acquisition consummated with a *plan for integration* of significant resources, operations, and/or technology. So, for example, Kmart's union with Sears was structured as an acquisition, but the companies referred to it as a merger.[2] In this book, we will use the term *merger* in this ordinary sense.

Don't all buyers and sellers count on postmerger integration?

No. Some buyers purchase companies merely in order to hold them for eventual resale, as one would hold a stock. These nonsynergistic acquirers are often referred to as "financial" (as opposed to "strategic") acquirers because their sole purpose is to achieve a return on the acquisition by putting it under new ownership—even if only by holding it and reselling it. They have no intention of integrating the resources, operations, or technology of the acquired company into their own company. These acquirers, which are typically (but not always) buyout funds, do not so much manage as *monitor* the resources that they acquire. And, as explained in Chapter 2, "The Path to Integration," this monitoring activity—often backed by financial restructuring—can yield substantial returns if the buyer has a financial *culture* and a relatively low cost of capital.

What is the difference between a financial culture and a strategic culture?

A *financial culture* treats each acquired company as a separate entity. In such a culture, exemplified by the buyout firm of Kohlberg Kravis Roberts (KKR), the buyer tries to add value by imposing superior, top-down management strategies in a short period of time. Financial acquisitions can be fairly diverse. Although these deals may be related to the acquirers' areas of expertise, the companies acquired need not be integrated into the acquirers' operations to yield good returns, as we will see in Chapter 2.

A *strategic culture*, by contrast, treats each acquired company as a new member of the acquirer's corporate family. In such a culture, exemplified by General Electric, the *acquired company itself* adds value to the acquiring company by being integrated into the buyer's existing operations. Strategic acquisitions (commonly referred to as mergers for the reasons mentioned earlier) often involve combinations of companies in the same or related industries.

Mergers within the same industry can reduce costs (usually by reducing the cost of payroll by laying off employees) and/or increase revenues (usually by increasing the customer base).

What about acquisitions outside the acquirer's existing business? Can't these be strategic?

Yes, they can be, but the burden is on the company to have the right strategy and to implement it well through integration. When companies cannot make the connection work, they spin off the parts that did not integrate well. (For more about spin-offs, see Chapter 2.)

Given the ever-changing nature of business and technology, how can we say that a given company is "inside" versus "outside" an acquirer's core domain?

As a matter of fact, we really can't. This determination is a matter of degree. We might think of corporate growth in linear terms. There are basically three directions for strategic growth (horizontal, vertical, and diagonal), as the following merger examples illustrate.

A company can expand

- *Horizontally* by buying a competitor in its present geographic territory or in a new one, as when Cingular bought AT&T and Sprint bought Nextel (in the wireless telephone industry) and when Kmart bought Sears (in the retailing industry)—all major transactions in 2004 and 2005. Other examples are the merger between the American brewer Adolph Coors and Canada's Molson, which shareholders approved as Molson Coors in February 2005; the May 2005 merger of US Airways and America West; and International Monetary Systems' July 2005 acquisition of International Barter Network Corp.
- *Vertically* by buying a current supplier or a customer, as in the 2004 merger of IMCO Recycling, an aluminum recycler, with Commonwealth Industries, a sheet manufacturer. For a press release on vertical integration, see Appendix E.
- *Diagonally*[3] by buying into a new market that is tangentially related to its existing core—typically a new product or

service line that can be marketed through current distribution channels, as in the classic 1985 merger of R.J. Reynolds Industries and Nabisco Brands, which blended tobacco and food products; or the 1996 merger of Duracell and Gillette, which added batteries to a shelf full of other consumer products; or IBM's 2002 acquisition of the consulting arm of PricewaterhouseCoopers. More recently, in May 2004, AXA, a major Paris-based insurer, bought MONY, a New York–based financial services firm, citing opportunities to cross-sell the companies' products through merged sales channels. Sometimes diagonal transactions involve product *development*, not just product distribution, as in the merger between Procter & Gamble and Gillette, which was approved by shareholders in July 2005.[4]

How successful are mergers generally? Isn't it true that most of them turn out to be failures?

The answer to this question depends on how you define *failure*. If you are not sure about your definition, you are not alone. In the past half century, scholars have published *hundreds* of studies of postmerger financial performance, and few have defined failure (or, conversely, success) in exactly the same way.

When failure is defined in extreme terms, such as the eventual liquidation or sale of the unit, then failure rates are low—under 20 percent. When failure is defined as an inability to reach certain financial norms, such as significant growth in net income or return on equity, then reported failure rates can be high—up to 80 percent.

Overall, M&A activity does produce positive results for participants. Robert Bruner's recent comprehensive review of M&A research—a 2004 study of more than 100 studies[5]—found that, in general,

- Shareholders of *selling firms* earn *large* returns.
- Shareholders of *buyers and sellers combined* earn *significant* returns.
- Shareholders of *buyers* usually earn the *required rate of return*.

Bruner's conclusions square with a 2003 Federal Trade Commission study comparing research from several major consulting firms. (See Appendix 1-A.)

Based on this research, what factors contribute to successful merger activity?

A number of factors can contribute to success. Here is a list of some commonly cited success factors, along with concrete actions that managers can take to secure them. Illustrative company quotes (based on typical press release language) follow.

1 *Strategic motivation.* **Action:** Take concrete steps to achieve the strategy: "This merger will fulfill our goal of expanding our distribution network. As part of our acquisition agreement, all the sellers' agreements with distributors will transfer to the new firm."

2 *Clear relation to core business.* **Action:** Buy a company in a similar or the same business: "Our core business is to provide superior customer service in apparel retail. Our purchase of this well-respected apparel franchise complements and helps build our legacy."

3 *Economic pricing.*[6] **Action:** Authorize or engage professional valuation services (not guesswork): "We will pay $X for this merger. This price is based on analysis by our internal financial staff, advised by external experts in this industry."[7]

4 *Prudent cash- or debt-based financing.* **Action:** Use cash, debt, or notes (not stock) to pay for the purchase:[8] "The purchase price will be paid in cash. To help finance this transaction, we took out a loan at favorable lending rates based on our sound credit rating. Our cash flow will support repayment of the debt."

5 *Efficient integration planning.* **Action:** Use the tools of project management—with leaders, goals, phases, deadlines, and resources. "This integration will take 100 days. This memo describes the actions we will take and the people responsible for the actions."

So far we've talked about acquisition integration. What is reintegration?

Reintegration has three meanings in business:

- First, *reintegration* is a macroeconomic term referring to consolidation in a market previously known for fragmentation. (Economists talk about reintegration in the telecommunications industry as mergers today undo some of the fragmentation following the breakup of the old AT&T into the regional Bell operating companies.)
- Second, *reintegration* can refer to the integration of two companies that used to operate as a single company, but split apart. For example, in early 2002, Deloitte Touche Tohmatsu decided to spin off Deloitte Consulting, but in early 2003, it announced a reversal of this plan and had to integrate it back.[9]
- Finally, *reintegration* can mean "clean-up" integration work done years after the original acquisitions and integration. This kind of effort can be useful for companies that have made multiple, complex acquisitions over time and need to make a fresh start.

What is the window of time for implementing a postmerger plan?

No one has ever suggested a minimum, but a number of consulting companies have suggested maximums. Realistically, the integration can take up to a year, but the more successful initiatives are completed in six months, with the most critical phases being completed in three months or, more poetically, 100 days.

What proof is there that rapid integration works better than slow integration?

Numerous studies have shown that there is a correlation between the speed of postmerger integration and success. Some of the most compelling evidence comes from research focusing on the integration of specific resources, processes, or responsibilities. For example, in a recent paper, the Boston Consulting Group concluded that "the rapid and comprehensive integration of IT systems greatly enhances the chance that a merger will succeed."[10]

Also, who needs proof? It stands to reason that the longer the acquirer waits to add value to the unit (presumably through some form of integration), the more expensive it will be to repay the premium paid to purchase the unit.

INTERNATIONAL CONSIDERATIONS

What general issues do cross-border buyers and sellers face in the postmerger integration process?

As in any multinational business matter, the inevitable differences of language and culture will affect the process of postmerger integration. In addition, deals must factor in differences in accounting and law. Fortunately for cross-border acquirers, these areas have undergone more convergence in recent years.

- In accounting, there is an International Accounting Standards Board (IASB), an independent accounting standard setter based in London, United Kingdom, that issues International Financial Reporting Standards (IFRSs). The IASB cooperates with national accounting standard setters such as the Financial Accounting Standards Board in the United States to achieve convergence in accounting standards around the world. Nearly 100 countries currently require or permit the use of IFRSs for their publicly traded companies. The current IFRS on merger accounting was issued in June 2005 with a comment deadline of October 28, 2005. For details, see Chapter 5.
- In law, the rise of the European Community has enabled more uniformity of merger law in that region. In May 2005 the European Parliament published the provisional text of a new directive on cross-border mergers. For details, see Chapter 12.

How important are international considerations to the average U.S. acquirer? Aren't cross-border deals relatively rare?

Based on tallies from the Securities Data Corporation of Newark, New Jersey, they are very common. About *one out of every four* mergers and acquisitions announced by U.S. companies over the past 15 years has involved a foreign company, either as a buyer or as a seller. This has held true whether merger levels have been high or low.

What is the total amount of money now changing hands in cross-border mergers, and how important will postmerger integration be for these deals?

Judging from statistics maintained by the United Nations Conference on Trade and Development (UNCTAD) since 1987, in any given year there are hundreds of thousands of mergers and acquisitions.[11] In the peak year of 2000, UNCTAD recorded more than *one million* transactions worldwide (1,143,816). Many of these transactions involved the integration of two or more firms—ideally after a period of strategic deliberation on the part of both organizations. This leads to our next subject: integration planning and communication.

APPENDIX 1 – A

Postmerger Performance: A Review of the Research

Results from a Federal Trade Commission Report (2003)

In 2003, the staff of the Federal Trade Commission compared the results of recent studies of postmerger performance. This chart shows data from the FTC study, emphasizing keys to success (in italics within chart).

Sponsor	Sample	Results
Accenture, 2005	334 interviews, equally divided between major companies in the United States and in Europe; interviews of senior business executives (54% of the total survey base) and IT executives (46%)	Two greatest impediments to postmerger performance were infrastructure incompatibility and cultural incompatibility; 31% of U.S. IT managers characterized merger as successful, vs. 15% of U.S. senior managers
Accenture, 2000, 2001	Oil industry and financial industry focus. Financial study reviews 72 deals from the 1990s	In the oil industry, 39% fully achieved their anticipated gains from alliances. In the finance industry, the best deals improved revenues 14–19%
A. T. Kearney, 1999	115 large deals 1993–1996; total shareholder returns three months before versus two years after the deal. No explicit nonmerger comparison group— comparisons made to average or quartiles in the sample	58% of deals reduced shareholder value. Top-performing deals were done in closely related businesses and had a higher percentage of *assets in the firm's core areas*. 74% of successful deals were run by *managers with deep merger experience*
Booz Allen Hamilton, 2001	Methods not fully described	53% of deals attained the objectives stated in the merger announcement; 55% of *same-industry deals* met expectations, but only 32% of cross-industry deals met expectations. 58% of CEOs of disappointing

		mergers were still at the company after two years vs. 84% of successful CEOs
Boston Consulting Group, 2000	Based on work with BCG clients	Doubling of asset size for financial firms leads to 20% reduction in unit cost of servicing accounts. For industrial firms, *savings of 10 to 15% in materials and components* are common as a result of scale gains
Boston Consulting Group, 2002	302 large deals 1995–2001	40% maintain or improve shareholder value one year later; on average, buyers do 4% worse than industry peers and 9% worse than S&P 500
Bureau of Economic Analysis, 2003	12,023 acquisitions by public firms from 1980 to 2001	Shareholders of these firms lost a total of $218 billion when acquisitions were announced. The only acquisitions by large firms that have positive aggregate gains are acquisitions of subsidiaries. Small firms overall gain from acquisitions, so that shareholders of small firms gained $8 billion when acquisitions were announced and shareholders of large firms lost $226 billion. Small-firm shareholders earn systematically more when acquisitions are announced.
KPMG, 1999	107 companies surveyed for 1996–1997 cross-border deals. Same comparison as for 2001 study	75% considered successful in executive survey. 17% add value; 30% no change; 53% reduce value. *Firms that focused on choosing a strong deal-management team and performed in-depth integration planning did 66% better than average. Pursuing synergies vigorously and communicating well improved performance by 45%*
KPMG, 2001	Survey of 118 executives for 118 companies doing 700 cross-border deals from 1997 to 1999. Companies' equity price trends relative to industry trend just before and one year after the deal	82% considered successful in executive survey. 30% added value; 39% no change; 31% lowered value. A focus on synergy attainment increased chances of success by 28% relative to the average deal
McKinsey, 2000, 2001	193 deals from 1990 to 1997. Industry-specific benchmarks are used	30% of deals enhance shareholder value; 36% of target firms maintained revenue growth in first postmerger

quarter, but only 11% by third quarter; revenue growth 12% below industry peers; 60% of mergers do *capture cost synergies*. In a related study, 58% of acquiring firms had growth equal to or higher than industry rivals for three years following the merger

Mercer Consulting 2001	152 trans-Atlantic deals from 1994 to 1999 using two-year postdeal comparison to industry-specific S&P stock price index	Over half of trans-Atlantic mergers work. Managers of the successful deals credit acquirer and target complementarities, especially careful planning, and speedy, well-directed implementation. Postmerger integration in successful deals has been focused on revenue-related issues, such as *customer communication, sales channels, and brands.*
Pricewaterhouse Coopers, 2000	Survey of executives in 125 companies across a broad range of industries in 1999; 72% of firms U.S.-based	Acquirer's stock 3.7% lower a year after a deal relative to peer group stock changes. 39% of firms reached their cost-cutting goals, while 60–70% achieved their market penetration goals. Success rates were uniformly higher if the firm moved *early and quickly* with *transition teams, communications, and integration.* Vast majority (79%) of executives regretted not moving faster in integration

Source of Data: Federal Trade Commission 2003 and Bureau of Economic Analysis. http://www.ftc.gov/be/rt/businesreviewpaper.pdf; NBER Working Paper No. 9523; Accenture (for 2005 Accenture study).

NOTES

1   The Web site for the new company, Aleris, says that the "merged company advances the successful business model that Commonwealth and IMCO have developed, which is built on the integration of focused competitive strengths, complementary facility locations and cost-effective, technologically advanced manufacturing processes." See http://www.ciionline.com/.

2   The Web site for the new parent company, searsholding.com, says: "The *merger* of Kmart and Sears as Sears Holdings Corporation closed on March 24, 2005, following affirmative shareholder votes of both companies" (emphasis added). Under the terms of the

agreement, Kmart shareholders received one share of new Sears Holdings stock for each Kmart share they owned. Sears shareholders chose either $50 cash or half a share of Sears Holdings, valued at $50.61, for each of their Sears shares.

3   In contrast to the terms *horizontal* and *vertical*, which are used in regulatory and corporate settings, the term *diagonal* is a term that the author coined. Each of these terms describes a *tendency at a point in time*, not a permanent category. Competitors are not clones, and customer–supplier relationships are not exclusive, so all mergers— even those that regulators would classify as horizontal or vertical— have a diagonal direction, in that they involve new markets and/or territories.

4   Discussing the Procter & Gamble merger, A. G. Gere of A. G. Edwards & Sons noted that the cost savings could go for new product development: "There are benefits on the cost side. In terms of synergies, combining what I viewed as $2 billion in cost savings for P&G as a separate entity with another $1–$1.2 billion in synergies with Gillette, I think there's at least $3 billion in cost savings that P&G can penetrate over the next five years, which is significant. It allows them to continue to develop new products, grow geographically and continue to get strong, innovative products to the marketplace with attractive price points. This should further enhance P&G's successful strategy."

5   Robert F. Bruner, "Does M&A Pay," in *Applied Mergers & Acquisitions* (New York: McGraw-Hill, 2004), pp. 30–66.

6   The average size of merger premiums has been declining in recent years, according to Securities Data Corporation, Newark, New Jersey. This could indicate that acquirers are improving their ability to price transactions.

7   This imperative reveals the importance of obtaining objective fairness opinions. The National Association of Securities Dealers, parent of the Nasdaq stock market, has proposed a new Rule 2290 for NASD member firms giving fairness opinions to disclose whether they will receive a fee contingent on completion of the transaction.

8   Over the past decade and a half (1990–2005), as corporate cash reserves have grown while equity values have stayed flat, more companies have been paying cash, according to Securities Data Corporation, Newark, New Jersey.

9   Jack Sweeney, "A Firm for All Reasons," *Consulting Magazine,* September 2004.

10   "Clusters and Nuggets: Mastering Postmerger IT Integration,"
     Boston Consulting Group, July 1, 2004 (white paper).

11   The UNCTAD database covers data on cross-border M&As,
     documenting all transactions with more than 10 percent equity
     capital. It contains information on the value of the deal, the name of
     the acquiring company and its home economy and industry, and
     the acquired company and its host economy and industry, as well
     as the nature of the deal.

CHAPTER 2

The Path to Integration

Two roads diverged in a yellow wood . . .

Robert Frost, "The Road Not Taken"

INTRODUCTION

This book shows companies how to integrate their resources, processes, and responsibilities after they merge. But mergers—and postmerger integration—are not the only viable paths to success.

A company may choose, for example, to grow internally rather than by acquiring other companies. Furthermore, if a company does expand by buying other companies, it may choose not to integrate them. The leadership of the new company may decide to downsize or divest resources, sell assets, terminate operations, or withdraw from commitments for a variety of strategic reasons (ideally acting within the bounds of ethics and law). Alternatively, a company may decide to conduct "business as usual," leaving some or all of the acquired resources, processes, and responsibilities undisturbed.

This chapter presents a step-by-step guide to these choices.

ALTERNATIVES

What choices lead (or should lead) to integration?

The first choice is between *growing* our company and *shrinking* it. If we choose growth, the next choice is between *buying* other companies and *building* our own through internal growth or alliances.

If we choose to buy, the next choice is between *keeping* what we have bought and *selling* it. If we choose to keep what we have bought, the next choice is between *integrating* these companies and *"ignoring"* them by limiting our involvement in financial oversight. (The "ignored" company will be managed, of course, but its management will be independent of the acquiring company, which will take a laissez faire approach to the unit.)

As a decision-making chain, choices unfold as follows: Grow or Shrink? > If Grow, Buy or Build? > If Buy, Keep or Sell? > If Keep, Integrate or Ignore?

Up to the point of purchase, the path can be taken for a company as a whole (X). After that, it may be taken for each unit (X1, X2, X3, . . .). (See Table 2-1.)

Let's take a look at the choices that face each and every company.

T A B L E   2–1

The Path to Integration

				If keep, INTEGRATE X1, X2, X3 or IGNORE X1, X2, X3?
			If buy, KEEP X1, X2, X3 or SELL X1, X2, X3?	
		If grow, BUY X or BUILD Y?		
Start: GROW or SHRINK?				

Choices leading to Y's purchase and integration of X Company, which has three units (X1, X2, and X3).

GROWING VERSUS SHRINKING

The path to postmerger integration obviously begins with a fundamental willingness to grow larger as a company (since any acquisition or merger will increase company size). Is it always a good thing for a company to grow?

Not necessarily. A 2005 study from McKinsey & Company concluded that for most companies, capital market scale has little impact on the cost of equity or the valuation multiple. The study also concluded that valuation multiples are best explained by underlying growth and return on invested capital (ROIC) performance and not by measures of size, such as revenues, earnings, and assets.[1]

This having been said, however, most stakeholders in corporations naturally prefer growth to shrinkage, as long as they can be a part of the growth. The challenge, then, is to keep on providing a return on invested capital while growing in size.

How can companies grow profitably?

Growing profitably means *increasing revenues without a commensurate increase in costs.* To increase revenues, a company can engage in *internal growth* or *external growth.* Many successful companies do both.

BUILDING VERSUS BUYING

What is internal growth?

This expression, when used in business, refers to sales growth that comes from a company's own business activities rather than from mergers or acquisitions. This sales growth can come from selling existing products or services in existing territories, selling new products or services in existing territories, selling existing products or services in new territories, or selling new products or services in new territories.

What is external growth?

This expression refers to enlarging the size of a company by buying or merging with another company.

What are the pros and cons of internal versus external growth?

Internal growth tends to contribute more strongly to corporate financial performance. Companies that have achieved profitable growth without acquisitions have outperformed acquirers in shareholder value appreciation.

Also, internal growth offers more stability than external growth. Internal growth tends to occur in gradual stages that involve existing resources, systems, and responsibilities, whereas external growth tends to occur in leaps and bounds that involve new resources, systems, and responsibilities—a process that can be disruptive.

But this leads to a key benefit of external growth: it can be much faster than internal growth, and some companies cannot afford to wait out the internal growth process. For this and other reasons, external growth is a strategic necessity in some industries at some times.

How do strategic alliances fit in here?

Strategic alliances are essentially agreements to share the risks and rewards of a specific project or set of projects. Alliances may be sealed through a contract (such as a cooperation agreement to share a resource or funding), through cross shareholdings, or through shared ownership of an incorporated joint venture. The frequency of alliances has been increasing dramatically in recent years—from fewer than 1,000 for all of the 1970s to an annual level of more than 1,000 per year in current times.[2] The number of alliances between major pharmaceutical companies and biotech firms alone has increased from 69 in 1993 to 502 in 2004.[3]

Although the growth that strategic alliances generate is generally considered internal by each party involved, this is a misnomer. Strategic alliances—especially the joint venture variety—involve a measure of external growth as well. Indeed, in many cases they function as a trial "merger" under controlled conditions—sort of like living together before marrying.

In theory, mergers that arise in this way have a head start in life, since much of the integration work has already been done in advance of closing. In practice, this is not so. The typical joint venture lasts three to seven years. As with mergers, the key to success in alliances is experience.

Can *M&A integration* apply to acquisitions of partial interests? Aren't such acquisitions usually for investment purposes only? How can integration occur?

Any time a company depends on a source of capital—whether debt or equity capital—that source will have an influence. If the provider of the capital is an operating company in a related industry, this influence may include an integration of resources, processes, and/or responsibilities.

What would be an example of a partial-interest acquisition that led to a full-scale acquisition?

These are not the kind of acquisitions that make headlines, but they happen every day. Consider Bayer CropScience's acquisition of the remaining interest in a Gustafson seed joint venture in 2004 and NanoDynamics's acquisition of the remaining 50 percent interest in MetaMateria Partners in that same year. In 2005, Cisa–Ingersoll-Rand acquired the remaining 70 percent interest in Italy-based CISA SpA. These are only a few examples of hundreds each year. Behind each of these transactions is a story of a strategy pursued with patient persistence.

KEEPING VERSUS SELLING

How common are postmerger divestitures of acquired company units?

It depends on how long a timeline for divestiture you are considering. Few companies divest units immediately following an acquisition (unless they are compelled to do so by antitrust regulators), but many companies divest them eventually. This process is very hard to trace over a significant period of time, since companies and their units are always undergoing restructuring and renaming.

In any given year, nearly half of the acquisitions that occur come about because the sellers are divesting a company unit.

Given the fact that most major companies grow both externally and internally, it would be reasonable to assume that about half of these divestitures stemmed from acquisitions, as opposed to internal growth. According to this logic, we would conclude that, over time, about one-fourth of all acquisitions are eventually divested. Yet in major companies, the level appears to be lower. In a follow-up study for the 10 largest mergers of 1985, the author of this book found that only a minority of the deals had ended in a divestiture even after 20 years—and most of the divestitures were partial (see Appendix 2-A).

What kinds of divestiture are there?

There are three basic types of divestiture: *sell-offs*, *spin-offs*, and *split-ups*. Some of these may involve a continuing involvement—a strategy referred to as a *satellite launch*.

What is a sell-off?

A sell-off, which is by far the most common type of divestiture (and the type usually referred to as such), is the sale of one or more company units to another company—for example, when BF Goodrich Corporation sold its JcAIR Test Systems business to Aeroflex Incorporated in 2005.

What is a spin-off?

A spin-off is a series of transactions through which a company divests or "spins off" one or more units—typically a small portion of its business with some common theme—by turning them into an independent company and selling the company's shares to the investing public. Recent U.S. examples include Sara Lee Corp.'s spin-off of its apparel business (as Sara Lee Branded Apparel Americas/Asia) in 2005 and the spin-offs of Abbott Laboratories' hospital products division (as Hospira) and General Electric's insurance businesses (as Genworth) in 2004.

Sometimes spin-offs precede mergers. For example, in Switzerland, Sandoz and Ciba spun off their chemicals business units—one as a taxable initial public offering and one as a tax-free "demerger"—before merging their pharmaceutical cores into Novartis. The slimmed-down Ciba, renamed Ciba Specialty Chemicals, then grew through acquisition. For example, it bought the Korean company Daihan Swiss, completing the acquisition in November 2004.

Spun-off units may be sold separately through separate spin-offs or may be combined into a single spin-off. This process usually begins with a pro rata distribution of stock to shareholders in the form of a special dividend, followed by (or combined with) an initial public offering of the unit's shares.[4] A common type of spin-off is the "IPO carve-out," in which the company goes straight to the IPO without the distributions to stockholders. If the parent retains an interest in an IPO carve-out, this may be termed a "divestiture IPO."

What is a split-up?

A split-up is the breakup of a company into two or more separate companies. It is different from a sell-off or a spin-off in that it involves the entire company, not just a unit or two. The most famous split-ups have involved AT&T. In 1984, AT&T broke up under order from the Department of Justice Antitrust Division, dividing into a telecommunications company (today's AT&T) and regional Bell operating companies (a.k.a. "baby Bells") to handle local calls. Then in 1996, having grown through acquisition, AT&T divided itself again—this time voluntarily—citing business complexities that outweighed the benefits of integration.[5] One of the surviving units, interestingly, followed this split-up with the spin-off of a unit, Lucent Technologies, in 1996, while another unit, AT&T Wireless, after being spun off in 2001, merged into Cingular in 2005.

What usually motivates postmerger divestitures?

Reasons for divestitures vary. A unit may be sold off or spun off, or a company may be split up, because it is performing poorly and the seller wants to stem the tide of losses. Conversely, it may be sold as a "crown jewel" because it can fetch a good price. Finally, and least appealingly, it may be tagged for sale to appease regulators—for example, the Antitrust Division of the Department of Justice or the

European Union—which may set this as a condition for regulatory approval of a merger. For example, Procter & Gamble had to sell its Crest SpinBrush toothbrush business in order to win European Union antitrust approval to buy Gillette in 2005.

How can an acquirer decide what to divest when?

Companies often purchase other firms with the intention of selling off some units eventually, holding this divestiture "option" open until the businesses in question develop further or until the industry consolidates to the point that it becomes a seller's market. Assigning a quantitative value to each divestiture option can help acquirers make the decision on keeping versus selling. It can also help set an appropriate price for the purchased company (see Appendix 2-B).

If a company's senior management knows that the company *may* divest a unit, should it disclose this to employees or wait until it makes a final decision?

In this area, silence is golden. True, employees deserve full, current, and constant information about all material matters before, during, and after the merger, but speculative information is not considered to be material. It would not be covered, for example, by the WARN law that requires notification of employees six months before a plant closing. (See Chapter 12.) Hypothetical information about the possible divestiture of a unit falls into the "don't ask, don't tell" category.

If managers must address this issue (because of information leaks, for example), here are some principles to keep in mind if divestiture plans are in the making:

- *Honesty.* When asked, never deny (a "no comment" is sufficient).
- *Discretion.* Don't volunteer nonessential information.
- *Utility.* Keep your communications useful. For example, if a divestiture decision hinges on a unit's productivity or profitability, these factors should be flagged for employees' urgent attention.

(For additional guidance, see Chapter 3, "Integration Planning and Communication.")

If senior management knows that it *will* divest a unit, when should it tell employees, and how much should it tell them?

The principles of honesty, discretion, and utility apply here as well, but *not* the rule of silence. Once a plan is certain, silence is *not* golden. Immediate, complete, and frequent disclosure is the rule here (again, see Chapters 3 and 12).

What benefits can divestitures bring?

In many cases, when a unit separates from a nonintegrating parent, both enjoy improved performance.

Should all companies with diverse units consider divestitures?

Not necessarily. A company with diverse products or services can achieve strong share performance if it can convince investors that it has a unified strategy. General Electric is a good example of this type of company.

Wall Street does not pay premiums for GE spin-offs because GE is adding value to its units. The lackluster response to GE's spin-off of Genworth Financial illustrated this point.

Can an acquirer simply divest at will? What kinds of restrictions might come into play here?

As the new owner of an acquired company, the acquirer has a great deal of flexibility in how it integrates or separates from the resources it has acquired. Certain restrictions can and often do apply, however. The most common restrictions stem from contracts signed prior to the merger by either the seller or the buyer.

In terms of human resources, the selling company may have signed a labor agreement limiting or penalizing layoffs, and this agreement may extend to a future change of control. In terms of physical assets, the seller may have pledged not to sell assets used as collateral. Other restrictions stem from federal or state laws protecting the interests of various stakeholder groups. Ideally, all of these restrictions will have been faced and resolved during the due diligence process prior to closing. The primary restrictions are identified in Part 4 of this book (Chapters 10, 11, and 12).

INTEGRATING VERSUS MANAGING SEPARATELY

Do some companies make acquisitions with no plans for integration? What would be the point of buying a company without integrating it?

Companies make acquisitions for a variety of motives. A Federal Trade Commission panel report in June 1980 (based on a focus group with 10 executives) counted 31 motives. Arthur D. Little, Inc., listed 21 in a 1978 report to the Financial Executives Institute. Financial economist J. Fred Weston has identified 10 main reasons. Warren Buffett once said in an op-ed that there was only one reason: to move investment out of cash and into assets. These and other studies can be boiled down into a shorter list of merger motives (provided here along with the "code names" academics use to designate them).[6]

One company may buy another in order to do any of the following:

- Achieve economies of scale by buying a customer, supplier, or competitor ("operating synergy")
- Accomplish strategic goals more quickly and more successfully ("strategic planning")
- Realize a return on investment by buying a company with less efficient managers and making them more efficient ("differential efficiency")
- Realize a return by buying a company with inefficient managers and replacing them ("inefficient management")
- Increase market share ("market power")
- Lower the cost of capital by smoothing cash flow and increasing debt capacity ("financial synergy")
- Take advantage of a price that is low in comparison to past stock prices and/or estimated future prices, or in relation to the cost the buyer would incur if it built the company from scratch ("undervaluation")[7]

- Assert control in an underperforming company with dispersed ownership ("agency problems")
- Obtain a more favorable tax status ("tax efficiency")[8]
- Increase the size of a company and therefore increase the power and pay of managers ("managerialism")

Note that only the first four of these motives depend on integration.

What are the benefits of integration versus separate management for an acquired company or one of its units?

If the acquirer has a strategic reason for buying the company, some form of integration will be necessary for the acquisition to be successful. If the acquirer's reason for buying a firm is financial, however, integration may not be helpful and may actually be harmful.

In order to succeed as a financial acquirer, however, a company must have a *financial culture*. Absent such a culture, acquirers would be wise to master the art of M&A integration.

INTERNATIONAL CONSIDERATIONS

In taking the long decision path to integration, what international considerations should be weighed?

Whenever a company asks whether it wants to grow or shrink, buy or build, keep or sell, integrate or manage separately, it must always add the question *where?*

Returning to our decision model, if a company chooses to

- Shrink by selling a unit, it can consider a domestic or a foreign acquirer.
- Grow internally or externally, it can consider domestic or foreign sources of growth.

If a company chooses to grow

- Internally, it can expand into domestic or foreign markets.
- Externally, it can acquire or form alliances with domestic or foreign companies.

If a company chooses to acquire from a foreign company, it can

- Keep all the domestic and/or foreign units it acquires.
- Sell one or more of the acquired units by selling to domestic or acquirers.

If a company chooses to keep the unit(s) it acquires, it can

- Integrate the unit(s) with its existing domestic and/or foreign operations.
- Manage the unit(s) separately as a domestic or foreign subsidiary.

In making these choices, company managers should rely on their collective wisdom and experience, as well as on ever-changing information. To find and assess foreign opportunities, companies need current and accurate information. A wealth of free information is there for the asking from local and national governments, accounting firms, consulting firms, law firms, and various international consortia.[9] In addition, most business publishers (including McGraw-Hill) offer a variety of useful international reference works at reasonable prices.

Assuming an informed choice for integration, a company can begin the next phase: planning and communication, the subject of the next chapter.

A P P E N D I X   2 – A

Postmerger Sell-Offs: How Common Are They?
Following Up on the 10 Largest Acquisitions of 1985

Buyer: Royal Dutch Shell Group
Company bought: Shell Oil Co. (remaining interest)
As of June 2005, Royal Dutch Shell still owns Shell Oil Co.

Buyer: Philip Morris Cos. Inc.
Company bought: General Foods Corp.
As of June 2005, Philip Morris still owns General Foods, now integrated with another acquisition (Kraft) into Kraft Foods Inc. The parent company is now called Altria.

Buyer: General Motors Corp.
Company bought: Hughes Aircraft Co.
As of June 2005, General Motors has a reduced ownership in the company that used to be called Hughes Aircraft. The aircraft company merged with GM's Delco Electronics to form Hughes Electronics, which was then sold to Raytheon. The research wing of the company, Hughes Research Laboratories, is now jointly owned by Boeing, GM, and Raytheon.

Buyer: R.J. Reynolds Industries Inc.
Company bought: Nabisco Brands Inc.
As of June 2005, R.J. Reynolds is no longer merged with Nabisco as RJR Nabisco. In 1999, the company spun off Nabisco as a separate company and returned to its original name, R.J. Reynolds. In July 2004, R.J. Reynolds merged with the U.S. operations of Brown & Williamson, to become Reynolds American Inc.

Buyer: Allied Corp.
Company bought: Signal Cos. Inc.
As of June 2005, the consolidated company, Allied-Signal, after a period of both integration and divestiture, had merged into Honeywell.

Buyer: Baxter Travenol Laboratories Inc.
Company bought: American Hospital Supply Corp.
As of June 2005, Baxter still owned parts of American Hospital Supply Corp. The new company, called Baxter International Inc., was an enormous entity that soon approached $10 billion in annual sales; about 10,000 of its 50,000 employees worldwide were in the Chicago area. During the 1990s, however, Baxter sold off several divisions, including many of the old American Hospital Supply Corp. operations. At the beginning of the twenty-first century, Baxter again began buying firms such as ESI Lederle.

Buyer: Nestlé SA
Company bought: Carnation Co.
As of June 2005, Nestlé was still the owner of Carnation Company, promoting many products under the brand Nestlé Carnation.

Buyer: Monsanto Co.
Company bought: G.D. Searle & Co.
As of June 2005, Monsanto Co. still owned G.D. Searle & Co., which is a division of Monsanto called Searle/Monsanto.

Buyer: Coastal Corp.
Company bought: American Natural Resources Inc.
As of June 2005, Coastal Corp. still owned American Natural Resources.

Buyer: InterNorth Inc.
Company bought: Houston Natural Gas Corp.
As of June 2005, the combined company, Enron, was no longer in business. The December 2001 bankruptcy of Enron caused widespread economic damage and sparked public outrage that led to the passage of the landmark corporate reform law Sarbanes-Oxley in 2002.

APPENDIX 2 – B

Valuing the Divestiture Option

The option to divest has quantifiable value, according to Kenneth W. Smith, of Mitchell Madison in Toronto, Canada, and Alexander Triantis, professor, School of Business, University of Wisconsin–Madison.

Consider the case of PJP,* a large conglomerate that is contemplating the acquisition of another firm with substantial real estate holdings. If the acquisition goes through, PJP plans to develop a particular piece of centrally located real estate for a distribution facility in two years. Based on its projected use, PJP has valued this piece of real estate at $20 million. Market conditions will, of course, cause the value of this real estate to fluctuate over the next two years. However, if the firm's business outlook turns sour and the distribution facility is projected to be unprofitable, the firm would be able to sell off this land quickly for at least $15 million.

To account for the value of this divestiture option in its valuation of the acquisition, PJP's management uses a simple two-year binomial model. Management assumes that the value of the real estate to the firm (without taking into account the divestiture option) will either appreciate by 50 percent or depreciate by 40 percent each year. In the worst-case scenario, the land would be worth only $7.2 million to the company after two years. In effect, the divestiture option establishes a $15 million floor for the value of the real estate after two years, thus mitigating the risk of the acquisition.

Even though the value to PJP of the real estate as a site for its distribution facility may be only $12 million at the end of the first year, it is still not optimal for the firm to sell it for $15 million at that time if it can sell it for that price at the end of the second year. The firm would prefer to retain the option to develop the land at the end of the second year should business conditions improve (at which point the value of the land as a distribution site would rise to $18 million).

---

* PJP is a fictional composite based on real cases.

The incremental value of waiting to divest amounts to $710,000 at the end of the first year. Overall, the divestiture option increases the current value of the land from $20 million to $21.77 million. In practice, of course, the resale price of an asset is not guaranteed, and more sophisticated option-pricing techniques would be required. The logic behind the valuation and exercise of a divestiture option, however, is still instructive.

NOTES

1   "Does Scale Matter to Capital Markets?," *McKinsey Quarterly*, Summer 2005. These findings suggest the need to grow with caution. But note that past research by Mercer Management Consulting shows that when it comes to shareholder value (as measured by total returns), profitable growth is superior to cost cutting, and unprofitable growth is superior to shrinking. Companies that grow profitably have a disproportionately higher stock appreciation than do companies that only cut costs: A dollar earned through growth is worth more to shareholders than the same dollar earned through cost cutting.

2   These figures are based on a lecture by Jill Foote, "Alliances as a Corporate Growth Strategy," Rice University, February 2005.

3   Matthew K. Hudes, national managing principal for biotechnology, Deloitte & Touche LLP, quoted in "Deloitte Survey Reveals Greater Competition for Alliances among Big Pharma, BioPharma and Biotech Companies," PR Newswire, June 19, 2005.

4   Some spin-offs do not involve widespread public ownership of the unit stock. As noted in past client letters of Fried, Frank, Harris, Shriver & Jacobson, a spin-off may be combined with or follow an acquisition or merger by a third party or may involve continued ownership by the original parent company. Generally speaking, though, the term *spin-off* implies independence for the previously owned units.

5   "The complexity of trying to manage these different businesses began to overwhelm the advantages of our integration," AT&T CEO Robert Allen told the *Wall Street Journal* the day after it announced its decision to break up. (John J. Keller, "Defying Merger Trend, AT&T Plans to Split into Three Companies," Sept. 21, 1996, p. A1.)

6   The author gratefully acknowledges J. Fred Weston, Cordner Professor of Money and Financial Markets, University of California–Los Angeles, as the source of this list.

7   This is where the so-called q ratio comes in. The q ratio is the market value of shares divided by the replacement costs of the assets represented by the shares. Of all motives, this may be the most fundamental. (Noted management author Peter Drucker, in his classic essay "The Five Rules of Successful Acquisitions," *Wall Street Journal*, Oct. 15, 1981, boiled M&A motives down to this one: a flight out of money into assets.)

8   For example, to avoid the penalty of depreciation on lower historical costs during a period of inflation, a company might make an acquisition in order to achieve a stepped-up basis for depreciable assets.

9   To cite just one example, consider the international business exchange now called GBX Business Opportunities, an electronic system designed to make it "easier, faster, and more affordable for firms, regardless of size or location, to find, qualify, and negotiate with partners worldwide." Over 50 chambers of commerce (including the U.S. Chamber of Commerce) and business organizations support this network.

A similar technology is owned by M&A Partners in Dallas, Texas, pertaining to relations with suppliers. See Chapter 10.

CHAPTER 3

Integration Planning and Communication

A merger provides a window of opportunity when change is expected and accepted. Push everything through that window that you can.

Sir Adrian Cadbury, Correspondence

INTRODUCTION

Very early in the M&A process—ideally, when the future company is no more than a "gleam in the eye" of its planners—key managers need to decide what elements to integrate as they shape the destiny of their new company. Will there be two chief executives or one? Will the companies combine their two names or seek a new one? What about their information systems? This chapter helps company managers make these choices and communicate them to their company's various constituencies.

First, our experts will look at how to plan and implement integration and who should do this planning. As part of this discussion, we will explore the use of interim executives, advisors, and facilitators. Moving on, the experts will answer some eternal questions about communicating postmerger plans, beginning with legal technicalities and ending with the grand prize—building a vision of the future company.

FORMING INTEGRATION PLANS

What elements should be integrated following a merger?

Everything that can usefully be combined. The very term *merger* as it is used by most businesspeople (not merely in the narrow technical sense defined earlier) implies no less an effort. It is useful to think of the merger effort as encompassing all *resources*, *processes*, and *responsibilities* of the buying and selling companies, both domestically and globally. These, in turn, need to be integrated with one another and with the company's overall *strategy* and *culture*.

What resources should be considered for postmerger integration?

First and foremost, there are human resources at the board, management, and support levels. Beyond this, acquirers will need to consider the integration of financial, tangible, and intangible resources. First among the intangibles are the sometimes priceless reputational resources, beginning with the company name and brand names of the seller. Part 2 of this book guides acquirers in integrating these resources.

What processes should be considered?

Acquirers and sellers should also consider how they might integrate their fundamental business processes, including management systems, compensation plans, and incentives for innovation. Part 3 of this book offers general principles for the integration of each of these process elements.

What about responsibilities?

It is useful to think of these in terms of commitments—binding by law or ethics—to various stakeholder groups, including customers, suppliers, shareholders, bondholders, employees, and communities. Part 4 shows how to fulfill these commitments in the course of postmerger integration.

Is there anything else?

For a fairly comprehensive list of resources, processes, and responsibilities, see Appendix B of this book. This list, along with the other tools provided or described in the book, can help a company combine the newly integrated resources, processes, and responsibilities into a single successful whole. The conclusion to this book explores this important endeavor.

Why is it important to integrate these matters? Isn't it sometimes best to leave such matters alone?

Organizationwide integration can leverage the value of resources by reinforcing strengths and offsetting weaknesses, improving the efficiency of processes by reducing redundancy, and ensuring fulfillment of responsibilities through continuity of commitments to stakeholders. More generally, integration can create a sense of shared purpose for everyone in the newly combined company. This sense of shared purpose can help employees embrace rather than resist the fact that after a merger, *the new organization must change.* Common sense and research alike show that for any organizational change to be successful, the change cannot be limited to one unit or one level of the organization. The *entire organization* must be involved in the change.

Integrating various resources, processes, and responsibilities is obviously a massive undertaking. When and how should companies begin?

As mentioned in Chapter 1 and illlustrated in Appendix A (in the back of the book), intergration planning should start as early as possible—ideally at the planning phase.

In the merger booms of the 1960s and 1980s, many of the more acquisitive companies had vice presidents of corporate development. This idea has had a revival recently, with the rise of the corporate development officer (CDO).[1]

Prior to closing, the buyer should engage in a thorough due diligence review of the seller's business. The purpose of this review is to detect any legal, financial, and business risks that the buyer might inherit from the seller. If the risk is too great, the buyer can walk away. Usually, however, buyers simply use the results of their due diligence investigations to extract price concessions and/or warranties and representations in the acquisition agreement.

At the same time as the due diligence review, however, there should be a *strategic review* in which the acquirer determines what synergies there are and how it will take advantage of them. Eventually, the acquirer (often in consultation with the acquired firm) will write up this review in the form of a postmerger integration plan.

What process should an acquirer use for planning?

Acquirers should follow the classic wisdom of project planning: prepare to plan, assess the current environment, define integration plan objectives, develop plans and identify resources, and validate the plan. For illustrations of this approach, see the appendixes to this chapter and to this book.

What exactly is an integration plan?

A postmerger integration plan is a document outlining exactly when and how the major resources, assets, processes, and commitments of the acquiring and acquired companies will be combined in order to achieve the strategic goals of the newly combined company. Ultimately, this outline will be distributed to key employees and (in modified form) to other interested parties. Like any corporate document, it should be reviewed by counsel.

What should be in a postmerger integration plan?

This varies greatly by industry and by situation. Clearly, however, there should be three elements in the postmerger integration plan: the goals of the new company; how integration of resources, systems, and responsibilities will support those goals; and the timetable for the integration.

For example, a postmerger integration plan for two hospitals might include a description of the primary goals for the new alliance, along with details of when and how these goals will be

Sample integration planning process

prepare to plan	assess current environment	define integration plan objectives	develop plans & identify resources	validate plan
define core operating model	identify key areas for "as is" analysis	define critical integration areas and objectives	develop action plans for each integration area	validate integration area action plans against integration area objectives
determine governance structure & exec. leadership	identify and collect data required for "as is" analysis	define scope of integration for each integration area	develop preliminary consolidated integration plan	validate consolidated integration plan against acquisition objectives
define integration scope, objectives, and critical success factors	plan/schedule and conduct site visits and interviews	define integration priorities	define resource requirements for integration projects	review plan with executive leadership for approval
develop high-level integration plan	document results		quantify costs and benefits for integration projects	launch integration plan
develop integration timeline			finalize consolidated integration plan and timeline	
define provisions for integration and assemble transition teams				
develop communications strategy				

Source: E-Know, Arlington, Virginia ©2005
(See also Appendix G.)

accomplished. Details might include how the board, management, and staff will be organized; how staff will be credentialed; who will be responsible for clinical policy making; how budgeting, accounting, accounts receivable, and bond covenants will be handled; what clinical services will be changed, expanded, or cut back; and what nursing models will be used. The thorough integration plan might also include how the mission, values, and vision of the two hospitals will be merged.

Some plans never get implemented or get implemented poorly. How can postmerger planners avoid this problem?

The following 15-point M&A planning checklist can help integration planners at the senior management level see if they are on the right track:

1. Are the plans consistent with the intrinsic logic of the deal?
2. Do the plans specify how the company will pay for the deal?
3. Are there written plans to cover both the short term (less than five years) and the long term (five years or more)?
4. Do the short- and long-term plans mesh?
5. Has the planning process involved both senior managers and the employees most affected by the plans?
6. Do the plans take into account the operational and cultural realities of the two companies involved?
7. Have senior managers and the board of directors reviewed the plan documents?
8. Are senior managers and the board using the plans to make their decisions?
9. Are the plans supported by appropriate policies?
10. Are the plans supported by adequate resources?
11. Do the plans specify measures and milestones of progress?
12. Who will be held accountable for achieving the plans?
13. Have the plans been distributed to all appropriate parties?

14. Is there a program for communicating the plans internally?
15. Is there a program for communicating the plans externally?

The answer to each question should be *yes*.

On points 11 through 15, it is useful to have a team of functional managers to plan operating details. Who should do what by when? For an example of such a planning document, see Appendixes 3-A and 3-B.

THE ROLE OF INSIDERS IN PLANNING M&A INTEGRATION

Traditionally, acquirers in mergers of equals (where there are inevitable job cuts after the merger) go through the following process:

1. Identify employees to retain and put them in charge of all aspects of postmerger operations.
2. Outplace the other employees humanely and deal with the survivor guilt experienced by employees who stay.

Most books about postmerger integration (including the first edition of this book) give advice on how to follow these two steps. There is at least one clear alternative to this approach:

1. Identify executives to retain and put them in charge of the *revenue-producing* side of postmerger operations (retention of customers, integration of the sales forces, customer relations).
2. Put the other executives (the ones to be outplaced) in charge of all other aspects of integration, including notably the *cost-cutting* aspects (including layoffs), and offer them a large financial incentive to take on this assignment.

Flowserve used this approach successfully when it acquired Ingersoll-Dresser in 2000 (advised by M&A Partners in Dallas,

Texas). The approach makes sense. Acquirers have a very small time frame in which to capture the revenue-producing synergies of a transaction. Key managers cannot be pulled away from their top-line jobs to tend to integration mechanics and fallout. They need to focus on the future of the company. Departing managers are better suited to the job of separating the company from its past. By leading the integration efforts, they will also learn new skills that can help them in future jobs.

Should someone be designated as chief planner of the integration?

No. Although one individual may be assigned to make sure that a plan is created and respected, the best postmerger plans are ultimately created by groups. Obviously, in the earliest "search and screen" stages, everyone in the planning group or "team" will be from the acquiring company, but once the acquiring company has entered negotiations with a specific merger partner, an equal number of representatives of the target company should join the team or teams. If this makes the planning group(s) too large—more than 12 per group is probably too many[2]—each side can drop members.

How many groups should be formed to plan postmerger integration?

The larger the company, the greater the number of planning groups that may be involved. In the early stages of preparing for their planned merger, Bell Atlantic Corp. and NYNEX Corp. had 25 joint planning groups working together at one time.

Who should be on the postmerger teams?

As mentioned, good planning involves both cost cutting and revenue production. Teams and team members should reflect this distinction. Team members involved in planning for long-term revenue production should be those with a stake in the long-term success of the merger, such as CEOs, senior managers, and key employees, including any interim executives who may be hired to guide and/or implement the emerging plan.

There may also be seats at the table for advisors—such as investment bankers, accountants, attorneys, or consultants—or for professional decision-making facilitators, but these outsiders should not have a vote in the outcome.

In the end, it is up to the board of directors of the newly combined company to approve the plan. Directors should not merely rubber-stamp the plan, but should question it thoroughly. The board of directors is often a secret weapon in postmerger planning. In most public companies, the board as a whole is independent, and thus has the objectivity of outside consultants. Furthermore, most boards, whether for public or for private companies, will include people who are chosen for their relevant expertise. Finally, an increasing number of directors today own stock in the companies they serve, making them long-term stakeholders in the future of the company.

Any postmerger plan that is created by stakeholders, advised by qualified experts, and approved by a well-structured board of directors is bound to serve the future company well.

THE ROLE OF OUTSIDERS IN PLANNING M&A INTEGRATION

What are the benefits of using outsiders in planning integration?

First, sometimes using an outside consultant is an absolute requirement because of antitrust issues. When a merger may cause market concentration, it requires approval from antitrust authorities. Until that approval is obtained, the companies are not allowed to begin integration. They may, however, have an independent third party begin the planning work. This is what Cingular Wireless and AT&T Wireless did. Pending regulatory approval, all planning for the integration occurred at "arm's length." Cingular hired a consultant, Accenture, to create its postmerger integration plan. Accenture set up a "clean room" in Cingular's headquarters city, Atlanta, where consultants studied the details of both companies, including advertising budgets, billing systems, and retail networks. The room was off limits to employees of both companies.

In addition to performing such services, consultants can provide experience, expertise, and objectivity. Managers should consider using the services of outsiders to compensate for their deficiencies in one or more of these regards. Experienced acquirers tend to achieve better postmerger returns because they are more likely than inexperienced companies to have the right vision and to implement it effectively and quickly. If an inexperienced acquirer wants to achieve these things, it may hire one or more outside parties who can help it form, implement, and accelerate a postmerger strategy.

What are the drawbacks of using outsiders to help in M&A integration planning?

It depends in part on how the advisors are paid. If advisors are paid on a contingency basis (a common practice with investment bankers[3]), they may be overly optimistic about how much synergy a deal contains and how easy it will be to achieve. Such advisors may have much valuable expertise to impart when it comes to financing, marketing, and structuring a transaction, but their enthusiasm should be taken with more than one grain of salt. This is especially true if the fee is paid on the basis of the size of the transaction (as in the traditional "Lehman's formula" fee: 5 percent of the first million, 4 percent of the next million, and so forth).

Conversely, if advisors are paid on a sliding scale based on the amount of time a transaction takes, whether or not it ever closes successfully (a common practice with lawyers, who typically bill by the hour), those advisors might be tempted to take an overly pessimistic view of a transaction, finding liability exposure under every hubcap. These advisors may have invaluable advice when it comes to the tax and legal implications of a transaction, but, as with their opposite numbers, the investment bankers, their voice should never predominate at the postmerger planning table.

Consultants are immune to these pressures, as they are paid a flat fee or on a retainer basis (not a contingency fee or an hourly fee). The temptation faced by consultants is the temptation to take over the decision-making role from managers, which is never good. Managers should use consultants and others to help them make decisions, not to make their decisions for them.

These warnings are not meant to impugn the integrity of M&A transaction advisors, who as a group are worthy of their hire.

The moral is twofold. First, when it comes to postmerger advice, clients get what they pay for and how they pay for it. Second, the best choices in any endeavor will come from those who have a vested interest in it.

In the case of postmerger integration, the best decision makers will be those whose destinies are linked to the long-term success of the merger, namely, the groups mentioned in Part 4 of this book (customers, suppliers, stockholders, bondholders, lenders, employees, and communities). Of course, a company's "suppliers" do include long-term advisors, but the point is that their perspective, however qualified, should never predominate in the planning process.

If an acquirer decides to engage a third party to help its postmerger integration effort, how should it begin?

First, the acquirer (or, more accurately, the potential acquirer, since planning for integration should start early) should determine who is working in this field.

Major acquirers often turn to the largest professional services firms, such as consulting firms associated currently or in past years with Big Four accounting firms. Additional sources of advisors include the following:

- The acquirer's current advisors
- Advisors recommended by trusted sources
- Advisors listed in books about postmerger integration (including this one)
- Trade and professional associations
- Professional reference books

With regard to this last source, you should never choose an advisor "straight out of a book." For one thing, not all qualified advisors are listed in reference books for their profession. Moreover, just because someone is listed in a reference book does not mean that he or she is superior to those who are not listed. Nonetheless, seekers can derive some comfort from the professional and editorial control that goes into the publication of professional reference books. Furthermore, these books contain valuable background information.

For background information on an attorney, one might consult the *Martindale-Hubbell Law Directory*, an encyclopedic reference source based in Providence, New Jersey, and published annually for well over a century. This reference lists law firms by state and city. For each law firm, it describes the firm's practice and the expertise of each lawyer.

To learn more about a recommended consultant, a good place to begin is with the comprehensive source *Directory of Management Consultants*, published by Kennedy Publications in Fitzwilliam, New Hampshire.[4] This directory lists people by up to four areas of expertise. Over 300 consultants list themselves as specialists in the M&A area (defined by the directory as "mergers and acquisitions, divestments, joint ventures, buy/sell agreements"). There is also *Management Consultants Resource Guide*, published biannually by the Institute of Management Consultants in New York. The IMC, established in 1968, awards a CMC (certified management consultant) title to members who pass its certification requirements. IMC members must adhere to a code of conduct that includes provisions for confidentiality, independence, fee disclosure, and so forth. These are real directories, not glorified Yellow Pages; no fee is required for listing.

If an advisor is hired to help with senior management integration, who should pay for these services?

Ideally, the advisor's payment should come from both entities. Payment can be made by the new entity in the event of a successful merger or by both entities if the merger never takes place. Alternatively, each company can retain its own advisor, each one acceptable to the other. If only one advisor is retained, and if only one party (for example, the acquirer) retains that advisor, it is imperative that the advisor gain acceptance from the other company (the acquired firm) before beginning work.

What are interim executives, and how can they help in planning M&A integration?

Interim executives, also called project executives, are qualified line managers who are hired on a temporary basis for a specific assignment, such as the integration of two companies. Such managers (usually employees of a temporary personnel agency specializing in interim management) are hired to assist in planning the more technical aspects of postmerger integration.[5] Such aspects include the following:

- Information systems (particularly for financial management and reporting)
- Process engineering in the manufacturing function
- Various "logistics" functions, such as purchasing, transportation, and order fulfillment

What is a facilitator, and how can a facilitator's services help a group form its postmerger integration plan?

A group facilitator is an independent third party who helps a group identify problems, find solutions, and make decisions. *Independent* means that the person should be neutral with respect to the matters being decided and should have no decision-making authority within the group. Obviously, to be effective, the facilitator should be someone who is acceptable to all members of the group. Also, the facilitation process requires accurate information from the group and free choices by the group. Although some group members may resent the presence of an "outsider," facilitators can be helpful to many groups, particularly those that are susceptible to dominance or deadlocking.

There are two basic types of facilitation: basic and developmental. Basic facilitation focuses primarily on a given *problem* (for example, achieving a better pay system), using a predetermined methodology for group decision making provided by the facilitator (for example, the "Delphi" method of decision making).[6] By contrast, developmental facilitation focuses on developing a useful *process* to solve the problem. Basic facilitation is good enough (and most cost-effective) for groups that will exist for only a short period of time; developmental facilitation is recommended for groups that will last over time (for example, six months or more).

In both types of facilitation, the group, not the facilitator, is solely responsible for the quality of its decisions: The facilitator facilitates; he or she does not advise. In developmental facilitation, however, the facilitator guides group members in using their faculties of reason and fairness to make the best possible decisions.

A common term used to describe developmental facilitation is *participative-process consulting*. An area of expertise first developed in the 1960s,[7] process consultation is a branch of consulting that is officially recognized by the Institute of Management Consultants. About 350 consultants in the United States offer such services, and of these, some 35 also have special expertise in mergers and acquisitions.[8]

INTEGRATION ELEMENTS IN THE MERGER AGREEMENT

What impact does a merger agreement have on the future life of the new company?

Quite often, the most important impact that the merger agreement has on the successor entity derives from the styles of due diligence and negotiation adopted by the parties as they work out the terms of the agreement. A distrustful, hostile negotiating process will result in deep-seated suspicions and antagonism between the management teams of the two previously separate companies. Often, these are exacerbated by postclosing litigation over alleged inaccuracies in the merger agreement. The analogy of a prenuptial agreement is most apt: it can strengthen a marriage by eliminating potential future controversies and establishing useful guidelines for future behavior, or it can weaken it by creating more problems than it solves. For this reason, the personalities of lawyers and other professionals involved in the due diligence and negotiating process should be carefully evaluated.

Does the merger agreement between the buyer and the seller usually set the conditions for postmerger integration?

It can, if either party insists on it and the other party is agreeable. The acquired company may insist on a certain level of job security for its employees or on continuing authority for its CEO. Conversely, the acquiring company may set some postmerger ground rules. (For more details, see Chapter 4, "Retaining and Integrating Human Resources.")

Even the bare-bones merger agreement will contain a few basic assurances about postmerger life beyond the seller's financial projections. An average agreement will establish the ground rules for the agreement and a few basic facts about the parties to the agreement: that the selling company is what it claims to be, that the seller has a right to sell it, and that the buyer has the right (and the ability) to buy it.

Of the dozen or so sections in a typical merger agreement, at least two will by definition contain assurances related to future events, namely, the covenant not to compete (covered in Chapter 4) and the representations and warranties of the seller.[9]

What postmerger matters might be covered in the section on representations and warranties of the seller?

This section, as its title suggests, will typically have all the representations and warranties (that is, assertions and promises) that the seller is making to the buyer concerning the seller's company. Most of these refer only to the past and present state of the company, not to its future state. For example, this section of the merger agreement will typically cover the seller's organization, capitalization, ownership of securities and property (real and intellectual), current levels of inventory and debt, exposure to lawsuits, and so forth. It is, in essence, the buyer's "due diligence" checklist. The more detail it has, the better the chances for smooth postmerger integration.

There is one type of representation, however, that explicitly refers to postmerger performance. This is the part of the agreement where the seller has provided financial projections, and the buyer will ask the seller to *assert the reasonableness of the assumptions and accuracy of the data* used to make the projections. Lenders may also insist on such representations in the loan agreement. Wise sellers will resist providing these unless doing so is absolutely necessary to the sale because if the company performs poorly in the future, the buyer or lender may sue the seller, claiming breach of representation.

While the representations may relate to current and past events, they have numerous forward-looking consequences. For example, a seller's representation that it has committed no employment law violations may be challenged later in the event of a suit alleging a pattern of discriminatory employment practices.

Beyond the obligations spelled out in the merger agreement, what other postmerger obligations might there be for the acquirer going forward?

These are myriad, limited only by the imagination of federal and state regulators and the plaintiff's bar. For further details, see Part 4.[10] Acquirers are advised to follow not only the letter but also the spirit of the law, or, in the words of one leading ethicist, "the law's *intent*."

INTERNAL COMMUNICATION: KEY CHALLENGES

Why is it so hard to know what's going on with the integration?

An integration may require that thousands of employees do something different from one day to the next. Everyone must know what is expected of him or her, and management at some level must know that information concerning these actions has been received by the right individuals, and that the actions are being performed. Management must know who is and who isn't pulling his or her weight, and what the actual results of the actions are.

That's a lot of information to exchange and track in any context. But the challenge is even greater with nonroutine activities like integration, because (1) there are no long-established processes to provide the necessary information by default, (2) employees are human beings and busy, and many may avoid accepting new tasks outside of their routine, and (3) many individuals believe that their contribution to the integration is invisible and therefore won't be immediately missed.

This is why a lightweight integration management tool can be potentially very helpful.

What should an integration management tool provide?

An integration management tool should

- Track hierarchies of integration tasks.
- Track value drivers and metrics or progress toward achieving them.
- Create simple databases of assets (people, facilities, customers, and so on) affected by the integration.
- Target employee communications based on employee role or profile information.
- Communicate tasks or requests to employees or integration team members.
- Allow task owners to directly update their tasks and create new tasks.
- Proactively collect task updates or other requested data from individuals.
- Roll up the collected data.
- Present graphs or other summaries.
- Present tasks, progress, and results by division, project, owner, value driver, and so on.
- Provide complete top-down visibility of individual and group performance.
- Reduce management and administrative effort.
- Present no learning curve or other adoption barrier for managed employees.
- Be quickly and easily modifiable as needs change, without information technology (IT) resource involvement to slow down the integration.

How can we quickly maximize user acceptance of an integration management tool?

Integration is a fast-paced, high-pressure activity with little tolerance for new baggage. If there are adoption barriers to your integration tool, the entire integration timeline could be affected. This risk is usually unacceptable.

To eliminate user adoption issues, your integration management tool should be designed so that it has little or no impact on how employees are working today. For example, it would be unwise to attempt to turn rank-and-file managers into disciplined project managers. Similarly, do not expect the entire organization to quickly begin using a powerful collaboration environment or document management system.

Instead, design your integration tool so that most users are exposed only to the information collection and dissemination *process*, with little or no *tool* visible to the users. E-mails with form links and Web-based reports are all fine. They are simple interfaces to the process. But tools menu commands, toolbars, learning curves, support requirements, or nontrivial navigation schemes will all create insurmountable process friction for many users. It is better to avoid them entirely.

The art in all of this is to make tools and software disappear as much as possible, so that only interfaces to the process itself are visible most of the time. In this way, your integration management tool will exert a light touch upon the organization while still serving its mission well.

How can the process of collecting data ("data calls") be accelerated?

The time required to complete a large-scale data call or similar project can easily be shortened by 50 to 90 percent, even when tens of thousands of employees must respond. There is no one magic bullet, but several practices will reward you with a significant increase in employee responsiveness.

First, invest some time up front in applying communications guidelines that are proven to elicit maximum response rates (see the next question). This alone can increase response rates tremendously and reduce the time required to collect all responses.

Second, also invest some effort in making it easy for employees to provide what you are asking for. If you are asking for data, provide an attached spreadsheet template with sample data or instructions. Better yet, provide a link to a database Web form. If possible, pre-populate forms with existing data so that the employee can simply edit what has changed, rather than typing in everything. If the employee must review and update a small portion of a larger data set (e.g., client accounts or IT assets), don't send the entire data set to everyone and ask each person to pore through it and find her or his own data. Split the data sets out for each recipient. Doing this manually will not be practical, but it can be readily accomplished with the right information tools.

Finally, never send a request to everyone when it applies only to some. Instead, precision-target only the applicable members of the affected group. Some tools can greatly simplify this targeting challenge.

How can a communication be designed to maximize response rates (for data calls, policy compliance, and so on)?

The following practices, particularly in combination, will often produce a startling improvement in responsiveness to large-scale requests:

1. *Send from the "right" person.* If many of the recipients have never heard of Tom in HR, *do not send from Tom in HR.* And *never* send requests from "Department XYZ." Send only from specific named individuals with a clear position of authority *in the employees' chain of command.* Show your short, simple e-mail draft to the ideal sender and ask for her approval to send it under her name.

2. *Specifically state the desired action right in the subject line.* (Subject: "Submit Conflict of Interest Declaration by 6/10.")

3. *Personalize the e-mail.* If you have the technical capability, always send mass e-mails to "Bob," "Pat," and so on, never to "Valued Employee." Otherwise you create the impression that the employee's individual contribution to the process is invisible or not critical, and that no one knows whether he has complied with the request, or even knows whether he is really supposed to. Also, never write "Dear Bob," as this is no longer appears natural in the e-mail era.

4. *Make the request short and direct.* A common error is to begin broadcast e-mail requests with "At Acme Corporation, we sincerely believe that our employees are our most valuable asset," followed by additional introductory diplomacy. However, many employees perceive this kind of message to be a disingenuous time waster, or will not immediately read the message because it is simply too long and is obviously a form letter. Employees are much more responsive to requests that get to the point quickly and personally. The e-mail should be short enough to read without paging down.

5. *Never request responses "ASAP"; state a precise deadline for responses.* If the task itself is simple, do not give the recipients more than a week to complete it, regardless of when you actually need the data. Simple requests that are due more than a week in the future will not just be done later; rather, many of them will not be done at all—the recipients will have forgotten about them.

6. *Do not let days go by before reminding the unresponsive employees.* This destroys the sense of urgency. If the request is sent Monday, choose Friday as the due date if that is realistic, and send the first reminder on Wednesday, just two days after the initial request. This reinforces urgency.

7. *Never broadcast reminders to individuals who have in fact complied with your request.* Target only the unresponsive, and word the message appropriately ("I see that you have not . . .") and not ambiguously ("If by chance you have not . . ."). The latter pattern communicates that the employee's contribution is anonymous and will not be missed.

What is surprising is the consistent and immediate impact these practices can have on response rates. Many initiatives that have taken a month or months can be completed with 95 percent compliance in five business days. Those cycle-time reductions can translate directly into financial value achieved in the integration.

How can I ensure that integration plans are sound?

It's quite possible to create a detailed and convincing-looking plan that is fundamentally flawed. A tool that can help is a plan validity checklist, such as this checklist in Table 3–1.

TABLE 3 – 1

Plan Validity Checklist

Criteria	Explanation
Executive mandate	Managers are accountable for valid planning and progress against plan.
Plan	Plan is documented, owned by someone, and maintained.
Objectives	Strategies and tactics align.
Action	Objectives are connected to action items "all the way down."
Ownership	Every action item is owned by someone.
Dependencies	Dependences are captured and understood.
Timeline	Schedules are defined and defensible.
Review	All owners have reviewed their action items.
Progress and success metrics	Benchmarks of progress are quantitatively defined, and reportable at all times.
Resources	Resources are realistically identified, and available or obtainable.

Source: E-Know, Inc., Arlington, Virginia.

How can I ensure that integration plans are executable?

It's also possible to create structurally sound but impractical plans. A tool that can help is a plan usability checklist such as the one in Table 3-2. This example is tailored for plans to be run by department managers who are not trained project managers.

T A B L E   3 – 2

Plan Usability Checklist

Criteria	Explanation
Fast	Creation and execution can begin tomorrow
"Bootstrapped"	Created and continuously improved in iterations, not in one fell swoop
Distributed/decentralized	*Not* centrally created or administered (but centrally reviewed)
Flexible	Easily modifiable on the fly
Simple	Easy to modify, update, and monitor without special training
Complete	Specifies everything that must be tracked
Visible	Anyone can view plan and progress, anywhere, anytime
Current	No status data points are more than 24 hours old (or one week, etc.)

Source: E-Know, Inc., Arlington, Virginia.

FORMAL EXTERNAL COMMUNICATION OF THE INTEGRATION PLAN

When should companies first announce their merger plans?

The earlier the better, unless making the announcement would cause harm to one or both of the parties. Privately held companies can make their own determinations of the trade-offs inherent in this timing decision. Publicly held companies must adhere to federal disclosure laws in this regard and should consult with counsel from the earliest stages.

The most important federal disclosure law in this area is Rule 10b-5, which forbids "any person, directly or indirectly . . . to make any untrue statement of a material fact or to omit to state a material fact necessary in order to make the statement made, in the light of circumstances under which they were made, not misleading."

The classic case here is *Basic, Inc.* v. *Levinson* (1988). In this case, a group of shareholders sued Basic Inc. for denying that it was engaged in merger talks when it was in fact already involved in them. The Supreme Court held that Basic should not have made the denial, but rather should have either confirmed that it was engaged in talks or stated that it had no comment.

It is usually best to make merger announcements as far along in the process as possible. The simple reason is that many seemingly successful merger negotiations break down even after the price and key terms are agreed upon in a "handshake" deal. Whether in a private or a public company, aborted merger talks that have previously been announced can cause ill will with the stakeholders of the two companies.

Pushing in the other direction are concerns about leaks and rumors, with the resulting uncertainty and erosion of confidence. The challenge is to do everything possible to avoid such leaks as long as possible and to be ready to make a carefully planned and well-staged public announcement if rumors cannot be suppressed.

What guidelines would you give for the announcement of merger plans?

At the stage when a letter of intent containing all key terms of the acquisition has been signed, public companies are required to make a disclosure to all their stockholders. This announcement must describe all the salient terms of the transaction. Obviously, a simultaneous announcement should be made to the other stakeholders of the company. There is nothing worse than having them learn about the deal from reading the newspaper.

Unfortunately, at the time of the initial announcement of a planned merger, there are no plans to announce. In many mergers between public companies, in-depth due diligence begins only after the public announcement. In other circumstances, integration plans can be developed only after the negotiation of the merger agreement—a process that should yield useful information about resources, processes, and responsibilities, as well as critical insights into culture.

For many constituencies, however, it is not enough to simply talk about the basic deal terms. Questions will arise from customers, suppliers, shareholders, lenders, employees, and others: What will happen to prices? Will the new company still buy from us? What will happen to share prices after the deal? Will the new company remain solvent? Will my job be eliminated? Will our local plant be closed?

Yet, at this early stage, there are no answers to most or all of these questions. In announcing their deal, companies should acknowledge that these questions exist and should explain how and when they will be answered. Any commitment to address such questions within a specified time frame must be honored, as a breach in this regard will cause even more consternation and insecurity.

Assuming that at the time of the merger announcement, companies do have detailed plans, how much of these plans should they disclose?

In general, acquirers should communicate as much about the deal's logic and plans as they can without compromising their competitive position. In public companies, such disclosures will help the market appreciate the value creation potential of the deal and will help to manage shareholder expectations concerning timing and results.

In the case of postmerger divestiture plans, companies will want to balance the positive impact that an announcement may have on the share price against the negative impact that the announcement may have on productivity. In most cases, companies can and should opt for early and complete disclosure. For example, at the same time that Revlon Inc. announced its plans to merge its cosmetics stores with Cosmetic Center Inc., it stated that the merger would probably lead to a spin-off of the unit.

It should be noted, though, that public companies must conform to various legal requirements outlining what they may and may not say (in public announcements and in filings with regulators) about their postmerger plans.

TAXABLE M&A REPORTING

Congress has created a new reporting rule for taxable mergers. The 2004 Jobs Act requires a corporation acquiring the stock or assets of a target corporation to disclose specified information to the IRS and the target corporation's shareholders. This reporting requirement applies only to the acquiring corporation (or, alternatively, to a stock transfer agent). However, new tax regulations could require disclosure by the acquired corporation as well. Also, the 2004 Jobs Act extends existing information reporting penalties to failures to comply with the requirements under this provision.

What must public companies say about their postmerger integration plans?

Acquirers making a tender offer bid for a U.S. public company must follow the disclosure laws for their state. With respect to federal laws, there are two important SEC filings: a Schedule 13D form, disclosing the acquisition of 5 percent or more of a company's stock, and a Schedule 14D-1 form, disclosing the intention to make a tender offer bid. In addition to asking for basic information (name, address, and so on), the forms ask for the bidder's long-term intentions.

Item 4 of Schedule 13D asks acquirers to describe the "Purpose of [the] Transaction," as follows:

> State the purpose or purposes of the acquisition of securities of the issuer. Describe any plans or proposals which the reporting persons may have which relate to or would result in:
>
> a. The acquisition by any person of additional securities of the issuer, or the disposition of securities of the issuer;
> b. An extraordinary corporate transaction, such as a merger, reorganization, or liquidation, involving the issuer or any of its subsidiaries;
> c. A sale or transfer of a material amount of assets of the issuer or any of its subsidiaries;
> d. Any change in the present board of directors or management of the issuer.[11]

In a similar vein, Item 5 of Schedule 14D-1 asks acquirers to disclose the "Purpose of the Tender Offer and Plans or Proposals of the Bidder," as follows:

> State the purpose or purposes of the tender offer. . . . Describe any plans or proposals which relate to or would result in:

a. An extraordinary corporate transaction, such as a merger, reorganization, or liquidation involving the subject company or any of its subsidiaries;

b. A sale or transfer of a material amount of assets of the subject company or any of its subsidiaries;

c. Any change in the present board of directors or management of the subject company;

d. Any material change in the present capitalization or dividend policy of the subject company;

e. Any other material change in the subject company's corporate structure or business.[12]

Although only acquirers of public companies have to make and update these disclosures, this regulation makes a sensible "short list" of what any stakeholder in any company—public or private—would want to know about postmerger plans.

Bidders must send a copy of their SEC filings to the stock exchange where their company's shares are listed. They should also make an announcement to the public via press releases.

Aside from the SEC, what other regulators must be informed of a plan to merge?

The Federal Trade Commission (FTC) and the Department of Justice (DOJ) must be notified of merger plans involving one or more large U.S. companies.[13] Under the Hart-Scott-Rodino Antitrust Improvements Act of 1976, the parties must provide financial information broken out by industry. The FTC and the DOJ use this information to determine whether or not the combination of the two companies would significantly lessen competition in any markets, as set forth under these agencies' joint guidelines. These guidelines, which are updated periodically, include a formula for calculating anticompetitiveness called the Herfindahl-Hirschman Index (H-H Index).

In addition to reviewing filings, the agencies may request copies of various acquisition documents, such as the postmerger plan or the acquisition agreement. Although these documents are treated confidentially, they may be used against the companies in a finding of undue market concentration—one good reason to ask counsel to review all merger documents, including the integration plan.

Other regulatory agencies may require additional notification. For example, U.S. banks must disclose their merger plans to the Federal Reserve System (Fed).

How long does the regulatory approval process usually take?

It can take anywhere from several months to several *years* in a contested case. Fortunately, though, the period of regulatory review is shrinking. The SEC has offered quick review to companies that write their filings (and related communications to shareholders) in plain English. Also, the FTC has rules that guarantee a "fast track" of no more than 13 months for a decision. Bank reviews remain slow, but could speed up in response to recent suggestions for reform.[14]

Suppose disclosing certain plans for postmerger change would be harmful to a company's business. Does it have to disclose them?

It has to disclose them to the SEC, but it may request an "order of confidential treatment" from the SEC for a limited amount of time.

As a practical matter, companies cannot hide behind the SEC's confidential disclosure policy—largely because the SEC is unwilling to allow confidentiality in circumstances where a proposed change in the merged entity would have a substantial impact on the capital markets. Additionally, while merger candidates sometimes believe that certain announcements might be harmful to their business, often the opposite is true, as shareholders and other stakeholders are far happier dealing with the certainty of announced intentions than with the risk and unpredictability of unannounced intentions. At the same time, many companies do not have definite postmerger plans at this stage, and conclude, for both securities law and business purposes, that an announcement of potential changes would be premature.

What may publicly held acquirers *not* tell the public about their integration plans?

In announcing postmerger plans, the parties to the transaction can say anything, but they must be cautious about making any "forward-looking statements" about the results they anticipate from the merger to come. Although forward-looking statements are protected under the safe harbor provisions of the Securities Litigation Reform Act of 1995, this protection has limits.

To conform to federal securities law (specifically, new Section 27 of the Securities Act of 1933 and new Section 21D of the Securities Exchange Act of 1934), forward-looking statements must be accompanied by meaningful "cautionary statements" identifying "important factors" that could cause actual results to differ "materially" from the results projected in the statement. The law does not impose a duty to update, but it is generally considered a good idea when there are material postmerger changes to report.

What about communications between the merging companies? Are there any restrictions here?

Unfortunately, yes, if the companies are considered competitors that are subject to federal antitrust law (that is, anticompetitive according to the H-H Index). Under Section 1 of the Sherman Act, competitors may not "conspire" to lessen competition in their markets—a restriction that, incredibly enough, can apply to competitors that are in the process of planning to merge.

Premerger discussions of postmerger plans may be considered a conspiracy to restrain trade if the discussions do the following:

1. Depart from the normal routine of merger activity.
2. Significantly affect customers' purchasing choices.
3. Occur well in advance of the closing date.

As mentioned in the beginning of this section on communication, companies should check with counsel very early in the communication process.

COMMUNICATING WITH STAKEHOLDERS

How can buyers and sellers stem the tide of rumors from various stakeholders before, during, and immediately after the deal?

Bear in mind that rumors are a symptom of a more pernicious problem: lack of information. The responsibility for the latter rests squarely with senior management.

In general, companies that are planning to merge should say so publicly as soon as they have reached an agreement to combine. This announcement should go out to all the companies' stakeholders and to the general public.

This initial announcement should be the beginning of a series of regular communications through letters, memos, meetings, and any other available media about each phase of the transaction. Once the transaction is close to completion or completed and a plan is in place, both the acquirer and the acquired firm should disseminate the plan (in brief format) to all stakeholder groups, developing a special *position statement* for *each* group. For more details, see Part 4.

The communication process must continue for the entire period of active integration—generally up to 12 months. The best strategy is to establish a regular process of communications, both formal and informal, at the front end. In the case of employees, for example, these would include monthly updates on the merged business. Communications should include not only a description of postmerger plans, but also how and why these plans were made and how they will be carried out. Ideally, the affected parties will have participated in forming the plans, so the announcements will not come as great surprises.

To build stakeholder ownership of the plans, announcements should contain financial details, which ultimately measure the success or failure of new policies. The goal is to have different stakeholders "buy into" postmerger plans by following the transformation process, understanding its components, and checking its success.

Meanwhile, at every stage of postmerger integration, management of the new company should communicate to all stakeholders in all appropriate media, as shown in Figure 3-2.

For more planning and communications paradigms, see the appendices to this chapter and to this book.

MERGER SCENARIOS

What are the basic kinds of merger scenarios, and how can they affect postmerger communications?

There are four basic scenarios for mergers: raid, contest, collaboration, and rescue, each of which can create "negative synergy" by destabilizing employee trust.[15]

FIGURE 3-2

Audience-Media Communications Matrix

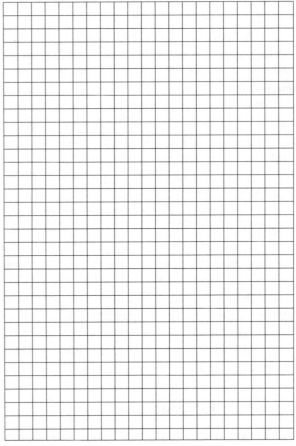

Courtesy of Gene Grossman, Siegel & Gale, New York

In a *raid*, an acquirer initiates and pursues a change of control in a public company against the express wishes of the company's management. If the raider is a going concern company, it will typically attain control via a tender offer—that is, a general, publicized bid to buy 5 percent or more of a company's shares at a premium price. A raid may also be accomplished by a proxy fight, that is, a solicitation of stockholders urging them to vote (by marking their "proxy" voting cards prior to the annual shareholders' meeting) for a slate of directors that opposes the current management. However, most proxy fights are waged by individuals or investment groups, not by going concern companies. In a *contest for control*, the acquirer is one of several entities seeking control of a public company. In a *collaboration*, the acquiring company and the acquired company seek their union on an entirely voluntary basis. Finally, in a *rescue*, the acquiring company comes on the scene in response to a plea from a company that is desperately seeking a buyer to save it from a raider or from creditors.

These four categories form a spectrum of willingness to integrate (from low to high) on the part of the acquired company. But whether the target's willingness is low or high, acquirers must be aware of the potential for negative synergy inherent in each scenario.

What are the main problems inherent in each M&A scenario?

The raid scenario, with its target-company resistance, mistrust, and poor morale, generates negative feelings about the acquirer. The contested situation, which generates fatigue, stress, and anxiety in target-company employees, generates negative feelings about the bidding process. In the collaborative merger scenario, with its potential for post-honeymoon disappointment and disillusionment, employees experience the loss of positive feelings about their future with the acquirer, whereas the financial rescue generates negative feelings about the new company's future. Finally, the panic and haste in a situational rescue by a white knight lead to a different kind of problem: confusion about the new company's future as a result of absence of information and direction.

Although *all* of these problems may be present in any *one* scenario, they do tend to cluster as described, and so do appropriate solutions.

How can a company solve these problems?

The problem of *negative feelings about the acquirer* has two solutions: either avoid creating them in the first place or, if you have created them, step aside after the acquirer wins. There is no other dignified way to deal with this catch-22.

The problem of *negative feelings about the bidding process* is much easier to solve. In the postmerger era, the message can simply be, to quote an old hymn, "The strife is o'er, the battle done." The new management can proclaim and demonstrate that the bidding wars are over and that it is time to get back to business in a new, improved setting.

To deal with the *loss of positive feelings about the future,* the new company can work on restoring such feelings by fulfilling all promises made. Although the fulfillment of promises will always fall short of optimistic expectations, good communication from the beginning can bridge this gap.

Combating outright *negative feelings about the future* may be impossible when it comes to the employees who will not be part of that future. As for dealing with survivors, it is important to stress that the process used to retain them (and to reject others) was fair and impartial and was based on the new company's legitimate plans for survival and growth.

Counteracting *confusion about the new company's future* requires a vision of the future and an ability to communicate that vision to all stakeholders and to the public.[16]

INTERNATIONAL CONSIDERATIONS

What are some planning and communications imperatives to keep in mind in cross-border deals?

In international deals, it is always desirable to hire local communications experts to deal with unique cultural and legal requirements. On the employee front, most foreign countries have far more protective laws for employees, and employee expectations concerning layoffs and restructurings are quite different (and generally far more hostile) from those in the United States.

MORE IS BETTER: A CASE IN POINT

This statement is certainly true—and this example is very close to home. It involves the very book you are reading! The first edition of *The Art of M&A Integration* was originally going to be published by Irwin Professional Publishing, a unit of Times Mirror. By the time the book was printed, however, Times Mirror had sold Irwin to McGraw-Hill Companies.

To his credit, the CEO-president of Irwin sent letters to authors informing them of these developments. The first letter stated that Times Mirror (which had acquired Irwin from Dow Jones several years earlier) had decided to divest Irwin and that further details would be forthcoming. The second letter told authors that Times Mirror was planning to sell Irwin to the McGraw-Hill Companies and that the transaction would be complete by September 1996, subject to government approvals.

Neither letter contained much information beyond these basic facts, yet the tone of the letters (and indeed their very existence) provided assurance that senior management empathized with the sense of uncertainty that authors might have in a merger situation. Similar letters went out to other stakeholders.

Prior to the combination of the two companies, employees attended daily meetings to learn about developments. According to one source, it was reassuring to be informed on a daily basis, even if at times all they heard was, "We've got no news to report today."

In the end, there were changes, including dismissal or departure of some employees and even the loss of the Irwin name (for all but one product line), but at least these changes did not come as a surprise to Irwin employees, thanks to Irwin's communication efforts at the outset.

After the merger was official, key employees became involved immediately in a series of nuts-and-bolts integration meetings attended by representatives of both companies. The result was a restructuring of the combined company that included leadership positions for former Irwin managers (who are now in charge of finance books such as this one). This helped McGraw-Hill retain the best human resources—the focus of the next chapter.

APPENDIX 3 – A

<u>Sample Mission, Team, and Timeline</u> <u>for Acquisition</u>

Team Mission

To facilitate a smooth assimilation of employees of newly acquired organizations into Company XY and to affect a smooth transition of their functional transactions into XY business plans, objectives, and strategies.

Source: Mid-sized company in Florida. Names fictional. Used with permission 2005.

Acquisition Integration Team

• Cross-Functional Team Members

- Mary Davis >> Payroll/Benefits Integration and Organizational Charts
- Sharon Peters and PR firm >> Marketing Communications
- Alma Rivers
  - >>Computer Requirements/Voice data interface/eConnectivity
- Jeff Coates
  - >>ISO 9000/Customer Service/Contracts/Facility/Environmental
- Sam Wilson/Tony Robins
  - >> Transaction Integration and Sales Expectations
- Bob Smith
  - >>Financial Institution Changes
- Felix Hernandez
  - >>Web Site Integration and Transaction Modeling
- Susan Ivory
  - >>Integration Progress Tracking/Single Point Contact for Acquirees

69

Acquisition Integration Team

• Roadblocks*

– Confusing, duplicate communication with acquirees
  – Solvable through good internal processes
– Firedrills at time of acquisition for employee integration
  – Solvable through closer communication with deal makers
– Connectivity issues - email and internet accessibility
  – Solvable through synchronizing Rivers/Wilson/Ivory on timing
– Cultural Integration
  – Solvable through more resources in HR and continued good communication from Sales Management
– Development of overall company database
  – Need overall systems to facilitate faster access to customer community
– Communication of requirements/sales goals for each facility to implementation team
  – Responsiveness to needs

*Notes from team meeting held to plan integration.

Acquisition Integration Process Timing

Closing Timeline

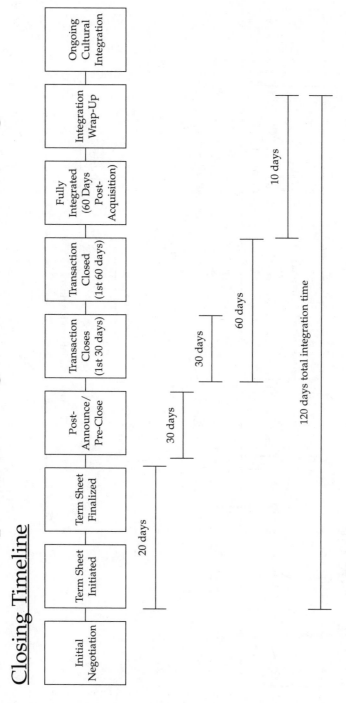

Acquisition Integration Process Timeline

Closing Timeline

Initial Negotiation → Term Sheet Initiated → Term Sheet Finalized → Post-Announce/Pre-Close → Transaction Closes (1st 30 days) → Transaction Closed (1st 60 days) → Fully Integrated (60 Days Post-Acquisition) → Integration Wrap-Up → Ongoing Cultural Integration

A 4/20-5/1 close
B 4-21-6/1 close
C 5/30-7/24 close (ex-real estate)
D 7/12-8/18 close
(four transactions)

20 days
30 days
30 days
60 days
10 days

120 days total integration time

Acquisition Closing Timeline

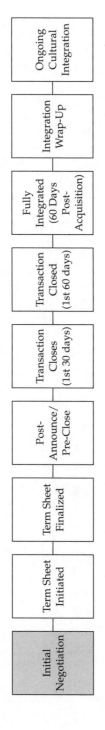

| Initial Negotiation | Term Sheet Initiated | Term Sheet Finalized | Post-Announce/ Pre-Close | Transaction Closes (1st 30 days) | Transaction Closed (1st 60 days) | Fully Integrated (60 Days Post-Acquisition) | Integration Wrap-Up | Ongoing Cultural Integration |

Correlated Integration Activities

During Initial Negotiation Process:

• Notification from James to Ivory and Davis (on alert)

<u>Comments:</u>

-A - Complete
-B - Complete
-C - Complete
-D - Complete

Acquisition Closing Timeline

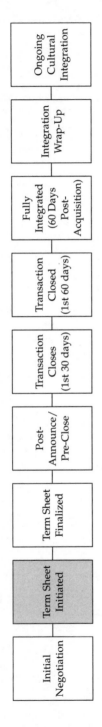

| Initial Negotiation | Term Sheet Initiated | Term Sheet Finalized | Post-Announce/ Pre-Close | Transaction Closes (1st 30 days) | Transaction Closed (1st 60 days) | Fully Integrated (60 Days Post-Acquisition) | Integration Wrap-Up | Ongoing Cultural Integration |

Correlated Integration Activities

During Term Sheet Initiation:

- James Notifies Ivory and Davis

- HR Information Collected (Current Employee and Payroll Info) (Davis)

- Notify Acquirees of Initial On Site Orientation (Davis)

- Marketing Communications prepares press release and customer letters (Peters)

- IT addresses internet connectivity and orders circuits required (Rivers)

- Ivory updates new acquisition contact sheet and distributes to Acquisition Team and Integration Team

- Sales prepares profile on new facility to Integration and Acq. Teams

Comments:

- Complete through D

- Open: D

- Open: C and D

- Open: C and D

- See Attached Plan

- Open: Add C and D

- Open: A, B, C, D

Acquisition Closing Timeline

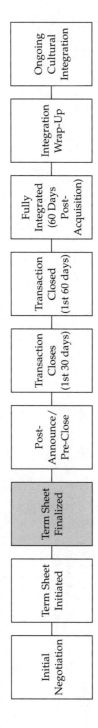

| Initial Negotiation | Term Sheet Initiated | Term Sheet Finalized | Post-Announce/Pre-Close | Transaction Closes (1st 30 days) | Transaction Closed (1st 60 days) | Fully Integrated (60 Days Post-Acquisition) | Integration Wrap-Up | Ongoing Cultural Integration |

Correlated Integration Activities

Once Term Sheet is finalized:

	Comments:
• Announcement date determined by James and communicated to Ivory/Davis	-Open: C, D
• Conference Call scheduled with Newly-Acquired employees (Davis)	-Open: C,D
• Internal announcement from Management to current employees regarding acquisition and significance (Davis)	-Open: C,D
• Finalize dates for initial on site employee orientation (Davis)	-Open: C,D
• Marketing Communications send letter to current and newly expanded customer database (Peters and PR firm)	-Open: B,C,D
• Marketing Communications releases announcement to public (Peters and PR firm)	-Open: B,C,D

Acquisition Closing Timeline

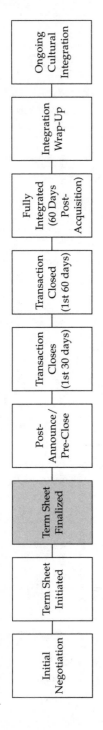

| Initial Negotiation | Term Sheet Initiated | Term Sheet Finalized | Post-Announce/Pre-Close | Transaction Closes (1st 30 days) | Transaction Closed (1st 60 days) | Fully Integrated (60 Days Post-Acquisition) | Integration Wrap-Up | Ongoing Cultural Integration |

Correlated Integration Activities

Once Term Sheet is finalized:

	Comments:
• Sales provides Requirements for Connectivity to IT (City/State/Zip/Contact Name/Phone #) - (Wilson)	-Open: ALL
• Finance orients acquirees on financial institution process, timing And logo use for transactions (James/Smith)	Open: B,C,D.
• Integration Handbook to new acquirees (Ivory/Davis)	Open: ALL
• Ivory established as primary integration contact	Open: D
• Sales provides IT with new employee name, job title, e-mail access, laptop or desktop PC through new hire form completion. IT places order appropriately (Wilson)	Open: ALL

Acquisition Closing Timeline

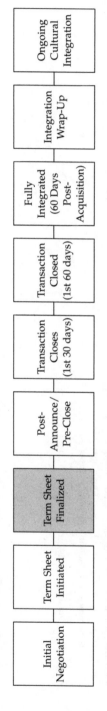

| Initial Negotiation | Term Sheet Initiated | Term Sheet Finalized | Post-Announce/Pre-Close | Transaction Closes (1st 30 days) | Transaction Closed (1st 60 days) | Fully Integrated (60 Days Post-Acquisition) | Integration Wrap-Up | Ongoing Cultural Integration |

Correlated Integration Activities

Once Term Sheet is finalized:

- IT sets up training dates for new employees for computer/e-mail orientation (Rivers)

- Ivory updates facility chart and distributes to acquisition and integration Teams

Comments:

Open: ALL

Open: C,D

Acquisition Closing Timeline

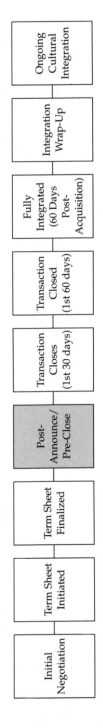

Initial Negotiation	Term Sheet Initiated	Term Sheet Finalized	Post-Announce/ Pre-Close	Transaction Closes (1st 30 days)	Transaction Closed (1st 60 days)	Fully Integrated (60 Days Post-Acquisition)	Integration Wrap-Up	Ongoing Cultural Integration

Correlated Integration Activities

During Post Announcement/Pre-Close Phase:

Comments:

• Conduct initial on site employee meeting (Davis, Ivory)

Open: C,D

• Present XY business strategy, significance of new acquiree to strategy, key contacts, organizational charts and XY locations (distribute facilities list to all employees) (Wilson, Davis, Ivory)

Open: D
Open: ALL

• Distribute/Discuss Assimilation Handbook internally (Davis, Ivory)

Open: ALL

• Conduct Acquiree Principal "Expectation Meeting" in Florida (Sales/Forecasts/Integration Process/Org Chart/Marketing Communications- logo/identity manual) - (Wilson/Ivory)

Open: C,D

• Letterhead/Business cards ordered   (Partridge)

Open: B,C,D

Acquisition Closing Timeline

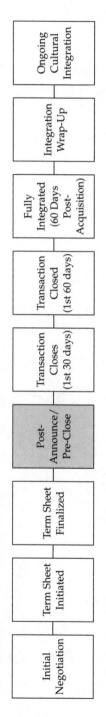

| Initial Negotiation | Term Sheet Initiated | Term Sheet Finalized | Post-Announce/Pre-Close | Transaction Closes (1st 30 days) | Transaction Closed (1st 60 days) | Fully Integrated (60 Days Post-Acquisition) | Integration Wrap-Up | Ongoing Cultural Integration |

Correlated Integration Activities

During Post Announcement/Pre-Close Phase:

Comments:

- Determine Customer Service Call Routing with Principals and determine plan (Coates) — Open: ALL

- Physical Facility plan (including signage) initiated including ISO 9000 regulations and environmental concerns (Coates) — Open: ALL

- Determine Contracts Administration plan (Coates) — Open: ALL

- Hernandez evaluates transactions and makes recommendations to Robins — Open: D

- Marketing Assessments for demographics initiated (Hernandez) — Open: ALL

- Travis Robins develops plan for transaction integration — Open: C,D

Acquisition Closing Timeline

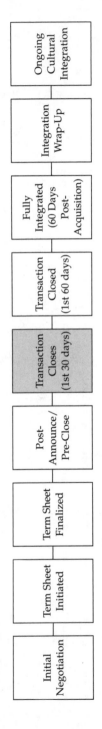

| Initial Negotiation | Term Sheet Initiated | Term Sheet Finalized | Post-Announce/Pre-Close | Transaction Closes (1st 30 days) | Transaction Closed (1st 60 days) | Fully Integrated (60 Days Post-Acquisition) | Integration Wrap-Up | Ongoing Cultural Integration |

Correlated Integration Activities

Once Transaction is CLOSED (1st 30 days):

Comments:

- Establish bank accounts for acquiree   (Smith)   Open: C,D

- Transaction Integration Implemented (Sales, Robins)   Open: C,D

- Letterhead issued (Partridge)   Open: C,D

- Business cards issued (Peters)   Open: C,D

- Logo Changes instituted (all paperwork) - (Peters/Smith)   Open: ALL

Acquisition Closing Timeline

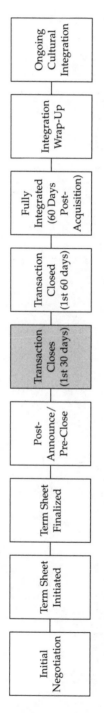

Initial Negotiation	Term Sheet Initiated	Term Sheet Finalized	Post-Announce/ Pre-Close	Transaction Closes (1st 30 days)	Transaction Closed (1st 60 days)	Fully Integrated (60 Days Post-Acquisition)	Integration Wrap-Up	Ongoing Cultural Integration

Correlated Integration Activities

Once Transaction is CLOSED (1st 30 days):

- Phone Answering Training initiated for all acquirees (Coates)

- New Contract Administration Plan becomes effective (Coates)

- Physical Structure changes begin and ISO 9000 process becomes effective (Coates)

- Computers Installed and e-mail training conducted for on site employees (Rivers)

- Voice Mail additions established/ training for newly acquired employees (Coates)

Comments:

Open: ALL

Open: ALL

Open: ALL

Open: ALL

Open: ALL

81

Acquisition Closing Timeline

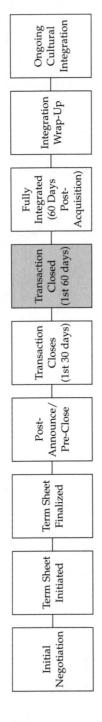

| Initial Negotiation | Term Sheet Initiated | Term Sheet Finalized | Post-Announce/ Pre-Close | Transaction Closes (1st 30 days) | Transaction Closed (1st 60 days) | Fully Integrated (60 Days Post-Acquisition) | Integration Wrap-Up | Ongoing Cultural Integration |

Correlated Integration Activities

Once Transaction is CLOSED (1st 60 days):

- Registration and Insurance Evaluation/Compliance (James)

  - Building
  - Vehicles

- P&S Notification (James)

- Web Site Integration Addressed (Hernandez)

- Acquiree employee training on (Wilson/Ivory)

  - XY Products
  - XY Business Plan

Comments:

Open: C,D

Open: ?

Open: ?

Open: ALL

Acquisition Closing Timeline

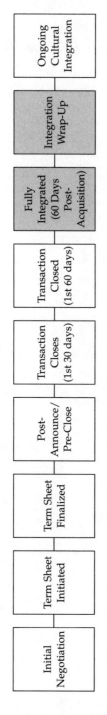

| Initial Negotiation | Term Sheet Initiated | Term Sheet Finalized | Post-Announce/Pre-Close | Transaction Closes (1st 30 days) | Transaction Closed (1st 60 days) | Fully Integrated (60 Days Post-Acquisition) | Integration Wrap-Up | Ongoing Cultural Integration |

Correlated Integration Activities

<u>Once Fully Integrated:</u>

- Close Out Meeting scheduled to Review Process with Acquiree Principal in Florida (Wilson/Ivory)

- Distribute Feedback Surveys on Integration or other Concerns to New Acquirees (Wilson/Ivory)

- Collect, collate and distribute results and open issues to Sales, Executive Management and Acquiree Principal (Wilson/Ivory)

<u>Comments:</u>

Open: ALL

Open: ALL

Open: ALL

APPENDIX 3 – B

Communications Plan Matrix

	Lead Group(s)	Support Group(s)	Activities That Must Occur First	Tactical Data Needed	Strategic Information Needed	Prioritization (H = Early Activity)	Elapsed Time (Days)	Actual Time (Hours)
Step 1: Message Development								
Gather due diligence information on acquiree	Corporate Development	All functions						
Develop messages					Why did we acquire (strategic or operational)?			
Acquiree employees	Corporate Communications	Acquired company president	Development of integration plan	Key dates from integration group		H	5	16
Senior management talking points (Why are we doing this? What will the process be?)								
Acquiree CEO broadcast e-mail								
Acquiree customers (notification of acquisition)	Marketing Communications	Acquired company president				H	8	12

(Continued)

	Ownership							
	Lead Group(s)	Support Group(s)	Activities That Must Occur First	Tactical Data Needed	Strategic Information Needed	Prioritization (H = Early Activity)	Elapsed Time (Days)	Actual Time (Hours)
Face-to-face talking points (top customers)								
Letter (other customers)								
News media	Corporate Communications	Acquired company president				M	3	7
Investment community	Corporate Communications	Investor Relations				M	1	3
Regulators	Legal/Regulatory		Corporate fact sheet; media and investment messages			H	7	6
ABC employees	Corporate Communications	HR				M	1	3
Approve messages	Legal, HR, acquired company							
Step 2: Launch Communications								
Acquiree employees								
Senior Management one-on-ones	Corporate Communications	Acquiree senior management				H		
Review talking points with senior management	Corporate Communications		Crafting talking points			H	1	4

(Continued)

| | Ownership | | | | | | | | |
	Lead Group(s)	Support Group(s)	Activities That Must Occur First	Tactical Data Needed	Strategic Information Needed	Prioritization (H = Early Activity)	Elapsed Time (Days)	Actual Time (Hours)
Oversee senior management meeting scheduling	Acquiree senior management	Corporate Communications		Employee list by function		H	5	2
Conduct one-on-ones	Acquiree senior management		Deal closing			H (Day One)	2	4
Broadcast e-mail from acquiree CEO	Corporate Communications	Acquiree senior management	Deal closing			H (Day One)	0	0
Welcome party	Integration Group	Corporate Communications/ HR					2	
HR compensation review	HR							
Acquiree customers								
Collect customer list with accurate contact names	Business Development (due diligence)					H	14	5
Print/ distribute letter (on stationery headed: ABC, an ABC company)	Marketing Communications	Advertising/print agencies	Collect customer list with accurate contact names	Customer list			14	5

(Continued)

	Lead Group(s)	Support Group(s)	Activities That Must Occur First	Ownership Tactical Data Needed	Strategic Information Needed	Prioritization (H = Early Activity)	Elapsed Time (Days)	Actual Time (Hours)
Schedule face-to-face with top customers	Acquiree senior management	Marketing Communications	Identification of top customers				14	4
Execute face-to-face with top customers	Acquiree senior management		Develop face-to-face talking points				14	0
News media								
Consolidate media contact lists and prioritize	Corporate Communications	Acquiree senior management						
Press release	Corporate Communications	Investor Relations/legal approval						
Set up interviews with press	Corporate Communications	Acquiree senior management						
Create and distribute collateral	Corporate Communications/ ad agencies	Investor Relations/Legal						
Plan and host event	Corporate Communications	Investor Relations			Strategic nature of deal; size of deal			
Investment community								

(Continued)

	Ownership							
	Lead Group(s)	Support Group(s)	Activities That Must Occur First	Tactical Data Needed	Strategic Information Needed	Prioritization (H = Early Activity)	Elapsed Time (Days)	Actual Time (Hours)
Consolidate investment community contact lists and prioritize	Investor Relations	Corporate Communications						
Press release and interviews, if relevant	Corporate Communications	Investor Relations/legal approval	Investment community message development, deal signed					
Create and distribute collateral	Corporate Communications/ ad agencies	Investor Relations/Legal						
Plan and host event	Investor Relations	Corporate Communications			Strategic nature of deal; size of deal			
Regulators	Legal/Regulatory	Corporate Communications						
ABC employees	Corporate Communications	HR						
Step 3: Brand Strategy/ Implementation								

(Continued)

	Ownership							
	Lead Group(s)	Support Group(s)	Activities That Must Occur First	Tactical Data Needed	Strategic Information Needed	Prioritization (H = Early Activity)	Elapsed Time (Days)	Actual Time (Hours)
Determine short-term and long-term brand strategy	Marketing Communications, Business Development, acquired company, Legal	Other functions			Decision factors: billing system, regulatory, brand strength, different customer/product set			
Maintain brand								
Co-brand (e.g., Z, an ABC company)								
One brand								
Sales collateral								
Create new sales collateral	Marketing Communications/ ad agency/ acquired company	Marketing approval						
Distribute sales collateral to sales force	Sales training	Marketing Communications						
Operationalize brand migration								

(Continued)

		Ownership						
	Lead Group(s)	Support Group(s)	Activities That Must Occur First	Tactical Data Needed	Strategic Information Needed	Prioritization (H = Early Activity)	Elapsed Time (Days)	Actual Time (Hours)
Billing system integration	Billing							
Customer service messages	Customer Services							
Advertising materials	Marketing Communications							
Sales collateral	Marketing Communications							
Direct mail pieces	Marketing Communications							
Acquiree receptionist message	Short-term — Corporate Communications; Long-term — Corporate Communications							
Acquiree stationery, business cards	Facilities							
Acquiree signage	Facilities			Legally required? Full brand conversion?				
Authorization letter								

(Continued)

	Lead Group(s)	Support Group(s)	Activities That Must Occur First	Ownership Tactical Data Needed	Strategic Information Needed	Prioritization (H = Early Activity)	Elapsed Time (Days)	Actual Time (Hours)
Craft ABC authorization letter (only if acquiree is in regulated industry)	Marketing Communications	Legal					14	5
Develop collateral for authorization letter	Marketing Communications/ ad agency	Legal/Marketing	Authorization letter				45	?
Send ABC authorization letter			45 days before complete brand conversion					
Step 4: Follow-on Communications								
Integration status update e-mails/ meetings with acquiree employees								

Source: Midsized acquirer based in Virginia. Provided courtesy of E-Know, Inc., Arlington, Virginia.

A P P E N D I X   3 – C

Integration Planning Worksheet

Key Business Process:

Primary Integration Activities*	Priority	Tasks/Subtasks	Task Owner	Prerequisites	Required Tactical Data	Relevant Strategic Questions
	• Day 1	1.				
	• 100 days	2.				
	• 6 months	3.				
	• Year 1	4.				
	• Eventually	5.				
		6				
		7				
		8				
		9.				
		10.				
	• Day 1	1.				
	• 100 days	2.				
	• 6 months	3.				

(Continued)

Key Business Process:

Primary Integration Activities*	Priority	Tasks/Subtasks	Task Owner	Prerequisites	Required Tactical Data	Relevant Strategic Questions
	• Eventually	5.				
		6.				
		7.				
		8.				
		9.				
		10.				
	• Day 1	1.				
	• 100 days	2.				
	• 6 months	3.				
	• Year 1	4.				
	• Eventually	5.				
		6.				
		7.				
		8.				
		9.				
		10.				

APPENDIX 3 – D

Integration Plan Outline (Sample Outline Focusing on HR, Communications, and IT)

1. Conduct integration planning kick-off meeting
2. HR Integration Plan
    2.1. Standardize HR policy
    2.2. Integrate HR processes
        2.2.1. Employee relations
            2.2.1.1.   Performance review and evaluation
            2.2.1.2.   Employee dispute resolution
            2.2.1.3.   Employee complaint investigation
            2.2.1.4.   Acquisition integration communication
            2.2.1.5.   Turnover reporting
            2.2.1.6.   Employee relations legal/regulatory compliance
            2.2.1.7.   EEO
            2.2.1.8.   OSHA
        2.2.2. Benefits administration
            2.2.2.1.   Benefits orientation
            2.2.2.2.   Presentation of compensation/benefits at welcome party
            2.2.2.3.   Benefits conversion and enrollment
            2.2.2.4.   Medical
            2.2.2.5.   Dental
            2.2.2.6.   Benefits plan administration
            2.2.2.7.   Benefits-related legal/regulatory compliance
            2.2.2.8.   401(k)
            2.2.2.9.   Health/welfare
            2.2.2.10. New hire process
            2.2.2.11. Termination process

2.2.3. Compensation
    2.2.3.1. Job mapping and redesign
    2.2.3.2. Map acquiree and acquirer job positions
    2.2.3.3. Set pay scales
    2.2.3.4. Manage changes in pay
    2.2.3.5. Performance reviews and promotions
    2.2.3.6. Equity/noncash compensation
    2.2.3.7. Sales compensation

2.2.4. Payroll
    2.2.4.1. Leave accrual and administration
    2.2.4.2. Customer service
    2.2.4.3. Payroll administration
    2.2.4.4. Accounting reconciliation
    2.2.4.5. Communications with treasury
    2.2.4.6. Pay-cycle disbursement

2.2.5. Recruiting/staffing

2.2.6. Facilities management
    2.2.6.1. Office/real estate consolidation
    2.2.6.2. Update database of site/contracts, leases
    2.2.6.3. Assign leases to acquirer
    2.2.6.4. Obtain acquiree staffing projections

2.2.7. Organization development/training

2.3. HR infrastructure integration

2.3.1. Employee set-up in HRIS
    2.3.1.1. Establish department numbers for acquirees
    2.3.1.2. Collect acquiree employee information
    2.3.1.3. Input acquiree EE data in Lawson (HRIS) database
    2.3.1.4. Provide acquirees with acquirer services
    2.3.1.5. Provide acquirees with acquirer intranet access

2.4. HR communications plan development

2.5. HR contracts and commitments

3. Corporate Communications Integration Plan
   3.1. Message development
      3.1.1. Gather due diligence information on acquiree
      3.1.2. Obtain communications message from acquirer CEO
      3.1.3. Craft messages
           3.1.3.1. Acquiree employees
           3.1.3.2. Senior management talking points
           3.1.3.3. Acquiree CEO broadcast e-mail
           3.1.3.4. Acquiree customers
           3.1.3.5. Face-to-face talking points to top customers
           3.1.3.6. Letter to second-tier customers
           3.1.3.7. News media
           3.1.3.8. Investment community
           3.1.3.9. Regulators
           3.1.3.10. Acquirer employees
           3.1.3.11. Approve messages
   3.2. Launch communications
      3.2.1. Acquiree employees
           3.2.1.1. Senior management one-on-ones
           3.2.1.2. Review talking points with senior management
           3.2.1.3. Oversee senior management meeting scheduling
           3.2.1.4. Conduct one-on-one meetings
           3.2.1.5. Broadcast e-mail from acquiree CEO
      3.2.2. Acquiree customers
           3.2.2.1. Collect customer list with contact names
           3.2.2.2. Print/distribute notice announcing merger
           3.2.2.3. Schedule face-to-face with top customers
           3.2.2.4. Execute face-to-face with top customers

3.2.3. News media

    3.2.3.1. Consolidate media contact lists and prioritize

    3.2.3.2. Press release

    3.2.3.3. Set up interviews with press

    3.2.3.4. Create and distribute collateral

    3.2.3.5. Plan and host event

3.2.4. Investment community

    3.2.4.1. Consolidate investment community contact lists and prioritize

    3.2.4.2. Press release and interviews

    3.2.4.3. Create and distribute collateral

    3.2.4.4. Plan and host event

3.2.5. Regulators

3.2.6. Acquirer employees

3.3. Brand strategy development

3.3.1. Determine short-term/long-term brand strategy

    3.3.1.1. Maintain brand

3.3.2. Operationalize brand migration plan

    3.3.2.1. Billing system integration

    3.3.2.2. Customer service messages

    3.3.2.3. Advertising materials

    3.3.2.4. Sales collateral

    3.3.2.5. Create new sales collateral

    3.3.2.6. Distribute sales collateral to sales force

    3.3.2.7. Direct mail pieces

    3.3.2.8. Acquiree receptionist message

    3.3.2.9. Short-term

    3.3.2.10. Long-term

    3.3.2.11. Acquiree stationery, business cards

    3.3.2.12. Acquiree signage

3.3.3. Authorization letter

    3.3.3.1. Craft authorization letter

    3.3.3.2. Develop collateral for authorization letter

    3.3.3.3. Send authorization letter

3.3.4. Advertising

3.3.5. Public relations protocol

3.4. Corporate Communications communication plan

    3.4.1. Internal communications

    3.4.2. External (media) communications

    3.4.3. Acquiree communications

4. Information Technology Integration Plan

    4.1 Architecture review and assessment

        4.1.1. Gather due diligence information on acquiree

        4.1.2. Inventory acquiree IT equipment/systems

        4.1.3. Assess acquiree IT environment

            4.1.3.1. Identify equipment/systems compatibilities/incompatibilities

            4.1.3.2. Inventory desktop hardware, peripherals, and communications equipment

    4.2. IT operations integration strategy

        4.2.1. Enterprise operations integration strategy

        4.2.2. IT applications integration strategy

        4.2.3. Network operations integration strategy

    4.3. Enterprise operations integration

        4.3.1. E-mail integration

            4.3.1.1. Define e-mail migration approach

            4.3.1.2. Create acquiree employee roster

            4.3.1.3. Forward acquiree employee roster to Help desk

N O T E S

1   "Striving for Transaction Excellence: Emergence of the Corporate Development Officer" (2003). This Ernst & Young Transaction Advisory Services study shows that in today's transaction environment, the nature of corporate development—its structure, role, skills, and processes—is changing. The corporate development officer (CDO) is emerging as the key figure responsible for transaction execution and a broad range of related corporate functions.

2   The average size of public company boards today is nine, according to the 2005 *Public Company Corporate Governance Survey* (Washington, D.C.: National Association of Corporate Directors, 2005), with the range being between six for the smallest companies and twelve for the largest companies. These numbers represent declines from previous years, recorded by NACD since 1992 and by Korn/Ferry, which has been tracking board size since 1976. Corporate America seems to agree that groups larger than twelve may be unwieldy for decision-making purposes.

3   Investment bankers may serve as initiators, financial advisors, and/or real estate advisors for a single transaction, sometimes receiving contingency pay upon closing. In addition, they may render fairness opinions and assist in private placements of securities connected with a transaction. These multiple roles in and of themselves may pose conflicts of interest—an issue that clients and advisors should address and resolve at the outset of any professional engagement. As mentioned in Chapter 1, the National Association of Securities Dealers, parent of the Nasdaq Stock Market, has proposed Rule 2290 to require disclosure of such conflicts of interest

4   See *Directory of Management Consultants 2005* (Fitzwilliam, N.H.: Kennedy Publications, 2005). This directory has profiles of over 2,800 consulting firms in North America, with indexes covering 118 services in 98 industry categories. A summary description of each firm and key contacts with their individual specialties are included.

5   Many executive recruiting firms have associates specializing in the search for interim executives, and there are even firms (for example, IMCO) that specialize in that.

6   For an application of the Delphi method of decision making, see Stanley F. Reed and Alexandra R. Lajoux, *The Art of M&A: A Merger/Acquisition/Buyout Guide*, 3d ed. (Burr Ridge, Ill.: Irwin Professional Publishing, 1999), pp. 927–968.

7   Two classics on the subject are Edgar H. Schein, *Process Consultation: Its Role in Organization Development* (Reading, Mass.: Addison Wesley, 1969), and Charles H. Kepner and Benjamin B. Tregoe, *Process Consulting* (Princeton, N.J.: Princeton Research Press, 1976). Continuing this grand tradition is Alan Weiss, *Process Consulting: How to Launch, Implement, and Conclude Successful Consulting Projects* (New York: Pfeiffer, 2002).

8   Each of the 2,800 firms listed in the *Directory of Management Consultants 2005* (note 4) was allowed to list up to four specialties, including M&A and also including participative-process consulting. The overlap between these two areas is about 10 percent—that is, approximately 35 consulting firms listed in this directory offer participative-process consulting services in the M&A arena.

9   The term *selling company* is used here in lieu of the common term *target*. The term *target* suggests passivity and vulnerability—traits foreign to most sellers, even in unfriendly transactions.

10 Also, see Alexandra R. Lajoux and Charles M. Elson, *The Art of M&A Due Diligence* (New York: McGraw-Hill, 2000).

11 Quoted in part from Schedule 13D (Rule 13d-101) of the Securities Exchange Act of 1934. For a sample form with instructions, see *Exchange Act Rules, Volume II, Rules 13a-1 through 15b9-1: General Rules and Regulations under the Securities Exchange Act, A Bowne Red Box Publication* (New York: Bowne & Co., 2005), printed July 15, 2005.

12 Quoted in part from Schedule 14D-1 (Rule 14d-100) under the Securities Exchange Act of 1934. For a sample form with instructions, see *Regulations 14D and 14E: Tender Offers under the Securities Exchange Act of 1934, A Bowne Red Box Publication* (New York: Bowne & Co., 2005), printed July 15, 2005.

13 HSR reporting is triggered in a change of control (as defined under HSR) involving a company with $100 million in gross assets or (for manufacturers) sales and a company with at least $10 million in assets or sales.

14 "The existing process is complex with differing competitive analysis by banking agencies and the Department of Justice (DOJ). The Gramm-Leach-Bliley Act of 1999 (GLBA) and its amendments to the Hart-Scott-Rodino Antitrust Improvements Act of 1976 (HSRA) add the Federal Trade Commission (FTC) to the competitive review process when certain merging companies have competing nonbank subsidiaries." Source; "Is the Bank Merger Regulatory Review Process Ripe for Review?" Walters Kluwer, April 2005. This paper

describes the most controversial elements of the merger approval process: the competitive review, the convenience and needs review, and the interstate banking review.

15   For more on this topic, see Price Pritchett, *After the Merger: The Autoritative Guide for Integration Succes, Revised Edition* (New York: McGraw-Hill, 1997). Mr. Pritchett, one of the experts consulted for this chapter, drew from this book (first published in 1987) as well as from his more recent experiences in the postmerger realm. For more resources on merger planning, see tecacq.com. Rob Baker, a principle in this firm, has provided advice to the author on the initial stages of the M&A process.

16   For tools and checklists to use for integration planning, see the appendixes to this chapter, and the appendixes to this book. See also Tim Galpin and Mark Herndon, *The Complete Guide to Mergers and Acquisitions: Process Tools to Support M&A Integration at Every Level* (San Francisco: Jossey-Bass, 1999). A number of companies provide technological solutions for merger integration, including E-Know, Inc. (eknow.com), used along with other software from M&A Partners, Inc. (mapartners.net) for planning and implementing mergers from the planning through the integration stage; TX2 Systems, Inc. (tx2systems.com), used for document management in large-scale, complex transactions; and Captaris Alchemy (captaris.com), also used for document management in large-scale transactions. The author has been affiliated with E-Know since March 2000 as an advisor and advisory board member.

PART TWO

Integrating Resources

... there is a dark
Inscrutable workmanship that reconciles
Discordant elements, makes them cling together
In one society.

William Wordsworth, *The Prelude*

INTRODUCTION AND ACKNOWLEDGMENTS

Businesses succeed in part because their particular combinations of resources work well together in a kind of corporate "personality." During a merger, this corporate personality faces many challenges. Part 2 offers business executives some practical guidance for getting through the integration period. How exactly can two newly combined companies merge their people, their wealth, and their reputations most effectively? Topic by topic, here are some expert answers.

Chapter 4, "Retaining and Integrating Human Resources," grounds itself first and foremost in employee retention—without which integration is impossible. After a review of current trends in postmerger employment practices (with insights provided by Jim Jeffries, CEO, M&A Partners, Dallas, Texas), we go straight to the legal aspects, consulting with Lawrence F. Carnevale, litigation partner at Carter, Ledyard & Milburn in New York, an expert on no compete agreements.

For an objective assessment of the dollars-and-sense "value" of human resources, we turned to the valuation expertise of specialists: Scott D. Hakala, Ph.D., director, CBIZ Valuation Group, Dallas, Texas; M. Travis Keath, CFA, CPA, Forensic Accounting Consultants, Houston, Texas; and Andrew M. Malec, Ph.D., a valuation consultant based in Grand Rapids, Michigan.

Turning to techniques of integration, we start at the top, with a discussion of how boards of directors merge. This section was based on interviews with John M. Nash, founding president, National Association of Corporate Directors (NACD); Roger W. Raber, president and CEO, NACD; Dr. Stanley Vance, William B. Stokeley Professor Emeritus, University of Tennessee, Nashville; and Paul D. Lapides, director of the Corporate Governance Center at Kennesaw State University in Marietta, Georgia.

For wisdom and experience on the subject of integrating board leadership, our expert of choice was Sir Adrian Cadbury, founding chairman of the United Kingdom's Committee on Financial Aspects of Corporate Governance, known as the Cadbury Committee, and former chairman of Cadbury-Schweppes and of the U.K. directors' association PRO-NED.

The section on merging senior management teams was based on interviews with William J. Altier, CMC, president, Princeton Associates, Inc., Management Consultants, Buckingham, Pennsylvania. Timeless observations on the nature of leadership, carried over from the original edition of this book, came from the late Robert K. Mueller, former chairman of A. D. Little, Inc. For wisdom and experience on merging sales forces, we turned to Linda Richardson, president, The Richardson Group, Philadelphia, Pennsylvania, a world-class sales training expert.

Chapter 5, "Integrating Financial and Tangible Resources," provides an introduction to purchase accounting. Guidance on this topic and on consolidated financial statements (both domestic and international) came from H. Peter Nesvold, Vice President, Bear Stearns, New York; Lawrence A. Gordon, Ph.D., Ernst & Young Alumni Professor of Managerial Accounting and Information Assurance and director, Ph.D. program, Robert H. Smith School of Business, University of Maryland; and Kermit D. Larson, Ph.D., CPA, Arthur C. Andersen & Co. Alumni Professor of Accounting at the University of Texas at Austin. Comments and illustrations are drawn from Larson's *Fundamental Accounting Principles* (Burr Ridge, Ill.: Irwin Professional Publishing), now in its seventeenth edition. Answers to our questions on tangible assets came from M&A valuation experts Hakala, Keath, and Malec, cited earlier. Dean Shaw, CPA, of Shaw & Sullivan, PC, Alexandria, Virginia, served as a general reviewer of this chapter.

Chapter 6, "Integrating Reputational and Other Intangible Resources," begins with the basic yet crucial matter of naming the new company. Then we move on to the important subject of preserving the value of brand names. For our answers in these two areas, we turned to Gene Grossman, partner, Siegel & Gale, and to Hakala, Keath, and Malec, cited earlier. Our discussion on trade secrets was based on information provided by Lawrence F. Carnevale, also cited in Part 1.This chapter's section on integrating mission statements was based on the expertise of Frederick Buggie, president and chief executive officer, Strategic Innovations, Lake Wylie, South Carolina. Guidance on how to write a vision and values statement came from Patrick J. Ward, retired CEO and chairman, Caltex Petroleum, Dallas, Texas, and Michael Lovdal, vice president, Mercer Management Consulting.

CHAPTER 4

Retaining and Integrating Human Resources

The meeting of two personalities is like the contact of two chemical substances: if there is any reaction, both are transformed.

Carl Jung, *Modern Man in Search of a Soul*

INTRODUCTION

If people are an organization's most important resource, then the most important element of postmerger integration must be the task of retaining key human resources from both companies and then merging them at all levels—from the board of directors to the front lines of sales.[1]

The "levels" of human resources discussed in this chapter are not organized by their value (for this will vary from organization to organization). Rather, they are organized by their *accountability*.

The success of any merger will depend most heavily on the new company's board of directors, followed closely by the company's chief executive and/or chair and its senior managers, especially human (HR) directors. The decisions of these accountable executives will, in turn, be most evident in the vitality of the merged company's middle managers and salespeople, who will act as the chief ambassadors of the new organization inside the company and out in the world. This chapter focuses on how a company can retain and integrate all of these key human resources.

Obviously, with a topic as vast as human resources, this chapter represents only a small part of the story. A full plan for human resources integration will include professional, technical, clerical, and production employees, among others. These important human resources are discussed later in this book—in Chapter 7, "Integrating Management Systems"; Chapter 8, "Integrating Compensation Plans"; Chapter 9, "Integrating and Enhancing Technology and Innovation"; and Chapter 12, "Fulfilling Commitments to Employees and Communities."

RETAINING HUMAN RESOURCES

Is it true that mergers cause job losses?

This characterization is somewhat misleading for three main reasons:

- First, job losses happen for other reasons, such as relocation or restructuring.[2] Research by Mark Mitchell of the University of Chicago shows that mergers and acquisitions tend to cluster in industries that are already going through fundamental change and are therefore more susceptible to large gains or losses in employment. Some of the most drastic workforce reductions that occur come from being in the wrong business at the wrong time—a problem that acquisitions can either cause or prevent. For example, Xerox reduced its workforce by 41 percent to 58,000 under CEO Anne Mulcahy immediately after she assumed leadership in October 2000.[3] In June 2005, General Motors announced plans to cut at least 25,000 jobs in North America by 2008 and close additional assembly and component plants. Mergers weren't to blame in either of these situations.
- Second, most mergers involve midsized companies buying smaller companies and do not involve large-scale layoffs. Few transactions trigger significant job losses—that is, not many are large-scale "mergers of equals."
- Third, aside from mergers of equals, when job redundancies do cause workforce reduction, the staying power of employees depends in part on how well the merger goes. A 2001 Booz Allen Hamilton study, cited in

Chapter 1, shows that only 58 percent of CEOs of disappointing mergers are still at the company after two years, versus 84 percent of successful CEOs.

On the other hand, it is obvious that mergers and downsizings *do* go hand in hand in many larger transactions. A significant percentage of transactions valued at $1 billion or more and involving workforces of thousands are mergers of equals that involve job cuts to eliminate the operational redundancies created when similar companies merge. These cuts are commonly cited as the driving strategic force in such mergers. Typical merger announcements in such transactions foresee cuts of 4 to 10 percent. Recent examples include 4 percent cuts at Procter & Gamble and Gillette; 7 percent cuts at Bank of America and FleetBoston Financial Corp. and at UniCredito and HVB Group; and 10 percent cuts at Cingular Wireless and AT&T Wireless.[4] Such events affect significant numbers of employees, often in concentrated geographic areas.

And even when there are no such redundancies to eliminate, postmerger job cuts can occur in any transaction where the acquirer paid money that it could not fundamentally afford, whether by paying with overvalued stock or by taking on too much debt in a highly leveraged transaction.

It is also true that following mergers of any size or type, while there may not be job losses, there is high turnover. The company is new, the culture is new, and the changes in the new company spark changes in individuals and their personal destinies.

People don't need to be fired; they quit.

A recent study showed that almost half of acquired executives leave in the first year after a merger or acquisition, and *three out of four* leave within the first three years.[5] This is not surprising, considering the difficulty some firms have in combining (or even coexisting) following some mergers, as detailed in Appendix 1-A.

In summary, after the typical acquisition, many employees leave—whether involuntarily or voluntarily.

What about *gaining* employees after an acquisition? Under what circumstances does this happen?

Again, the answer can be traced to the strategic rationale for the merger. When the rationale is to reduce costs by eliminating redundancies, layoffs automatically ensue. But cost reduction is not the only good reason for a merger. Another good reason (and, some believe, a superior reason) is revenue growth. In this case, a newly merged company is more likely to hire than to fire.

Sage observers have coined two very simple equations that illustrate this contrast in strategies:

- The equation for synergy through cost cutting is $-2 + -2 = -3$. (The merger will reduce costs, which otherwise would be -4.)
- The equation for synergy through revenue growth is $2 + 2 = 5$. (The merger will increase revenues, which otherwise would be 4.)[6]

Why is retaining employees so important?

Qualified, experienced human resources add value to any business. Indeed, professional appraisers can and do put numbers on this value—at both the senior management and employee levels.

How do appraisers value human resources in the merger context?

For tax accounting purposes, companies have to record the difference between what they paid for a company and the value of all the assets (financial, tangible, and intangible) that they purchased. This difference is called *goodwill*.

Most of the goodwill recorded in the purchase of very small personal services businesses stems from *personal* goodwill: the value of the implicit and explicit employment and noncompetition agreements that the business has with its key employees. As a company grows, this personal goodwill diminishes in favor of *business goodwill*, as the contacts, skills, and knowledge of key people become infused into the value of the firm. This process takes time, however. Letting people leave an enterprise before they have made their full contribution can harm postmerger value. And making an acquisition in order to get more key talent can backfire if veterans as well as newly acquired employees leave.[7]

Concerns about talent drain are not unreasonable, considering that most senior executives in U.S. companies today are being wooed by competitors and are actively seeking to change employers.[8]

How can an acquirer prevent the loss of key employees?

The acquirer's strongest defense against employee defections is a good reputation as an employer, substantiated by actions consistent with that reputation. The new owner must demonstrate immediately and clearly to all of the new company's employees at all levels that their future is bright—individually and collectively. This means attending to all the critical success factors discovered by the researchers cited in Chapter 1, ranging from deal price to integration pace.

It also means following the legal and ethical imperatives outlined in Chapter 12, "Fulfilling Commitments to Employees and Communities."

LEGAL ISSUES

Are there legal means to increase the chances of employee retention? What about a no compete (also called noncompete) agreement?

Good point. At the time it invites each key employee to stay (ideally with a raise or promotion), the acquirer can ask the employee to sign an agreement that restricts the employee's ability to work for a competitor if he or she breaks the contract. The contract may set forth specific restrictions—for example, banning the solicitation of former customers or the use of company trade secrets. Or it may be extremely broad, prohibiting any and all competition with the former employer. In either case, the agreement must be considered "reasonable."

Why the raise or promotion? If employees really want to keep their jobs, won't they sign the agreement anyway?

They may, but if they change their minds, they may be able to challenge the contract in court. Courts do not view the offer of continued employment as adequate reward (or "consideration") for the restriction. The legal concept of *consideration* means that the employee should receive something of value in exchange for promising not to compete. For example, in the Form 8-K for Sunair Electronics, Feb. 14, 2005, the company describes the no compete agreement with its incoming president and CEO, John J. Hayes, as follows: "Mr. Hayes will be further subject to a two-year no compete covenant to the extent his employment is terminated in a manner that does not entitle him to the severance payments described above. Mr. Hayes will also be subject to a two-year no compete covenant to the extent his employment is terminated in a manner that does entitle him to the severance payments described above; however, if the Company fails to make these severance payments, Mr. Hayes' no compete obligations will no longer be in effect."

If an agreement does not pass the consideration test, it may be unenforceable. (For a sample no compete agreement, see Appendix 4-A. For comments on the accounting aspects of no compete and employment agreements, see Chapter 8, "Integrating Compensation Plans.")

How would a court define a "reasonable" no compete agreement?

The agreement should satisfy four tests: it must be necessary to protect the employer's legitimate interests, reasonable in duration and scope, not unreasonably restrictive to the employee, and not harmful to the general public.

When would a no compete agreement be considered "necessary" to protect an employer's interests?

The agreement would be considered necessary if it were used to prevent disclosure or use of trade secrets, to protect significant customer relationships, or to retain an employee whose services are extraordinary or unique.

To determine whether a trade secret is at stake, the courts would probably use the definition of trade secret given by the Uniform Trade Secrets Act.[9] (For more information on that definition, see Chapter 9.) To determine whether a customer relationship is significant to a business, the courts would judge the extent to which the company's profitability depends on employees' relationships with customers. (The greater the extent, the greater the protection.) To determine whether an employee is extraordinary or unique, the courts would consider how much the company would be harmed if it lost the employee. (The greater the harm, the greater the protection.)

What kind of scope would a court consider reasonable for a no compete agreement?

The geography and duration of the restrictions cannot be broader than necessary to protect the employer's interests. For example, the geographic scope cannot extend beyond the company's present territories, and the duration cannot outlive the company's trade secrets protected or the time necessary to rebuild lost business relationships. A duration of six months to two years is generally considered reasonable; longer time periods would be subject to more scrutiny. Also, the restriction must fit the concern. If the company is seeking to protect certain customer relationships, the covenant cannot prevent an employee from working in another field or in a capacity where the customer relationships are not in jeopardy. Some no compete agreements contain *change of control* provisions that release the employee from these restrictions in the event of a merger or acquisition.

How would courts define "burden on the employee" and "harm to the general public"?

These two disqualifiers normally arise in relation to an unreasonable scope. If the restrictions in the no compete agreement are so broad that they would prevent the employee from making a living or prevent the general public from obtaining the employee's services, the courts would refuse to uphold the agreement.

In addition to satisfying these four tests, what other features should the no compete agreement have in order to strengthen its enforceability?

It helps enforceability to add a provision guaranteeing continued payment of salary during the period of the no compete agreement.

Also, it can be helpful to add a "choice of law" provision to the agreement, specifying the state law that will govern the agreement. The state selected should be one that has not passed a law attempting to nullify no compete agreements.

CULTURAL ISSUES

Some say that cultural clashes cause most postmerger problems. What exactly is culture, and can cultural clashes do harm?

Culture is a force that influences what people believe, think, and do. In an organization, it can shape

- Attitudes and mental processes (how people feel and think)
- Behavior (what actions get performed and rewarded)
- Functions (how people do things)
- Norms (what rules get enforced)
- Structures (how the above are organized and repeated)
- Symbols (what images and phrases have special meaning)
- History (what stories and traditions get passed on to future generations)[10]

All of these elements tend to be synchronized within a culture. So, for example, if attitudes are risk-averse, so too will be the behavior, functions, norms, structures, symbols, and history.

Is it true that culture clashes cause most postmerger problems?

Culture clashes are a thorn in the side of strategic acquisitions. Although they don't cause "death" (financial failure) in and of themselves, they can cause pain and weaken performance. Culture clashes often involve attitudes toward risk. The more risk-averse cultures (those of older, more mature companies) may be praised as prudent or criticized as passive. Conversely, risk-tolerant cultures (typically those of smaller, newer companies) may be either branded as brash or lionized as innovative. One of the greatest challenges in any merger is to find a way to balance the two cultures.

Mergers commonly cited as examples of cultural clashes[11] include (in reverse chronological order):

- Hewlett-Packard and Compaq Computer (2002)
- AOL and Time Warner (2001),[12] Mattel and The Learning Company (1999)[13]
- Citicorp and Travelers Group (1998)
- Daimler-Benz and Chrysler (1998)
- Walt Disney Co. and Capital Cities/ABC (1996)
- Pharmacia and Upjohn (1995)
- Quaker Oats and Snapple (1994)
- AT&T Corporation and NCR Corporation (1991)
- Sony Corporation and Columbia Pictures (1989)

In most of these cases, analysts depicted the acquirer (listed first here) as being more risk-averse than the acquired or merged firm.

Do extreme cultural differences doom deals to failure?

No. They merely need to be managed appropriately. Paying attention to them can help.

When it acquired Compaq, Hewlett-Packard conducted 144 focus groups and 150 interviews in 22 countries, all focused on determining cultural problems. The focus groups and interviews raised awareness of culture generally. Furthermore, they gave the CEO, Carly Fiorina, information that she needed in order to appoint the right management team and to focus joint training programs.[14]

MERGING BOARDS OF DIRECTORS

What usually happens to boards of directors when two companies merge?

The answer depends in part on the type of transaction involved. In a typical merger of equals, it is generally assumed that all directors will remain as the two boards combine, unless the two parties agree on board reductions in advance, which is typical in public company mergers. Otherwise, any reduction in board size occurs through attrition, speeded along by various mechanisms for board turnover, such as retirement policies and director term limits.

By contrast, in a typical merger between extreme unequals (when a very large company acquires a much smaller one), the smaller company's board will not merge into the larger company's. Instead, one of two things will happen. If the acquired company will be operated as a subsidiary, its board may remain intact as a subsidiary board, often with links to the corporate board. (This is very common in the case of hospitals and mutual funds.) If, on the other hand, the company will be integrated fully into the parent, the board will typically be dissolved in favor of a single parent-company board and all directors will be expected to resign—unless the CEO-owner wishes to serve on the board, and/or requests that certain directors continue their service.[15]

A third alternative is to reserve a certain number of seats on the board for the acquired organization, following negotiations that reflect the balance of power. In the June 2005 merger of UniCredito and HVB Group, 8 of the new bank's 24 board members came from HVB.[16]

In this context, it may be useful to know some current trends in board size and composition. As of 2005, the average large company ($1 billion plus in sales) had ten members, compared with eight at the average midsized company (between $100 million and $1 billion) and six at the very smallest companies (under $50 million in sales). Approximately one in three companies has mandatory retirement policies for directors (with 72 being a typical age), while one in three has tenure limits instead (with 10 years being the typical length of tenure).[17]

How can an acquirer ensure continued involvement and commitment from acquired-company managers who lose their board positions following a merger?

One good idea is Merck & Co.'s "management committee," a group of senior executives (including the heads of acquired units) that functions like an internal board of directors. In complementing the work of Merck's statutory corporate board, this committee ensures a balance of inside and outside perspectives in important company decisions. In this sense, the Merck management committee resembles the lower boards in many European two-tier boards. As Merck states on its Web site, it has a "highly experienced Board of Directors and Management committee, who are responsible for the company's objectives and policies, and the stewardship of Merck resources. The Board and Management Committee concentrate mainly on strategy, financial performance and critical business issues."

RESHAPING THE CHAIRMAN AND CEO ROLES

When two companies merge their boards, what usually happens to leadership roles?

Often the leader of one of the companies becomes the CEO of the newly combined entity, and the leader of the other one becomes the chairman (also referred to as "chair"). In June 2005, for example, when UniCredito of Italy agreed to buy HVB Group of Germany in Europe's largest-ever cross-border merger, the leader of UniCredito (Alessandro Profumo) became chief executive, and the leader of HVB Group (Dieter Rampl) became chairman of the board of the combined company.

The exact formula will vary depending on the number of potential leaders already involved in the transaction and the leadership model they wish to construct.[18]

In terms of potential leaders, there may be two (a chairman-CEO from one company and a chairman-CEO from the other), three (the chairman-CEO of one company, plus the chairman and the CEO from the other company), or four (the chairman and the CEO from one company and the chairman and the CEO from the other company). And this does not even count the "co-," "vice," or "deputy" titles at the head of the table.

In terms of leadership paradigms, there may be a single job (the CEO-chairman position), two jobs (the CEO and chairman positions), or more than two jobs (adding co-, vice, or deputy positions through an "office of the president" or "office of the chairman"). For example, when America West and US Airways announced their intended merger in May 2005, the companies said that Douglas Parker, chairman and chief executive officer of America West, would keep those two titles in the new airline, while Bruce R. Lakefield, US Airways' president and chief executive officer, would serve as vice chairman.

The challenge for the newly constituted board will be to use the maximum amount of leadership resources in the most efficient leadership structure.

The key is to agree on what board and management structure will deliver the merger benefits most effectively. As mentioned in Chapter 3, "Integration Planning and Communication," this must be addressed in advance.

What are the current trends? How common is it to combine versus split the chairman and CEO roles?

In small, new companies everywhere, the two jobs are naturally combined in one person. Indeed, leaders of new companies usually serve not only as chairman and chief executive officer, but also as president and even as an untitled "chief cook and bottle washer." However, when the founders of such companies near retirement, they often separate the two roles for transition purposes, giving up their jobs one at a time until only the chairman's role remains.

In the United States, about half of companies have a separate chairman and CEO, whereas in England, the level is now closer to 80 percent.[19]

What is the role of the chairman, and how does it differ from the role of the CEO?

There is a clear division of duties. The chairman is responsible for the board, and the CEO is responsible for putting the board's plans, policies, and decisions into effect. Inside the boardroom, at general meetings, and in agreed-upon areas of external relations, the chairman is in charge; otherwise, the CEO is in charge. The jobs are complementary, not competing, and they must be seen in that light by their holders if the split is to work.

The company chairman (whether serving as CEO or not) has both internal and external responsibilities. *Internally*, he or she must oversee the operations of the board and its committees, ensuring that the board provides leadership and vision; has the right balance of membership; sets the aims, strategies, and policies of the company; monitors the achievement of those aims; reviews the resources of the people in the company; and has the information it needs to be effective. *Externally*, the chairman (or a designated agent of the chairman) reports financial results to shareholders and other concerned parties, represents the company to shareholders, monitors the conduct and character of the company, and arbitrates disputes.

If the CEO and chairman roles are combined, say corporate governance experts, a leader should be chosen by and from the independent directors. This leading independent director can be called by a variety of names, the most common one being lead director. Other names include chair of the governance committee (if the director assumes this role) or presiding director (if the director chairs executive sessions of the board—that is, meetings without management present).

What are the main arguments for *combining* the chairman and CEO roles?

Clearly the chief advantage here is unity. With a single CEO-chairman, there is no question about who is leading the company. Also, this model is more common (especially in smaller companies) and therefore more culturally acceptable. Finally, it is easier to find one person who can do both jobs than to find two people who will work well together in what are arguably two halves of a single job. (Note, though, that the problem of different criteria for the two jobs—in skills, experience, and even age—still remains.)

What are the main arguments for *separating* the two roles?

As just mentioned, the two jobs require different types of people. Furthermore, chairmanship is work! Thus, the main argument for separation is that turning a group of directors into an effective board is a difficult and demanding task. There is also the constitutional argument against concentrating power in one pair of hands. This is relevant after a merger when there are sensitivities about which of the former companies has come out on top.

Suppose two organizations merge and each has a strong leader who wishes to maintain his or her leadership position. What happens then?

A typical strategy is to have the older leader serve as chairman while the younger one serves as chief executive, with plans to give the younger leader both roles in the future. When roles cannot be divided so easily, leaders of merging firms typically try to preserve their old titles and/or authority. As mentioned earlier, each merger situation will bring a certain number of candidates (two, three, or more) for a certain number of leadership jobs (one, two, or more).

In the most common U.S. situation (one involving two leaders, each of whom comes to the deal table as CEO-chairman), the leaders have basically three options. They may share leadership, with each one named "co-chief executive officer and cochairman"; one leader may become chairman and the other CEO; or one leader may keep the combined chairman and CEO role (thus conforming with common U.S. practice), while the other becomes vice chairman.

Each of these alternatives has its pros and cons. Making the titles identical (as in the first model) can preserve institutional knowledge. However, questions of real authority can linger as people inside and outside the company try to determine which person is the "real" leader.[20] Also, there can be leadership deadlocks. When titles are equivalent (as in the second model), the same problem can occur. The problem of ambiguity vanishes when one leader is clearly subordinated to the other (as in the third model). In many cases, however, a new problem surfaces: professional pride. The low man or woman on the totem pole rarely relishes that status.

To reduce ambiguity or deadlocks in a co-leader situation, some companies set an informal or formal deadline for selecting one of the co-leaders as a sole leader. To preserve professional pride in a totem pole situation, companies can let one leader have the top title first, but let the other leader have it next. A third alternative is to have a separate chairman and two CEOs for an indefinite (but ultimately finite) period.

These social considerations are obviously important, but some analysts complain that they get too much attention. One proxy advisory firm, reporting to its institutional investor clients, accused AT&T's management and board of paying more attention to issues of executive rank and pay than to the price that shareholders would be getting for their exchange of shares.[21]

In a choice between combining and splitting the CEO and chairman roles, which model is better following a merger?

Each model offers a potential postmerger advantage.

Having a *single CEO-chairman* clearly has value in the post-merger situation, where ambiguity can be an enemy of progress. No one has to ask who is in charge when a single leader is at the helm as both chairman and CEO.

Having *a chairman as well as a CEO* offers several advantages in the merger context, particularly following a merger of equals. Unless reductions in the number of board seats have been negotiated in advance, the new board will probably contain members from both former companies and will almost certainly be too large. In this situation, a chairman will have to spend considerable time working with directors individually and collectively to build a new board team, while a chief executive will be fully stretched in implementing the merger. If one person has to do both jobs, the priority has to be putting the two businesses together, leaving the board to look after itself. As for the "social" considerations mentioned earlier, a separate chairmanship is good because it offers an "extra" job that can help solve the "leadership surplus" that can arise in a merger of equals.

Each of these benefits is important, but neither should out-weigh the real question: what leadership model will best suit the needs of the company and the board? The choice of the model should be based on the people available and the cultures of the companies concerned. The essential point is to decide at the outset how the company is to be run and stick with it. Structure is important, but its precise form is not. It has to meet the needs of the situation.

Could you give some different examples of how two leadership teams and boards were combined in a recent merger?

When J. P. Morgan bought Bank One Corporation on July 1, 2004, the two boards achieved a classic balance of power. J. P. Morgan's chairman of the board and chief executive officer, William Harrison, continued in those positions, while Bank One's James Dimon became president and chief operating officer. The merger agreement stipulated that by July 1, 2006, Dimon would succeed Harrison as CEO, while Harrison would continue to serve as chairman of the board. The size of the board was set at 16 members, consisting of 8 members from each predecessor company, including Harrison and Dimon. The company bylaws were amended to state that all vacancies on the board would be filled by a nominee proposed by the corporate governance and nominating committee, which was co-chaired by one director from each predecessor and composed of an equal number of directors from each predecessor.

When Sears and Kmart merged (also in 2004) into Sears Holdings Corporation, Kmart board members dominated the new structure. The discount chain named seven of the ten members of the board, and its chairman (Edward Lampert) now leads the office of the chairman of the holding company. His two direct reports are the new vice chairman and CEO of the holding company (Alan Lacy, former chairman and CEO of Sears) and a president of the holding company and Sears' CEO for retail (Aylwin Lewis, former president and CEO of Kmart).[22]

MERGING SENIOR MANAGEMENT TEAMS

What are the primary questions facing companies that wish to merge their senior management teams?

In general, three questions will be paramount:

1 To whom will the senior management of the acquired business report? (For example, will the senior financial manager report to his or her own unit's CEO, to the senior financial manager in the acquiring company, or to the CEO of the acquiring company?)

2 Conversely, who in the acquiring organization may directly interface with the acquired company, and who must work through the acquired company's CEO?

3 What personnel will be reassigned from the acquiring company to the acquired company, and vice versa?

Clearly, answering these questions will be difficult. To accomplish a meaningful combination—one that serves a new organization rather than perpetuating the old organizations that are creating it—the existing power structure must, in effect, destroy itself to clear a new path that is appropriate to the new organization. Given human nature, this requires extraordinary determination. And yet it must be done to the greatest extent possible.

TURF: TYPICAL AND SPECIAL SCENARIOS

How can companies manage turf concerns to plan for the future?

Most situations call for early teamwork by executives from both companies. The comments immediately following pertain to such a typical situation. (Antitrust and downsizing issues call for special tactics, discussed at the end of this section.)

As mentioned in Chapter 3, prior to closing or immediately after closing, representatives from both sides of the table should form a balanced *postmerger integration team*, with an equal number of representatives from each company. (If deadlocking is a problem, the group can bring in an impartial third party who is acceptable to both the acquiring and the acquired firm as a tiebreaker—or, better yet, a facilitator.)

This team should first determine what the *strategy* of the new organization will be, based on the stated motives or "logic" of the deal, and then select the *people* who are best suited to carry out this strategy. The question for the team is not "What will the hierarchy be?" but "*What* will we do and *who* will do it?" The time to ask this question is before, not after, the deal is closed. After the closing, people will be too intent on making things happen and will have little patience with strategic planning.

Why is it important to have a balanced integration team? Is this so that each of the two merging companies will have its own representatives in the new company?

No. The reason to have equal representation on the team is to take full advantage of history, not to perpetuate it. The team should try to use past history to chart the firm's course for the future, considering the energies and qualifications of all key players. This goes far beyond merely doling out top jobs (and presumably top pay) to an equal number of senior managers from each company. Rather, it means taking a critical look at existing titles and pay systems. New systems for both may emerge out of the joint planning process.

Should the postmerger integration team have the final say on the choice of senior managers?

It depends on where the ownership lies. In a smaller private or closely held company, where team members are owners, yes, the integration team would have the final say. Board approval will be a mechanical matter in such a case. In a publicly held company, the owners are usually not the managers. The owners may want to have a real say via the board of directors of the acquiring firm or that board's nominating committee.

OK, let's assume that the two companies devote their time ahead of the merger to strategizing. Why is this important for senior management integration?

By putting strategy first, you accomplish three main things.

First, you improve your chances of realizing any potential synergies that motivated the combination in the first place. If the merger is to have value beyond mere economies of scale, it must generate better ways of doing things tomorrow.

Second, you strengthen senior management selection. A strategy-oriented company will be likely to select people based on what they can do for the organization, rather than on which company they worked for, what titles they held, or how well they have promoted themselves. Early emphasis on strategy dilutes the impact of these factors, which often carry much more weight in senior management selection than they should.

Third, you save the pride of those who leave involuntarily. Seldom in any merger situation are there meaningful, productive slots for all the senior managers from both organizations. A clear picture of the combined organization's future strategy can show why some senior managers should stay and some should leave.

This does not reflect on the senior managers' intrinsic worth, only on their worth to the emerging company.

Aren't there some risks in putting strategy first? Suppose the deal falls through. Couldn't both sides take advantage of confidential information?

Yes. Premerger strategy sessions do expose both organizations to the risk of information leaks. The chances of this risk can be lowered if both sides sign a confidentiality agreement and avoid sharing confidential, proprietary information until shortly before the closing date.

As for the closing date, most deals take about six months from the initial announcement.[23] Some deals (notably ones subject to the waiting period imposed by Hart-Scott-Rodino, a disclosure law mentioned in Chapter 3) can take over a year to move from announcement to closing. Obviously, the farther away the date is set, the more information is exchanged, and the more each side has to lose in a breakdown. On the other hand, it is rarely wise to rush a merger.

The best course of action is to set a proposed closing date at some reasonable time in the future (say, for example, six months from the announcement date), making the date subject to the completion of the acquirer's due diligence review and to necessary regulatory approvals.

How should the postmerger integration team select senior managers for the "revised" organization?

The team (and the individual or group to which it reports, if any) should look for the senior managers who are *most able to integrate the two organizations*. For example, in a choice between two senior vice presidents of marketing, one with superior marketing skills and one with superior management skills, including linkages with stakeholders, the second candidate would be the better choice.

One way to determine the best candidate for a given function would be to ask each of the senior executive candidates for a one-page statement about the future of the new and better organization as he or she sees it, identifying the two or three major issues most likely to affect its future success. The responses will say a lot about which candidate would be able to assign the people in the revised company appropriate work—work that flows naturally from better ways to build a better company tomorrow. The work will be the work of the emerging new organization, not a perpetuation of that of its predecessors.

If one of the two merging companies is more successful than the other, shouldn't that company be the one to fill most of the senior management positions?

Not necessarily. In any given merger, one of three things is likely to happen: the acquirer will try to keep all, some, or none of the senior managers of the acquired company. In a merger of equals or a high-technology acquisition, the first scenario is common. In the purchase of a distressed firm, the last scenario is more the norm. Most mergers fall into the vast middle realm, where some acquired-company managers stay and some leave.

In all of this, the integration team often focuses too much attention on the history of a company, when it should focus instead on the history—and potential—of the company's managers. A company may be in a distressed condition because of its CEO, not because of its senior management. Conversely, a successful company may be successful thanks to its CEO, not its senior team.

How quickly or slowly should an organization proceed in assigning new roles for senior managers and those who work for them?

Ideally, the new senior management team should hit the ground running as soon as the merger is completed, with new titles and lines of reporting already established. As mentioned in Chapter 3, dragging out the process out of deference to the premerger power structures does more harm than good. First, it does little to allay the fears of those who are "waiting for the other shoe to drop"— and may even aggravate them. (There's something eerie about business as usual in the face of change.) Second, a slow postmerger transition perpetuates old ways of doing things, robbing the new organization of the brief window of time it has to fulfill its potential for true synergy.

What guidance do you have about titles and pay for managers in the new company?

The real question is how the new company can use the tools of titles and pay to accomplish its new goals. If postmerger titles and pay are linked closely to actual postmerger responsibilities and achievements, they can preserve the important factor of positive self-image among senior managers—an image based not on self-centered egotism (*I* can do it), but on the value that the manager's division or function brings to the company (*we* can do it).

Titles and pay are vehicles for retaining the people who are the most capable of implementing a new strategy. They are a means, not an end. No senior manager (or employee at any level) will give up a prestigious title and generous perquisites gladly. At the same time, both titles and pay are becoming increasingly relative.

Take titles, for example. In organizations with very few line-management layers, titles may be deemphasized or eliminated. One reason for this may be that titles are at best only approximations of power and prestige. Each culture adds its own nuance to titles. This nuance is based partly on the power traditionally wielded by the holders of the title and partly on the power that the *individual* supplies. So even if an employee who was a "president" on Friday becomes a "senior director" on Monday, he or she may find it worthwhile to stay and contribute if circumstances surrounding the change are positive. The term *demotion* has less meaning in today's flatter organizations.

Pay does tend to go up following a merger, both for employees of the acquiring firm and for those in the acquired firm. But compensation today (especially at the higher levels of the organization) is typically linked to future performance and is therefore more difficult to compare (because the future is hard to forecast).

For more on titles and pay, respectively, see Chapter 7 and Chapter 8.

Should the top management of the acquiring firm be concerned about integration at the middle management and professional levels, or will senior management integration take care of this?

As mentioned earlier, in a choice between two senior managers, the leader's job should go to the one with superior integration skills. Such a manager will need no help in selecting and integrating the managerial and professional employees in his or her bailiwick. Sometimes, however, senior managers' talents lie in other areas. In such cases, the top management of an acquiring firm may need to bypass the acquired company's senior management to ensure proper integration.

Does this advice apply to all situations?

No. Some situations call for different approaches.

- First, if a transaction requires approval by antitrust authorities, it may be necessary to use an independent outside advisor to do merger planning, without any involvement from management. As discussed in Chapter 3, Cingular Wireless did this when it merged with AT&T Wireless.
- Second, if a transaction will involve downsizing, it is best to separate revenue-producing activities from cost-cutting activities, and to put outgoing executives in charge of the latter. Appropriate financial incentives must be structured to make this job appealing.

What advice do you have for the merging of human resource personnel (HR departments and their leaders)?

These personnel will be critical in the new structure, since they are or should be the custodians of all critical knowledge about the company's most valuable assets—its employees.

A good framework for analyzing HR departments as a business unit can be found in Appendix 4-B, "Human Resources Integration Planning Grid."

MERGING SALES, MERCHANDISING, AND DISTRIBUTION FORCES

What are the chief benefits of merging sales forces?

By investing time and money up front to create unity in the sales force, management can achieve *cost savings* in sales force training, development, and compensation. Also, a single sales force for multiple products enables more efficient *cross-selling*, which can benefit customers and the company alike. Finally, having one sales force can economize *communication* of the corporate vision to the selling troops.

What are the main challenges in merging sales forces?

Mergers often thrust salespeople into selling new (unfamiliar) products with new technology in new territories in new ways, following new rules (red tape) and receiving new kinds of complaints and objections.

The combined effect of all this unfamiliarity can cause salespeople to take their eye off the prize—the hunt to find new customers even as they serve old ones. Thus the first challenge may be to keep alive the famed "fire in the belly" that makes new sales possible. As Josiane Feigon writes in *TeleSmart Communications Newsletter* (tele-smart.com), "Even if you hate *Death of a Salesman* and *Glengarry Glen Ross*, you can learn from them. The demise of the salespeople in those movies is a result of the loss of the hunt. Don't be too proud to put yourself out there, muscling up the hunt. Create abundance!"

When integrating sales forces, it is better to provide support and encouragement than to threaten. (Do not say things like, "And as the hours are waning, I suggest to you those of you who are interested in a continuing job with this organization get to work," or "Second prize, a set of &%$# steak knives. Third prize, you're fired," to quote *Glengarry Glen Ross*.[24]) Fear can motivate, but enthusiasm is preferable.

If your sales force must sell new products, devote the time to training in both sales skills and product knowledge. Make sure that both sales teams know the critical skills of creating rapport, questioning, listening, product positioning, and checking. Although these skills are transferable to any product and to any industry, not every organization has taught them. Second, product training is obviously imperative. Even in a merger of equals, such as that of Cingular and AT&T, products may appear to be similar but may in fact have different features and benefits.

What would be a good example of the use of teamwork to improve a sales force's product knowledge following a merger?

IBM offers a great example. Following some acquisition activity in the early 1990s, IBM chairman Louis Gerstner had a different vision. He and his senior management team reorganized the IBM sales force, which had been divided into geographic territories, into 12 industry units to serve different types of customers. Each unit has not only a dedicated sales force, but also researchers, software engineers, and its very own outside consultants. This structure continues under Gerstner's successor, CEO Sam Palmisano, now serving 16 industries.

What about integrating merchandisers? What are the benefits here?

Merchandisers are essentially salespeople, so the same benefits of enhanced cost saving, cross-selling, and communication apply here. Also, on the benefits side, merging merchandisers may yield a net gain in shelf space. The job of the merchandiser, after all, is to obtain favorable space (supplying and checking on shelf stock and negotiating for better positioning). Giving a successful merchandiser more products to represent can enable him or her to obtain more prime space as one product piggybacks on another.

The spatial clout of merchandisers was crucial to the 2005 merger between Gillette and Procter & Gamble.

What are the challenges in this arena?

Merchandisers may not need detailed product knowledge of the goods they represent, but they do need product *enthusiasm*.

Merchandisers do not sell to end users, but they sell to those who do. As a key link in a chain of sellers, merchandisers must care about what they are representing. Training can help here.

When it comes to postmerger integration, aren't there trade-offs in sales and distribution?

Absolutely. After merging, companies should look at their sales and distribution forces as a whole, weighing the pros and cons of each. In some cases, such as new high-ticket services, companies will need a dedicated sales force to make direct contact with end users. In other cases, such as established low-ticket commodities, distributors (which normally cost less than a sales force) will be the better choice. Complex scenarios will often require mixed approaches.

INTERNATIONAL CONSIDERATIONS

If a large company buys a smaller one in a foreign country, should it send someone from headquarters to run it or choose someone local?

The choice depends on company dynamics. A headquarters manager will be preferable for entry into a new country where key decisions will be investment-oriented, whereas a local manager will be preferable when the company's foreign consumers differ greatly from its domestic consumers, when marketing costs are high in relation to selling price, and/or when production is fully local. How can a newly merged global company make the best use of its human resources?

To quote Hippocrates, "First, do no harm." If cultures are extremely different, it may not be wise to force them to work together. This is one reason why mergers between companies in two different countries often maintain dual headquarters, dual stock listings, and dual chairmen. Another good rule is, "When in Rome, do as the Romans do." Obviously, acquirers must comply with legal and accounting requirements in their host countries. But beyond that, they should make a good-faith effort to comply with different management practices—including those involving financial and intangible assets, the subjects of the next two chapters.

APPENDIX 4-A

Sample No Compete Agreements

EXAMPLE 1

This example is a complete agreement that you can fill in and use for an employee who does not have a separate written employment contract.

Nondisclosure and Noncompetition.

(a) At all times while this agreement is in force and after its expiration or termination, [employee name] agrees to refrain from disclosing [company name]'s customer lists, trade secrets, or other confidential material. [Employee name] agrees to take reasonable security measures to prevent accidental disclosure and industrial espionage.

(b) While this agreement is in force, the employee agrees to use [his/her] best efforts to [describe job] and to abide by the nondisclosure and noncompetition terms of this agreement; the employer agrees to compensate the employee as follows: [describe compensation]. After expiration or termination of this agreement, [employee name] agrees not to compete with [company name] for a period of [number] years within a [number] mile radius of [company name and location]. This prohibition will not apply if this agreement is terminated because [company] violated the terms of this agreement.

Competition means owning or working for a business of the following type: [specify type of business employee may not engage in].

(c) [Employee name] agrees to pay liquidated damages in the amount of $[dollar amount] for any violation of the covenant not to compete contained in subparagraph (b) of this paragraph.

IN WITNESS WHEREOF, [company name] and [employee name] have signed this agreement.

_____

[company name]

_____

[employee's name]

Date: _____

EXAMPLE 2

This example is part of a larger agreement, such as an employment contract or an employee handbook. You can use it as a separate agreement or incorporate it into another, larger document.

Nondisclosure and Noncompetition.

(a) After expiration or termination of this agreement, [employee name] agrees to respect the confidentiality of [company name] patents, trademarks, and trade secrets, and not to disclose them to anyone.

(b) [Employee name] agrees not to make use of research done in the course of work done for [company name] while employed by a competitor of [company name].

(c) [Employee name] agrees not to set up in business as a direct competitor of [company name] within a radius of [number] miles of [company name and location] for a period of [number and measure of time (e.g., "four months" or "10 years")] following the expiration or termination of this agreement.

(d) [Employee name] agrees to pay liquidated damages of $[dollar amount] if any violation of this paragraph is proved or admitted.

IN WITNESS WHEREOF, [company name] and [employee name] have signed this agreement.

_____

[company name]

_____

[employee name]

Date: _____

EXAMPLE 3

This example is a clause and should be used as part of a larger agreement, such as an employment contract, and not as a stand-alone item.

Covenant Not to Compete.

(a) [Employee name] agrees not to compete with [company name] in the practice of [type of business or service] while working for [company name] and for a period of [number and measure of time (e.g., "six months" or "10 years")] after termination of employment within a radius of [number] miles of [company name and location].

(b) For purposes of this covenant not to compete, competition is defined as soliciting or accepting employment by, or rendering professional services to, any person or organization that is or was a client of [company name] during the term of [employee name]'s work with [company name].

APPENDIX 4-B

Human Resources Integration Planning Grid

Note: Order of steps is suggested. Merging companies may wish to use a different order. Many of the steps will be pursued simultaneously.

> *Note:* Prior to HR work, Corporate Development gathers HR due diligence information on acquiree.
> - Gather information on all key areas (see Step 3 for complete list).

> *Step 1:* Integration Planning Steering Committee invites HR reps to attend integration planning kickoff meeting (IPKO) and, at meeting, requests formation of functional committees for all functions, including HR.

Actions:
- Invite HR directors of both acquirer and acquiree to attend meeting, as applicable (acquiree may not have HR).
- Ask HR director(s) to suggest agenda items for IPKO meeting.
- At meeting, cover most important HR agenda items (use the list in Step 4 as a reminder).
- At meeting, ask HR director(s) to form HR Functional Committee (with both HR heads, as applicable).

	Who		Dependence on Previous Activity	Data		Priority	Elapsed Time	Actual Time
	Lead	Support		Strategic	Tactical			
Step 1: Steering Committee meeting	Corporate Development (represented by ___)	HR directors (and other function directors)	Signing of acquisition agreement	Find out whether acquired company has HR and how it is to be integrated (transferred? reduced/cut? left as is?)	Find out name of HR director of acquired company, if any	H	1 day	4 hours
Step 2: Hold early HR meetings	HR director of acquiring company	HR key staff	IP kickoff meeting	See Step 1	Need to know basic facts about acquired company's HR policies and processes	H	4 weeks (at least one meeting per week)	20 hours (up to 4 hours per meeting/ working session)
Step 3: HR makes/ implements/ announces decisions: See Step 3 List below.	HR director of acquiring company	HR key staff	Kickoff meeting	See Step 1	Same as Step 3; need to know basic facts about acquired company's HR policies and processes	H	3 months (90 days)	20 hours (up to 4 hours per meeting/ working session)

Step 2: List HR director of acquiring company forms HR Committee for acquiree; chairs committee meetings or appoints chair.

- Invite key HR staff to attend first functional committee meetings.
- Ask key HR staff to suggest agenda items for the meetings (use the list in Step 4 as a reminder).
- Set up calendar for decisions/actions related to integrating key activities within the HR support function.
- Set up subcommittees of the HR committee as appropriate and assign responsibility for meeting deadlines.

Step 3: HR Committee makes/announces/implements decisions on all key HR areas.

- Recruitment, retention, termination.
  - New hire process (HR asks line management if Company A plans to hire new people).
  - Retention (HR asks line management which employees to retain).
  - Termination process (HR asks line management if company will terminate any jobs; report turnover via resignations, layoffs).

- Career development, promotions/succession, training.
  - Job review and performance evaluation (HR begins reviewing acquiree jobs and evaluating incumbent performance in acquired company).
  - Job mapping and redesign (HR helps line management map and redesign jobs).

- Compensation, including benefits and payroll (HR helps set policy for integration and managing change).
  - Base pay program (HR, with line managers, sets pay scales).
  - Special pay programs (HR, with line managers, determines incentive pay, bonuses in cash and equity, especially for sales force).

- Benefits (HR advises line managers on benefits; then HR handles conversion, enrollment, and plan administration of benefits).
  - Health and welfare.
    - Details of insurance coverage: life, disability, health (basic, dental, vision), preventive.
  - Retirement compensation.
    - 401(k).
    - Other.

- Payroll process (HR integrates acquired employees into payroll process).
  - Accounting reconciliation.
  - Communications with treasury.
  - Pay-cycle disbursement.
  - Leave accrual.

- Employee relations—regulatory compliance.
  - Regulatory compliance.
    - Equal Employment Opportunity (EEO).
    - Office of Safety and Health Administration (OSHA).
  - Employee dispute resolution.
  - Employee complaint investigation.
  - Communications to employees on regulatory matters.

- HR within organizational structure.
  - Outsourcing, if any, of HR functions.
    - Vendor management.
  - Reporting lines from HR to senior management.

- HR Information System (HRIS).
  - Employee setup in HRIS.
  - Establish department numbers for acquirees.
  - Collect acquiree employee information.
  - Input acquiree data into HRIS database.
  - Provide acquirees with company IT services, such as intranet access.

- HR contracts and commitments.
  - Covenants in acquisition agreement relating to any aspect of HR.

Source: Midsized acquirer based in Virginia. Provided courtesy of E-Know, Inc., Arlington, Virginia. The author played a role in developing this tool for E-Know and its clients. HR categories were inspired by James Hatch, Brian Friedman, and David M. Walker, *Delivering on the Promise: How to Attract, Manage, and Retain* (New York: John Wiley & Sons, 1998). James Hatch and Brian Friedman are human resource consultants. David M. Walker is now the comptroller general of the United States, serving a nine-year term 1998–2007.

NOTES

1   Some managers reject the term *levels* because it implies a hierarchy of ascending value. They favor other depictions of people in organizations (concentric circles, clustered circles, and so forth) that show a broad dispersion of value throughout an organization. The merits of these two perspectives will be discussed in Chapter 7, "Integrating Management Systems."

2   Mural Arik, "Where Did Tennessee Companies and Jobs Relocate?", white paper dated Mar. 10, 2004, http://www.mtsu.edu/~berc/pdfs/relocation.pdf. Professor Arik is associate director, Business and Economic Research Center, Middle Tennessee State University.

3   The pruning worked: by the end of 2004, Xerox had increased its (free) cash flow from zero to $1.5 billion.

4   The cuts were announced in 2004 (for Bank of America/FleetBoston and Cingular Wireless/AT&T Wireless) and 2005 (Procter & Gamble/Gillette and UniCredito/ HVB).

5   Mark Herndon, Watson Wyatt Worldwide, quoted in Ann Freedman, "Assessments Key to Merger Success," *Human Resource Executive*, Feb. 4, 2002.

6   The formula "2 + 2 = 5" has been around for decades as an expression of synergistic growth, but its corollary in synergistic shrinkage ("–2 + –2 = –3") is new. It was originated by Mark N. Clemente and David S. Greenspan, principals of Clemente, Greenspan & Co, Inc., Glen Rock, New Jersey.

7   In a study of law firm dissolution, Hildebrandt International, Inc., found that misguided mergers were a contributing factor.

"From our analysis, one common theme in many of these failures was the lack of any clear sense of strategic direction in the dissolving firms. This absence of a shared vision for the future made partners—and especially partners controlling significant amounts of business—vulnerable to 'cherry picking' by competitors, leading often to a growing talent drain that resulted in a downward spiral to ultimate dissolution. The problem was exacerbated in some cases by last-ditch efforts to rejuvenate the enterprises through poorly planned expansions or failed merger attempts, efforts that also suffered from a lack of strategic vision or purpose." *Client Advisory 2004*, Hildebrandt International, Inc.

8   A March 2004 survey of chief information officers showed that 37 percent of top IT executives who responded to this year's survey on the role of the CIO indicated that they will look for a new job if the economy improves. The analysis uncovered certain "clusters" of CIOs who are most likely to be job hunting: those who feel their work is not appreciated (65 percent), those at manufacturing firms (51 percent), and those at companies that are not hitting their strategic goals (48 percent).

9   See the section on combining intangible assets in Chapter 5, "Integrating Financial and Tangible Resources."

10 This discussion is based in part on the writings of John H. Bodley, *Cultural Anthropology: Tribes, States, and the Global System*, Mountain View, Calif.: Mayfield Publishing Co., 1994. Professor Bodley is the chair of the Department of Anthropology at Washington State University. Lowell F. Christy, Jr., Ph.D., of the Cultural Strategies Institute, Seneca, Maryland, has created a "cultural mapping" series based in seven categories: conflict resolution, education, linguistics, male/female relations, politics, spirituality, and symbolism/rituals. Like John Bodley's definition of culture, this definition could be useful in analyzing corporate culture.

11 For more about Citicorp, Pharmacia, and Upjohn, see *McKinsey Quarterly*. For more about the other mergers in this list, see Robert Bruner, *Deals from Hell* (New York: John Wiley & Sons, 2004).

12 "Time Warner employees considered their AOL counterparts to be too pushy and aggressive, while AOLers considered Time Warner staffers to be coddled, passive, and lazy." Morningstar report cited by Peter Haapaniemi, "Coping with M&A Culture Clash," *Business Empowered (Bearing Point)*, Issue 2, 2005.

13 "Former executives refer to the culture of 'learned powerlessness' that pervaded the toy giant's operations. In contrast, employees at

TLC exhibited a sense of urgency, camaraderie, and entrepreneurial zeal. The conflict between these styles peaked over the company's Internet strategy. TLC employees were eager to launch online operations, while Mattel executives dragged their heels, fearing that Web sales would alienate retailers." *Leverage Points,* Oct. 19, 2000.

14   J. Robert Carleton, *Achieving Post-Merger Success: A Stakeholder's Guide to Cultural Due Diligence, Assessment, and Integration* (San Francisco: Pfeiffer, 2004). Carlton's firm, Vector Group Inc., conducted the focus groups and interviews as consultants to HP.

15   In building a newly consolidated board of directors out of two previous ones, companies may wish to consider the guidelines developed in 1996 by a 28-member panel of experts selected by the National Association of Corporate Directors in Washington, D.C. The panel, chaired by NACD board member Ira M. Millstein, senior partner at Weil, Gotshal & Manges LLP, New York, agreed that each board should have a majority of independent, committed directors as well as mechanisms to preserve independence and ensure involvement. Each individual director, said the panel, should possess integrity and accountability, informed judgment, financial literacy, mature confidence, and high performance standards. The board as a whole, said the panel, should possess core competency in accounting and finance, business judgment, management, crisis response, industry knowledge, international markets, leadership, and strategic vision. See *Report of the Blue Ribbon Commission on Director Professionalism* (Washington, D.C.: National Association of Corporate Directors, 1996/2001/2005).

16   Heather Timmons, "Cross-Border Bank Deal to Be Largest in Europe," *New York Times,* June 13, 2005.

17   *2005 Public Company Governance Survey* (Washington, D.C.: National Association of Corporate Directors, 2005).

18   For an authoritative report on board leadership, see *Report of the NACD Blue Ribbon Commission on Board Leadership* (Washington, D.C.: National Association of Corporate Directors, 2004), chaired by Jay Lorsch of Harvard Business School and David Nadler, chair of Mercer Delta Consulting.

19   *2004–2005 Public Company Corporate Governance Survey.*

20   As a solution, in many cases, only one of the CEOs may actually function as a leader. In many family-controlled firms, however, combined leadership is relatively common.

21   "The proxy statement indicates that during the week of January 24–28, 2005, the attorneys for the respective sides essentially

completed the proposed merger agreement, including presumably all of the 'social considerations,' such as Dorman becoming president of the combined company and being elected to the SBC board (along with two other AT&T directors) as well as his very lucrative compensation contract, while the critical question of the financial exchange ratio was put to one side." Alasandra Monaco, AT&T, Proxy Governance Advisory Service, May 27, 2005, p. 12. This internal client report is quoted with permission.

22   Ed Garsten, "Kmart Chairman's Power Base Grows," *Detroit News*, Nov. 18, 2004.

23   This rough rule of thumb is based on common lore and on an informal comparison of merger announcements and merger closings as published in *Mergers & Acquisitions* magazine.

24   David Mamet's *Glengarry Glen Ross*, 1984, after being performed on stage in several venues, became a movie starring Jack Lemmon. Most recently (2005), it played at the Bernard Jacobs Theatre on Broadway to critical acclaim.

CHAPTER 5

Integrating Financial and Tangible Resources

Est modus in rebus. (There is measure in all things.)

Horace, *Satires*

INTRODUCTION

When companies come under common ownership, everyone involved—from veteran employees to new vendors—may wonder about the future. Will the two companies' resources remain autonomous, or will they truly merge; and if so, to what degree? Answers may unfold slowly. One thing is certain, however: When two companies tie the knot, they are guaranteed to merge immediately, *on paper*. Although under generally accepted accounting principles (GAAP), separate financial reporting by company units is permitted and even encouraged, GAAP accounting also requires *consolidated financial statements*.

In this chapter, therefore, we will review the basics of accounting for combinations, emphasizing both current and emerging GAAP. We will also discuss some "enhanced business reporting practices" that are not required under GAAP, but are considered "best practice." (GAAP accounting does not tell the whole story of any company, which is why, through the Financial Accounting Standards Board and the American Institute of Certified Public Accountants, the accounting profession is continually adjusting GAAP to make it reflect financial reality ever more closely.)

Moving on, we will address the challenges in combining various types of tangible assets (plant, equipment, inventories, and land). We will see how these assets can be valued after a merger, and then anticipate some challenges in consolidating them—not just on paper but in reality. (For a discussion of intangible assets, see Chapter 6, "Integrating Reputational and Other Intangible Resources.")

In closing, we will examine emerging financial issues for cross-border transactions.

ACQUISITION ACCOUNTING FOR M&A (UNDER GAAP)

At what point should the combining companies combine their financial statements?

As soon as they need to see this information. Even prior to the close of a transaction, the companies' managements can begin working together to consolidate their financial statements on a pro forma basis for informational purposes. It is common to see pro forma financial statements prior to merger closings.

What exactly is pro forma accounting, and how is it used in M&A?

Pro forma accounting is accounting for illustrative purposes. This kind of unofficial accounting always supplements GAAP; it never replaces it. It need not follow GAAP, and it is not audited. Pro formas carry disclaimers accordingly, but in some cases, investors have found them to be misleading. The role of abusive pro forma accounting in the failure of Enron Corporation was one of the problems that led to the Sarbanes-Oxley Act. Section 401(b) of that law required the SEC to propose reforms in this area. In March 2003, the SEC issued "Conditions for Use of Non-GAAP Financial Measures," including so-called Regulation G.[1] Business combinations are exempt from Regulation G requirements.[2] Nonetheless, it is good to be familiar with these standards for non-GAAP reporting, as they express some of the principles that regulators and shareholders would like to see followed in financial reports.

What are the most important current or emerging accounting standards for acquisitions under GAAP?

As this book goes to press (late 2005), U.S. companies must follow Statement 141, "Business Combinations," from the Financial Accounting Standards Boards (FASB), while companies located outside the U.S. must follow a parallel International Financial Reporting Standard, IFRS 3, "Business Combinations," from the International Accounting Standards Board (IASB).[3] These are the *current* standards at press time.

There is, however, an *emerging* standard on business combinations that every acquirer should understand. On June 30, 2005, in their first ever joint standard, the FASB and the IASB issued parallel exposure drafts on business combinations.[4] When issued, this standard will be the single most important and influential standard for all merger and acquisition transactions.[5]

Could you summarize the FASB's recent exposure draft on accounting for consolidations and indicate any differences from the existing standard, Statement 141?

There are similarities and differences between the emerging standard and the current standard.

Similarities between the Exposure Draft and Statement 141   The June 30, 2005 document, "Exposure Draft on Business Combinations" would retain the fundamental requirement in Statement 141 that the *acquisition method of accounting* be used. (This was called "purchase" accounting, back in the days when something called "pooling" accounting used to be permitted.)

Also, like Statement 141, the proposed requirement would require that an *acquirer be identified for every business combination* (even a merger of equals, formerly sometimes treated through pooling accounting).

Finally, the newly proposed standards would retain the general guidance in Statement 141 for *identifying and recognizing intangible assets separately from goodwill.* Goodwill is the difference between the price an acquirer pays and the book value of the entity purchased, and is generally a positive difference. For more on goodwill, see Chapter 6, especially its discussion of another important accounting standard, Statement 142.

Differences between Statement 141 and the Proposed New FASB Standards   The proposed standard defines a business combination as "a transaction or other event in which an acquirer obtains control of one or more businesses." The standard says that consideration transferred by the acquirer in exchange for the acquiree must be measured at fair value as of the acquisition date[6] as the sum of (1) assets transferred by the acquirer, liabilities incurred by the acquirer, and equity instruments issued by the acquirer, including contingent consideration; and (2) any *noncontrolling* equity investment in the acquiree owned by the acquirer immediately before the acquisition date, with certain exceptions.[7]

What is the significance of this new definition of business combinations?

It means

- Recognizing the full fair values of assets acquired, liabilities assumed, and noncontrolling interests in acquisitions of less than a 100 percent controlling interest
- Recognizing holding gains and losses in step acquisition and partial disposition transactions (including those that involve contingent consideration)
- Accounting for changes in the ownership of a subsidiary (that do not result in a loss of control) as capital transactions

These are all new developments. Statement 141 does not include partial interests in its definition. Also, Statement 141 does not require the recognition of contingent consideration as of the acquisition date. Finally, Statement 141 does not provide guidance for measuring the noncontrolling interests' share of the consolidated subsidiary's assets and liabilities at the acquisition date.[8]

What are some other important aspects of the newly proposed standard?

The acquirer must assess whether any portion of the transaction price paid and any assets acquired or liabilities assumed or incurred are not part of the exchange for the acquiree. Only the consideration transferred and the assets acquired or liabilities assumed or incurred, are accounted for as part of the business combination accounting under the proposed new standard. This will mean *expensing acquisition-related transaction costs and restructuring costs,* which is new. (Statement 141 requires direct costs of the business combination to be included in the cost to the acquiree.)

Under the newly proposed standard, the acquirer must recognize the acquiree's intangible assets that are identifiable (for example, intangible assets that arise from contractual legal rights, or acquired research and development assets) as *separate from goodwill.*[9] This has implications for compensation, discussed in Chapter 8. Also, this change will mean capitalizing in-process research and development (IPR&D) assets acquired. (This is not currently required under Statement 141.)

Also, under the newly proposed standard for business combinations,

- The acquirer must exclude any changes in the amount of its deferred tax benefits that are recognizable as a result of the business combination.[10] (This would amend Statement 109, which requires a reduction in goodwill or an increase in negative goodwill.)
- In a *bargain purchase* (where the acquisition date fair value of the acquirer's interest in the acquiree exceeds the fair value of the consideration transferred for that interest), the acquirer must account for the excess by *reducing goodwill until the goodwill related to the business combination is reduced to zero,* and then recognizing any remaining excess in income. (Statement 141 requires that excess to be allocated as a pro rata reduction of the amounts that would have been assigned to the particular assets acquired.)

Acquirers should work closely with qualified professionals to plan for these new standards. Given the fact that the IASB is considering identical or similar changes (see the end of this chapter), there will be more global pressure to make these the new accounting standards for business combinations.

When might the FASB's proposed new standards be approved, and when will they be effective?

The FASB's proposed standard should become final in mid-2006, and will be effective for fiscal years beginning after December 15, 2006. (*Note:* Future printings and editions of this book will reflect this change.)

How much flexibility is permitted for structuring under these accounting rules? For example, if one company buys all the stock of another company, does it have to take over that company's assets, cancel its stock, and merge the stock into its own stock, or can it structure the transaction differently?

Accounting and structuring are really two different subjects. First, managers should determine what structure would be best for the organization and its shareholders. Then it should determine what accounting to use. There may be legal and/or organizational tax advantages to maintaining a separate identity as a parent corporation that holds the stock of the subsidiary. Indeed, some parent companies—called *holding companies*—exist solely for this purpose.

How does the parent-subsidiary relationship work from a legal and investment standpoint?

When a business operates as a parent company with subsidiaries, separate accounting records are kept by each corporation. From a legal standpoint, the parent and each subsidiary is still a separate entity, with all the rights, duties, and responsibilities of an individual corporation. From an investment standpoint, however, shareholders in the parent company are also investors in the subsidiaries. They need combined information about both the parent and its subsidiaries. This information is provided in *consolidated financial statements* (see Figure 5-1).[11]

FIGURE 5-1

Summary of Consolidated Financial Statements

A consolidated entity's relationship to the parent and subsidiary corporations

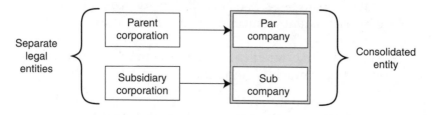

Consolidating the balance sheets of the parent and subsidiary corporations

Source: Kermit B. Larson, John J. Wild, and Barbara Chiapetta, *Fundamental Accounting Principles*, 17th ed. (New York: McGraw-Hill, 2004).

What financial statements may be consolidated following a merger or acquisition?

After a merger, only one corporation continues to exist, and consolidated financial statements are not necessary. After an acquisition, all the primary financial statements generally must be consolidated, including balance sheets, income statements, and cash flow statements.

What are the basic elements of the balance sheet, income statement, and cash flow statement?

- The balance sheet shows what a company owns and what it owes. It lists the assets, liabilities, and equity of an entity. It is called a balance sheet because assets must equal, or balance, the total of all liabilities and equity. (Equity is what is left after subtracting liabilities from assets.)

■ The income statement shows how much money a company makes. It shows sales (also called revenues), minus expenses, equaling income (also called profits, or the "bottom line").

■ The cash flow statement shows how much cash is coming in and how much is going out.

How can balance sheets be consolidated?

To consolidate multiple balance sheets under U.S. GAAP, one must combine into one statement all the assets, liabilities, and equity of the parent and the corporations owned by the parent. This consolidation is not merely a matter of addition, however. If there are duplications among the statements, these must be eliminated.

What are some examples of duplications that must be eliminated in the consolidated balance sheet?

One duplication is the parent's investment in the shares of a subsidiary's stock. On the parent company's balance sheet prior to consolidation, this would show up as an asset of the parent. On the subsidiary's balance sheet prior to consolidation, it would show up as equity. If both of these line items appeared in the consolidated balance sheet, however, there would be duplication. In the consolidated balance sheet, both of these items are offset and eliminated.

Another duplication is any debt that the subsidiary may owe to the parent. Obviously, a single enterprise cannot owe a debt to itself. For example, suppose that the parent company has loaned $10,000 to the subsidiary. The parent's accounts would reflect a $10,000 receivable, while the subsidiary's would reflect a $10,000 payable. From the consolidated point of view, however, there is no receivable and no payable. Therefore, receivables and payables between the parent and the subsidiary are eliminated in preparing a consolidated balance sheet.

T A B L E   5 – 1

Worksheet for 100 percent owned subsidiary; stock purchased at book value

	Par Company	Sub Company	Eliminations Debit	Eliminations Credit	Consolidated Amounts
Par Company and Sub Company **Worksheet for a Consolidated Balance Sheet** **December 31, 2005**					
Assets					
Cash	5,000	15,000			20,000
Notes receivable	10,000			(a) 10,000	
Investment in Sub Company	115,000			(b)115,000	
Other assets	190,000	117,000			307,000
	320,000	132,000			327,000
Liabilities and Equities					
Accounts payable	15,000	7,000			22,000
Notes payable		10,000	(a) 10,000		
Common stock	250,000	100,000	(b)100,000		250,000
Retained earnings	55,000	15,000	(b) 15,000		55,000
	320,000	132,000	125,000	125,000	327,000

Source: Kermit B. Larson, John J. Wild, and Barbara Chiapetta, *Fundamental Accounting Principles*, 17th ed. (New York: McGraw-Hill, 2004). See also the 13th edition, dated 1993.

How are the balance sheet data usually organized into a consolidated balance sheet?

Usually this is done through a worksheet (see Tables 5-1 and 5-2).

How are these worksheets created?

In the worksheet, the account balances are presented as of the date on which the parent company (called Par Company) acquired its interest in the subsidiary company (called Sub Company). In this example, Par Company paid cash to purchase all of Sub Company's outstanding $10 par value common stock from the Sub Company stockholders. The stock had a book value of $115,000, or

T A B L E   5 – 2

Worksheet for an 80 percent owned subsidiary;
stock purchased above book value

	Par Company	Sub Company	Eliminations		Consolidated Amounts
	Par Company	**Sub Company**	**Debit**	**Credit**	**Amounts**
Par Company and Sub Company Worksheet for a Consolidated Balance Sheet December 31, 2005					
Assets					
Cash	16,000	15,000			31,000
Notes receivable	10,000			(a) 10,000	
Investment in Sub Company	104,000			(b)104,000	
Other assets	190,000	117,000			307,000
Excess of cost over book value			(b) 12,000		12,000
	320,000	132,000			350,000
Liabilities and Equities					
Accounts payable	15,000	7,000			22,000
Notes payable		10,000	(a) 10,000		
Common stock	250,000	100,000	(b)100,000		250,000
Retained earnings	55,000	15,000	(b) 15,000		55,000
Minority interest				(b) 23,000	23,000
	320,000	132,000	125,000	137,000	350,000

Source: Kermit B. Larson, John J. Wild, and Barbara Chiapetta, *Fundamental Accounting Principles*, 17th ed. (New York: McGraw-Hill, 2004). This updated worksheet is based on one from the thirteenth edition of this book.

$11.50 per share, on Sub Company's books. We assume that Par Company simply paid $115,000, or book value, for the outstanding shares.

In Table 5-1, notice that the *eliminations* columns include two sets of debits and credits. One set is identified as *a*, and the other set is identified as *b*. These two sets of debits and credits are sometimes called *elimination entries*. They appear only on the consolidation worksheet; they are not journal entries made on the books of either the parent or the subsidiary.

What is elimination *a* in this example all about?

On December 31, 2005, the parent company loaned the subsidiary company $10,000 in cash to use in its operations. (Loans are fairly typical following a merger.) In exchange for the cash, the subsidiary company signed a promissory note to the parent company. The intercompany debt was in reality a transfer of funds within the consolidated entity. Because this transaction did not increase the total assets and total liabilities of the affiliated companies, elimination *a* is made to keep both balances from appearing on the consolidated balance sheet.

What about elimination *b*?

When a parent company buys a subsidiary's stock, it records the investment as an asset. This investment represents equity in the subsidiary's net assets. However, you must not show both the subsidiary's net assets (equity) and the parent company's investment in the subsidiary on the consolidated balance sheet. Doing so would double-count those items. On the worksheet, the credit portion of elimination *b* eliminates the parent company's investment and avoids double counting of the subsidiary's net assets.

What happens after worksheet eliminations are done?

After the intercompany items are eliminated on the worksheet, the assets of the parent and the subsidiary are combined, as are the remaining equities in these assets. Then all these combined values are carried into the worksheet's last column. The amounts in this last column are used to prepare a consolidated balance sheet that shows all the assets, liabilities, and equities of the parent and its subsidiary.

In Table 5-1, the parent bought all of the subsidiary's stock at book value. What if the parent company bought less stock for more than book value?

The new company could use the same worksheet, but with some important differences that will become immediately apparent (see Table 5-2).

Considering the same companies, assume that the parent purchased only 80 percent of the subsidiary, paying $13 per share, or $1.50 more than the company's book value. These new assumptions do not change the worksheet treatment of the intercompany debt. Therefore, elimination *a* is exactly the same as the one presented in Table 5-1. Assets are another matter, though. There must be eliminations of the parent's investment and the subsidiary's stockholders' equity accounts. The eliminations are complicated for two reasons. First, they must reflect the minority interest in the subsidiary. Second, they have to show the premium (excess over book value) paid by the parent company for the subsidiary's stock.

Why does a consolidated balance sheet have to show minority interest in the subsidiary?

When a parent company buys a controlling interest in a subsidiary, it becomes the subsidiary's majority stockholder. If the parent owns less than 100 percent of the subsidiary's stock, the subsidiary obviously has other stockholders who hold a minority interest in its assets and earnings. When you prepare a consolidated balance sheet for a parent and a subsidiary that has a minority interest, the equity of the minority stockholders must be recognized.

How can the worksheet be used to calculate this minority interest?

You can use the consolidation worksheet to calculate the minority interest in the process of eliminating the stockholders' equity balances of the subsidiary, as shown in Table 5-2. In this case, the minority stockholders have a 20 percent interest in the subsidiary. Therefore, 20 percent of the subsidiary's stockholders' equity, or $23,000 [($100,000 + $15,000) × 20 percent], is reclassified on the worksheet as the minority interest in the consolidated entity.

Moving on to the question of accounting for a premium, how does the worksheet record the payment of a premium (that is, an excess of investment cost over book value)?

It depends in part on why the premium was paid. There are basically three reasons for acquisition premiums, which accountants refer to as "excess of investment cost over book value." (*Premium* has another common meaning, but we won't get into that here.[12]) The first reason is that the assets of the seller may have been carried on the seller's books at less than their fair values. (For example, the value of land may have been recorded 50 years ago and never upgraded to reflect current market values.) Second, the seller's liabilities may be carried at book values greater than their fair values. (For example, the value of a disputed account payable may be lower because of a pending settlement of the account.) And finally, the seller's earnings prospects may be good enough to justify paying more for the stock than the net fair (market) value of the subsidiary's assets and liabilities. (Ask any proud seller!)

So how is the accounting done in each of these scenarios?

Let's start with the first two. If a company pays more than book value because the seller's assets are undervalued or its liabilities are overvalued, the excess over book value must be allocated to those assets and liabilities so that they are restated at their fair value. Any remaining cost in excess of book value is reported in the consolidated balance sheet as *goodwill from consolidation*.

In our example, we are assuming the third scenario, high earnings prospects. This involves somewhat more complicated accounting. First we calculate the premium paid over book value (in this case, $12,000).[13] This amount is noted in the debit column of Table 5-2 as one of four eliminations labeled *b*. Furthermore, in addition to the $12,000 debit, there are two credits and two debits. The $104,000 credit to "Investment in Sub Company" eliminates the balance of that account. Moreover, the stockholders' equity accounts of Sub Company are eliminated with a $100,000 debit to Common Stock and a $15,000 debit to Retained Earnings. The $23,000 recognizes the equity of Sub Company's minority-interest stockholders.

So what's the bottom line? What would the second example (of an 80 percent interest purchased at a premium) look like in a balance sheet?

After the worksheet is completed, the consolidated amounts in the last column are used to prepare a consolidated balance sheet, as shown in Table 5-3.

T A B L E   5 - 3

Par Company and Sub Company Consolidated Balance Sheet December 31, 2005

Assets	
Cash	$ 31,000
Other assets	307,000
Excess of cost over book value	12,000
Total assets	$350,000
Liabilites and Equities	
Liabilities:	
Accounts payable	$ 22,000
Minority interest	23,000
Stockholders' equity:	
Common stock	$250,000
Retained earnings	55,000
Total stockholders' equity	305,000
Total liabilities and stockholders' equity	$350,000

Source: Kermit B. Larson, John J. Wild, and Barbara Chiapetta, *Fundamental Accounting Principles*, 17th ed. (New York: McGraw-Hill, 2004). This worksheet is based on one from the 13th edition of this book.

ENHANCED FINANCIAL REPORTING FOR M&A (NON-GAAP)

How can managers get around the limitations of GAAP as they combine their financial statements?

To supplement the shortcomings of GAAP, managers must do what they can to recognize and communicate true value. Two veteran hospital executives and a leading consultant noted the difficulty of finding comparable data across the merging organizations. "For example, head counts varied at hospitals and the multinationals depending on how part time and contract workers were counted. Similarly, the organizations maintained very different financial data, even computing similar things using quite different methods." The authors suggest having a "data team" to help define and compare the data.[14]

What tools might be useful for collecting financial data?

It may be helpful to use some of the worksheets that appear at the ends of certain chapters of this book. These worksheets provide a natural checklist for obtaining the most critical information.

More generally, as the combined organization moves into the future, it will be important to make sure that all important information is collected and communicated to stakeholders, even if this reporting is not required under GAAP. For example, consider reporting on product quality, customer satisfaction, productivity, and market share.[15]

In December 2002, the American Institute of Certified Public Accountants (AICPA), following previous work in this area, created the Special Committee on Enhanced Business Reporting, composed of representatives from corporations, academia, government, and the accounting profession. The mission of the special committee was "to establish a consortium of investors, creditors, regulators, management and other stakeholders to improve the quality and transparency of information used for decision-making." Special committee members formed an advisory council composed of prominent business and civic leaders. The advisory council is working to build a broad consortium that aims to eliminate stale and redundant disclosures, to encourage disclosures that capital markets find truly relevant, and to make information easier to use. (Its motto might well be, "Out with the old and arcane, and in with the new and useful."[16])

VALUING AND COMBINING TANGIBLE ASSETS

What are the main types of tangible assets that might be combined on a consolidated balance sheet following a merger or acquisition?

All of the assets will typically be combined. Therefore, in addition to financial assets (for example, cash, marketable securities, and accounts receivable), a consolidated balance sheet will include combined values for plants, equipment,[17] inventories, and land.

In addition to being combined on a balance sheet, are these tangible assets ever actually combined from an operational standpoint?

Plants, equipment, and *inventories* may be combined in whole or in part when two companies integrate their operations. *Land* and *real estate,* of course, cannot be combined physically, but the leasing or ownership terms for the use of the land may be consolidated.

Plants
How can plants be combined operationally (as opposed to merely on the balance sheet)?

First, let's define our key term. A *plant* is a production operation at a defined physical location. It is usually envisioned in a manufacturing context. A plant's major assets include real estate, structures (foundations, buildings, framework, and related improvements), equipment (for production, communication, control, and administration), distribution assets (such as piping, conveyers, and docks), wiring and instrumentation (for electrical supply, communications, and control of operations), and software. In a service context, a plant may be a physical location in which services are performed. Examples of service plants include a computer processing facility, a branch bank facility, and a phone operation.

In both the manufacturing and service sections, plants can be consolidated in many different ways, ranging from plant closings to integration of plant operations through common, integrated systems. (See Chapter 7, "Integrating Management Systems.")

What are the main costs associated with plant conslidation?

In consolidating plants, employers may incur costs associated with disposal of assets (including environmental aspects); relocation, termination, and/or recruitment of employees; investments in physical assets or software to support consolidation; and redesign of products and/or services to accommodate integration. In addition, acquirers may have to spend money on new marketing efforts to preserve goodwill if plant consolidation has involved layoffs. Finally, closing or relocating plant operations may cause the loss of a group of customers or increase transportation and distribution costs to a set of customers (see Chapter 12, "Fulfilling Commitments to Employees and Communities").

Equipment
How can equipment be combined operationally?

Physically combining equipment is uncommon unless the equipment is mobile or unattached, such as forklifts, trucks, office equipment, and furniture. Combining companies are often at distant locations. Even when operations are consolidated, it is often preferable (if money permits) to purchase and install new equipment, rather than to remove, transport, and install older equipment from a discontinued operation. Furthermore, in addition to equipment purchased for replacement, some equipment may be purchased for enhancement—for example, to facilitate the integration of systems and operations.

Note also that the shareholders of the acquired business may retain some equipment, either to keep or to sell separately. The owners of closely held companies may wish to retain personal property (including equipment) for their own use, and such property will not be conveyed with the sale.

The difference between the fair market value of the sum of the financial and tangible assets should be either recorded as *goodwill* or allocated to identified intangible assets.[18]

What are the cost implications of combining equipment?

The value of some equipment held by the acquired entity and/or the acquirer may be written off in value because of costs associated with disposing of it or transferring it (the aforementioned cost of transportation, installation, and setup that is part of fair market value in use).

What tips do you have on valuing and combining inventories on a consolidated balance sheet and in reality?

The inventories of the acquired entity should be audited during the due diligence process and appraised at the current fair market value, as explained at the beginning of this chapter.[19]

Inventory valuation adjustments are much more likely if there is some consolidation of the inventory of the acquirer and the acquired entity. If this consolidation results in some units becoming obsolete or being discontinued, these will be sold at a discount or discarded. Consolidation of distribution or retail operations will typically involve some such consolidation and/or repositioning of inventory.

Land/Real Estate

How can land and/or real estate from two different companies be valued and combined on a consolidated balance sheet?

The real estate of the acquired entity should be valued at fair market value, whereas the real estate of the acquirer is recorded at historical cost. Each tract of real estate is typically valued separately, but in connection with any surrounding tracts commonly owned by the same entity.

What are some valuation issues to consider when combining the land and/or real estate of two companies?

It is possible for the value of two adjoining properties to increase as a result of their having common ownership. A change in the expected use of a specific piece of real estate may impair the value of that real estate, especially if the property is to be sold after being acquired and the future use of the property would require some modification or remedial efforts. Land associated with a profitable manufacturing operation may be worth more than equivalent raw land, especially when fully utilized.

How often are terms of land ownership or leasing consolidated, and why?

In a purchase of assets, there is a transfer of title to land and/or a transfer or renegotiation of leases. In a purchase of stock, by contrast, title may be retained by the acquired corporation, especially when the acquired entity retains its original identity. Leases in purchase accounting may give rise to a capitalized asset or liability associated with the leasehold interest (the contractual right of the tenant to occupy the leased property). If the acquired lease is favorable (a below-market lease rate), then a leasehold interest has value as an asset and is amortizable over the remaining term of the lease. If the acquired lease is unfavorable, then a leasehold interest liability may be recorded and amortized over the term of the lease.

If a company merges with another company to which it was leasing property, the merger eliminates the lease on a consolidated basis, even though the individual entities may continue to account for the lease as lessor and lessee on an operational basis.

INTERNATIONAL CONSIDERATIONS

What are the main challenges that arise when consolidating financial and tangible resources across international boundaries?

There are two primary challenges in this area of integration: conforming to international as well as domestic accounting standards and offsetting fluctuations in currency exchange rates.

You mentioned earlier IASB 3 and the new exposure draft for business combinations. Could you please summarize these current and emerging international standards for merger accounting?

The standards are generally the same in principle as the U.S. (FASB) standards described earlier, except that they have slightly different disclosure standards—requiring more detail or an optional rather than required treatment for some items.[20] The most significant difference is in the treatment of replacement share-based performance awards. See Chapter 8 for a discussion of this issue.

If a U.S. company buys a controlling interest in a foreign company and makes that company a subsidiary, how does it prepare a consolidated balance sheet?

First, if the foreign subsidiary does not follow U.S. GAAP (but rather follows its foreign equivalent), its accounts must be restated to conform to U.S. GAAP. Second, after such a restatement (if necessary), the accounts in the foreign financial statement must be put into U.S. dollars, using the appropriate exchange rate.

How do currency exchange-rate fluctuations affect a company after a merger?

First, some definitions are in order. There are two kinds of fluctuations: *nominal* and *real.* Nominal exchange-rate movements are the movements that occur daily in the relationship between one currency and another. These may require some complicated accounting adjustments, but they have very little effect on consolidation issues.

Real exchange-rate movements, on the other hand, are changes in the nominal exchange rates between two countries that do not reflect changes in price levels between the two countries. This kind of movement can substantially alter fundamental economic values and relationships.

For example, an appreciation in the real exchange rate of a given country can make products and services provided in that country's currency more expensive from the perspective of the rest of the world and make foreign goods and services cheaper from the perspective of the residents of that country, thus increasing the domestic market for imports and decreasing foreign markets for exports.

This means that a company may buy an overseas plant that is reasonably profitable and that has substantial intangible (goodwill) value at the time of its acquisition, only to see it suffer a loss in sales and income (and eventually goodwill value) in both its domestic and foreign markets following a rise in the country's real currency exchange rate.

How can exchange-rate movements be offset following a merger between companies from two countries?

Rather than buying supplies only from the two countries, companies can buy from a mix of countries. Also, pricing contracts can be pegged to a so-called basket of currencies or to a relatively stable currency.

Another way to hedge against the risk of exchange-rate fluctuations in any currency is to buy derivative financial instruments based on that currency.

Aren't derivatives risky?

Yes, but so is business. Derivative instruments hedge against the risks inherent in the things from which they "derive." Used properly, they lower risk rather than increase it.

The key lies in proper internal financial control. For more on this subject, see the section on internal control in Chapter 7, "Integrating Management Systems."

How should U.S. acquirers account for income in foreign currency?

They should consult the most recent FASB standard, which at present is Statement 52, as amended by subsequent rules.[21] Basically, Statement 52 says that when a local functional currency is translated to U.S. dollars, the amounts should be recorded as a separate component of shareholders' equity. For foreign subsidiaries with the U.S. dollar as the functional currency, the amounts should be included in income. Exchange gains and losses arising from transactions denominated in a foreign currency should be translated at average exchange rates and included in income.

What are some of the postmerger accounting issues associated with currency-exchange-rate movements?

There are three main accounting problems to watch for following an international merger:

- Valuation changes
- Transfer-pricing changes
- Value impairment

With regard to the first item, shifts in real exchange rates may substantially change the values of various transactions and investments at two times: at the outset, when translating from the original currencies into the functional currencies of the foreign operations, and later, when translating into the reporting currency of the consolidated company. Exchange gains and losses associated with the first translation are included in net income, while exchange gains and losses associated with the second translation are accumulated and reported as adjustments to consolidated shareholders' equity.

Furthermore, international acquisitions that lead to consolidations across countries raise a series of complex *transfer-pricing* issues. Transfer pricing is the allocation of income between two related companies for corporate tax purposes. In some cases, transfer pricing requires that a company recognize royalty payments or adjust the price of goods and services that it receives from the related company. As exchange rates change from year to year, imputed royalties associated with transfer-pricing allocations may turn out to be inappropriate and require adjustments.

Finally, to the extent that real exchange-rate movements impair certain intangible assets or goodwill tied to a specific operation, some recognition of the impairment will have to be recognized on the consolidated financial statements.

In this context, what is the difference between valuation impairment and the so-called risk factors that are often associated with foreign acquisitions?

Valuation impairment is the loss of value in a specific operation as a result of real changes in operations or in real currency-exchange values. This loss of value, which occurs in some (but not all) instances, is real and must be recognized. Risk factors, by contrast, are factors that have the *potential* to affect the future income streams expected from foreign-based tangible and intangible assets.

Some risk factors can substantially lower the appraised values of foreign assets by lowering the expected future income from those assets. This is especially true of intangible assets, as we shall see in Chapter 6, "Integrating Reputational and Other Intangible Resources." Nonetheless, in the valuation of foreign assets, international risk factors should not affect the discount rate used to value the future income streams from the assets. This can result in an inaccurate valuation that is inconsistent with evidence from financial markets.

Many exchange-rate risk factors are two-sided and, if anything, neutral between most developed economies. Besides, as mentioned, they can be hedged. Further, international investments provide important diversification benefits that would tend to *lower* the risk and therefore the required rate of return relative to comparable domestic investments.

APPENDIX 5 – A

Selected Unaudited Pro Forma Condensed Combined Financial Data (in thousands, except per share data)

The following selected unaudited pro forma condensed combined financial information was prepared using the purchase method of accounting. The Adobe and Macromedia unaudited pro forma condensed combined balance sheet data assume that the merger of Adobe and Macromedia took place on March 4, 2005, and combines the Adobe historical consolidated balance sheet at March 4, 2005 with Macromedia's historical consolidated balance sheet at March 31, 2005. The Adobe and Macromedia unaudited pro forma condensed combined statements of income data assume that the merger of Adobe and Macromedia took place as of November 29, 2003. The unaudited pro forma condensed combined statements of income data for the fiscal year ended December 3, 2004 combines Adobe's historical consolidated statement of income for the fiscal year then ended with Macromedia's results of operations for the nine months ended December 31, 2004 and the three months ended March 31, 2004. The unaudited pro forma condensed combined statements of income data for the three months ended March 4, 2005 combines Adobe's historical consolidated statement of income for the three months then ended with Macromedia's historical consolidated statement of income for the three months ended March 31, 2005.

The selected unaudited pro forma condensed combined financial data are presented for illustrative purposes only and are not necessarily indicative of the combined financial position or results of operations of future periods or the results that actually would have been realized had the entities been a single entity during these periods. The selected unaudited pro forma condensed combined financial data as of and for the three months ended March 4, 2005 and for the fiscal year ended December 3, 2004 are derived from the unaudited pro forma condensed combined financial statements included elsewhere in this joint proxy statement/prospectus and should be read in conjunction with those statements and the related notes. See "Unaudited Pro Forma Condensed Combined Financial Statements."

	Three Months Ended March 4, 2005	Fiscal Year Ended December 3, 2004
Unaudited Pro Forma Condensed Combined Statements of Income data:		
Revenue	$588,936	$2,088,701
Gross profit	531,956	1,868,658
Income before income taxes	139,522	518,659
Net income	116,673	374,282
Net income per share:		
Basic(1)	0.20	0.65
Diluted(1)	0.19	0.63
Weighted average number of shares used in computing earnings per share:		
Basic(1)	588,228	573,320
Diluted(1)	608,150	598,395
Cash dividends per share(1)	$0.005	$0.020

	As of March 4, 2005
Unaudited Pro Forma Condensed Combined Balance Sheet data:	
Cash, cash equivalents, and short-term investments	$ 1,845,381
Working capital	1,545,680
Total assets	5,561,205
Long-term liabilities	29,099
Stockholders' equity	4,880,655

(1) Adjusted to reflect the two-for-one stock split in the form of a stock dividend of Adobe common stock paid on May 23, 2005 to Adobe stockholders of record as of May 2, 2005.

COMPARATIVE HISTORICAL AND PRO FORMA PER SHARE DATA

The following information gives effect to the two-for-one stock split in the form of a stock dividend of Adobe common stock paid on May 23, 2005 to Adobe stockholders of record as of May 2, 2005.

The information below reflects:

- the historical net income, book value, and cash dividends per share of Adobe common stock and the historical net income (loss), book value, and cash dividends per share of Macromedia common stock in comparison with the unaudited pro forma net income, book value, and cash dividends per share after giving effect to the proposed merger of Adobe with Macromedia on a purchase basis; and
- the equivalent historical net income, book value, and cash dividends per share attributable to 1.38 shares of Adobe common stock which will be received for each share of Macromedia common stock.

Because of different fiscal period ends, the unaudited pro forma condensed combined statements of income data for the three months ended March 4, 2005 combines Adobe's historical consolidated statement of income for the three months then ended with Macromedia's historical consolidated statement of income for the three months ended March 31, 2005. The unaudited pro forma condensed combined statements of income data for the fiscal year ended December 3, 2004 combines Adobe's historical consolidated statement of income for the fiscal year then ended with Macromedia's results of operations for the nine months ended December 31, 2004 and the three months ended March 31, 2004.

You should read the tables below in conjunction with the respective audited and unaudited consolidated financial statements and related notes of Adobe and Macromedia incorporated by reference in this joint proxy statement/prospectus and the unaudited pro forma condensed financial information and notes related to such consolidated financial statements included elsewhere in this joint proxy statement/prospectus.

Adobe

	Three Months Ended March 4, 2005	Fiscal Year Ended December 3, 2004
Historical Per Common Share Data:		
Net income per common share—basic	$0.31	$0.94
Net income per common share—diluted	0.30	0.91
Book value per share(1)	3.34	2.94
Cash dividends per share	0.00625	0.025

Macromedia

	Three Months Ended March 31, 2005	Twelve Months Ended December 31, 2004
Historical Per Common Share Data:		
Net income (loss) per common share—basic	$(0.03)	$0.85
Net income (loss) per common share—diluted	(0.03)	0.79
Book value per share(1)	8.94	8.80
Cash dividends per share	—	—

Adobe and Macromedia

	Three Months Ended March 4, 2005	Fiscal Year Ended December 3, 2004
Combined Pro Forma Per Common Share Data:		
Net income per Adobe share—basic	$0.20	$0.65
Net income per Adobe share—diluted	0.19	0.63
Cash dividends per Adobe share	$0.005	$0.020
Combined Pro Forma Per Equivalent Share Data:(2)		
Net income per equivalent Macromedia share—basic	0.27	0.90

(Continued)

Adobe and Macromedia

	Three Months Ended March 4, 2005	Fiscal Year Ended December 3, 2004
Net income per equivalent Macromedia share—diluted	0.26	0.86
Book value per Adobe share(1)	8.27	—
Book value per equivalent Macromedia share	$11.41	—
Cash dividends per equivalent Macromedia share	$0.007	$0.028

(1) The historical book value per Adobe share is computed by dividing stockholders' equity by the number of shares of common stock outstanding at March 4, 2005 and December 3, 2004. The historical book value per Macromedia share is computed by dividing stockholders' equity by the number of shares of common stock outstanding at March 31, 2005 and December 31, 2004. The combined pro forma book value per share is computed by dividing combined pro forma stockholders' equity by the combined pro forma number of shares of Adobe common stock outstanding at March 4, 2005 and December 3, 2004 assuming the merger had occurred as of those dates.

(2) The combined pro forma per equivalent share amounts are calculated by multiplying the Adobe and Macromedia combined pro forma amounts by the exchange ratio of 1.38 shares of Adobe common stock for each share of Macromedia common stock.

FORWARD-LOOKING INFORMATION

This joint proxy statement/prospectus includes "forward-looking statements" within the meaning of the safe harbor provisions of the United States Private Securities Litigation Reform Act of 1995. Words such as "anticipate," "believes," "budget," "continue," "could," "estimate," "expect," "forecast," "intend," "may," "plan," "potential," "predicts," "project," "should," "will" and similar expressions are intended to identify such forward-looking statements. Forward-looking statements in this joint proxy statement/ prospectus include, without limitation, statements regarding forecasts of market growth, future revenue, benefits of the proposed merger, expectations that the merger will be break-even to slightly accretive to Adobe's results, future expectations concerning available cash and cash equivalents, Adobe's expectations with respect to future stock repurchases following the merger, including the timing and amount of such repurchases, and other matters that involve known and unknown risks, uncertainties and other factors that may cause actual results, levels of activity, performance, or achievements to differ materially from results expressed in or implied by this joint proxy statement/prospectus. Such risk factors include, among others:

- difficulties we may encounter in integrating the merged businesses;
- uncertainties as to the timing of the merger, and the satisfaction of closing conditions to the merger, including the receipt of regulatory approvals;
- the receipt of required stockholder approvals;
- whether certain markets will grow as anticipated;
- the competitive environment in the software industry and competitive responses to the proposed merger; and
- whether the companies can successfully develop new products on a timely basis and the degree to which these gain market acceptance.

Actual results may differ materially from those contained in the forward-looking statements in this joint proxy statement/ prospectus. Additional information concerning these and other risk factors is contained in Adobe's and Macromedia's most recently filed Annual Reports on Form 10-K and Adobe's most recently filed Quarterly Report on Form 10-Q. You are cautioned not to place undue reliance on these forward-looking statements, which speak only as of the date of this joint proxy statement/ prospectus. All forward-looking statements are qualified in their entirety by this cautionary statement.

Source: Securities and Exchange Commission (8-K filing from Adobe).

N O T E S

1   "Regulation G will not apply to a non-GAAP financial measure included in disclosure relating to a proposed business combination, the entity resulting therefrom or an entity that is a party thereto if the disclosure is contained in a communication that is subject to the communications rules applicable to business combination transactions."

2   Diane Schmalensee, Andrew Riddle, and Del Joiner, "Making Mergers More Successful," an undated research paper posted on www.schmalensee.com. Schmalensee is president of Schmalensee Partners in Chestnut Hill, Massachusetts. Riddell is former CEO of AtlantiCare Medical Center , and Del Joiner is former vice president of quality for North Shore Medical.

3   The FASB issues the principal guidelines covering all generally accepted accounting principles (GAAP), including M&A accounting, in the United States. (See www.fasb.org.) The U.S. Securities and Exchange Commission (SEC) and the American Institute of Certified Public Accountants (AICPA) also issue standards in some areas, but they both recognize FASB financial accounting standards as authoritative. The FASB and equivalent bodies in nearly 100 countries recognize the IASB as an additional and parallel authority.

4   The FASB standard is "Exposure Draft 1204-001, Proposed Statement of Financial Accounting Standards: Business Combinations, June 30, 2005." The IASB standard is "International Financial Reporting Standard: Business Combinations, June 30, 2005." Any differences between the two documents (detailed on pp. 210–215 of the FASB document) are likely to be reconciled by the time both entities publish a joint standard on business combinations in mid-2006.

5   Furthermore, it should be noted that the FASB has recently issued Exposure Draft No. 1205-001, "Proposed Statement of Financial Accounting Standards: Consolidated Financial Statements, Including Accounting and Reporting of Noncontrolling Interests in Subsidiaries," to replace Accounting Research Bulletin No. 51. Comments were due October 28, 2005. Space does not permit adequate discussion of this standard.

6   Note: The acquirer must recognize any adjustments made during the measurement period to the provisional value of any assets acquired and liabilities assumed as if the accounting for the business combination had been completed at the acquisition date.

(Comparative information for prior periods presented in financial statements would be adjusted.)

7   The exceptions are as follows: (1) Goodwill is to be measured and recognized as the excess of the fair value of the acquiree, as a whole, over the next amount of the recognized identifiable assets acquired and liabilities assumed. If the acquirer owns less than 100 percent of the equity interests in the acquiree at the acquisition date, goodwill attributable to the noncontrolling interest is to be recognized. (2) Long-lived assets (or disposal groups) classified as held for sale, degreed tax assets or liabilities, and particular assets or liabilities related to the acquiree's employee benefit plans are to be measured in accordance with other GAAP rules.

8   *SFAS No. 141*, paragraph 10, provides the following definition of a business combination: "The provisions of this Statement apply equally to a business combination in which (a) one or more entities are merged or become subsidiaries, (b) one entity transfers net assets or its owners transfer their equity interests to another, or (c) all entities transfer net assets or the owners of those entities transfer their equity interests to a newly formed entity (some of which are referred to as roll-up or put-together transactions). . . . An exchange of a business for a business also is a business combination."

9   This proposed standard would supersede *FASB Interpretation No. 4*, "Applicability of FASB Statement No. 2 to Business Combinations Accounted for by the Purchase Method," which said that acquired R&D assets with no alternative future use must be measured at their fair value and expensed at the acquisition date.

10 Statement 109 would be amended to require such changes in deferred tax benefits to be recognized either in income from continuing operations (in the period of the combination) or directly as part of contributed capital, depending on the circumstances.

11 This discussion on consolidation of financial statements was based in part on Clyde P. Stickney and Roman L. Weil, *Financial Accounting: An Introduction to Concepts, Methods, and Uses*, 11th ed. (Mason, Ohio: Thomson-Southwestern, 2005).

12 In the purchase of publicly held companies, the term *premium* commonly refers to the price paid per share over the market value—measured typically as the closing price five working days before the announcement of the transaction.

13 In our example, the parent company paid $13 per share (or $1.50 over book) for the subsidiary company's stock. The cost of these shares exceeded their book value by $12,000 ($8,000 × $1.50).

14   Schmalensee, Riddle, and Joiner, "Making Mergers More
Successful." In this case study of a hospital merger, the authors
show how a three-part process involving preparation, discovery,
and communication succeeded in overcoming many common
pitfalls of mergers, including the challenges of differing financial
reporting conventions at the respective institutions.

15   These four items are emphasized in Lawrence A. Gordon,
Managerial Accounting: Concepts and Empirical Evidence, 7th ed.
(New York: McGraw-Hill, 2006).

16   The advisory council is chaired by Edward (Ned) Regan, professor,
City University of New York, former president of Baruch College
and former New York State Comptroller; David Walker, comptroller
general of the United States; Paul Volcker, chairman, Trustees of the
IASC Foundation, and former chairman of the Federal Reserve;
Maria Livanos Cattaui, secretary general of the International
Chamber of Commerce; Roderick Hills, president of Hills & Stern
and former chairman of the Securities and Exchange Commission;
Norm Augustine, director and former chair and CEO, Lockheed
Martin; Don Tapscott, CEO of New Paradigm Learning
Corporation, adjunct professor of management, Joseph L. Rotman
School of Management, University of Toronto; and Peter Wallison,
resident fellow at the American Enterprise Institute, former general
counsel of the U.S. Treasury Department, and former White House
counsel to President Reagan. For more about the EBRC, see
www.ebrcconsortium.com.

17   Plant and equipment may also be referred to as property, plant, and
equipment (PP&E), and is sometimes also called furniture, fixtures,
and equipment (FF&E) in a retail or office-type business).

18   The allocation of value to identified intangible assets should be
based upon the application of valuation methods appropriate for
each asset. For more on this subject, see the discussion of combining
intellectual property in Chapter 6.

19   For large inventories—even with heterogeneous units—it is
possible to use sampling techniques to value the inventories with
reasonable precision by comparing the market value of a set of
units sampled to the current book value for those same units. For
example, an acquired salvage operation reports $2,560.35 million
on its balance sheet as the cost basis of its inventory of used parts.
A sample of 5,000 out of 100,000 items (representing $245,199.10
of inventory at original cost) reveals that the current cost
(at wholesale auction) of these items would be $250,619.50. This

yields a value-to-book ratio of 1.022106. Thus the overall inventory can be valued based on this cost-to-book ratio at $2,616,751.50.

20 The FASB standard, cited in note 4, includes a chart at the end comparing differences between the FASB and IASB standards. None of the differences appear to be major, with the exception of the treatment of replacement share-based performance awards.

21 Paragraph 101 of Statement 52 has been amended by *SFAS No. 141*, paragraphs 44 through 46.

CHAPTER 6

Integrating Reputational and Other Intangible Resources

The purest treasure mortal times afford
Is spotless reputation.

William Shakespeare, *King Richard II*

INTRODUCTION

Of all the treasures exchanged in a merger, surely reputation ranks highest in value. This chapter sets forth the opportunities and risks that arise in the merging of two corporate reputations as captured in the names and images of the companies and their brands.

The following pages will cover several challenges for combining companies:

- What to name the new company
- How to preserve the names of newly acquired brands
- When and how to merge statements affecting the new company's reputation, such as merging vision statements or merging vision statements
- How to value and combine intangible assets

In closing, we turn to international considerations. The appendix to this chapter features a particularly succinct postmerger vision statement from a small yet global company based in India.

THE CHALLENGE OF COMPANY NAME CHANGES

What usually happens to the names of two companies when they merge?

When one company buys another, it has four basic choices:

- To keep its own name (as Cingular did when it acquired AT&T Wireless in 2004). This is the most common option.
- To assume the seller's name (as Kmart did when it acquired Sears in 2005). This is the least common option.
- To combine both names (in full, as in Northrup Grumman or Lockheed Martin; or via an acronym, as in CIGNA—from Connecticut General and INA).
- To create an entirely *new* name (as when Great Lakes Chemical Corporation merged with Crompton Corporation to become Chemtura in 2005).[1]

Why do most acquiring companies keep their names unchanged after a merger or acquisition?

Name changes are generally reserved for deals in which the acquired company has a reputation equal to or more prominent than that of the acquirer. The majority of M&A deals involve purchases of companies that are smaller and less well known than their acquirers.

Even in a merger of equals, there is usually one company that has a stronger name value and wishes to assert that. The company may take on a new name that evokes the name of the second company, but that can fade in time—especially if the new entity is acquired later. The story of the BayBank name shows the gradual loss of an acquired company name. When BayBank merged with Bank of Boston in 1996, the combined entity called itself BankBoston—a small but symbolically significant concession to the elided BayBank name. In 1999, when BankBoston merged with Fleet, the new company was called FleetBoston Financial Corporation. By 2004, the BayBank elision and name were gone: Bank of America bought FleetBoston and kept its own name.

What are the pros and cons of these four different approaches?

Let's look at them one by one.

- *Keeping the acquirer's name* is the simplest approach, and it is often a wise course for high-profile companies that buy low-profile companies. The chief drawback is the sense of loss felt by the acquired company's employees. From plant to boardroom table, people can literally grieve for the loss of what they have worked for years to build.[2] There is also a dollars-and-cents issue for the company as a whole and its owners: if the selling company has name recognition, as most companies that are worth buying do, the value of this "trade name" might be diminished, along with any "trademark" value it may have.
- *Adopting the seller's name* is good for acquirers that need to gain cachet from the seller's company. The chief advantages and disadvantages here are the same as in the first example, but with the acquirer and seller roles reversed.
- *Putting the two names together*, with or without acronyms, has the advantage of bolstering the pride of both parties. On the other hand, it poses the challenge of making a dual identity understood both within and outside the company.
- *Creating an entirely new name* avoids this challenge while creating another one: what to call the new company. Of all the communication challenges facing newly combined companies, this one is paramount. (In fact, the comprehensive communications grid that appears in Chapter 3 was originally developed as a grid to announce company name changes.) In this option, the potential sense of loss is doubled. Employees from both the acquired and the acquiring company may feel a sense of abandonment.

How do buyers and sellers decide whether to use old or new names? And how do they create new names?

Sometimes the best course for naming a newly combined entity will be obvious. If a large, successful company buys a small, struggling firm in the same industry, the acquirer's name should probably prevail unchanged, especially if the acquirer has already changed its name within the past few years. Usually, however, the choice is not so easy.

Merging companies would be wise to appoint a small group of managers to look into this important question—a subgroup of the postmerger integration team(s) described in Chapter 3. These designated managers can consider taking the following steps.

Step 1: Compare the Present Names with the Future of the Combined Company   The designated managers can ask themselves honestly whether the existing company names (separately or in combination) adequately convey the range of products and services that the new company will offer. Is the company expanding? Is it planning to sell off noncore businesses? What qualities does the company want to project?

Step 2: Determine the Needs and Expectations of Stakeholders   The managers or their agents (designated employees or consultants) can then interview representatives of each stakeholder group to find out what they think of the businesses that are combining. This includes customers, suppliers, stockholders, bondholders, lenders, employees, and people in the communities where the companies are headquartered.

Step 3: Develop Criteria for a New Name   In listing criteria, managers should ensure congruence with as many facets of the company as possible. Here is a quick checklist of 10 important attributes of a name:

1. *Descriptive* of the combined companies' core business
2. *Suitable* to the products, services, and (if regional) location of subsidiaries
3. *Broad* enough to suit the present while leaving room for growth in the future

  4. *Acceptable* to the company's stakeholders
  5. *Distinctive* rather than clichéd
  6. *Memorable* rather than arcane
  7. *Pronounceable* rather than a tongue-twister
  8. *Real-sounding* rather than outlandish
  9. *Self-explanatory* rather than a stretch
  10. *Legally available*

Step 4: Develop a Long List of Names   Now is the time for maximum creativity. The decision-making group may wish to include additional employees and/or outside consultants for brainstorming at this point. In generating a list of possible names, managers can use key prefixes, suffixes, and word fragments to imply general image attributes, such as "Uni" for centralization, "Max" for high-quality services, and "Ameri" for domestic orientation. The dictionary and thesaurus will be helpful here. To add to the list, a computer can be programmed to generate random names. In the end, the list should include as many as several *hundred* names for a large, complex company. It is important to check to be sure the names aren't already being used. The most sought-after names in the investment sector, for example, convey something "soaring, mighty, fast or majestic," as one source wrote. The challenge, however, is that, there is currently a "logjam" of names. Greek gods, animals, mountain ranges, rivers, roads, and even solar systems are "largely taken."[3]

Step 5: Review and Screen Names, Making a Short List   Next, managers should winnow the list down to 25 to 35 acceptable candidates. In this process, they should bear in mind that no single name can meet all the criteria. It is up to senior management to set priorities. Managers might assign points for each attribute desired, with extra points for the attributes that matter the most. They might also decide that failure on certain key points will mean automatic rejection, despite the overall score.

Step 6: Conduct a Preliminary Legal Search   Although the process of obtaining legal clearances can be long and frustrating, a full corporate designation must be legally cleared, registered, and protected in accordance with statutes governing its use. Depending on the size of the business and its market, a preliminary search must be conducted at the national, state, and/or local level to identify the legal availability of the names on the list. (Sometimes the search must be conducted internationally, nation by nation.) It is fairly typical at this point to find that most of the names are already taken.

Step 7: Evaluate Graphic and Phonetic Attributes   In the process of narrowing down the choice, managers should begin to get a feel for what it will be like to "live" with each of the names. At this point, they should begin to pay especially close attention to the way the name looks and sounds. The name selected must be adaptable to a variety of media, both visual and auditory. It will appear in newspapers, in magazines, and on the Internet, as well as on a range of forms, stationery, and signage. It will also be heard on radio, over the telephone, and in conversation—sometimes in many languages.[4]

Step 8: Select Final Candidates   By now, a company may have about a dozen name finalists. At this point, it is time to make a final choice. One way to do this is to take two names at a time and select only one each time—a process called pairwise comparison—continuing to evaluate the attributes listed so far. (See Appendix C of the book.) At the end, only one name will survive.

Step 9: Obtain Final Legal Clearance for Use of the Name   Having selected a name, managers should ask their legal counsel to begin the paperwork for obtaining the legal right to use the name and any images associated with the name, pending board and stockholder approval. As discussed later, *trademarks* and *service marks* have value, so this is an important step.

Step 10: Seek Approval from the Board and/or Stockholders   In most situations, it will be necessary to seek approval for the name change from the board of directors and from owners. In seeking approval, managers should disclose the criteria and process that they used to select the new name, and the benefits that a new name may bring.

Step 11: Create a Graphic System for the New Name
Once the name has been selected and approved, it is time to design a graphic system for it. This system will include such visual elements as logos, symbols, and typefaces for the name's expression in all foreseeable applications. Will the name consistently be linked to a specific color or symbol? Will the name appear on stationery in all capital letters or in upper- and lowercase?

Step 12: Develop a Communications Plan   If a tree falls in the forest and no creature is there to hear it, does it make a sound? No, suggests the old riddle. It is equally unlikely that a new name will catch on without an audience. It is up to the managers of a newly combined company to ensure that the new name reaches the right audience at the right time in the right way.

Managers should decide when to announce the name change, leaving adequate time for reprinting and reordering materials such as forms, stationery, and signs. After the announcement, the company should use only the new supplies. The announcement (which is sometimes coupled with the announcement of the merger itself) should be made not only through the usual channels of communication, but also in special mailings or meetings tailored to specific stakeholder concerns. (For more on this point, see Chapter 3.) The company should be sure to include information about the new name in the part of its Web site devoted to the merger. One of the FAQs (frequently asked questions) posted about Bank of America's merger with Fleet was, What is the name of the new company? (The response: Bank of America Corporation.)

In the end, the burden of proof will be on the new owner, who must demonstrate that the values underneath the company name and logo will survive and indeed thrive under a new banner.

These steps are summarized in Table 6-1.

MANAGING BRAND IDENTITY AFTER A MERGER

How common is it for an acquirer to buy a company because of its brands?

Very common. Virtually every acquisition involves the purchase of at least one product or service with a recognizable name in its market segment. In some cases, the brand may be a "household

T A B L E   6 – 1

Steps for Naming a Newly Combined Company

1. Compare the present names with the future of the combined company.
2. Determine needs and expectations of stakeholders.
3. Develop criteria for a new name.
4. Develop a long list of names.
5. Review and screen names, making a short list.
6. Conduct a preliminary legal search.
7. Evaluate graphic and phonetic attributes.
8. Select final candidates.
9. Obtain final legal clearance for use of the name.
10. Seek approval from board and/or stockholders.
11. Create a graphic system for the new name.
12. Develop a communications plan.

name" nationwide or even internationally. Companies like these often build brands by imposing their identity (through a visual logo or by sharing a product title, for example) on a series of different products. Indeed, to build the strength of a corporate brand, a company will sometimes rename itself after a brand that it owns through a subsidiary. This is what Consolidated Foods did in 1985, when it successfully renamed itself Sara Lee Corporation after one of its acquired brands.

In some cases, though, acquirers choose not to link their corporate identity with any of the brands they develop or acquire. Maintaining separate brand identities for their subsidiaries gives the acquirer more flexibility should it wish to sell the subsidiaries later. Autonomous brands that do not rely on their parent's identity can change hands many times over the lifetime of a consumer, and the consumer will notice only the brand, not its changing owners. This brings the valuable element of continuity to the best product brands.

Sometimes after a merger, there is a shift from a corporate identify to a brand identity. DaimlerChrysler did this after its merger. The firm's brands include Maybach, Mercedes-Benz, Chrysler, Jeep, Dodge, and Smart.

In the United States, communications and dealership signage gave more emphasis to the corporate brand (represented by the Chrysler Pentastar) than to the product brands. Furthermore, most product brands had inconsistent identities across different applications (dealerships, cars, marketing materials, signage). For more cases, see Appendix 6-B.

If brand value is independent of the owner's identity, why do acquirers have to work to preserve brand identity after a merger? Can't they just do nothing (so to speak)?

Acquirers need to bear in mind that when they buy a brand, they aren't just buying a name and a logo. These aspects (technically called a trademark and a service mark) are just the tip of the iceberg. Acquirers of brands buy four things: the brand's definition (the values it promises), its culture (how the brand's previous owner has honored the brand's promise), its infrastructure (internal and external support via advertising, distribution, marketing, promotion, and sales networks), and, finally and most apparently, the visual identity as expressed in the brand's name and logo. To the extent that any of these elements changes, the brand's value will change. Also, sometimes an acquiring organization fails to recognize the value of a brand that it is acquiring. As one blogger put it recently, when writing about a "rollup" type acquirer of independent producers of alcoholic beverages, "You can bet your bottom dollar, major brand rationalization will occur, and will occur swiftly. [The acquirer] has a reputation for bean counting and anything that is not profitable or returning an adequate return on investment is given the chop. Many of the boutique brands will go."[5]

How can an acquirer preserve brand identity during the postmerger integration process?

By putting the brand first and integration second. The management of a newly combined company should not say, "Let's combine our advertising efforts" (or other brand support), thinking that what works for one brand will work for another. This can bury a brand. Instead, managers should say, "Let's build this brand." In other words, managers should use integration as a means, not an end. In the process of building a brand, an acquirer should have special reverence for existing names and logos and what they mean to employees and others.

INTEGRATING MISSION STATEMENTS

Many companies have developed "mission" statements expressing their driving purpose. When two companies merge, should they merge their mission statements, and if so, how?

Certainly both companies should devote part of their postmerger planning sessions to this question. Answers will vary depending on the two companies' situations.

If the acquirer has a fully developed mission statement that applies perfectly to the acquired company, and if the acquired company has no mission statement of its own, the job of integration will be easy. It will be merely a matter of educating the employees of the acquired company as to the mission of the acquirer. If, on the other hand, both companies have mission statements, a greater effort may be required.

There are two basic possibilities here. The companies may be in completely different businesses. If so, it is best to leave their respective mission statements undisturbed, at least temporarily, for the sake of continuity. Integration should not be engaged in for its own sake. If, however, the companies are in related businesses that require integration of their missions, they can and should consider drafting an entirely new mission statement for the newly combined entity.

The creation of a new mission statement should not begin with a blank slate. Instead, it should be based on the existing statements. First, the postmerger integration team (or its designated agent, such as a public relations manager or consultant) should inventory all formal self-descriptions that the company has generated, including mission statements, policy statements, and vision statements.

Next, the team should determine the extent to which these statements have been publicized (if at all). If the statements have been widely disseminated, it would be wiser to build on them than to scrap them entirely. If, however, they have not received wide distribution, they can be used or discarded, as appropriate to the new situation.

Finally, with past statements as a base, the newly combined entities should work to develop a new set of statements that can apply to both companies.

What is the difference between "mission" statements and "policy" or "vision" statements?

The primary purpose of the *mission* statement is to provide identity and focus. A mission statement says, "This is the business we are in today, as exemplified by our present products and services." These statements typically have a broad audience that includes the general public as well as all company stakeholders (such as employees, stockholders, creditors, customers, suppliers, and local communities). About half of all companies have formal mission statements.

The main goal of any *policy* statement is to ensure ethical and legal behavior. A policy statement says, "This is how we operate our business. All our employees must adhere to these rules." Almost all companies have developed policy statements for some aspects of their business, and most major companies have comprehensive codes of conduct. *Vision* statements provide direction and motivation for a company or a company unit. A vision statement (sometimes called a "vision and values" statement) says, "Here is the difference we want to make in the world—the vital goal that animates us as we pursue our mission and adhere to our policies." These statements are relatively new to the corporate scene; they number in the hundreds. Some experts believe that the distribution of a vision statement should be broad, while others believe it should be strictly limited to top management. For a sample vision statement intended for broad distribution, see Appendix 6-A.

Assuming that an acquirer wants to develop and disseminate new mission, policy, and vision statements to suit its new identity, how should it go about this?

First of all, management must determine who will be drafting the statements. The mission statement should be developed by senior line managers, whereas policy statements (or a code of conduct) should be developed by senior legal staff. The vision statement should be developed by the chief executive and the board of directors, ideally based on the advice of outside experts who have a sense of the company's potential future.

Beyond this, the development of each statement should proceed step by step. The working group that is drafting each statement should obtain comparable statements and work from these, developing a content and style appropriate to the company's circumstances. Mission and values statements tend to be expressed in a page or so, whereas policy statements (especially comprehensive companywide codes of conduct), by their very nature, should be longer. Some become booklets—or even books.

VALUING AND COMBINING INTANGIBLE ASSETS

Moving from the subject of values to the subject of valuation, how would an appraiser look at these various intangible elements that we have been discussing?

Intangible assets can be classified into three broad groups:

1. *Operational* intangibles
2. *Production* intangibles
3. *Marketing* intangibles

Operational Intangibles
What are operational intangibles?

Operational intangibles are, in essence, the value generated by the coexistence of various assets, both tangible and intangible, in a going concern. In fact, another term for this concept is *going concern value*, which has been defined as "the additional element of value which attaches to property by reason of its existence as an integral part of a going concern," and as "the ability of a business to continue to function and generate income without interruption as a consequence of a change in ownership."[6] Going concern value has often been equated with avoided start-up costs.

Examples of operational intangibles include the existence of an assembled and trained workforce (as evidenced, for example, by franchise, employment, and no compete agreements), operating and administrative systems, and corporate culture. (For more on these subjects, see Chapters 4, 5, and 7.)

Could you say more in this context about the value of corporate culture?

Earlier, we defined corporate culture as a force that influences what people believe, think, and do—shaping attitudes, behavior, functions, norms, structures, symbols, and history.

Social scientists generally agree that culture takes on a life of its own. Although culture cannot exist without the people who create, shape, and continue it, it does have a life beyond people. B. Kenneth West, retired CEO and chairman of Harris Bank of Chicago, has called it the "soul" of a corporation.[7] Can we put a precise value—a price—on corporate soul? No. Yet corporate identity clearly has some value that is deeper than just its trade name and trademarks. (See Box 6-1.)

Production Intangibles
What are production intangibles?

Production intangibles (also called *production and product intangibles*) are values placed on the combined entity's accumulated intellectual capital in product design and production. These intangible assets enable the company to produce a product or service with a competitive advantage vis-à-vis alternative products or services. This competitive advantage may take the form of lower production costs, higher product quality, faster production, or another production-related characteristic that makes the product more attractive to the consumer or client.

Examples of assets typically considered to be production and product intangibles include patents, technical know-how, production standards, copyrights, software, and favorable contracts.

Marketing Intangibles
What are marketing intangibles?

Marketing intangibles are factors that help a company sell its products or services. These include customer lists and relationships; price lists and pricing strategies; marketing strategies, studies, and concepts; advertising and promotional materials; and trademarks, service marks, and the trade name.

B O X   6 – 1

Company "Soul"

The following exercise in visualization can help heighten sensitivity to the value of "corporate soul," a concept described by B. Kenneth West. (See Note 7).

1. Visualize these scenarios (all based on real-life events):

    ■   A professional services firm has locations all over the world, with tens of thousands of employees and a century of untarnished history. Through the ethical lapses of a few, the company becomes subject to a federal indictment and clients flee, forcing the company to go out of business. *The company ceases to exist.*

    ■   A manufacturing firm has made a high-quality product for many years, being a responsible employer to a community. Through a series of poor financial decisions, the company is forced into liquidation and closes its doors. *The company ceases to exist.*

    ■   A financial information company has a single location (a floor in a high-rise located in a large city) but broad influence. This service company is known for proud employees, satisfied customers, and loyal vendors. Over the years, employees come and go, but the company remains a steady presence in its industry niche. Then, through a catastrophic event, the entire company—its people, its technology, its records, everything—is physically destroyed. *The company ceases to exist.*

2. How do you feel in each case when you learn that "the company ceases to exist"? Do you believe that a *company* (not merely its people, products, and services) can be missed or mourned? If so, what are the implications for a merger in which an acquired company's name, logos, policies, and processes are being phased out?

The last three terms require additional definition. A *trademark* is the right to use a name associated with a company, product, or concept, whereas a *service mark* is the right to use an image associated with these factors. A trademark and/or service mark is often a signal to potential customers that a specific location, product, or service is associated with the general reputation of a company. A *trade name* is the name under which the company operates, which is usually (but not always) the name of its top brand. If a trade name is strongly associated with the company's brands and the trade name disappears, the acquirer can take one of two approaches: keep the trade name going (as Sears is doing with Kmart) or deemphasize the trade name (as Daimler-Benz did with Chrysler). For more on a shift from a corporate identity to a brand identity, see Appendix 6-B, case 1.

Most highly successful global brands (85 percent) carry the full clout of their owner's name—in particular, all of the top 10 do.[8] In fact, of the top 100 global brands identified by *BusinessWeek* in August 2005, only 15 had no discernible connection with the trade name of the companies that owned them.[9]

When a firm changes its trade name as a result of a merger or acquisition, its new trade name may continue to have value because of the transfer of the reputation and image of the business—even if there is no continuing brand to remind consumers of the old company name. (For more on the subject of company names, see the preceding discussion.)

What is the difference between a trade name and goodwill?

The terms *trade name* (defined previously) and *goodwill* are often used synonymously. This usage is consistent with the term *goodwill* in law and economics, but the term *goodwill* is defined much more narrowly in accounting.

The classic legal definition recognizes goodwill as "the expectancy of continued patronage."[10] Courts have held also that the "nature of goodwill is the expectancy that 'old customers will resort to the old place.'"[11] Economists have defined goodwill as the intangible value of a company that follows from its advantage in its relationships with various markets.[12]

Accounting and tax rules have significantly narrowed the concept of goodwill by excluding from the value of goodwill the *identified* intangible assets (including the operational, production, and marketing intangibles just described) that are known to have ascertainable values and finite, determinable lives. Goodwill is recognized for accounting and tax purposes only when the purchase price paid for a business exceeds the sum of the fair market values of all of the identified assets (both tangible and intangible) of the business.

This means that in the allocation of a purchase price for tax and financial accounting purposes, goodwill is the sum of those marketing intangible assets that have *indefinite* lives (generally but not always the trade name plus the value associated with the expectation of future customers). As mentioned in Chapter 4, goodwill may be associated with an individual person or with a business.

Could you summarize Statement 142: "Goodwill and Other Intangible Assets"?[13]

This statement addresses financial accounting and reporting for acquired goodwill and other intangible assets. It addresses how intangible assets that are acquired individually or with a group of other assets (but not those acquired in a business combination) should be accounted for in financial statements upon their acquisition. Intangible assets acquired in a business combination are covered under Statement 141, described previously. Statement 142 also addresses how goodwill and other intangible assets should be accounted for after they have been initially recognized in the financial statements.

How does Statement 142, "Goodwill and Other Intangible Assets," define intangible assets?

Appendix F of Statement 142 defines *intangible assets* simply as "[a]ssets (not including financial assets) that lack physical substance." While goodwill would generally be thought of as an intangible asset, for the purposes of Statement 142, the term *intangible asset* refers to intangible assets other than goodwill. One of the FASB's objectives in developing Statement 142 was to make the recognition criteria for intangible assets more operational so that more intangibles would be recognized separate from goodwill.

Under Statement 142, when must an acquirer recognize an intangible as an asset apart from goodwill?

Under Statement 142, an intangible asset acquired in a business combination must be recognized as an asset apart from goodwill if

(1) it arises from a *contractual or legal right*, or (2) it is *separable*. An intangible asset is considered separable if the acquirer is able to separate or divide it from the target and subsequently sell, license, rent, exchange, or otherwise transfer the asset to another entity. Examples include

- *An acquired customer list.* While not a contractual right, the list is separable and thus represents an intangible asset. However, a "walk-in" customer base is not an intangible asset because it is not separable.
- *An acquired patent that expires in 15 years.* Regardless of the company's intent to sell or otherwise dispose of it, the patent represents a legal right and thus is an intangible asset.
- *Technology that cannot be patented.* While not based on a contractual or legal right, the technology is separable and thus represents an intangible asset.
- *An employee's five-year no compete agreement.* The agreement is based on a contractual right and thus is an intangible asset. However, an "at-will" employee workforce is generally not considered an intangible asset unless the employees are subject to some form of employment agreement.

If an asset acquired in a business combination does *not* qualify as an intangible asset under one of the two criteria provided by Statement 142, the asset must be *included in goodwill* (as part of the amount initially recorded as goodwill).

How is goodwill calculated under Statement 142?

Goodwill is calculated under Statement 142 as the excess of the purchase price of the target over the fair market value of the net assets acquired. As was the case under *APB No. 16*, "net assets" are defined as the target's tangible and intangible assets (excluding goodwill) less assumed liabilities. Another way of thinking about goodwill under Statement 142 is that goodwill is equivalent to the sum total of intangible assets that do not specifically meet the legal/separability requirements previously discussed.

How are intangibles treated in a business combination?

If an acquirer purchases an intangible asset in a business combination, the acquirer must follow the initial measurement procedures of Statement 142, which generally involve four steps:

- First, the acquirer must recognize each *qualifying* intangible asset at fair value. *Fair value* is generally defined as the estimated value at which the asset could be bought and sold between two willing parties (i.e., not liquidation value). This is the same principle prescribed by *APB No. 16.*
- Second, the acquirer must estimate the intangible asset's *useful economic life*—the period over which the acquirer expects the asset to contribute directly or indirectly to the acquirer's future cash flows. At the end of its useful economic life, the intangible asset is assumed to have no residual value unless it meets certain criteria. There is no maximum potential useful economic life.
- Third, the acquirer deducts an amortization expense against the intangible asset in each reporting period. Typically, the amortization method is assumed to be straight-line (with amounts allocated equally to each year) unless some other method better reflects the underlying pattern of economic consumption of the asset. In each reporting period, the acquirer must reevaluate the remaining useful economic life of the asset to determine if the assumed estimated life is still reasonable.
- Fourth and finally, the acquirer must test the intangible asset for impairment if and when there is an indication that the asset might be impaired. The impairment methodology to be followed is contained in *Statement of Financial Accounting Standards (SFAS) No. 144,* "Accounting for the Impairment or Disposal of Long-Lived Assets" (Statement 144). Note that the timing of an impairment test—i.e., the time when there is an indication that the asset might be impaired—for an intangible asset with a definite life is different from the timing of an impairment test for goodwill or for an intangible asset with an indefinite life, which generally must occur at least

annually. However, from a practical perspective, it is likely that the acquirer's external accountants will evaluate an intangible asset with a finite life for impairment each year in conjunction with their annual audit, as accounting standards generally require assets to be carried at the lower of cost or market.

How does this analysis differ if the intangible asset's useful economic life is indefinite?

If the useful economic life of the intangible asset extends beyond the foreseeable future, its life is deemed to be indefinite (not infinite), and the asset is not amortized until such time as its life is determined to be finite. An intangible asset might have an indefinite useful life if no factor—legal, contractual, economic, and so on—limits its useful life. Any brand owned by a company, if separable, is an intangible asset with an indefinite life, while a patent or copyright (both of which have finite lives under the law) is not.

As long as the useful economic life of an intangible asset is deemed to be indefinite, the acquirer must test the intangible asset for impairment at least annually, or more frequently if circumstances warrant. The impairment test methodology in this situation is relatively straightforward—the acquirer compares the fair value of the intangible asset to the asset's book value to determine whether a write-down is appropriate.

What are some examples of intangible assets' estimated useful economic lives under Statement 142?

Appendix A of Statement 142 provides nine examples. Three are summarized here.

- *Example 1: An acquired customer list.* A direct mail company acquired the customer list and expects that it will be able to derive benefit from the information on the acquired customer list for at least one year but no more than three years. Statement 142 treatment: the customer list would be amortized over 18 months, management's best estimate of

its useful life, following the pattern in which the expected
benefits will be consumed or otherwise used up. Although
the acquiring entity might intend to add customer names
and other information to the list in the future, the expected
benefits of the acquired list relate only to customers on that
list at the date of acquisition (a so-called closed-group
notion).

- *Example 2: An acquired patent that expires in 15 years.* The
  product protected by the patented technology is expected
  to be a source of cash flows for at least 15 years. The
  reporting entity has a commitment from a third party to
  purchase that patent in five years for 60 percent of the fair
  value of the patent at the date it was acquired, and the
  entity intends to sell the patent in five years. Statement 142
  treatment: the patent would be amortized over its five-year
  useful life to the reporting entity, following the pattern in
  which the expected benefits will be consumed or otherwise
  used up. The amount to be amortized is 40 percent of the
  patent's fair value at the acquisition date (residual value is
  60 percent).
- *Example 3. An acquired broadcast license that expires in five
  years.* The broadcast license is renewable every 10 years if
  the company provides at least an average level of service
  to its customers and complies with the applicable Federal
  Communications Commission (FCC) rules and policies
  and the Communications Act of 1934. The license might be
  renewed indefinitely at little cost and was renewed twice
  prior to its recent acquisition. The acquiring entity intends
  to renew the license indefinitely, and evidence supports its
  ability to do so. Historically, there has been no compelling
  challenge to the license renewal. The technology used in
  broadcasting is not expected to be replaced by another
  technology any time in the foreseeable future. Therefore,
  the cash flows from that license are expected to continue
  indefinitely. Statement 142 treatment: The broadcast license
  would be deemed to have an indefinite useful life because
  cash flows are expected to continue indefinitely. Therefore,
  the license would not be amortized until its useful life is
  deemed to be no longer indefinite.

What are some recent examples of large write-offs resulting from goodwill impairment?

Here are two different examples, one from Time Warner, representing a merger of two large companies (Time Warner and AOL), and the other from JDS Uniphase, a company that made a series of smaller acquisitions.

> *Time Warner.* The largest write-off ever was recorded by Time Warner in the fourth quarter of 2002. When the company performed its annual impairment review for goodwill and other intangible assets, it recorded an additional noncash charge of *$45.538 billion*, which was recorded as a component of operating income (loss) in the accompanying consolidated statement of operations. This amount included charges to reduce the carrying value of goodwill at the AOL segment ($33.489 billion), the cable segment ($10.550 billion), and the music segment ($646 million), as well as a charge to reduce the carrying value of brands and trademarks at the music segment ($853 million). (*Note:* In 2005, Time Warner set aside money to pay for the settlement of a $2.4 billion class-action suit by shareholders who had sued it over poor postmerger financial performance.[14] This write-down was one of the events that triggered the lawsuit.)
>
> *JDS Uniphase.* In the last two quarters of 2001, this company recorded charges of $39.8 billion and $6.9 billion to reduce goodwill and other long-lived assets, respectively, because of impairment. Of the total write-down, $46.6 billion was related to the goodwill primarily associated with the acquisitions of E-TEK Dynamics, SDL, and OCLI. Fair value was determined based on discounted future cash flows for the operating entities that had separately identifiable cash flows.

How should an acquirer estimate an intangible asset's fair value?

The ideal fair value is based on a quoted market price in an active market. However, this scenario typically exists only when the asset is a commodity, and unfortunately (from a practical perspective), intangible assets are rarely such fungible goods, even if they are separable for the purposes of Statement 142. Alternatively, the acquirer should consider using one of three methods:

- *Income approach*. This is the most commonly used approach and involves a discounted cash flow (DCF) analysis of the asset's expected future cash flows. Like other DCF analyses, the present value to which the cash flow is discounted is particularly sensitive to the acquirer's choice of discount rate.
- *Cost approach*. This method estimates the asset's value at its replacement cost. The approach is not very effective when the asset at issue is unique or highly proprietary, as it might not be easily replicated at a reasonable or otherwise appropriate cost.
- *Market approach*. This third and final approach looks at the purchase prices of comparable assets in other arms-length transactions. This type of analysis is common in M&A, which frequently incorporates comparable companies or comparable transactions analyses in the valuation process. However, the market approach is more difficult to apply to the valuation of intangible assets because a market for the asset often does not exist or the prices are not widely reported.

Does the application of Statement 142 depend on whether the business combination was initiated before or after the statement's effective date?

No. An acquirer must account for intangible assets under the provisions of Statement 142 regardless of when the acquirer purchased the assets. This is an important point to understand because Statement 142 defines intangible assets more narrowly than *APB No. 17* did. As a result, an acquirer might have purchased certain intangibles in a business combination prior to the effective date of Statement 142 that were properly recorded as goodwill under *APB No. 17*, but that are considered intangible assets under Statement 142. In that scenario, the acquirer must reclassify historical goodwill into the appropriate intangible asset classes, as provided by Statement 142. Likewise, items that were previously classified as nongoodwill intangible assets under the *APB No. 17* rules must be reexamined to determine if they still qualify as intangible assets under Statement 142. If not, they must be reclassified as goodwill.

How has Statement 142 affected M&A deal structures?

From a practical perspective, Statement 142 has had at least three impacts on deal structuring. First, it has affected the amount of goodwill that a company unit reports. Second, it has made valuation models more complex, as the measurement of intangible assets has become more specific. And third, the new accounting pronouncement has had an impact on an acquirer's accretion/dilution analysis, as a greater number of intangible assets increases the amortization expense of nongoodwill intangibles and, hence, lowers reported earnings in the first few years following the transaction. After those intangible assets are fully amortized, however, the earnings of combined companies have increased because the companies are no longer required to deduct goodwill amortization expense.

What disclosures are currently required under Statement 142 in the period of acquisition?

Statement 142 expands the disclosure requirements for goodwill and recognized intangible assets. Three items must be disclosed in the period of acquisition:

1. Intangible assets subject to amortization:
   - The total amount assigned and the amount assigned to any major intangible asset class
   - The amount of any significant residual value, in total and by major intangible asset class
   - The weighted-average amortization period, in total and by major intangible asset class

2. Intangible assets not subject to amortization—the total amount assigned to any major intangible asset class
3. The amount of purchased research and development assets acquired and written off in the period and the line item in the income statement in which the amounts are written off

What disclosures are required under Statement 142 in each balance sheet?

Statement 142 requires three disclosure items in each balance sheet:

1. Intangible assets subject to amortization

   - The gross carrying amount and accumulated amortization, in total and by major intangible asset class
   - The aggregate amortization expense for the period
   - The estimated aggregate amortization expense for each of the five succeeding fiscal years

2. Intangible assets not subject to amortization—the total carrying amount and the carrying amount for each major intangible asset class
3. The changes in the carrying amount of goodwill during the period, provided in total and for each reportable segment, including

   - The aggregate amount of goodwill acquired
   - The amount of goodwill included in the gain or loss on disposal of all or a portion of a reporting unit
   - The aggregate amount of impairment losses recognized

What is an impairment loss?

An *impairment loss* is the difference between the asset's recorded value carried on a financial statement and its market value when the market value is lower than the carrying value. It is described in *SFAS No. 144*, "Accounting for the Impairment or Disposal of Long-Lived Assets."

What disclosures are required under Statement 142 in periods in which an impairment loss on an intangible asset is recognized?

There are four items that a company must disclose when an impairment loss on an intangible asset is recognized:

1. A description of the impaired intangible asset and the facts and circumstances leading to the impairment
2. The amount of the impairment loss and the method for determining fair value
3. The caption in the income statement where the impairment loss is recorded
4. If applicable, the segment that includes the impaired value

What disclosures are required under Statement 142 in periods in which a goodwill impairment loss is recognized?

The following three items must be disclosed when a goodwill impairment loss is recognized:

1. A description of the facts and circumstances leading to the impairment
2. The amount of the impairment loss and the method for determining the fair value of the reporting unit (whether based on quoted market prices, prices of comparable businesses, a present value or other valuation technique, or a combination thereof)
3. If a recognized impairment loss is an estimated loss that has not been finalized, that fact and the reasons and, in subsequent periods, the nature and amount of any material adjustments made to the initial estimate of the impairment loss

How is goodwill treated under Statement 142?

Instead of requiring goodwill amortization, Statement 142 generally requires that goodwill be tested for impairment at least annually. The acquirer must evaluate preexisting goodwill (i.e., goodwill on the balance sheet of the acquirer at the time it adopts Statement 142) for impairment within one year of adopting the new standard and then generally at least annually thereafter. This is in contrast to the treatment of goodwill under *APB No. 17*, whereby goodwill was capitalized and amortized over a period not to exceed 40 years.

On the acquisition date, an acquirer must allocate goodwill and all other assets and liabilities associated with the target to one or more *reporting units*. (As discussed in more detail later in this chapter, Statement 142 defines a reporting unit as "an operating segment or one level below an operating segment" [as that term is defined in paragraph 10 of *SFAS No. 131*, "Disclosures about Segments of an Enterprise and Related Information" (Statement 131)].) An asset (including goodwill) or liability may be allocated to more than one reporting unit if two criteria are met: (1) the asset or liability is employed in or relates to the operations of more than one reporting unit, and (2) the asset or liability would be included in a sale of the reporting unit as a stand-alone entity.

Goodwill is divided among the reporting units that are expected to benefit from the synergies of the business combination, permitting some management discretion. That is, management must assign goodwill among the reporting units using a methodology that is reasonable, supportable, and applied in a consistent manner. For example, the acquirer could allocate the goodwill based on the anticipated revenue or cash flows from the acquisition for each reporting unit. Alternatively, the acquirer could allocate the goodwill based on the relative fair value of each different reporting unit that is expected to benefit from the transaction. In any event, the acquirer should give careful consideration to the initial methodology it chooses, because it will be required to use the same methodology consistently going forward. For existing goodwill, allocation occurs on the date the reporting company implements Statement 142. We note that allocating existing goodwill accumulated over a number of years from various acquisitions can be very difficult.

What is negative goodwill?

In some transactions, the amounts assigned to the acquired net assets of the target exceed the cost of the acquisition. The FASB's view is that the excess, sometimes known as *negative goodwill*, is usually due to measurement errors in the purchase price allocation. Where negative goodwill is deemed to exist, the amount should be allocated on a pro rata basis to all intangible assets, with the exception of assets that have an unalterable value, such as financial assets (e.g., cash), assets earmarked for sale, deferred tax assets, and prepaid assets relating to pension or other postretirement benefit plans.

How should a company identify a reporting unit for the purposes of testing goodwill?

A reporting unit is the same level as, or one level below (known as a *component*), a Statement 131 operating segment. Determining whether a component of an operating segment is a reporting unit is a matter of judgment based on an entity's individual facts and circumstances. While Statement 142 includes a number of characteristics that must be present for a component of an operating segment to be a reporting unit, no single factor or characteristic is determinative. How an entity manages its operations and how an acquired entity is integrated with the acquiring entity are key to determining the reporting units of the entity.

Management is required to define the reporting unit at the component level (i.e., one level below the operating segment) if two criteria are met: the component has (1) discrete financial information available and (2) economic characteristics different from those of the operating segment's other components. Accordingly, the acquirer should group together multiple components within an operating segment that have similar economic characteristics to form a single reporting unit. Factors that should be considered in evaluating economic similarities include

- The manner in which an entity operates its business and the nature of those operations
- Whether goodwill is recoverable from the separate operations of each component business or from two or more component businesses working in concert (which might be the case if the components are economically interdependent)

- The extent to which the component businesses share assets and other resources, as might be evidenced by extensive transfer-pricing mechanisms
- Whether the components support and benefit from common research and development projects

The fact that a component shares assets and other resources extensively with other components of the operating segment might be an indication that the component either is not a business or is economically similar to those other components.

Components that share similar economic characteristics but relate to different operating segments may not be combined into a single reporting unit. For example, an entity might have organized its operating segments on a geographic basis. If its three operating segments (e.g., Americas, Europe, and Asia) each have two components (A and B) that are dissimilar to each other but similar to the corresponding components in the other operating segments, the entity would *not* be permitted to combine component A from each of the operating segments to make reporting unit A.

How does testing for goodwill impairment under Statement 142 differ from testing under the prior accounting rules?

Like other assets on the balance sheet, goodwill has always been subject to a test for impairment. That is, if there was reason to suspect that the amount recorded on the balance sheet was no longer recoverable from future operations, it was tested to see if it had, in fact, diminished in value. If so, it was written down with a charge to earnings. Statement 142 differs from previous GAAP in two important respects: the frequency and the mechanics of impairment testing.

How frequently must a company conduct a goodwill impairment test?

Under Statement 142, a company generally must conduct a goodwill impairment test at least once a year. The test can be undertaken at any point during the year, so long as it is performed at the same time every year. The company can test different reporting units for goodwill impairment at different times during the year.

However, after a company has conducted an initial goodwill allocation under Statement 142, the company may presume that the current fair value of a specific reporting unit exceeds its carrying value if three criteria are met: (1) the assets and liabilities of the reporting unit have not changed significantly; (2) the previously calculated fair value of the reporting unit substantially exceeded its carrying amount; and (3) no adverse events have occurred that would indicate a likelihood that the unit's current fair value has fallen below its carrying amount. But to paraphrase an old saw, "stuff happens." The following question discusses a handful of adverse events that might prompt a goodwill impairment test.

When must a company conduct an interim impairment test?

A company should conduct an interim test for goodwill impairment if "an event occurs or circumstances change that would more likely than not reduce the fair value . . . below its carrying value." Examples include the following:

- A significant adverse change in legal factors or in the business climate
- An adverse action or assessment by a regulator
- Unanticipated competition
- A loss of key personnel
- A more-likely-than-not expectation that a reporting unit or a significant portion of a reporting unit will be sold or otherwise disposed of
- A significant asset group being tested for recoverability
- Recognition of a goodwill impairment loss in the financial statements of a subsidiary that is a component of a reporting unit

What are the mechanics of Statement 142 goodwill impairment testing?

Goodwill is measured under Statement 142 using a two-step impairment test:

Step 1: Compare the fair value of the reporting unit with its book value. In the first step of the impairment test, the acquirer determines the fair value of the reporting unit using one or more of the approaches discussed previously (income approach, cost approach, or market approach). The acquirer compares this estimated fair value to the reporting unit's book value. If the fair value is greater than the book value, the impairment test ends and there is no charge to earnings. If the fair value is less than the book value, the impairment test continues on to Step 2.

Step 2: Compare the implied fair value of goodwill to its recorded value. In the second step, the acquirer estimates the fair value of the reporting unit's goodwill. This is accomplished by allocating the fair value of the reporting unit calculated in Step 1 to the individual assets and liabilities in the reporting unit. In effect, this requires a hypothetical purchase accounting allocation at the testing date. (Note that this is done only to test goodwill for impairment. The actual assets and liabilities of the reporting unit are not revalued on the balance sheet.)

The excess of the fair value of the reporting unit over the sum of the fair values of the net assets is the implied goodwill. The impairment charge is the excess of the goodwill recorded on the balance sheet over the implied fair value of the goodwill. However, while the charge resulting from this test is limited to the recorded goodwill, there may be additional write-downs resulting from the application of Statement 144 to other assets in the reporting unit. Also, once written down, goodwill cannot be written back up.

Can you provide examples of the operation of this goodwill impairment test?

Example 1: No impairment charge. Consider Corporation A, which has a custom magazine publishing component that constitutes a reporting unit. Assume that the fair value of the unit is determined to be $5 million, the carrying value of the unit on Corporation A's balance sheet is $3 million, and the carrying value of the unit's goodwill is $1 million. Under Step 1 of the goodwill impairment test, Corporation A would compare the unit's fair value, $5 million, and its carrying value, $3 million, and conclude that the fair value of the reporting unit is greater than its book value. As a result, the impairment test would end and there would be no need to evaluate the carrying value of the unit's goodwill.

Example 2: Impairment charge required. Assume further that Corporation A also has a paper manufacturing component that constitutes a second reporting unit with a fair value of $25 million, a carrying value of $30 million, and goodwill with a carrying value of $10 million.

- *Under Step 1,* the fair value of the reporting unit, $25 million, is less than its carrying value, $30 million, so Corporation A would move on to the second step.
- *Under Step 2,* management would determine the fair value of each identifiable physical and intangible asset and each identifiable liability, using a purchase price allocation method as if Corporation A had just acquired the reporting unit. Assume that the fair value of the unit's tangible assets is $14 million, the fair value of its intangible assets is $6 million, and the unit has no debt. The reporting unit's implied goodwill is $5 million, calculated as the difference between the unit's tangible and intangible assets, $20 million, on the one hand, and the fair value of the reporting unit, $25 million, on the other hand. Corporation A would have to record an impairment charge of $5 million, calculated as the carrying value of the unit's goodwill, $10 million, less the implied goodwill at the time of the impairment test, $5 million.

Can the manner in which the acquirer structures its reporting units influence the results of a goodwill impairment test?

Yes. The acquirer can generally organize its internal reporting units in order to best fit its needs with respect to goodwill impairment tests. For example, if the acquirer has a unit with previously unrecognized goodwill (i.e., goodwill that does not appear on the unit's balance sheet), the acquirer can fold the target into the unit and use the unrecognized goodwill as a cushion against future impairment tests.

An acquirer may have unrecognized goodwill from internal development efforts such as research output, advertising, brand names, workforce in place, market share, and franchise value. (For this reason, a large reporting unit might be less susceptible to a goodwill impairment charge than a small unit.) In addition, an acquirer may have unrecognized goodwill from a target acquired under the previous pooling-of-interest accounting rules.

INTERNATIONAL CONSIDERATIONS

What are some guidelines for naming a new company that results from a cross-border transaction?

First, it is important to remember that one country's household name is another's blank stare. This was a challenge in a recent partnership between the owners of the names "Hilton" and "Conrad." The Hilton name has a six-star reputation within the United States, where the name Conrad has meaning only by association with founder Conrad Hilton. By contrast, outside the United States, it is the Conrad name, first introduced in 1985, that dominates the hotel galaxy. In the end, the partnership opted to preserve both names. The first newly built Conrad in North America opened in Miami last year. It has 203 guest rooms and 103 residences.[15] New Conrad Hotels are scheduled to open in Tokyo and Phuket, Thailand, this year; in Las Vegas and Indianapolis next year; and in Dubai, United Arab Emirates, in 2007.

Coming up with an entirely new name, as Sandoz and Ciba-Geigy did when they merged to form Novartis, is always an option. Such cross-border transactions require the same steps as domestic transactions (see Table 6-1), but with a special awareness of national differences. For example, in determining the needs and expectations of stakeholders, managers need to consider national differences between stakeholder groups. (For more on this, see the sections on international considerations in Chapters 10, 11, and 12.) In evaluating the linguistic and graphic attributes of a new name, it is important to consider language and cultural differences. This is certainly a challenge in countries that have different languages,[16] but it may be a challenge even in countries that share the same language. (In its recent international expansion efforts, Rubbermaid discovered that in the United Kingdom, its brand name connotes rubber dolls.)

Do you have any tips on building brands following an international merger?

This subject is worth at least a book, but here are a few thoughts. The newly combined companies can produce multilingual catalogs catering to different national tastes. Their senior salespeople can also hold meetings with their major customers to build brand enthusiasm.

What about merging of mission, policy, and vision statements in international deals?

The same principles discussed earlier in this chapter apply here. As in domestic deals, there are no blueprints. (This said, however, readers are urged to see *Principles for Business* from the Caux Round Table, cited throughout this book, which contains some virtually universal values that can help companies expand their policy statements.)

APPENDIX   6 – A

Sample Vision Statements from Companies Involved in Mergers

DS Smith Packaging

Values and Principles

Vision Statement   To be a dynamic organization where everyone enjoys anticipating and responding to customer needs to the mutual benefit of our customers, our employers, and our shareholders.

Mission Statement   To be the leading company in all that we do and be the standard by which others are judged.

Principles   Thanks to the merger with LINPAC Containers, DS Smith Packaging is now stronger than ever. In order to reinforce the successful blending of two dynamic cultures, we have developed a clear vision, mission, and set of values behind which all our different businesses are united.

The very first of these principles is "We are one company." The merger of two leading companies with long and well established traditions and track records of success means we will need to work closely together, recognizing the strengths that we have as a combined business. We believe there is value in having strong independent sites with a collegiate culture in which people come together to share information and cooperate openly to the benefit of all.

The second principle is **"We will establish the highest standards of health, safety and environmental practice."** This principle highlights our wish to have a culture which puts safety at the top of our agenda.

The third principle is "We will operate with integrity in an open style." Developing trust between our colleagues will help foster a culture of openness and that in turn will engender closer relationships between ourselves and with our customers.

The fourth principle is, "We will focus on objectives, not just tasks, which drive business goals." The fourth principle relates to the way we should keep the "bigger picture" in mind as we work on specific projects. It is the leadership's job to provide clear overall goals and targets but we all need to assess our priorities and make sure they are in line with what we are trying to achieve as a whole.

The fifth principle is all about a culture of initiative and innovation. It says "We will create an environment which encourages winning initiatives and achievement of business goals." This principle highlights how important it is, in a modern company, to release the potential for good ideas which every individual has. After all, who knows better how to make improvements than the people doing the work?

In the same vein, the next principle says, "We will recognize, encourage, and support high performance." Our expectations are high. We have the people. We need to create and maintain an environment which allows individuals to perform to their full potential.

Our final principle is "We believe that long term relationships can only be based on fairness and mutual benefit." This very important statement interweaves with all other principles and applies to colleagues, customers, suppliers, and everyone else with whom we do business.

Welspun Vision

[*Welspun is an Indian producer of terry cloth towels. This vision statement was announced after the company merged with Glo Fame Cospin, a supplier, in 2004.*]

Our message to stakeholders is exemplified in our following vision statement. We wish to share our vision with our shareholders.

> We aim to . . .
> Emerge as a global leader
> Preferred by every home
> Serve . . . with passion
> Grow . . . with speed
> Innovate . . . with quality
> Excel . . . with ethics
> Delighting all stakeholders . . .
> We are . . . WELSPUN

APPENDIX 6 – B

Branding Case Studies

DaimlerChrysler (Merger of Equals–Automotive)

- Developed a *"product-centric"* brand strategy to replace the Pentastar, expressing the DaimlerChrysler identity at the corporate level only.
- Established new unified brand marks for the key product brands (Chrysler, Dodge) across different marketing mediums (i.e., product badging, dealership signage, advertising, and brochures).
- Created a new dealership identification system in order to ensure visibility and recognition of the dealership location, express the "product-centric" brand strategy, and improve consistency across dealership facility sign systems and secondary signage (trade dress, co-branded sites).

ExxonMobil (Merger of Equals)

Exxon and Mobil joined forces to create a petrochemical corporation of unparalleled strength and the world's largest publicly held company. By late 2005, the company's revenues topped $100 billion.

"Our new ExxonMobil identity is bold and distinctive. It preserves some of the wonderful heritage of both companies—and it is a dramatic new look for the future. Going forward, our new identity will help to communicate the global presence, technological strength and reputation for quality of our truly premier company." Lee R. Raymond, Chairman and Chief Executive Officer

Postmerger, key challenges remained. How could ExxonMobil convey its strength to the marketplace, unify the powerful Mobil and Exxon brands as equals under a single corporate identity, and leverage the combined resources of the new company to support its wide-ranging business franchises?

- Created a new corporate identity that drew upon the well-known and memorable graphic elements unique to each company.

- Developed a clear system for linking all businesses to the ExxonMobil name. The system unifies the business units' products and services (e.g., ExxonMobil Chemical, ExxonMobil Fuels Marketing, ExxonMobil Exploration) and ensures a consistent overall presentation of the corporation.
- Implemented an identity system across an entire spectrum of corporate communications, from facility signs to the corporate Web site, lending itself to possible future use as a marketing brand.

Underwriters Laboratories

Underwriters Laboratories Inc. (UL) is an independent, not-for-profit product safety testing and certification organization. The company has tested products for public safety for more than a century. Each year, more than 17 billion UL marks are applied to products worldwide.

- Known for its certification marks—most notably the "UL" label—Underwriters Laboratories underwent a period of acquisition and worldwide restructuring that caused a shift in its audience and organizational needs. Management needed to develop an organized brand architecture and visual system suitable for a global, unified organization while meeting local customer needs in each market.
- Performed a global audit of identities for affiliates, subsidiaries, liaison offices, and certification marks.
- Created a brand architecture that distinguished between the corporate identity and the UL mark, supporting the image of Underwriters Laboratories as a provider of a broad array of testing products, materials, and systems beyond those associated solely with the UL mark.
- Developed a visual system that unifies all Underwriters Laboratories offerings, yet provides flexibility for subsidiaries that need to promote their own identities for particular market segments.

- Designed a new corporate logo to distinguish the corporate identity from the UL mark.
- Developed guidelines to ensure the worldwide support of the identity structure and visual system.

United Technologies (Diversified Aerospace and Technology)

United Technologies makes building systems and aerospace products through some of the industries' best known brands—Carrier, Otis, Pratt & Whitney, and Sikorsky.

- United Aircraft's evolution into a diversified high-technology conglomerate with such prominent brands as Pratt & Whitney, Sikorsky helicopters, and Carrier air conditioning went underrecognized in the financial community because the parent company name misrepresented the company's broad reach.
- Analyzed United Aircraft's worldwide core businesses to determine the best approach for revising its corporate identity.
- Recommended the new, more accurate United Technologies name and supported it visually with a distinctively modern logotype.
- Introduced an eye-catching symbol as a universal technology mark for all identity communications.
- Used the new name and symbol as keystones of an endorsement system designed to leverage the well-known names of many of the divisions by linking them to the parent corporation.

Source: Lippincott Mercer (a Marsh & McLennan Company), June 2005.

NOTES

1   In a joint press release dated May 11, 2005, the companies announced the new name as a harbinger of the future. "Our new name will reflect that our merger has created a new company," said Wood. "We will not be Crompton. We will not be Great Lakes. We will be the Chemtura team, focused on the future."

2   Employees can get attached to company identity. In the article "Making Connections" in the May 19, 1996, issue of the *Washington Post*, we learn that "hardened linesmen cried when they had to punch out the bell logo from their identity cards" following the 1984 break-up of AT&T's Bell System. The company had featured a bell in its logo for nearly a century—ever since its founding in 1889. The author of this book is acquainted with an AT&T mobile telephone salesman.

3   Ianthe Jeanne Dugan, "Why Hedge Funds Hunt for Animals, Search the Stars: As Firms Proliferate, Finding the Right Name Is Tough; 'Clade' Beats 'Catalyte,'" *Wall Street Journal*, July 25, 2005, p. A1.

4   For a list of the top 25 global brand names, see note 8.

5   Blogged on www.torbwine.com.

6   VGS Corp. v. Commissioner (1977), 345 F. 2d,35,44.

7   B. Kenneth West, "Does the Corporation Have a Soul?", *Director's Monthly*, February 2003, pp. 16–17. West writes, "One of the primary responsibilities of management is to bring the external actions of the corporation—its operating self—into harmony with its soul—its inner self, its values, its ethics—so that the corporation can achieve wholeness."

8   The top 25 global brands (which all have the same names as or a recognizable variation of the names of their parent companies), according to *BusinessWeek*, are Coca Cola, Microsoft, IBM (International Business Machines), GE, Intel, Nokia, Disney (Walt Disney Company), McDonald's, Toyota, Marlboro, Mercedes-Benz, Citi, Hewlett-Packard, American Express, Gillette, BMW (Bayerische Motoren Werke AG), Cisco, Louis Vuitton (LVMH Moet Hennessy Louis Vuitton), Honda, Samsung, Dell, Ford, Pepsi, Nescafe (Nestlé), and Merrill Lynch. Sixty of the remaining 75 Top 100 Global Brands also have names that are identical to or obviously related to those of their parent.

9   The following brands in the Top 100 do not have any recognizable relationship to their parent: Budweiser (Anheuser Busch), MTV (Viacom), KFC and Pizza Hut (YUM! Brands, Inc.), Kleenex (Kimberly-Clerk Corporation), Zara (Industria de Diseno Textil, S.A.), Panasonic (Matsushita Electric Industrial Co., Ltd.), Duracell (Gillette Company), Smirnof (Diageo PLC), Cartier (Compagnie Financière Richemont SA), Shell (Royal Dutch Petroleum Company), Prada (I Pellettieri d'Italia S.p.A.), and Nivea (Biersdorf AG). Source: "Top 100 Global Brands," *BusinessWeek*, Aug. 3, 2005.

10 *Pridemark, Inc.* v. *Commissioner* (1965), 345 F. 2d, 35, 44.

11 *Citizens and Southern Corp.* v. *Commissioner* (1988), 91 TC 463.

12 Markets are so broadly defined by economists as to include the entire range of possible transactions that the business has with its labor markets (employees and potential employees), rental markets (real estate leases and equipment leases), supply markets (vendors), rights markets (licensees and licensers), and wholesale and retail markets (customers). See Charles T. McCormick, *Handbook on the Law of Damages* (New York: West Publishing, 1935), p. 537, note 6.

13 This discussion of Statement 142 is based in part on Alexandra R. Lajoux and H. Peter Nesvold, *The Art of M&A Structuring: Techniques for Mitigating Financial, Tax, and Legal Risk* (New York, McGraw-Hill, 2004).

14 Julia Angwin, "Time Warner Sets Aside $3 Billion: Reserve Would Pay to Settle Claims From AOL Merger; $321 Million Loss Is Posted," *Wall Street Journal*, Aug. 4, 2005.

15 "Hilton: Conrad Hotels Locations to Nearly Triple in 5 Years," *Los Angeles Business*, Feb. 3, 2005.

16 For example, the brand name "Psssssshit!" (used in Berlin, Germany, for a carbonated soft drink that was popular in the early 1970s) would not do well in an English-speaking market.

PART THREE

Integrating Processes

Truth happens to an idea. It becomes true, is made true by events. Its verity is in fact an event, a process . . .

William James, *Pragmatism*

INTRODUCTION AND ACKNOWLEDGMENTS

Organizational processes may not show up in financial statements or factories, but they are no less real—as the following pages show.

Chapter 7, "Integrating Management Systems," benefited greatly from review and information provided by Allan R. Cohen, Edward A. Madden Distinguished Professor of Global Leadership at Babson College in Wellesley, Massachusetts. Data and reflections on current structural trends came from Michael E. Hora, vice president, retired, A. T. Kearney in New York. Commentary on shared-services units came from Leland I. Forst, Ph.D., CMC, chief executive and managing director of the Amherst Group Limited, Greenwich, Connecticut. Expertise on parent company support of subsidiaries was provided by Dr. Alok Chakrabarti, Distinguished Professor and past dean, School of Management, New Jersey Institute of Technology, Newark, New Jersey.

On the subject of employee performance management, guidance came from T. Quinn Spitzer, Jr., partner, McHugh Consulting, Holland, Pennsylvania. The discussion of corporate parenting comes from the work of Marcus Alexander, Andrew Campbell, and Michael Goold, principals of Ashbridge Strategic Management Centre, London. Our discussion of integrating accounting controls came from "Internal Control—Integrated Framework," a publication of the Committee of Sponsoring Organizations of the Treadway Commission (COSO), chaired by John J. Flaherty. In addition, John Fletcher, Ph.D., CEO and chairman, Delta Group, Niederfeulen, Luxembourg, provided general guidance for the accounting material in this chapter.

Chapter 8, "Integrating Compensation Plans," contains insights and experience from several noted compensation experts. For a big-picture view of compensation, this chapter relied on guidance from the members of the Blue Ribbon Commission on Executive Compensation, convened in 2003 by the National Association of Corporate Directors and co-chaired by Bill George, former CEO, Medtronic, and Hon. Barbara Franklin, former U.S. secretary of commerce. Commission member Edward Archer, vice president, Pearl Meyers & Partners, New York, can be credited for his ongoing guidance on compensation matters. For checklists, we turned to Alan Johnson, managing partner of Johnson Associates, Inc., New York, and Ed Archer, Pearl Meyer & Partners, New York. Our discussion on merging health-care plans was based on the expertise of Richard J. Dobkin, managing partner of Ernst & Young's compensation practice in Tampa, Florida—a firm with firsthand expertise in integration. (In mid-2005, the Tampa office of Ernst & Young absorbed the Tampa office of Arthur Andersen.) The accounting aspects of postmerger compensation were provided by valuation experts Scott Hakala, Travis Keath, and Andrew Malec, cited in the credits to Part 2.

Chapter 9, "Integrating and Enhancing Technology and Innovation," owes its greatest debt to Julia Allen, senior member, technical staff, Carnegie Mellon Software Engineering Institute. Ms. Allen reviewed the entire chapter and provided detailed guidance on many technical points. Thanks also goes to Barbara Blumenthal, Ph.D., principal, Blumenthal Associates, Princeton, New Jersey, who provided insights concerning the management challenges facing high-technology mergers. Comments on the control aspects of this subject came from "Internal Control—Integrated Framework," a publication of the Committee of Sponsoring Organizations of the Treadway Committee, chaired by John J. Flaherty. Guidance on combining information-management systems came from Charles W. Wilson, data processing manager, Griffith Energy Services, Inc., Cheverly, Maryland. Fundamentals on patents and trade secrets were provided by Hakala, Keath, and Malec; as well as legal expert Lawrence Carnevale, cited in the introduction to Part 2.

CHAPTER 7

Integrating Management Systems

It struck me that nature's system must be a real beauty because in chemistry we find that the associations are always in beautiful whole numbers—there are no fractions.

R. Buckminster Fuller, *New Yorker* Interview

INTRODUCTION

When two companies consolidate in fact as well as on paper, they join their systems, too. Company systems are ways of doing things—notably ways of organizing accountability (*organizational structure*), making products or rendering services (*operational processes*), and ensuring reliable financial reports (*internal controls*).

This chapter begins with the broadest of these three systems: organizational structure. In this opening section, we will offer guidance on how to integrate two dissimilar structures—one organized by products and one organized by functions. This chapter also contains concepts and "tools" that are useful for folding a decentralized company into a centralized one.

Next we review the essentials of so-called process management, with a brief look at International Standards Organization (ISO) standards for management, design, production, and distribution, among other topics.

Finally, we will look at the important subject of internal financial controls, noting tips for quick postmerger cash flow protection.

Throughout this chapter, readers should be mindful of a basic riddle: which comes first, people or systems? Of course people come first—a company's systems will be automatically determined by the goals, talents, and limitations of the system's architects and operators. On the other hand, systems have a life of their own. They do not automatically change simply because people change; people have to change them—and unless they do, the systems can change the people. Let's see how.

INTEGRATING ORGANIZATIONAL STRUCTURES

Merging companies means merging their management structures. What is the best way to do this?

First, try to obtain copies of the organization charts (if they exist) for both organizations. To be sure, the *responsible leader* in any group, division, or company (the one on the organization chart, who has the title and accountability) may not be the same as the *effective leader* (the one who tends to prevail in decisions) or the *psychological leader* (the one who commands the greatest respect).[1] The responsible leader, however, is as good a proxy as any for understanding the complex dynamics of an organization. Thus (to paraphrase Winston Churchill) organization charts are a terrible way to represent company structure—and the only way.

OK. So how can an acquirer build new reporting patterns for the new company?

Building a new reporting structure for combining companies requires two things: knowledge of the old companies' past patterns and a sense of the companies' potential patterns as a newly combined company.

To gain knowledge of past structures, managers should try to get hold of the latest organization charts for both organizations and check them out through interviews. (If there are no charts, interviews will have to do.) The information from these charts and interviews might seem like old news after the merger, but in fact it is the foundation for the future. Those boxes, lines, and dotted lines reveal not only past experience but future expectations with regard to accountability and relationships.

The next step is to move beyond the past and into the future to build a new structure. A few truisms are in order here. The structure should be based on the business needs of the companies, not on some theory of what makes people happy. The "right" structure is a matter not only of comfort for employees, but also of fit with the company's economic environment. No structure guarantees behavior; a structure merely makes it easier or harder to get work done. Experience, not theory, will always be the best arbiter here.

What are the basic types of organizational structures, and how common are they?

Actual organization structures differ widely (just study the hundreds of representative charts available from the Conference Board in New York), but it is possible to identify five basic types of organizational structure:

- Functional
- Geographic
- Market segment
- Product/service
- Divisional[2]

Any of these structures may coexist with a so-called cluster framework that organizes people by projects.[3] (For diagrams, see Appendix 7-A.)

In a *functional* organization, people are assigned to groups according to their functions or specialties, such as accounting, distribution, engineering, manufacturing, marketing, purchasing, and sales. This is common for small, new companies. A good example would be Tidal Software in Palo Alto, California, which has an executive team that is organized by function and a management team under it that is also organized by function.

In a *geographic* organization, employees' work is organized by physical territory. For example, the top level of Arch Insurance Group (a company within Arch Capital Group) is organized by Midwest, West, Southeast, and Northeast regions, with an executive vice president for each region. Sometimes companies that are organized by function or product then superimpose a geographic dimension. Amgen, a biotechnology company, and ADP, a computer services company, are both examples of this type of organization.

In a *market segment* organization, the customer also determines the structure, but it is not the location of the customer that matters; rather, it is the customer's profile. Thus a financial company might be structured according to institutional versus retail clients. For example, Pay by Touch, a single-product software company, has the usual senior titles (CEO, CFO, and so on) and then three more: executive vice president, Franchise Services; senior vice president, Retail Sales; and senior vice president, Financial Institution Sales.

In a *product/service* organization, functional specialists are grouped according to their responsibilities toward a given product or service. For example, K-Tron International, a Nasdaq-listed company in Pitman, New Jersey, is organized into three business lines based on products: feeding equipment, pneumatic conveying equipment, and size reduction equipment. This organizational structure emerged as the logical result of a series of acquisitions broadening the company's product reach.[4]

In a *divisional* organization, families of products are grouped into independent divisions (or "strategic business units"). This organizational structure, which is highly decentralized, has always been dominant for very large, complex companies and is becoming more so. General Electric, for example, is currently organized into nine divisions, ranging from GE Commercial Finance to GE Transportation.

Aren't some divisional companies (such as GE) organized by product line? If so, what's the difference between a divisional structure and a product structure?

In a true product/service line structure, all the lines share one central headquarters management team. For example, the individuals who head up K-Tron's product divisions have the rank of senior vice president for those divisions, but they also have a headquarters title, such as chief financial officer for the company. In a divisional structure, which is more decentralized, each division has its own senior management teams. For example, each of GE's divisions has its own president and CEO, who in turn has vice presidents. (At the very top of GE is a separate set of senior officers who oversee the company as a whole.)

Given the success that GE and others have had with a decentralized divisional structure, is the centralized, product/service line structure a dying breed?

No. This structure will never disappear. Over time, companies tend to swing like a pendulum between *centralized* and *decentralized* organizational structures. During periods of economic recession, when companies are focusing on cost reduction, centralized organizations have greater appeal because they are associated with control and efficiency. During periods of economic expansion, when companies are focusing on growth, decentralized organizations have greater appeal because they are associated with flexibility and effectiveness. As we head into the new millennium, these extremes seem to be moderating as organizations seek to become both efficient and effective.

Mergers create their own miniature economic climates. After a highly leveraged transaction focused on reducing redundancies, merging firms may face an internally recessionary economy that pushes their managers toward a centralized structure. Conversely, after a self-financed transaction focused on market opportunities, companies may have expansionist economies that push their managers toward a decentralized structure. Over time, as a company's economy changes, these structures change, migrating toward a middle ground.

When two companies have very different reporting patterns, how can they be integrated?

If the companies are following the path of least resistance, the pattern with the most complexity should prevail. Thus a divisional structure will prevail over a product/service or functional structure, and a product/service structure will prevail over a functional structure. As Appendix 7-A shows, these structures are like

Russian dolls. Each of them can stand alone, but they can also contain smaller structures. A divisional structure (the biggest doll) can easily contain a product/service structure (the next biggest doll) within it, and that structure can easily contain territories and/or functions (the smallest dolls).

But engineering isn't everything. As discussed throughout this book, other factors can come into play, such as size. Large acquirers can and usually will impose their structures on the smaller, less powerful units that they acquire.

This is unfortunate. If an acquirer uses its own organizational structure as a template, ignoring that of the acquired company, the employees of the acquired company will continue to have the same expectations of their fellow employees as they did before the merger. If these expectations are unfulfilled, this may provoke disappointment. If they are fulfilled, it may cause trouble. The positive alternative must be a new structure that is sensitive to the expectations arising from the old structures, while serving the needs of the newly combined organization.

The following are some important checkpoints to bear in mind:

- Appropriateness of reporting lines
- Adequacy of staffing and experience levels
- Clarity of delegation of authority and duties

It seems that centralized companies tend to be hierarchical, whereas decentralized companies tend to be flat. Is this true?

Yes. Centralization and *hierarchy* (also called *layering*) tend to go hand in hand. Centralization is impossible without a center point, and that point is typically a higher level of management (at *headquarters*—a telling term) that has authority over the units it connects. The headquarters-subsidiary relationship is often mirrored within individual units by a reporting structure that goes from "lower" to "higher." By contrast, in decentralized organizations, hierarchical traits may exist, but they are perceived as less critical to value generation. In general, decentralized organizations tend to be flatter in scope.

This said, though, we should note that it is possible to have a centralized structure that is flat—for example, one with only two levels of management: central and subsidiary. And it is possible to have a decentralized structure that is hierarchical, with many layers of management within each unit. The traits tend to pair the other way, however, so much so that the terms *centralized* and *hierarchical* are sometimes used interchangeably with each other and with the pejorative term *bureaucracy.*

Don't hierarchies have a bad name as an organizational strategy?

Yes, but it is undeserved. The term *hierarchy* is often associated with a multitude of interrelated sins—notably slow, insensitive decision making and unjust distribution of authority, recognition, and pay. The classic tale (somewhat Marxist in orientation) goes like this: a competent, overworked, and underpaid assistant vice president with innovative ideas cannot put them into action without approval from an incompetent, underworked, and overpaid vice president who takes weeks to approve them and later takes credit if they succeed or blames the assistant if they fail. This scenario represents a dysfunctional hierarchy, not a functional one.

   Yet the scenario has a grain of truth in it. Traditional hierarchies do have a continuum of management responsibility up through the chain of command. In these organizations, managers tend to involve themselves in the work of their subordinates. Over time, the line management continuum can cause problems, such as competition between managers and subordinates. Management experts have proposed and companies have adopted solutions to these problems. The late Elliott Jaques, a brilliant and prolific defender of hierarchies, proposed the concept of the superior-once-removed (SOR).[5] In this approach, each employee has not only a superior (his or her boss), but also an official superior-once-removed (that boss's boss). In a structure that takes the SOR concept seriously, the SOR of each employee has certain rights and obligations to mentor and assess the employee. This prevents an employee's immediate superior from either understating or overstating the employee's accomplishments in the interests of self-advancement.

   For the past few decades, following the work of strategy-oriented consulting firms such as Boston Consulting Group, many companies have tried a different type of hierarchy, one based not on management levels but on business levels. At the senior or "corporate" level, managers set strategy and determine policies. At the business-unit level, people focus on growth and profitability. Finally, at the work-team level, people concern themselves with operational matters such as productivity and quality. This is consistent with Jaques's theory that hierarchy is an outgrowth of the nature of human beings and of work.[6]

Which organizations tend to be more profitable, those with centralized hierarchies or those with flatter, more decentralized structures?

Both can be profitable, but these organizational types derive their income in different ways. As mentioned earlier, centralization is associated with cost cutting, whereas decentralization is associated with revenue building. Adding or subtracting management layers intensifies this contrast. If a middle manager has to seek approval before spending money, he or she will tend to invest less of it—but also tend to generate less of it. By the same token, if the manager has no restraints on spending money, he or she may tend to invest more of it and, if successful, generate more.

Which basic option is better for postmerger integration, a hierarchical, centralized structure or a flat, decentralized structure?

Hierarchy makes integration a lot easier, as it enables managers to promulgate universal policies throughout the organization, deliver financial and technological support, and resolve conflicts between and among units.[7] Extreme decentralization, in contrast, can make integration more difficult, unless the organization has identified a position or unit with the authority to create and disseminate policies and a network for sharing or redistributing resources.

On the other hand, centralization does not guarantee success. In the case of a *detrimental parent*, headquarters' policies may be wrong for the organization, or the parent may fail to deliver enough of the right kind of support to its units. Conversely, a *beneficial parent* knows how to overcome the challenges of decentralization and to link units without a centralized, hierarchical structure.[8]

Are there many "detrimental parents" among acquiring firms?

Apparently so. The corporate headquarters of many large, multi-business companies (often operating as parent companies to various acquired units) can actually do more harm than good by exerting influence that is inappropriate and/or expensive.[9]

Why don't all corporate parents add value to the units they integrate?

Potential problems include too many rigid controls, not enough communication and support, lack of understanding of the business, a focus on the wrong issues, hiring or promoting the wrong managers, and pressing for the wrong levels or measures of performance.

In short, postmerger management requires the same kinds of judgment calls as other kinds of management, but focusing on the unique challenges of integration with techniques and tools—our next subject.

What can managers actually do to enhance integration?

Following a merger, designated managers can work to ensure that company units share space, goals, standards, and/or services to some useful degree.[10]

SHARING SPACE

How can sharing space help M&A integration?

It is a well-known fact in manufacturing circles that the layout of a work site can prevent or encourage collaboration—and that collaboration is linked to higher productivity.

A study funded by the National Center for Manufacturing Sciences showed that in *process-complete* departments, layouts that permitted people to see others' work had cycle times *4.4 times faster* than those with layouts that did not permit this.[11] The study defined process-complete departments as those responsible for most manufacturing steps and defined cycle times as total throughput (order to delivery) time for the three products that accounted for the highest percentage of the department's output for the most recent six-month period.

Common sense suggests that the link between collaboration and productivity applies to work in any realm, including corporate headquarters. In any work environment, acquirers should avoid falling prey to the "fifth floor" phenomenon (isolating all the acquired staff on their own floor) or the "that function" mentality (isolating employees according to their function). While this may be sensible from an operational, business-as-usual standpoint, it can hinder the kind of spontaneous interaction that leads to innovation. Some mixing or conjoining of office locations is almost always desirable and achievable.

Another way to achieve integration is to have certain work spaces used by employees from different functions, product/ service lines, and/or divisions. Shared computer rooms, laboratories, and libraries can foster increased communication and hence integration among units, even in very large companies.[12]

SHARING GOALS

How can sharing goals help M&A integration?

Common goals can serve to integrate two or more units for a period of time. Setting exact timetables and procedures for new product development can impel the different units of the organization to work together in small groups or clusters (as mentioned earlier) to accomplish the development by the target date. Or, to cite another example, a five-year plan to improve shareholder value (if employee compensation is linked to the stock price) can create unity of purpose in an entire organization for half a decade. The more units that share the goals and the longer the time span necessary to accomplish the goals, the more integration is accomplished.

SHARING STANDARDS

How can common standards help M&A integration?

Shared standards can create a sense of cohesion throughout the company; they are the very essence of integration. Types of standards that are useful in M&A integration include operating procedures, technological specifications, ethical values, internal control guidelines, and, most important of all, employee performance yardsticks: setting comparable performance *standards* using comparable *measures* to obtain comparable *rewards* throughout a company.

For example, no matter how a company defines its subunits (be it by function, geographic territory, customer segment, product/ service, or division), it will need to find a way to measure the financial performance of the identified units. There is no one set method of doing this. In fact, there are several possible ways—including cost center, profit center, investment center, or producer of residual income.[13]

SHARING SERVICES

How can sharing services help M&A integration?

Sharing services can help eliminate duplication in a decentralized structure. Instead of each unit's having its own accounting staff, for example, there may be an accounting staff at headquarters. The same goes for legal, public relations, information processing—the list is virtually infinite.

The classic way to share services is to use a common staff, typically located at headquarters. Another way to share services is to create *shared-services units* for nonoperating activities, and to allow other business units to buy services from these units. Companies currently using shared-services units include BMW, Boeing, DHL, HBSC, Monsanto, Rhone-Poulenc, and Shell Oil.

The underlying principle driving shared internal services is that a business-oriented unit can employ common management practices focused entirely on delivering needed services at the lowest cost with the highest value to internal customers. This is more effective than having multiple points of responsibility and varied management practices. Also, it provides more accountability than the classic headquarters model.

The shared-services unit is based on the classic *functional* organizational structure, described earlier. In this structure, companies have units or departments to provide an enterprise with discrete functions, such as information systems, internal control, or pay systems. Moreover, these functions are devoted to transactional areas, such as data systems entry, payroll check processing, or benefit claims processing. Because of the discreteness of these functions, they are the same ones that are sometimes outsourced (an activity sometimes referred to as shared services) A true shared-services unit idea takes this concept further, creating a single unit that provides all of these services and more.

How is using shared services different from using headquarters staff?

When headquarters staff provides services, it is typically under monopoly conditions: all units must use the company's central services at a cost determined by headquarters and borne by the company as a whole. It's the only game in town. The shared-services model, by contrast, puts competition into the equation. Heads of company divisions and their key employees negotiate with the shared-services unit for the services they will receive and the price they will pay. They may go outside for services if they are not satisfied. Unlike headquarters staff, the shared-services unit is not a cost center, it is a profit center. Corporate headquarters still has a role, but this is confined to the high-level areas of strategy and governance.

INTEGRATING PROCESSES FOR PRODUCT OR SERVICE DESIGN, PRODUCTION, AND SUPPLY

If two merging companies make and/or distribute the same product and/or service, how should they go about integrating these activities?

First of all, it's a good idea to step back and compare the two companies' quality control programs. There are several different ways of controlling quality, and if two companies have different systems, these will need to be integrated.

Could you give an example of merging companies that merged their quality control systems?

Honeywell, which merged with Allied-Signal in 1999, has five key initiatives, according to its Web site as of August 2005: growth, productivity, cash, people, and various quality "enablers," including Six Sigma, a program pioneered by Motorola in the mid-1980s. Prior to the merger, Honeywell had a program called "Quality Value Assessment," but this was folded into Six Sigma after the merger.[14]

What are some systems for quality improvement that can be used in a postmerger setting to improve operations?

Consider a standard benchmark such as ISO 9001, *Quality Systems-Model for Quality Assurance in Design, Development, Production, Installation, and Servicing*. The ISO, which stands for International Standards Organization, is a network of the national standards institutes of nearly 150 countries, with a central office in Geneva, Switzerland, that coordinates the system and publishes the finished standards. There are also other benchmarks used in particular industries in particular countries.[15]

What exactly are the ISO 9001 series standards, and how can they help companies integrate their plant operations?

The ISO 9001 standards are guidelines for ensuring the quality of design, manufacturing, and supply systems. They are jointly determined by national standards bodies in countries around the world (146 as of late 2005), drawing on recommendations from technical advisory groups (nearly 3,000 of them). The standards are used by an estimated 100,000 organizations around the world. For companies that do only manufacturing and supply, there is a shorter version called ISO 9002, and for those that perform only supply, there is the even briefer ISO 9003. The top-level series, called ISO 9000, provides guidance as follows:

- Management responsibility
- Resource management
- Product realization
- Measurement, analysis, and improvement

See www.iso.org.

This sounds like good general guidance. Why would a company particularly need it following a merger?

A change in ownership usually means a change in managerial control, and hence a change in operations. Whenever there is a change in operations, companies may suffer certain setbacks.

First, the *quality of the plant's products or services* may suffer after a merger. This may be a temporary change resulting from the redesign or integration of processes and standards, or it may be permanent if standards and incentives deteriorate or morale declines. There is usually some initial inefficiency when plant employees have to relearn or reorient their activities. The distractions resulting from a merger may reduce actual production throughput or increase production costs. Larger operations may have greater information asymmetries: critical information may fail to reach the right people at the right time. Having good standards for process mapping and information flow will help.

Second, there may be *logistical problems*. The consolidation of plant activities will affect the production and flow of products and services. For manufacturing firms and retailers alike, there may be disruption in inventory control, stock, transportation, and distribution. In this situation, having good standards for logistics will help.

For instance, at the time of their 2004 merger, Cingular Wireless and AT&T Wireless were running some 2,800 retail stores, and tens of thousands of authorized agents and third-party resellers like Best Buy and Wal-Mart sold their handsets and calling plans. To decide which of these stores to close and which to expand, Cingular's consulting firm, Accenture, weighed multiple factors, including the number of subscribers each store had signed up, its cost for signing up customers, its location and distance from other company stores (and stores operated by rival carriers), and its size and lease provisions.[16]

What is an example of an effort to integrate manufacturing plants?

Delphi (formerly Automotive Components Group Worldwide), which operates 167 plants around the world, engineered a successful integration of its plans in the mid-1990s. Although it filed for protection from creditors under Chapter 11 of the bankruptcy code, the company is still operating under the restructuring plan, which is generally considered to be successful. At the time of the filing, Delphi Chairman and CEO Robert S. Miller said the company hopes to emerge from Chapter 11 by mid-2007. Meanwhile, Delphi is continuing to manufacture and ship products, and to pay employees and suppliers.

The company was created in 1991 as an amalgamation of various units that General Motors had acquired nearly a century earlier.

In 1996, the company integrated its 50 most troubled plant operations. In this restructuring, Delphi

- Phased out old mass-production lines where one mistake could stop hundreds of operators.
- Introduced work cells, small teams of workers with a voice in daily plant operations and production levels.
- Worked toward a 24-hour production cycle.
- Streamlined job classifications.

In 1999, GM spun off Delphi, which became a public company via an initial public offering (IPO). In recent years, Delphi has been selling or closing units as part of a more drastic restructuring of plan operations, driven by financial rather than operational needs. For more on Delphi, see Chapter 12.[17]

You mentioned downsizing. What guidance do you have here?

First, slow down. Speed is important, as mentioned in Chapter 3, "Integration Planning and Communication," but so is accuracy. First, avoid scapegoating the locations with the poorest numbers unless and until you are sure that those numbers reflect future prospects, not just past performance. Take the time to find out.

Second, once you have identified the weakest or most redundant locations, consider all options, beginning with continuation of operations. There is more than one way to consolidate a company! To take an example from manufacturing, it may be better to consolidate two plants than to close one and expand the other.

How can you "consolidate" plants?

First, as mentioned previously, management can *adopt a common set of systems and standards* for activities.

Second, management can *forge closer links* between plants. New links may emerge from common information systems, inventory control, supply relationships, pipelines, or rail links. (For more on the technological aspects of the "virtual factory," see Chapter 9.

Third, management can *pursue more vertical integration*, having different operations focus on different stages of production. Some facilities may specialize in producing specific components or intermediate goods, while other operations become more oriented toward producing finished goods or toward finishing and packaging goods for local or regional markets.

Fourth, when and if there is excess capacity and/or redundancy in capacity, a company may *close certain operations* and move certain productions activities and assets from the closed operations to the other facilities.

And fifth, a company may *shift production allocations* across facilities to allow each operation to become more focused in its production of a subset of products or to serve a narrower geographic region or customer base.

What are the chief benefits and drawbacks of postmerger plant closings?

It depends on the company's situation. If there is excess capacity or significant redundancy, closing plants may make economic sense. However, acquirers should bear in mind the economic costs associated with plant closings, which are often taken as a significant one-time charge against earnings.

Also, having too few manufacturing sites may be risky and inefficient. Having manufacturing facilities at multiple sites may reduce operational risks while increasing flexibility and efficiency. Following the tragic events of September 11, 2001, many corporations are seeking redundancy in their most critical operations.

Therefore, when demand is low, it may be more efficient to shut down several small units completely on a temporary basis than to experience a partial, long-term idling of larger, consolidated units.

Finally, there can be reputational costs associated with plant closings, costs that eventually affect a company's bottom line (as described in Chapter 12, "Fulfilling Commitments to Employees and Communities").

INTEGRATING INTERNAL FINANCIAL CONTROLS

What exactly are internal financial controls?

Internal financial controls are the processes that a company uses to make sure that its financial statements are reliable. In a mom-and-pop microbusiness, these controls can be as simple as keeping the checkbook balanced and requiring two signatures on every check (those of the two owners). In a major public company, they may involve literally thousands of procedures.

The Securities and Exchange Commission defines "internal control over financial reporting" as follows:

> A process designed by, or under the supervision of, the registrant's principal executive and principal financial officers, or persons performing similar functions, and effected by the registrant's board of directors, management and other personnel, to provide reasonable assurance regarding the reliability of financial reporting and the preparation of financial statements for external purposes in accordance with generally accepted accounting principles and includes those policies and procedures that:
>
> Pertain to the maintenance of records that in reasonable detail accurately and fairly reflect the transactions and dispositions of the assets of the registrant;
>
> Provide reasonable assurance that transactions are recorded as necessary to permit preparation of financial statements in accordance with generally accepted accounting principles, and that receipts and expenditures of the registrant are being made only in accordance with authorizations of management and directors of the registrant; and
>
> Provide reasonable assurance regarding prevention or timely detection of unauthorized acquisition, use or disposition of the registrant's assets that could have a material effect on the financial statements.[18]

The SEC issued this definition in the aftermath of the financial scandals that ushered in the Sarbanes-Oxley Act of 2002.

Under Section 404 of Sarbanes-Oxley, all public companies must have internal controls and assess them. Furthermore, they must have their auditors assess those controls.[19]

As for management's assessment, SEC rules implementing Section 404 state that "the assessment of a company's internal control over financial reporting must be based on procedures sufficient both to evaluate its design and to test its operating effectiveness."[20]

In particular, "an assessment of the effectiveness of internal control over financial reporting must be supported by *evidential matter*, including documentation, regarding both the design of internal controls and the testing processes."

Controls subject to such assessment (again quoting verbatim from the SEC final rule) include

- controls over initiating, recording, processing, and reconciling account balances;
- classes of transactions and disclosure and related assertions included in the financial statements;
- controls related to the initiation and processing of non-routine and non-systematic transactions;
- controls related to the selection and application of appropriate accounting policies; and
- controls related to the prevention, identification, and detection of fraud.

As for the auditors' assessment of controls and their assessment, the standard is the Public Company Accounting Oversight Board's Auditing Standard No. 2, "Audit of Internal Control over Financial Reporting Performed in Conjunction with an Audit of Financial Statements," issued in March 2004.

For a broader definition of internal controls, advanced by the Committee of Sponsoring Organizations of the Treadway Commission, or COSO, see Appendix 7-B. According to COSO, "Internal control consists of five interrelated components":

- Control environment
- Risk assessment
- Control activities
- Information and communication
- Monitoring

How can an acquirer assess and ensure the quality of these five components in its newly merged entity?

In the last section of its report "Internal Control—-Integrated Framework," COSO provides three things:

- Blank guidesheets (called "tools") for assessing each component
- A reference manual for filling in the guidesheets
- Sample filled-in guidesheets

The guidesheets feature COSO recommendations for the five components on the left-hand side of each page, along with blank spaces on the right-hand side of each page. The filled-in guidesheets show how an assessor might fill in the guidesheets. (For a sample focusing on one of the components, the control environment, see Appendix 7-C.)

This sounds important but time-consuming. What can the acquirer of a small organization do on Day 1 to "hit the ground running" on internal control, particularly with respect to cash?

Excellent question. Of all these elements of internal control, certainly the one that will require the most urgent and immediate attention from the acquirer will be procedures for cash management.

The day the acquisition is completed, the acquirer should assume control over all cash receipts and disbursements by the acquired business. For each location, a new checking (or lock box) account should be established, and all receipts should be deposited into this account. Access to this account should be limited to individuals designated by the acquirer. In addition, a separate cash disbursements checking account should be established for payroll and accounts payable.

Having separate accounts for receipts and disbursements makes sense, but it sounds complicated. How exactly does it work?

Typically, the financial management of the acquired company requests a weekly transfer of funds to the disbursement account (the checking account for payroll and accounts payable) with appropriate justification, such as payroll or vendor payments (by name and invoice number). The manager designated by the acquirer should collect all receipts and transfer funds to the cash disbursement account as requested.

What other techniques can the acquirer use to establish financial control?

In addition to setting up separate accounts for receipts and disbursements, the acquirer can establish a budgeting process and a signatory-level requirement.

The budgeting process will vary from company to company, but it usually involves identifying revenue sources and expenses for the upcoming 12 months, along with a forecast of balance sheet changes that will be required to meet the business's requirements. Once the acquirer and the acquired company have agreed to this budget, they can monitor the acquired company's progress each month against the forecast. If there are changes or trends indicating that the budget is inaccurate, the acquirer can ask the budget managers to revise the budget. If the revisions are not satisfactory, the managers can be replaced.

Signatory levels will also vary from company to company, as levels of materiality differ depending on company size. An expenditure of $1,000 might require the signature of an officer in a $1 million company but not in a $1 billion company. Here is a sample signatory requirement for a midsize company with sales levels between these extremes. In this example, the acquired company is operating independently from the acquiring company, with its own senior management team.

Sample Signatory Levels

1. All checks over $5,000 must be signed by the senior financial officer and the chief operating officer of the acquired company.
2. All checks over $25,000 must be cosigned by a staff member of the acquiring company.
3. All sales contracts over $1 million or with potential liabilities over this level will require signature by the

CEO of the acquiring company or a manager he or she designates.

4. All compensation to senior management (defined by job function or by name) must be approved by the CEO of the acquiring company.

This system, we should emphasize, is ideal for small companies or for units of large companies. A large company with many units will need a more complex system for cash control and should consult a public accounting firm with experience assessing Section 404 compliance under the PCAOB's Standard 2.

INTERNATIONAL CONSIDERATIONS

What are some special challenges in integrating organizational structures across national borders?

Briefly, in an international merger, the form of organization for the new company will be crucial. The temptation will be to organize around regions, in light of the many legal, accounting, and business differences among different countries—not to mention language differences. This temptation should not outweigh other organizational considerations, however. The organizational structure chosen should be the best possible one for the company, not necessarily the easiest one.

Can true centralization ever make sense in a multinational company? Aren't countries and regions too different for that kind of management?

Some companies that merge across national boundaries bypass the integration challenge, maintaining parallel structures for everything. And, consistent with advice given in Chapter 4, it is not a good idea to centralize postmerger sales management in a company with diverse markets, high marketing costs, and/or localized production. In such companies, it is best to have a local manager operating with some autonomy.

On the other hand, when making investment-oriented acquisitions, a centralized structure can make good sense, especially for staff functions outside the sales arena. For example, during its heyday of international expansion in the 1970s and early 1980s (prior to its merger with Philip Morris Cos. in 1985), General Foods made scores of acquisitions annually from a single office—indeed, they were made by a single individual. It was not easy to find someone with a business and engineering background who spoke fluent German, French, and Italian and was willing to fly to Europe up to two hundred times a year, but General Foods did find such a person and employed him for two decades, to their mutual benefit.[21]

APPENDIX 7 – A

Types of Organizational Structure

FUNCTIONAL ORGANIZATION

Widget Company, Inc.
    Accounting function
    Distribution function
    Engineering function
    Manufacturing function
    Marketing function
    Purchasing function
    Sales function
       North
       South
       East
       West

PRODUCT/SERVICE ORGANIZATION

Machine Tools Company, Inc.
    Product 1
       Accounting function
       Distribution function

Engineering function
Manufacturing function
Marketing function
Purchasing function
Sales function
    North
    South
    East
    West

Product 2
Accounting function
Distribution function
Engineering function
Manufacturing function
Marketing function
Purchasing function
Sales function
    North
    South
    East
    West

Product 3
Accounting function
Distribution function
Engineering function
Manufacturing function
Marketing function
Purchasing function
Sales function
    North
    South
    East
    West

DIVISIONAL ORGANIZATION

Modern Industries, Inc.

Division 1

Product 1

Accounting function
Distribution function
Engineering function
Manufacturing function
Marketing function
Purchasing function
Sales function
> North
> South
> East
> West

Product 2

Accounting function
Distribution function
Engineering function
Manufacturing function
Marketing function
Purchasing function
Sales function
> North
> South
> East
> West

Division 2

Product 3

Accounting function
Distribution function
Engineering function

Manufacturing function
Marketing function
Purchasing function
Sales function
   North
   South
   East
   West

Product 4
   Accounting function
   Distribution function
   Engineering function
   Manufacturing function
   Marketing function
   Purchasing function
   Sales function
      North
      South
      East
      West

Note: These data points can also be organized as block matrices (two dimensions—products and functions or products and territories) or cube matrices (three dimensions—products, functions, and territories).

Internal Control–Integrated Framework

Excerpts from the Original COSO Report

In the wake of the Sarbanes-Oxley Act of 2002, which included a section (404) on internal controls (also called internal control) merger decisionmaker, implementers, and advisors need more than ever to understand this activity.

The classic guide to internal control in 1992 is the report "Internal Control—Integrated Framework," published by the Committee of Sponsoring Organizations of the Treadway Commission, known as COSO, composed of six organizations: the American Institute of Certified Public Accountants, the American Accounting Association, the Institute of Internal Auditors, the Institute of Management Accountants, the National Association of Accountants, and the Financial Executives Institute. These organizations sponsored the original (1987) work of the National Commission on Fraudulent Financial Reporting (chaired by James Treadway and known as the Treadway Commission). Although COSO and others have set more detailed guidelines, this executive summary remains a valuable overview. For links to current guidance, see the end of this appendix. The following text is excerpted verbatim from the executive summary.

EXECUTIVE SUMMARY

Senior executives have long sought ways to better control the enterprises they run. Internal controls are put in place to keep the company on course toward profitability goals and achievement of its mission, and to minimize surprises along the way. They enable management to deal with rapidly changing economic and competitive environments, shifting customer demands and priorities, and restructuring for future growth. Internal controls promote efficiency, reduce risk of asset loss, and help ensure the reliability of financial statements and compliance with laws and regulations.

Because internal control serves many important purposes, there are increasing calls for better internal control systems and report cards on them. Internal control is looked upon more and more as a solution to a variety of potential problems.

WHAT INTERNAL CONTROL IS

Internal control means different things to different people. This causes confusion among businesspeople, legislators, regulators and others. Resulting miscommunication and different expectations cause problems within an enterprise. Problems are compounded when the term, if not clearly defined, is written into law, regulation or rule.

This report deals with the needs and expectations of management and others. It defines and describes internal control to:

- Establish a common definition serving the needs of different parties.
- Provide a standard against which business and other entities—large or small, in the public or private sector, for profit or not—can assess their control systems and determine how to improve them.

Internal control is broadly defined as a process, effected by an entity's board of directors, management and other personnel, designed to provide reasonable assurance regarding the achievement of objectives in the following categories:

- Effectiveness and efficiency of operations.
- Reliability of financial reporting.
- Compliance with applicable laws and regulations.

The first category addresses an entity's basic business objectives, including performance and profitability goals and safeguarding of resources. The second relates to the preparation of reliable published financial statements, including interim and condensed financial statements and selected financial data derived from such statements, such as earnings releases, reported publicly. The third deals with complying with those laws and regulations to which the entity is subject. These distinct but overlapping categories address different needs and allow a directed focus to meet the separate needs.

Internal control systems operate at different levels of effectiveness. Internal control can be judged effective in each of the three categories, respectively, if the board of directors and management have reasonable assurance that:

- They understand the extent to which the entity's operations objectives are being achieved.
- Published financial statements are being prepared reliably.
- Applicable laws and regulations are being complied with.

While internal control is a process, its effectiveness is a state or condition of the process at one or more points in time.

Internal control consists of five interrelated components. These are derived from the way management runs a business, and are integrated with the management process. Although the components apply to all entities, small and mid-size companies may implement them differently than large ones. Its controls may be less formal and less structured, yet a small company can still have effective internal control. The components are:

Control Environment
The control environment sets the tone of an organization, influencing the control consciousness of its people. It is the foundation for all other components of internal control, providing discipline and structure. Control environment factors include the integrity, ethical values and competence of the entity's people; management's philosophy and operating style; the way management assigns authority and responsibility, and organizes and develops its people; and the attention and direction provided by the board of directors.

Risk Assessment
Every entity faces a variety of risks from external and internal sources that must be assessed. A precondition to risk assessment is establishment of objectives, linked at different levels and internally consistent. Risk assessment is the identification and analysis of

relevant risks to achievement of the objectives, forming a basis for determining how the risks should be managed. Because economic, industry, regulatory and operating conditions will continue to change, mechanisms are needed to identify and deal with the special risks associated with change.

Control Activities

Control activities are the policies and procedures that help ensure management directives are carried out. They help ensure that necessary actions are taken to address risks to achievement of the entity's objectives. Control activities occur throughout the organization, at all levels and in all functions. They include a range of activities as diverse as approvals, authorizations, verifications, reconciliations, reviews of operating performance, security of assets and segregation of duties.

Information and Communication

Pertinent information must be identified, captured and communicated in a form and timeframe that enable people to carry out their responsibilities. Information systems produce reports, containing operational, financial and compliance-related information, that make it possible to run and control the business. They deal not only with internally generated data, but also information about external events, activities and conditions necessary to informed business decision-making and external reporting. Effective communication also must occur in a broader sense, flowing down, across and up the organization. All personnel must receive a clear message from top management that control responsibilities must be taken seriously. They must understand their own role in the internal control system, as well as how individual activities relate to the work of others. They must have a means of communicating significant information upstream. There also needs to be effective communication with external parties, such as customers, suppliers, regulators and shareholders.

Monitoring

Internal control systems need to be monitored—a process that assesses the quality of the system's performance over time. This is accomplished through ongoing monitoring activities, separate evaluations or a combination of the two. Ongoing monitoring occurs in the course of operations. It includes regular management and supervisory activities, and other actions personnel take in performing their duties. The scope and frequency of separate evaluations will depend primarily on an assessment of risks and the effectiveness of ongoing monitoring procedures. Internal control deficiencies should be reported upstream, with serious matters reported to top management and the board.

There is synergy and linkage among these components, forming an integrated system that reacts dynamically to changing conditions. The internal control system is intertwined with the entity's operating activities and exists for fundamental business reasons. Internal control is most effective when controls are built into the entity's infrastructure and are a part of the essence of the enterprise. "Built in" controls support quality and empowerment initiatives, avoid unnecessary costs and enable quick response to changing conditions.

There is a direct relationship between the three categories of objectives, which are what an entity strives to achieve, and components, which represent what is needed to achieve the objectives. All components are relevant to each objectives category. When looking at any one category—the effectiveness and efficiency of operations, for instance—all five components must be present and functioning effectively to conclude that internal control over operations is effective.

The internal control definition—with its underlying fundamental concepts of a process, effected by people, providing reasonable assurance—together with the categorization of objectives and the components and criteria for effectiveness, and the associated discussions, constitute this internal control framework.

WHAT INTERNAL CONTROL CAN DO

Internal control can help an entity achieve its performance and profitability targets, and prevent loss of resources. It can help ensure reliable financial reporting. And it can help ensure that the enterprise complies with laws and regulations, avoiding damage to its reputation and other consequences. In sum, it can help an entity get to where it wants to go, and avoid pitfalls and surprises along the way.

WHAT INTERNAL CONTROL CANNOT DO

Unfortunately, some people have greater, and unrealistic, expectations. They look for absolutes, believing that:

- Internal control can ensure an entity's success—that is, it will ensure achievement of basic business objectives or will, at the least, ensure survival.

Even effective internal control can only help an entity achieve these objectives. It can provide management information about the entity's progress, or lack of it, toward their achievement. But internal control cannot change an inherently poor manager into a good one. And, shifts in government policy or programs, competitors' actions or economic conditions can be beyond management's control. Internal control cannot ensure success, or even survival.

- Internal control can ensure the reliability of financial reporting and compliance with laws and regulations.

This belief is also unwarranted. An internal control system, no matter how well conceived and operated, can provide only reasonable—not absolute—assurance to management and the board regarding achievement of an entity's objectives. The likelihood of achievement is affected by limitations inherent in all internal control systems. These include the realities that judgments in decision-making can be faulty, and that breakdowns can occur because of simple error or mistake. Additionally, controls can be circumvented by the collusion of two or more people, and management has the ability to override the system. Another limiting factor is that the design of an internal control system must reflect the fact that there are resource constraints, and the benefits of controls must be considered relative to their costs.

Thus, while internal control can help an entity achieve its objectives, it is not a panacea.

ROLES AND RESPONSIBILITIES

Everyone in an organization has responsibility for internal control.

Management

The chief executive officer is ultimately responsible and should assume "ownership" of the system. More than any other individual, the chief executive sets the "tone at the top" that affects integrity and ethics and other factors of a positive control environment. In a large company, the chief executive fulfills this duty by providing leadership and direction to senior managers and reviewing the way they're controlling the business. Senior managers, in turn, assign responsibility for establishment of more specific internal control policies and procedures to personnel responsible for the unit's functions. In a smaller entity, the influence of the chief executive, often an owner-manager, is usually more direct. In any event, in a cascading responsibility, a manager is effectively a chief executive of his or her sphere of responsibility. Of particular significance are financial officers and their staffs, whose control activities cut across, as well as up and down, the operating and other units of an enterprise.

Board of Directors

Management is accountable to the board of directors, which provides governance, guidance and oversight. Effective board members are objective, capable and inquisitive. They also have a knowledge of the entity's activities and environment, and commit the time necessary to fulfill their board responsibilities. Management may be in a position to override controls and ignore or stifle communications from subordinates, enabling a dishonest management which intentionally misrepresents results to cover its tracks. A strong, active board, particularly when coupled with effective upward communications channels and capable financial, legal and internal audit functions, is often best able to identify and correct such a problem.

Internal Auditors

Internal auditors play an important role in evaluating the effectiveness of control systems, and contribute to ongoing effectiveness. Because of organizational position and authority in an entity, an internal audit function often plays a significant monitoring role.

Other Personnel

Internal control is, to some degree, the responsibility of everyone in an organization and therefore should be an explicit or implicit part of everyone's job description. Virtually all employees produce information used in the internal control system or take other actions needed to effect control. Also, all personnel should be responsible for communicating upward problems in operations, noncompliance with the code of conduct, or other policy violations or illegal actions.

A number of external parties often contribute to achievement of an entity's objectives. External auditors, bringing an independent and objective view, contribute directly through the financial statement audit and indirectly by providing information useful to management and the board in carrying out their responsibilities. Others providing information to the entity useful in effecting internal control are legislators and regulators, customers and others transacting business with the enterprise, financial analysts, bond raters and the news media. External parties, however, are not responsible for, nor are they a part of, the entity's internal control system.

Note: For current guidance, visit pcaobus.org, coso.org, or any of the members of COSO, including notably theiia.org.

APPENDIX 7–C

Benchmarking Postmerger Integration of Internal Control

A Sample Guidesheet

In the last section of its report "Internal Control—Integrated Framework," COSO provides three things:

- Blank guidesheets (called "tools") for assessing the five main components of internal control (control environment, risk assessment, control activities, information and communication, and monitoring)
- A reference manual for filling in the guidesheets
- Sample filled-in guidesheets

The guidesheets feature COSO recommendations for components on the left-hand side of each page, along with blank spaces on the right-hand side of each page. The filled-in guidesheets illustrate how an assessor might fill in the guidesheets. The following sample illustrates how an assessor might begin to fill in a guidesheet for the first component: *control environment*.

ORGANIZATIONAL STRUCTURE

The organizational structure should not be so simple that it cannot adequately monitor the enterprise's activities nor so complex that it inhibits the necessary flow of information. Executives should fully understand their control responsibilities and possess the requisite experience and levels of knowledge commensurate with their positions.

- **Appropriateness of the entity's organizational structure, and its ability to provide the necessary information flow to manage its activities.** For example, consider whether:
  - The organizational structure is appropriately centralized or decentralized, given the nature of the entity's operations.
  - The structure facilitates the flow of information upstream, downstream, and across all business activities.

The organizational structure of the company has recently been modified to accommodate the divestiture of the defense division and the acquisition of Laker Parts. Management believes the new structure is appropriate. However, the new structure has not been in place long enough to evaluate its effectiveness.

- **Adequacy of definition of key managers' responsibilities, and their understanding of these responsibilities.** For example, consider whether:
  - Responsibilities and expectations for the entity's business activities are communicated clearly to the executives in charge of those activities.

Key managers' responsibilities have been redefined recently in conjunction with the new organizational structure. Such responsibilities appear adequate for the company's need, but have not been tested over an extended period. Managers' performance indicates they understand their responsibilities, which are reviewed with them annually.

- **Adequacy of knowledge and experience of key managers in light of responsibilities.** For example, consider whether:
  - The executives in charge have the required knowledge, experience, and training to perform their duties.

All officers have been with the company for at least five years, except for one former Laker executive, and all are highly knowledgeable of the industry and their responsibilities. Certain managers (i.e., the controller and director of manufacturing) at Laker Parts joined the company within the last six months, but held similar positions with other companies in the aerospace industry.

- **Appropriateness of reporting relationships.** For example, consider whether:
  - Established reporting relationships— formal or informal, direct, or matrix—are effective and provide managers information appropriate to their responsibilities and authority.
  - The executives of the business activities have access to communication channels to senior operating executives.

Reporting relationships are logical, and each activity manager reports to the proper company officer. Reporting relationships ensure effective communication between employees, supervisors, managers, and officers.

- **Extent to which modifications to the organizational structure are made in light of changed conditions.** For example, consider whether:
  - Management periodically evaluates the entity's organizational structure in light of changes in the business or industry.

The organizational structure is assessed on an as-needed basis. For example, after the acquisition of Laker Parts, modifications such as integrating administrative functions and consolidating purchasing activities were made to streamline operations.

- **Sufficient numbers of employees exist, particularly in management and supervisory capacities.** For example, consider whether:
  - Managers and supervisors have sufficient time to carry out their responsibilities effectively.

■ Managers and supervisors work excessive overtime and are fulfilling the responsibilities of more than one employee.

*Because of the recent merger with Laker
Parts, ABC has more employees than needed.
Layoffs are occurring, but management carefully considers who is terminated and the effect
the layoffs may have on control. Management
evaluates employees' workload, particularly
those with supervisory and key control responsibilities, to ensure they are able to discharge
their responsibilities effectively.*

CONCLUSIONS/ACTIONS NEEDED

*The company's organizational structure and reporting relationships are logical and fit the
company's activities. However, the recent changes require close monitoring of the effectiveness
and appropriateness of the structure in the near term. Pending layoffs as a result of the Laker
Parts acquisition must be monitored for effects on supervisory and key control responsibilities.
For an auditor's guide, see the PCAOB's Standard 2, cited earlier.*

N O T E S

1   These terms come from the classic leadership textbook by Dr. Eric
Berne, *Structure and Dynamics of Organizations and Groups* (New York:
J. B. Lippincott Co., 1963), pp. 105–107. Berne is the author of the
popular psychology book *Games People Play* (New York: Penguin,
1968).

2   For a good explanation of these organizational types, see Danna
Greenberg, "Designing Effective Organizations," in *The Portable
MBA in Management,* ed. Allan R. Cohen (New York: John Wiley &
Sons, 2002), pp. 243–275.

3   The government of Ontario uses a cluster organization rather than
traditional ministries. See cio.gov.on.ca.

4   "K-Tron International, Now Organized with Three Business Lines,
Provides a Broad Range of Material Handling Products and
Services," company press release dated June 9, 2003. As of late 2005,
the company still has this structure.

5   Elliott Jaques, *Requisite Organization: A Total System for Effective
Managerial Organization and Managerial Leadership for the 21st Century,*
2d ed. (Rockville, Md.: Cason Hall, 1996).

6   "There is a marked qualitative shift in the complexity of work with
each shift in work-stratum. This increase in complexity makes it

possible to encompass a much greater field of activity, that is to say, to encompass marked increases in the scope and scale of responsibility, and hence to work in longer time-spans. . . . It is this pattern which generates a constant hierarchy of values for employment work: market forces could not produce this consistent value hierarchy." Elliott Jaques, *Free Enterprise, Fair Employment* (London: Heineman, 1982), p. 80.

7 One hierarchically organized company that moves with speed is WellPoint, which recently acquired Anthem. This became an issue in the two companies' integration in 2005. "WellPoint traditionally moved with greater *speed* and greater direction *right from the top.* Anthem, on the other hand, made more of its decisions by consensus; it was a more collaborative, more discussion-oriented company" (emphasis added). Connie Van Fleet, "Culture Shock: How Two Cultures Become One in a Merger," *Across the Board,* May–June 2005. Van Fleet is vice president of integration planning and implementation at WellPoint.

8 These terms were first introduced in a National Science Foundation study by Professor Alok Chakrabarti of the New Jersey Institute of Technology, "Organizational Factors in Post-Acquisition Performance," *IEEE Transactions in Engineering Management,* vol. 37, No. 4 (November 1990), pp. 259ff.

9 Studies cited in the first (1998) edition of this book suggested that parent companies of diversified subsidiaries add less value than parents of subsidiaries in the same industry. More recently, a study of spin-offs suggests the same. "This . . . studies 91 parent-subsidiary pairs operating in the service sector, analyzing performance in the decade following the subsidiary's listing and finds that, on sales growth, the subsidiaries tend to show stronger advances than their parents. . . . Subsidiaries that operate in the same sector as their parent tend to underperform the parent while those that enter a different industry tend to outperform their parent." See Elizabeth Rose and Kiyohiko Ito, "Widening the Family Circle: Spinoffs in the Japanese Service Sector," *Long Range Planning,* February 2005.

10 This section is based in part on Danna Greenberg (ibid, note 2).

11 Ann Majchrzak and Qianwei Wang, "Breaking the Functional Mind-Set in Process Organizations," *Harvard Business Review,* September–October 1996, pp. 93ff. This study looked at productivity in 86 manufacturing departments, 31 of them process-complete and 55 of them functional. Process-complete organizations were found to have faster cycle times if they had at least one of the following:

participative decision-making and work styles, overlapping responsibilities, team-based rewards, or work spaces that let workers see or learn about each other's work (such as open work areas or shared conference rooms). See also Satyandra K. Gupta, Ujval Alva, Deepak Rajagopal, and Zhiyang Yao, "Process Planning for Small Batch Manufacturing," white paper posted as of August 2005 on University of Maryland, Department of Mechanical Engineering and Institute for Systems Research Web site (www.glue.umd.edu/~skgupta/PPforSmallBatchMfg.htm).

12 See "Elements in Merging Laboratory Operations," *Journal of Clinical Ligand Assay*, vol. 24, no. 4 (December 2001), pp. 239–244. Sandia Corp., which is managed by Lockheed Martin, reported $50 million in savings after it merged its laboratories. The Sandia example was cited recently during meetings about merging Los Alamos National Laboratories. See "Lab Workers Press DOE for Answers," www.lamonitor.com, posted August 8, 2005.

13 For a discussion of these different types of accounting for business units, see Lawrence A. Gordon, *Managerial Accounting: Concepts and Empirical Evidence* (New York: McGraw-Hill, 2004), pp. 179–186.

14 For the history, see Glenn Haske, "Merger Marries Quality Efforts," *Industry Week*, Aug. 21, 2000.

15 For example, in the United States, standards have been published by the Federal Aviation Administration (FAA Production Certification), the Federal Drug Administration (FDA Good Manufacturing Processes), and the Department of Commerce (Malcolm Baldrige Award), among others.

16 Ken Belson and Matt Richtel, "Cingular, Becoming No. 1 Also Poses Risks," Sept. 27, 2004 (posted at www.Wirelessadvisor.com).

17 In 2005, Delphi closed its Lansing Cockpit Assembly plant in Lansing, Michigan, and sold its battery product line to Johnson Controls Inc. The sale included facilities in France, Mexico, and Brazil. Source: Delphi 10-Q, filed August 8, 2005.

18 "Management's Reports on Internal Control over Financial Reporting and Certification of Disclosure in Exchange Act Periodic Reports," SEC, http://www.sec.gov/rules/final/33-8238.htm#iia.

19 Sarbanes-Oxley requires that annual reports contain an "internal control report" stating "the responsibility of management for establishing and maintaining an adequate internal control structure and procedures for financial reporting" and must "contain an assessment, as of the end of the most recent fiscal year of the issuer, of the effectiveness of the internal control structure and procedures of the issuer for financial reporting." The law made the SEC responsible for setting this standard.

Also, it requires that company auditors must "attest to, and report on, the assessment made by the management of the issuer." The law made the PCAOB responsible for setting this standard. Both the SEC and the PCAOB in Standard 2, have prescribed the methods for assessment in great detail.

20 "Final Rule: Management's Reports on Internal Control over Financial Reporting and Certification of Disclosure in Exchange Act Periodic Reports," Securities and Exchange Commission, releases nos. 33-8238; 34-47986; IC-26068; File Nos. S7-40-02; S7-06-03, http://www.sec.gov/rules/final/33-8238.htm#iia. This rule was effective August 14, 2003, for fiscal years starting on or after June 15, 2004, with the exception of small companies, which have until April 15, 2006 to comply.

21 The individual was the late Anthony Hass, Sr., of White Plains, New York, and Washington, D.C., former vice president of external development for General Foods and consummate M&A gentleman.

C H A P T E R   8

Integrating Compensation Plans

Money is a terrible master but an excellent servant.

Phineas Taylor (P.T.) Barnum, American impresario

INTRODUCTION

Mergers bring opportunities for employees, but they also carry risk—and many questions: Will I keep my job, and if I do, will it be worth keeping? If I lose my job, what kind of severance will I receive? If I keep my job, will I get a raise? Will I still get this year's bonus and profit sharing? Will we be switching health insurers? What will happen to my retirement benefits?

Postmerger pay planners will need to forge the answers to these individual questions in the context of broader corporate concerns: Will we need to downsize? What kind of severance plans and outplacement services will we offer at different levels? Should we give newly "acquired" managers and/or our own managers a raise to equalize their pay? Should we combine our bonus plans? Our health plans? Our retirement plans? And if so, how? What legal, financial, and strategic issues should we consider?

This chapter offers a general framework that may be helpful in the search for answers. We begin with the basics, move on to strategy, and then dwell on two important subjects: pensions and disclosure. And as usual, our experts touch on the global aspect of these topics. Finally, the appendix to this chapter presents a Blue Ribbon Committee answer to what may be a company's single most important compensation question: How can we link pay to performance?

POSTMERGER COMPENSATION BASICS

What kinds of pay plans must be integrated (or otherwise administered) after a merger?

Several types of pay plans should be considered for possible integration: pay plans for executive employees (such as the top most highly paid officers), pay plans for other employees, and pay plans for corporate directors. Each of these will have a different set of elements. The focus of this chapter is on executive pay.[1]

When integrating executive pay plans (or designing new ones), what are the various pay elements and pay arrangements that postmerger planners should consider?

There are basically five pay elements in executive pay:

1. *Base pay*, otherwise known as *salary*, is a fixed amount of cash. It is typically determined annually and paid on a weekly or (in small companies) monthly basis. For most employees, this is the dominant portion of pay (although to large-company senior executives, it is of minor importance).
2. *Bonus pay* is a lump-sum award in cash and/or stock paid to an employee for past performance. Bonus pay is typically determined and paid on an annual basis. Some companies call their bonuses "incentive pay," but compensation purists reserve that term for pay that is awarded according to a predetermined plan, not after the fact.
3. *Incentive pay* is compensation awarded to employees because they (or their team, division, or company) have met a predetermined performance target. This pay, which may be in cash and/or in stock (either outright grants or options), is truly variable; it may not be paid at all. It may

be awarded annually and/or "long-term," with the term defined by the company. Incentive pay is often awarded as *deferred compensation*. Funds are usually put into an escrow account that appreciates according to a standard interest rate (such as Treasury bills).

4. *Benefits* are additional economic offerings considered integral to making or sustaining a living, such as plans for pensions, health care, and, at the board level, liability insurance.

5. *Perquisites*[2] are additional economic offerings considered to be "extras," such as use of a company car or payment of club memberships. Ideally, perquisites will enable or motivate better job performance.

In addition, there is a potentially infinite universe of *special pay arrangements* that can come up before, during, or after a merger.

1. Through *no compete agreements* (discussed in Chapter 4), companies can take the first of many steps to keep key executives—not only retaining their talent, but also preventing them from joining (or becoming) competitors of the new company.

2. Through *signing bonuses* (called *golden handshakes*), companies can increase the motivation of executives they wish to hire.

3. Through *severance agreements*, companies can promise to compensate employees in the event of job loss.

4. Through *change-of-control plans* (offered in addition to plain-vanilla severance agreements), a company agrees to pay employees in the event of job loss following a merger or acquisition. At the senior level, these M&A-related severance packages are called *golden parachutes*. At lower levels, they are called *tin parachutes*.

5. Finally, through *retention agreements* (also called *golden handcuffs*), companies promise rewards if an employee stays for a stated length of time.

The sum total of all basic pay elements and all special compensation arrangements is generally referred to as *total compensation*. Most consultants today offer services in *total compensation planning*.

When two companies merge, to what extent should they merge their compensation plans?

It depends on whether the new company will be integrated or managed separately. As explained earlier in this book, not all acquisitions lead to integration. If an acquirer has only a financial (as opposed to a strategic) reason for buying a company, it may choose to keep the two companies' pay plans separate. And even if an acquirer has a strategic reason for buying a company and does plan to integrate resources and systems, the company's leaders may still decide to keep some aspects of pay separate (especially if they are venturing outside their company's core industry).

Given all of these factors, the burden of compensation design is generally shared between the acquiring parent company and its units. In a typical situation:

- The parent company will determine a policy for how much of senior management pay will be in stock (for example, five times salary) and how managers will receive it (by award or purchase, and, if the latter, whether the purchase will be mandatory or voluntary). The division will encourage and enforce compliance with the parent's target ownership plan (often called a TOP).
- The parent company will determine the desired competitiveness of base pay (below market, at market, or above market), while the unit will identify the labor market in which it will be competing (local, regional, or national).
- The parent company will decide on a policy for bonuses, while the unit will decide who will receive them.
- The parent company will set targets for incentive pay. Achievement of the targets can be based on various metrics (including accounting ratios, stock price, qualitative factors, and/or discretionary factors) and valuation methodologies (economic value added, cash flow return on investment, or some other model), while the unit will select whether to award the incentive pay based on unit, team, or individual performance. The parent is also responsible for ensuring that pay plans do not provide incentives to increase short-term performance at the expense of ethical behavior.

- The parent company will decide on a benefits policy, while the unit will administer the policy, making occasional exceptions as necessary by contract or law.

Note, however, that even when parents have the power to set uniform policies and targets, they may use their power to vary pay plans from unit to unit, or may delegate their power outright.

Why would a newly combined company want to have different pay plans for different units?

Because the units may have very different pay environments:

- Base pay for similar jobs may differ from industry to industry. Also, a company in a mature industry will have a greater percentage of pay as base pay as opposed to variable pay from bonuses or incentives.
- There may be regional differences in pay. The U.S. Office of Personnel Management has recognized this and has developed detailed tables of pay by region.[3]
- Bonus pay may be hard to align following a merger between one firm that pays huge bonuses and another one that pays none. Any acquirer of a Wall Street investment bank or brokerage firm knows that trying to moderate year-end bonuses in these cultures can be difficult, if not impossible. (Even Warren Buffett, the widely revered and successful chairman of Berkshire Hathaway, failed to do this as outside chairman of Salomon Brothers in the early 1990s.)
- Incentive pay targets for early-stage high-growth companies should be linked to sales growth, market share, and product development, not short-term profit performance, whereas the opposite would apply for a mature company. Or, to use an industry example, consider the differences between a mutual fund, which lives and dies on stock prices, and the mutual insurance industry, which depends more heavily on long-term relationships with policyholders. Incentive plans in such companies are likely to be different and should remain so after a merger.
- Finally, incentive plans may reflect differences in managerial philosophy, valuing the formal versus the informal, and quantitative versus qualitative.

Benefits are another area where postmerger disparity may be necessary. Suppose that in the negotiation phase, the acquirer agreed to let the selling company's senior management keep certain perquisites, knowing full well that it will not extend these same perks to its own senior team. If that was the deal, the acquirer has no choice but to live with these strings attached, and to explain them to the envious as a "grandfather clause." Furthermore, there may also be regulatory restrictions on merging certain benefits, such as retirement plans.

All these differences can add up, resulting in sharp contrasts between companies and, once merged, units. For example, a mature, centralized business with heavy capital investments, stable profit margins, little technological change, and few competitors should strive for the following:

- Senior management depth
- Predominantly fixed compensation
- Moderate incentives
- Moderate equity participation
- Discretionary evaluations

At the other end of the spectrum, a changing, decentralized business with low capital investment, pressured profit margins, significant technological change, and many competitors should strive for the following:

- Little senior management depth
- Predominantly variable compensation
- Heavy incentives
- Heavy equity participation
- Objective evaluations

Are you saying there is no role for pay-plan integration—that each unit should have its own pay plan?

No, to the contrary. To be fair to all employees, pay plans should be as uniform as possible—within the limits of what makes sense for each business unit. Few mergers will involve companies as diverse as the two just described. (Indeed, mergers between such opposites face immense barriers to success, partly because of the incompatibility of their pay cultures!) The important thing is to recognize and value differences, not ignore them. At the same time, pay planners should work holistically. A pay plan, whether for an entire company or for a single unit, must be a true plan, not a patchwork quilt.

Aren't there some *general* principles of compensation that apply in *any* type of company? If so, what are they?

Yes, there are universal principles of good pay planning. The first one is that if it works, it is good. Compensation theory is continually testing itself against the reality of experience. That blend of theory and proven practice appears continually in articles and books written by compensation experts.

Take, for example, the principle of equity ownership. The basic idea of linking management and ownership is good,[4] but there are challenges, such as the volatility of stock prices and the risk that managers will get windfalls and leave. In recent years, a number of innovations have emerged to solve this problem—for example, linking pay to share price through an indexed option plan and putting restrictions on the exercise of some options following a term of service.[5] Moreover, compensation experts have put a greater emphasis on stock-based pay in the more glamorous high-tech, high-growth area and have not recommended equity pay as heavily in lower-tech, mature industries. Here is a list of principles that are already widely accepted in corporate and compensation circles.

Do:

- Encourage real share ownership at all levels.
- Link pay to performance.
- Reward executives for both shareholder value and quality of products or services.[6]
- Make sure that pay is competitive in local markets.
- Communicate appreciation of an employee through promotion and recognition as well as through pay.
- Limit benchmarks to accounting measures (which can be manipulated) or stock price (which can be influenced by external events). Use a variety of benchmarks.

Don't:

- Award excessive, repriceable stock options to senior management.
- Keep increasing pay no matter what.
- Rely too heavily on benchmarks such as quartiles, which by their very nature keep rising as long as everyone tries to stay at the top.
- Agree to compensation contracts that can pay very large amounts under some scenarios.[7]

What generally happens to senior management pay levels after a merger, and why?

Pay levels for senior management tend to go up following a merger. This is not surprising, since mergers make companies bigger, and bigger companies tend to pay their top managers more than smaller companies do. Size is not the only factor, though. Companies that have expanded by takeover have systematically higher top management pay growth than same-size peers that are expanding by internal growth.

There are two reasons for postmerger pay inflation. First, postmerger equality is easier to achieve through pay raises than through pay cuts. If senior executives from Company A and Company B are doing similar work, but Company A executives are getting paid more, it is more likely that Company B executives' pay will be raised to Company A levels than the other way around.

Second, there are the special M&A compensation arrangements mentioned earlier, such as golden handshakes, golden parachutes, and golden handcuffs. Total costs for these elements, under various scenarios, can run into the tens and even hundreds of millions.

Speaking of golden parachutes, aren't they discouraged by law?

Yes and no. Ironically, the law that was passed to discourage golden parachutes may have actually *encouraged* them.

The 1984 Deficit Reduction Act set fines for companies that pay golden parachutes and executives who receive them. Triggered by public outrage over the $5 million golden parachute that William Agee got after the Bendix–Allied Signal merger in 1983, the law added two new sections to the tax code, which exist to this day. Section 280G of the Internal Revenue Code defines an "excess parachute payment" as one that equals or exceeds three times the executive's average W-2 compensation over the previous five years. Section 4999 of the code imposes a 20 percent excise tax on the amount exceeding average annual compensation and denies the company a tax deduction for that amount.

But the government maximum quickly became an industry norm. Many companies began to raise their levels of parachutes to 2.99 times average annual compensation—just in time for the merger boom of the mid-1980s (and in plenty of time for the boom of the mid-1990s).

Parachutes proliferated. At the time of the golden parachute laws, only about one-third of major companies had parachutes. Today, the figure is over two-thirds. And nearly half of all companies *offer to pay taxes* on amounts in excess of the 2.99 norm!

What about stock purchase rights or options that get triggered when a change of control occurs? Do they count?

Yes. If a stock option will be granted or vested because of a change in control, this may constitute a parachute payment under Revenue Procedure 2003-68, which provides guidance on the valuation of stock options for this purpose. This could include any shareholder rights ("poison pill") antitakeover arrangements that function as golden parachutes.[8]

If an acquirer gives golden handshakes to acquired company managers, what prevents the managers from walking away with the gold the very next day?

An acquirer can prevent a golden handshake from becoming a golden escape hatch by adding either a *back-end* provision or a *take-back* provision to the manager's contract. In a back-end provision, a company defers part of the promised sums, making them payable late in the contract period. In the take-back provision, an acquirer states in the manager's employment agreement that he or she will have to repay all or part of the bonus in the event of his or her departure prior to contract expiration. This second strategy can be layered, with heavier penalties for earlier departure. For example, a four-year contract might set the following penalties for repayment of a $4 million signing bonus:

Year 1: $4 million repayment
Year 2: $3 million repayment
Year 3: $2 million repayment
Year 4: $1 million repayment

These retention provisions are often referred to as *golden handcuffs*. Another type of golden handcuff is the no compete agreement, discussed in Chapter 4.

PLANNING PAY INTEGRATION: A STRATEGIC OVERVIEW

Assuming that two companies want to combine their pay systems, how should they do this?

A newly combined company must reconcile the individual and the collective, the past and the future. As individuals, employees will naturally want a pay package comparable to or better than what they had in the past. But pay planners must also look ahead, designing a pay system that makes sense for the long-term future.

One very simple way to do this is to chart the basic elements of compensation (base pay, bonus pay, incentive pay, and benefits) against the past approaches of each of the merging companies and the future needs of the combined enterprise in the view of senior management. By weighing these, planners can come up with a bridging strategy that takes both into account (see Table 8-1).

When designing new compensation plans (or adjusting old ones), what general principles should compensation planners keep in mind?

First, reach out. Consult some of the many guides available on this topic. Ask for expert advice. Most leading compensation firms offer services in "total compensation planning," and many have expertise in the postmerger arena.

Of course, there are many things that a company can do on its own. The important thing is to strive for viability—financial, emotional, and technical.

T A B L E   8 – 1

Sample "Sketchpad" for Compensation Planning

Compensation Elements	Past Approach of Company A	Past Approach of Company B	Future Needs of Company AB	Bridging Strategy
Base pay	Below market	At market	At market	Raise A's salaries; keep B's on course.
Bonus pay	None	Generous	Minimal	Finish out year keeping the status quo. Then start modest awards for all based on B's system, but reduced.
Incentive pay	None	None	Generous	Design pay-for-performance system. Employees: Additional 20 percent on base if goals for unit profits met. Senior management: Additional 30 percent on base if goals for company ROA met.
Benefits	Average benefit plans (cafeteria); generous, flexible benefit plans; no perks.	Below average in health and retirement. Lavish perks.	Average health and retirement. Modest perks.	Improve B's health and retirement plans. Cut B's perks. Upgrade health coverage.
Special	1 year severance.	6 months severance.	1 year severance.	Extend B's severance.

Note: This is a sample, not a paradigm. Planners should use their own terminology and make their own choices.

How can a planner ensure the financial viability of a new pay plan?

Planners need to consider the financial condition of the newly combined company. Although this condition will be based in part on the previous condition of the two merging companies, the new entity will have its own financial dynamics.

Aside from the merger price tag and related charges (which can be substantial, as explained in Chapter 5), the new company's condition will naturally be affected by the way the deal is financed.

There are four common ways to finance a merger. In order of frequency, these are cash, stock, a combination of cash and stock, and a combination of notes and cash and/or stock. Each of these payment strategies can have an impact on the financial condition of the new company—and therefore on the new company's compensation system.

1. *Pay after an all-cash deal.* If the acquirer uses its own cash to finance the deal, depending on the amount of cash used, the impact on compensation planning may be slight, especially if the cash used came from a full treasury. In such a case, planners have a clean slate for their creations. If the acquirer borrows cash to finance the transaction, the deal may be a highly leveraged transaction, or HLT. *Highly leveraged transaction* means an extension of credit to or investment in a business by an insured depository institution where the financing transaction involves a buyout, acquisition, or recapitalization of an existing business and one of the following criteria is met:

   - The transaction results in a liabilities-to-assets leverage ratio higher than 75 percent; or
   - The transaction at least doubles the subject company's liabilities and results in a liabilities-to-assets leverage ratio higher than 50 percent; or
   - The transaction is designated an HLT by a syndication agent or a federal bank regulator.[9]

   Pay packages following HLTs should not be cash-heavy, since the company will need cash to pay debt. Incentive pay should be paid in stock or stock options and based on improvements in cash flow.

2. *Pay after an all-stock deal.* If the acquirer finances the deal through an exchange of stock using newly issued shares, the transaction may cause dilution. In such a scenario, pay planners should be conservative about granting more stock or stock options to managers, unless the company

can buy back its own stock. Companies facing potential dilution by using stock-based pay might consider "phantom" stock grants (payments based on stock performance).

3. *Pay after cash-and-stock deal.* If the acquirer combines cash and stock in the payment, the impact on postmerger compensation may be nil, unless the cash is borrowed (in which case, the HLT caveats may apply) or the stock is generous (in which case, beware of dilution).

4. *Pay after a contingency deal.* If the acquirer offered notes to the seller, promising additional payments or "earn-outs" based on contingencies (such as 20 percent sales growth), postmerger compensation should be structured to give managers a chance to make good on those targets. Managers who were owners of the merged company (and therefore are noteholders after the merger) will be most concerned about being given the authority, autonomy, and resources they need to meet performance targets. Obviously, the performance targets in pay-for-performance plans should be in sync with the targets set in the earn-out notes.

How can planners make sure that a new compensation plan will be, as you say, emotionally viable?

Mergers bring out many negative emotions: loss, anxiety, jealousy. Planners need to make sure that their pay plans signify the opposite: gain, security, fairness. One of the best ways to do this is to strive for *positive comparability*. Employees of the newly merged firm may not get the same compensation they got before, but it should be *similar or better*.

Consider the employees of AB Company (shown in Table 8-1). The employees who worked for old Company A will rue the decline in their benefits, and the employees of old Company B will dread the phase-out of their bonuses, even though both groups stand to benefit from other, positive adjustments in the total pay package. For example, in this scenario, employees of Company A have a lot to gain: raises, bonuses, and additional incentive pay. Employees of Company B gain in the areas of incentive pay and benefits.

It is up to management to help employees focus on the positives, not the negatives. In this example (and in the case of any postmerger pay plan worth its salt), the message is this: "Your pay package is not the same as it was in the past, but it is comparable, and in some ways it is better." (In other words, don't just practice your compensation philosophy, preach it!)

In addition to comparability, another byword in the emotional realm is *patience*. It is widely believed that employees resist change; hence the burgeoning field of "change management." Certainly new compensation plans meet with resistance. According to one pay consultant, it takes three years for a new plan to take hold. The first year is for trial and error, the second for progress, and the third for noticeable impact.

Of course, change doesn't end with a new plan. As time goes on, managers will want to continually adjust their pay practices to meet changing realities. A word of advice, though: compensation is a very expensive way to tell employees that they are valued. Pay can do only so much to attract, retain, and motivate people. Meaningful work, a sense of worth, and a chance to advance must also come into play. If these are absent, no amount of raises, bonuses, incentives, benefits, and special deals can take their place. The best and the brightest will take their talents elsewhere.

How can planners make sure that a new pay plan is technically viable?

Compensation rules change frequently. Every day, some new rule or some new interpretation of a rule appears to change the technical nuances of a pay plan. Therefore, compensation planners should rely on specialized experts inside and, often, outside their companies to learn the latest appropriate changes in the accounting and legal treatment of base, bonus, incentive, and benefits pay.

Benefits pay is particularly complex, so much so that many employers use outside vendors to keep records for their benefit programs. But outsourcing does not free an employer of its obligations, whether long-standing or newly acquired. Buyers and sellers alike often fail to realize how many different kinds of benefits there are—and what obligations each benefit entails.

MERGING BENEFIT PLANS

What are the main kinds of employee benefit plans?

There are three primary types of employee benefits: *pension* plans, *health* plans, and *employment/advisory security* plans. Other benefits can be considered perquisites and are limited only by the human imagination.

What are the different types of pension plans?

There are two types of pension plans: *qualified* (meaning that they meet certain federal standards and qualify for tax-favorable treatment) and *nonqualified*. Furthermore, there are two types of qualified pension plans: defined-benefit plans and defined-contribution plans.

A *defined-benefit plan* is a pension plan that uses a formula to determine the total value of benefits and requires the employer to meet certain actuarially determined standards in making contributions to the plan. Contribution must be enough to pay obligations when they fall due.

A *defined-contribution plan* is a pension plan with shorter-term requirements. Minimum contributions are required for each year in which the plan is in existence. These plans can take the form of profit-sharing plans with or without salary deferral (the well-known 401(k) plan) and usually have variable contribution levels.

Both of these types of qualified, defined plans are subject to a $200,000 compensation cap under recent tax law.[10] More broadly, they are subject to rules set forth in the Internal Revenue Code and the Employee Retirement Income Security Act of 1974 (ERISA), administered by the Department of Labor. (For more on ERISA, see Chapter 12.)

If a buyer and seller both have defined-contribution plans, how can these be merged?

This is a complex area that is best understood on a plan-by-plan basis. Let's take the example of the most common type of defined-contribution plan, the 401(k). Whether these plans can be merged depends on whether the acquirer bought the stock of the acquired company or its assets. In an asset acquisition, the plans must remain separate, and the acquired company's plan must be managed by the seller. In a stock acquisition, three approaches are possible: maintaining separate plans, terminating the acquired plan, or merging the two plans.

To maintain separate plans, the acquirer simply has to make sure that each group files its own forms (Form 5500) and satisfies federal requirements for the nature and extent of coverage. One benefit of maintaining separate plans is that there is no break in coverage, as both plans continue to exist. If the plan years are the same, the acquirer can take a full calendar year to come into compliance. (If the plan years are different, the acquirer should check on its timetable; it may be shorter.)

Terminating the seller's plan requires a one-year waiting period. The IRS's "successor plan rule" says that an acquired company's plan will be disqualified if more than 2 percent of its employees participate in another defined-contribution plan (except for an employee stock option plan) within one year of the acquisition. And even if an employer respects the 2 percent limit, it must pay sanctions to prevent those employees from being taxed.

Merging the two plans can save administrative expense, but it can be complicated. Assets from the old plan move to the new one. While this is being done, employees are "locked out" of their plans for a period of time—typically two weeks to four months. During this time, the old record keeper runs a final tally on the accounts, the shares are sold, and the money is moved to the new record keeper. Sometimes employees have to select new investments when they can again access the plan, and sometimes the money is automatically invested in the nearest matching fund in the new plan. During the lockout period, employees typically aren't allowed to take out a loan, make a withdrawal, or pick new investments. However, their contributions and loan obligations and repayments continue. The pension fund blackout provisions of Sarbanes-Oxley added additional restrictions.[11]

What types of health plans do most major public companies today offer?

Most offer one of two types. An *indemnity plan* is a fee-for-service plan. A *managed-care plan*, which has become more prevalent in recent years, can fall into three categories, ranging from most restrictive to least restrictive. All three types of managed-care plans are offered by major health-care insurers, such as Aetna, CIGNA, Health Net Inc., Prudential Insurance Company of America, and Anthem/WellPoint, as well as some 50 other organizations of varying size and quality. Also, some corporations act as self-insurers for their plans.

At the most restrictive end of the managed-care spectrum, you will find *health maintenance organizations* (HMOs). These plans restrict participants to a tight network of health-care providers (physicians and hospitals) and require participants to use a primary-care physician as a gatekeeper. HMOs can keep their costs down by contracting rates with participating providers for specific services at specified rates during a set time frame. These plans have the strongest cost controls and quality oversight and therefore tend to be on the low end of the cost spectrum. Insurers providing HMOs have come under legal attack from physicians and others in recent years. [12]

At the least restrictive end of the spectrum, you will find *preferred provider organizations* (PPOs). These plans rely on a loose network of providers that have agreed to provide medical services at a discount to PPO plan participants. These plans do not require the use of a physician-gatekeeper; participants can go directly to specialists and be reimbursed under the plans. Because of their flexibility, these plans tend to be on the high end of the cost spectrum.

Between these two extremes are *point-of-service plans* (POSs), a relatively new hybrid product. POSs have the physician-gatekeeper and tight provider network of the HMO, thus offering relatively low costs. On the other hand, they enable participants to opt for providers outside the network at lower rates of reimbursement, as long as the care is accessed through the gatekeeper.

In addition to managed-care plans, many companies offer other health benefits. These include not only dental, vision, long-term disability, dependent care, accidental death or disability (business travel, accident), and of course traditional life insurance, but also sick leave and various "wellness" benefits, often linked at no cost or low cost with local health-care providers. These can be single health-care events such as "Flu Shot Day" or "Spring Health Fair," or they can be ongoing wellness programs such as employee assistance programs (EAPs), which provide ongoing treatment referral for substance abuse or mental health problems.

What usually happens when a company with one type of health-care provider network buys a company with another type? What should happen?

Many acquirers phase out their affiliations with the networks of acquired firms and put the firm's employees on their own network. For example, if the acquirer has an HMO and the acquired company has a PPO, the acquirer will cancel the PPO and put everyone on the HMO.

But this may not always be the best course of action. Companies often make their selections based on the conditions prevailing in their *geographic region*. In one area, an HMO may be the best choice, while in another area, a PPO may be the best choice.

Therefore, the best strategy is to reexamine the needs of the new company and maintain (or switch to) one or more network types according to need. Even if a company uses multiple networks, it can still use a single insurance carrier. This will require extra work on the part of the company and the insurer, but it is worth the effort. By using one carrier for all networks, the company can enjoy economies of scale and spread risk. It can also achieve efficient price structuring.

Do different networks use different pricing methods? If so, how can an acquirer integrate them?

Pricing can and often should vary according to the type of health-care network used.

Services may be offered at a discounted fee for service, at a predetermined fee for service, or at a capitated fee.

A *discounted fee for service* is common in plans that use PPOs. In this approach, the network organization and the employer agree on a discount from each provider's "regular" fee for each visit to a hospital, doctor, or other provider by a covered employee, and premiums are set accordingly. The advantages of this approach are that employees enjoy freedom of choice, and doctors have no disincentives for treating any patient. The disadvantage is that prices are hard to predict. This approach is best for a company or unit with low claims experience.

A predetermined fee for service is more common in HMOs or POSs. In this approach, the network sets a price for each service performed, and charges accordingly. Price changes occur slowly over time. The advantage here is cost control. The disadvantage is lack of employee flexibility.

Capitated fees, also used in HMOs and PPOs, stipulate that a certain amount of money will go to the provider regardless of how much his or her services are used. Like the predetermined-fee approach, this one offers the trade-off of higher control and lower flexibility. It has the added disadvantage of physician disincentives at levels above the preset cap.

Aside from the type of network, what about the level of service provided by the network? Can the same company have different levels for different locations or units?

Generally speaking, it is best to have the same level of coverage for all employees at all locations. The only exception will be for a company unit that maintains its own identity and its own policies, including compensation policies.

Suppose an acquirer with one level of health-care coverage acquires a company with a different level? How can these be combined?

There are two dimensions to this question. One dimension involves employee satisfaction; the other involves business strategy. Employees of the newly combined company should be reasonably satisfied with their level of health-care coverage. On the other hand, this level should be suitable to the newly combined company's business purposes.

Obviously, to ensure employee satisfaction, acquirers should strive to make health-care coverage better (or at least the same) following a merger and avoid making it worse.

Fortunately, mergers often trigger an upgrade from the acquired company's inferior coverage to the acquiring company's superior coverage. For example, if a $5 billion public company acquirers a $5 million private company, chances are that the acquirer's level of health-care coverage will be higher than that of the acquired company and that the employees of the acquired company will be automatically added to the acquirer's plan.

Sometimes, though, a merger will lead to the downgrading of health-care coverage for acquired-company employees. This should always be for sound business reasons, which should be communicated prior to the merger. Communications should stress any positive trade-offs received by the acquired firm's employees. (For further discussion, see Chapter 12.)

What business reasons should be taken into consideration when integrating health-care coverage levels?

First of all, health-care coverage should be considered part of an over-all strategic compensation plan, as discussed earlier in the chapter. That plan should take into account prevailing compensation trends in companies comparable to the parent. In addition to such benchmarking, however, the company should look to its own strategic needs.

A strategic review of health-care coverage will involve a series of steps, as follows:

1. *Determine health-care-plan objectives.* Before making any decision about integrating health plans, an acquirer should give each of its affected units an unsparing financial and strategic checkup. In considering the level of health-care coverage provided to employees, companies should consider the state of their *industries.* A company in a profitable, high-growth industry with intense competition for human resources will need to make a heavy investment in top-of-the-line products. By contrast, a firm in a moribund industry with survival issues may opt for a sturdy but low-cost safety net.

2. *Research health-care-plan options.* What products are being offered by comparable companies? Although competitive information may be difficult to obtain on a local basis, national trends are tracked by compensation consulting groups—both independent firms and those affiliated with public accounting firms. It's also worth finding out what employees want in a health-care plan.

3. *Draft the company's health-care "wish list."* After learning what products are being offered in various industries and

various markets and how company employees perceive these products, an acquirer will be well on the way to designing an "ideal" package that fits its overall compensation approach.

4. *Balance value and cost.* When reevaluating existing health-care-plan contracts or entering new ones, look at quality as well as cost. For an objective assessment of quality, you can consult groups such as the National Committee for Quality Assurance (ncqa.org), which evaluates managed-care networks (especially HMOs) and grants them yearly accreditation accordingly. Some major companies insist on an "NCQA seal of approval" for their health plans—something that not every plan can obtain.

5. *Administer and monitor your postmerger program with care.* Excellence in postmerger benefits management requires constant vigilance through both administration and oversight.

   Administration means putting in place and running a system for controlling the quality and cost of benefits, and for managing productivity related to wellness. How frequently are employees submitting claims? How long are they waiting to be reimbursed? Are they taking advantage of the lowest rates offered by your plan, or are they opting to use providers outside the plan at higher rates? Are they satisfied with the care being provided? When employees are off work for health or disability reasons, how long do they stay off the job, and at whose expense?

   Oversight means ensuring the efficiency of this process. Who is in charge of making sure that your administrators are doing their work? Whether it is the human resources director, a board committee, or an outside auditor, a responsible party must be assigned to keep watch over the administration of health-care benefits, not only just after the merger, but in the months and years to follow.

What different types of employment and advisory security plans are there?

The most common are relocation, retraining, and severance pay. (Sometimes these benefits are lumped together with health care and referred to as *welfare* plans.) Most senior managers and outside directors also receive director's and officer's liability insurance—today considered more a necessity than a perquisite or even a benefit.

Obviously, the pension plans of U.S. companies are subject to a good deal of federal law. What about other benefits?

Like pension plans (but to a lesser degree), health and welfare plans are also subject to the tax code and ERISA.

Aside from these laws, what others apply?

There is no real body of compensation law, but there is considerable employment law, and the pay planner must master its fundamentals. To adhere to both state and federal law, companies must pay minimum wage or better, make proper withholdings, pay proper taxes, honor contracts, avoid discriminatory practices, and so forth. Many of the laws establishing these principles are well known and have no special relevance to the postmerger scene.

A more arcane area, yet one with clear relevance to mergers, is disclosure. Postmerger planners should be familiar with SEC pay disclosure rules and the disclosure and trading regulations under Section 16 of the Securities Exchange Act of 1934.

DISCLOSURE AND TRADING RULES

What are the SEC pay disclosure rules?

Item 402 of Regulation S-K, administered by the SEC, contains some 20 pages of dense print detailing a myriad of disclosure obligations for public companies.[13] Under this regulation, companies must publish in their registration statements, proxy statements, and periodic reports the pay details for their five most highly paid officers. These details include salary, bonus, other annual compensation, restricted stock awards, options, stock appreciation rights, long-term incentive payouts, and "all other compensation."[14]

Under the regulation, these reports must also include

- A summary table detailing the compensation of the five most highly paid executives earning over $100,000

- A report from the compensation committee of the board on its pay philosophy
- A graph charting the company's five-year shareholder returns against peers
- Other disclosures, including details on executive holdings of the company's stock, any repricing of executive stock options, compensation committee membership, and details of any new compensation plans subject to stockholder approval.

Since passage of this regulation in 1992, regulators have handed down two more important pay rules. One (effective in 2003) requires shareholder approval of all equity plans.[15] Another (effective in 2006) requires disclosure of the value of stock options.[16]

What are Section 16 rules, and why are they important in the M&A context?

Section 16 of the Securities Exchange Act defines the disclosure obligations and trading restrictions that apply to the directors, officers, and principal stockholders of public companies (companies with reporting obligations to the Securities and Exchange Commission). Section 16(a) outlines disclosure obligations, Section 16(b) outlines trading restrictions and exemptions from those restrictions, and Sections 16(c) through 16(e) define additional exemptions to these rules.

What are the trading restrictions under Section 16(b), and what are the main exemptions applying to mergers?

This section, containing so-called short-swing trading rules, is an attempt to prevent officers and directors from trading on inside information. It says that a company may recoup any profits an insider makes on short-term (six months or under) trades.

In recent years, companies have complained that the short-swing rules have been hampering their efforts to create stock-based pay plans. To facilitate such plans, regulators exempted certain kinds of stock-based pay plans from the rules. However, in the aftermath of Sarbanes-Oxley, the New York Stock Exchange and NASDAQ Stock Market passed a new rule requiring stockholder approval of all stock-based pay plans. Therefore, such plans still require stockholder approval.[17]

What are the accounting rules with respect to employment agreements?

The acquirer can recognize the value of employment and no compete agreements in one of three ways: as *part of the purchase price* (to the extent that the key personnel are shareholders and agree to limit their compensation after the acquisition), as a *separate payment* made or negotiated in the present, or through *future compensation*. This payment may be made through lump-sum payments of cash, through awards of securities (stock or stock options), and/or through future contingent payments that are negotiated and capitalized by the buyer at or around the date of the acquisition or paid by the seller at some time prior to the acquisition.

In any of these cases, there may be recognition of the asset value of "personal goodwill." (See Chapters 4 and 6 for discussion of goodwill.)

INTERNATIONAL CONSIDERATIONS

What issues confront pay planners following a cross-border merger?

Following an international merger, pay planners are likely to face differences in pay levels (particularly at senior ranks), pay philosophy, and pay disclosure. This is particularly true in a merger between a U.S. company and a company based in Europe.

What differences in pay levels are U.S. planners likely to encounter in a deal with a European company?

In terms of pay levels, the most obvious differences are at the top. U.S. senior executives tend to receive higher base pay and much higher total pay, but with a greater percentage of total pay "at risk"—that is, based on performance.

What differences in pay philosophy are planners likely to encounter?

As mentioned, in the United States, pay tends to be more "at risk" than pay in Europe. Conversely, U.S. pay tends to lag behind

European pay when it comes to benefits, including retirement benefits. Interestingly enough, however, long-term research shows that over time, pay differences tend to even out in cross-border mergers. In recent years, foreign pay practices in these firms have been shifting toward U.S. norms in some respects, with a rise in incentive pay relative to base pay.

What about disclosure differences?

No other securities exchange in the world requires such detailed disclosure. Some experts say that if they all did, the United States' apparent lead in executive pay would shrink considerably.

A P P E N D I X   8 – A

Pay for Performance

An Excerpt from the *Report of the NACD Blue Ribbon Commission on Executive Compensation and the Role of the Compensation Committee*

Link Pay to Performance

- **Understand fully the mathematical implications of each plan, including the potential rewards under a variety of scenarios.**

    In designing each compensation package, the compensation committee should consider the advantages, disadvantages, and proper weighting of all compensation elements. The committee should periodically review the company's *total* compensation liabilities to its CEO and other senior executives—under scenarios of voluntary termination, retirement, involuntary termination, and changes of control.

- **Define the relevant marketplace with care.**

It is important to define the relevant "compensation marketplace" at the outset of the process before entering active discussions about compensation. Defining the compensation market is a complicated matter that involves judgment as much as empirical evidence. Compensation committees and boards sometimes have failed to question analyses presented to them or to explore alternative models.

For example, it is not meaningful to establish the "market value" of CEOs in a highly concentrated industry, where a movement of a CEO from one company to a competitor is highly unlikely. As for the "market value" of other CEOs or executives, such comparisons should be tempered to reflect the specific financial circumstances and business strategies of a given company.

The committee should oversee selection of the peer group against which the company's performance is to be measured, and have a clear understanding of the survey methodology used by their consultant. When judging peer companies for appropriateness, committees should use multiple criteria (such as number of employees, market value, and revenues), not just revenues alone.

- **Establish executive compensation objectives that reflect the company's strategy and take account of financial circumstances.**

    Setting performance objectives for the CEO and senior managers is an important board responsibility that requires the consensus of the managers who will meet the objectives. As such, the objectives should be realistically achievable and should take account of both company strategy and financial circumstances. The performance measures selected to trigger compensation, including annual and long-term bonuses, should be logically related to the strategy and goals of the particular company.

    For example, a company set on raising customer satisfaction might give less weight to benchmarks that focus on revenue growth. A company that has experienced unusual personnel losses might include employee turnover as part of its performance measures. Or a company with declining margins might place more emphasis on improving margins than gross revenues.

The objectives and the performance metrics should be agreed upon by all parties and written down annually, in advance of any period of evaluation, so that everybody understands what constitutes "success."

- **Ensure that the company's compensation framework helps to identify, develop, and motivate internal candidates for executive positions.**

  Successful organizations typically have a high percentage of long-term employees ready to assume responsibility and lead when the opportunity arises. This "core" (and corps) of veteran employees can shape and protect a company's culture, transmit its values to newer employees, and ensure that the company can thrive even when its leaders retire.

  Compensation can play an important role in promoting stability and strengthening succession management by rewarding employees for achievement and tangibly demonstrating that they are valued. In this context, directors should try to lessen pay multiples, as discussed earlier under the principle of fairness, and avoid extremes. They should not emulate the extremely high multiples for CEO pay in relation to worker pay seen in recent years.[18]

- **Use appropriate metrics to measure the achievement of objectives.**

  Measures of performance need to be linked to corporate objectives that flow from corporate strategy. While each organization will identify different metrics for measuring performance, every organization should set clear criteria and apply them consistently—whether that means more pay or less.

- **Use a range of metrics to provide a balanced assessment of performance—including both financial and nonfinancial measures.**

  The CEO and other executives should be evaluated on the basis of multiple measures to allow for a complete view of performance. Financial benchmarks should include, but not restrict themselves to, reported financial results, stock market performance, and comparative pay patterns. They should also leave room for the measure of other things that are important to the long-term growth of the company, such as improved customer satisfaction or product quality. Growth in earnings per share, return on investment, and cash flow are good measures of performance. Growth in market share is also an important consideration. Achievements in product quality or customer satisfaction, diversity and stability of the workforce, responsiveness to the community, and leadership through difficult periods are all examples of nonfinancial metrics that should be considered. Boards also need to focus on intrinsic qualities such as leadership and ethics, for these cannot be taken for granted. Finally, these criteria should be incorporated into a meaningful executive evaluation process.

Regardless of which metrics are used, how success is measured needs to be determined at the outset.

EXAMPLE OF PERFORMANCE METRICS

Quantifiable Metrics

- Revenues
- Net income
- Profit margins
- Cash flow
- Earnings per share
- Reduced debt
- Return on equity, capital, or assets
- Market share

Qualitative Metrics

- Compliance with the highest ethical standards and with legal requirements
- Community relations
- Customer satisfaction
- Product development milestones
- Product quality
- Risk assessment, management, and oversight

- Succession planning
- Team building
- Workforce diversity

Honor agreed-upon performance metrics; do not change performance metrics after the fact in order to provide additional compensation despite failure to achieve stated objectives. Compensation metrics should generally be based on reported financial results determined in accordance with generally accepted accounting principles (GAAP), without adjustments. Compensation plans must include downside risk in incentive compensation for those who fail to meet objectives.

Excerpted with permission from *The Report of the NACD Blue Ribbon Commission on Executive Compensation and the Role of the Compensation Committee* (Washington, D.C.: National Association of Corporate Directors, 2003). This commission's 34 members included chief executives, corporate directors, institutional shareholders, attorneys, accountants, compensation consultants, university professors, and others.

NOTES

1 For guidance on executive pay, see *The Report of the NACD Blue Ribbon Commission on Executive Compensation and the Role of the Compensation Committee* (Washington, D.C.: National Association of Corporate Directors, 2003).

2 Language buffs may be interested to know that *acquisition* and *perquisite* both share the same root, *quaerere*, "to seek to obtain." Acquisition comes from *ad-* ("extra") + *quaerere* and refers to something extra that is obtained. *Perquisite* comes from *per-* ("through") + *quaerere*. It originally referred to goods obtained by means other than inheritance.

3 See "2005 General Schedule (GS) Locality Pay Tables" at the Web site for the Office of Personnel Management, http://www.opm.gov/oca/05tables/indexGS.asp.

4 Target ownership plans are positively associated with improvements in firm performance. See John Core and David Larcker, "Performance Consequences of Requiring Target Stock Ownership Levels," Mar. 21, 2000, a white paper from the Research Center, Accounting Department, University of Pennsylvania, Wharton School of Business.

5 This idea was first advanced by Ira M. Millstein, senior partner, Weil, Gotshal & Manges, New York, and by Paul W. McAvoy of Yale

School of Management, New Haven, in a letter mailed to the members of the National Association of Corporate Directors on Apr. 11, 1996.

6 For example, links to quality can be offered through a variety of means, including customer satisfaction survey results, rate of returned merchandise, defect rate, and other quantitative measures. It may seem difficult to use more than one measure, but this is a fundamental principle of the "balanced scorecard" approach that is sweeping management consulting circles. For an application of this approach to research and development, see Chapter 9.

7 *In re Walt Disney Co. Derivative Litig.*, Consolidated C.A. No. 15452, slip op. at 2-3 (Del. Ch. Aug. 9, 2005) shows how important it is to understand the results of executive contracts. The case involved payments made to former Disney CEO Michael Ovitz.

8 Doug Tormey, "Regulatory Update: 280G Stock Option Valuation," *Perspectives: Insights for Today's Business Leaders*, Sept. 30. 2003. Statement No. 123 (revised 2004), "Share-Based Payment" (issued December 2004). For a good discussion of how golden parachutes can function as poison pills, and what kind of poison pills would be deemed golden parachutes under Sections 280G and 4999, see John P. Beavers, "The Role of Golden Parachutes Is Often Misunderstood," *Accredula*, vol. 1, no. 1, October 2000. *Accredula* is a newsletter of the law firm of Bricker and Eckler LLP, of Columbus, Ohio.

9 Federal Deposit Insurance Corporation Rules and Regulations, Part 235, "Capital Maintenance," Subpart A, "Minimum Capital Requirements," Section 328.2, "Definitions."

10 The Economic Growth and Tax Relief and Reconciliation Act of 2001 (EGTRRA) raised the ceiling from previous lower limits. The limit is now $200,000.

There is also a $1 million cap on the deductibility of compensation under IRC Section 162(m). This cap may be waived for plans that include performance incentives approved by an independent committee of the company's board of directors.

11 Securities and Exchange Commission, *Insider Trades during Pension Fund Blackout Periods* 17 CFR Parts 240, 245 and 249, Release No. 34-47225; IC-25909; File No. S7-44-02, RIN 3235-AI71, effective date Jan. 26, 2003. These rules clarify the application and prevent evasion of Section 306(a) of the Sarbanes-Oxley Act of 2002. Section 306(a) prohibits any director or executive officer of an issuer of any equity security from, directly or indirectly, purchasing, selling or otherwise acquiring or transferring any equity security of the

issuer during a pension plan blackout period that temporarily prevents plan participants or beneficiaries from engaging in equity securities transactions through their plan accounts, if the director or executive officer acquired the equity security in connection with his or her service or employment as a director or executive officer. In addition, the rules specify the content and timing of the notice that issuers must provide to their directors and executive officers and to the commission about a blackout period. The rules are designed to eliminate inequities that may result when pension plan participants and beneficiaries are temporarily prevented from engaging in equity securities transactions through their plan accounts. The 401(k) part of this answer is based in part on information provided by the Web site 401khelpcenter.com.

12 *Pegram* v. *Hedrich* (U.S. Supreme Court 2000) recognized that the nation's health-care system now operates under a "congressional policy of allowing HMO organizations." The court rejected claims that an HMO structure providing an inherent financial incentive to limit patient care breached the plan's fiduciary duty to its beneficiaries. The court said that the law would not permit attacks on the structure of HMOs, "untethered to claims of concrete harm." Nonetheless, health-care providers have sued insurers over problems. Currently, major insurers are named in litigation called *In re: Managed Care Litigation*, MDL No. 1334, and are in the process of making payments to settle this litigation.

13 See *Regulation S-K Under the Securities Act of 1933, the Securities Exchange Act of 1934, and the Energy Policy and Conservation Act of 1975* (New York: Bowne Red Box Service, Sept. 15, 2005), pp. 58-74. These rules, in effect for well over a decade now (since October 1992) have had the beneficial effect of making compensation more "transparent" (visible) to stockholders. On the other hand, some believe that they have enabled inflation of executive pay, as companies benchmarked against each others' disclosures.

14 The SEC defines the "other compensation" that must be disclosed as including, but not limited to, termination and change-of-control payments; accrued or contingent above-market or preferential earnings on deferred compensation; contributions to defined-contribution plans, and premiums on executive split-dollar insurance.

15 Securities and Exchange Commission, *Self-Regulatory Organizations; New York Stock Exchange, Inc. and National Association of Securities Dealers, Inc.; Order Approving NYSE and NASDAQ Proposed Rule Changes and NASDAQ Amendment No. 1 and Notice of Filing and Order Granting Accelerated Approval to NYSE Amendments No. 1 and 2 and*

NASDAQ Amendments No. 2 and 3 Thereto Relating to Equity Compensation Plans (Release No. 34-48108; File Nos. SR-NYSE-2002-46 and SR-NASD-2002-140), June 30, 2003.

16 For options disclosure, see *SFAS No. 123* (revised 2004), "Share-Based Payment" (issued December 2004) This statement had the following effective dates: public entities that do not file as small-business issuers—as of the beginning of the first interim or annual reporting period that begins after June 15, 2005; public entities that file as small-business issuers—as of the beginning of the first interim or annual reporting period that begins after December 15, 2005; nonpublic entities—as of the beginning of the first annual reporting period that begins after December 15, 2005. This statement applies to all awards granted after the required effective date and to awards modified, repurchased, or cancelled after that date. The cumulative effect of initially applying this statement, if any, is recognized as of the required effective date.

17 Exchange Act Rules Volume IV, Rules 16a-1 through 31-1: General Rules and Regulations Under the Securities Exchange Act of 1934. See also Order Approving NYSE and Nasdaq Proposed Rule Changes and Nasdaq Amendment No. 1 and Notice of Filing and Order Granting Accelerated Approval to NYSE Amendments No. 1 and 2 and Nasdaq Amendments No. 2 and 3 Thereto Relating to Equity Compensation Plans (Release No. 34-48108; File Nos. SR-NYSE-2002-46 and SR-NASD-2002-140) June 30, 2003.

18 The total compensation ratio, measuring options on Black-Scholes grant value, went from 25 times in 1970 to 570 times in 2000, declining to 360 times in 2002. Average cash compensation has continued to increase relative to worker pay—from 25 times worker pay in the 1970s to 90 times worker pay in 2002—and the multiples are much higher when equity-based pay is included. Brian J. Hall and Kevin Murphy, "The Trouble with Stock Options," *Journal of Economic Perspectives*, Vol. 17, No. 3, Summer 2003.

CHAPTER 9

Integrating and Enhancing Technology and Innovation

Builders of visionary companies concentrate primarily on building an organization—building a ticking clock—rather than on hitting a market just right with a visionary product idea and riding the growth curve of an attractive product life cycle.

James C. Collins and Jerry I. Porras, *Built to Last: Successful Habits of Visionary Companies*

INTRODUCTION

The first decade of this new millennium saw significant M&A activity in the high-technology sector. The merger of Hewlett-Packard and Compaq made history in 2002 as the largest high-tech merger ever, requiring half a million planning hours from 900 managers.[1] That same year WorldCom, an acquisitive telecommunications company, filed for the world's largest bankruptcy, dragged down by financial control failures that acquisitions had helped disguise.[2]

The year 2005 also marked phase one for the integration of a $10.3 merger between Oracle and PeopleSoft, a high-tech megamerger that gave Oracle access to PeopleSoft's "enterprise resource planning" (ERP) customers—a vanishing breed in the new environment of mix-and-match middleware. Enterprise resource planning is a broad term describing a suite of applications that can help organizations communicate and plan. Confident of the value of the company's ERP customers, PeopleSoft's board held out for a 60 percent premium offer.[3]

Yet the real action for technology mergers may not have been in these megadeals, which were motivated more by a desire to pool customer bases than by a desire to improve or expand technology. For truly tech-intensive transactions, smaller transactions tell the story better. In late 2005,[4]

- Perot Systems Corp. of Plano, Texas, bought a safety, environmental, and engineering services company called PrSM Corp. of Knoxville, Tennessee, for $7.2 million, enabling Perot Systems Government Services to provide a wider range of safety and engineering services to the Energy Department and expand its offerings to other departments, such as the Defense Department and NASA.
- IBM Corp. agreed to acquire PureEdge Solutions Inc. of British Columbia, Canada. PureEdge offers business process automation frameworks to create, manage, and deploy Extensible Markup Language (XML) forms-based processes. PureEdge worked with IBM on its WebSphere Portal, which integrates with PureEdge XML-based e-forms and lets users work on e-forms online and offline. Government customers for PureEdge include the U.S. Air Force and Army and the National Institutes of Health, according to the company's Web site.
- VeriSign Inc. of Mountain View, California, acquired security intelligence provider iDefense of Reston, Virginia, for about $40 million in cash; iDefense, which has a multilingual network of more than 200 research contributors in more than 30 countries, publishes intelligence on network security threats and vulnerabilities for financial services firms, government agencies, retailers, and other enterprises. Customers use the reports to modify their security infrastructure and respond to threats on a real-time basis. VeriSign provides intelligent infrastructure services for the Internet and telecommunications networks.
- The Pacific Alliance, a $200 million apparel manufacturer based in New York, purchased the Unified Buying Engine and the TradeStone Unified Order Management module from TradeStone Software. The TradeStone Unified Buying

Engine is a technology platform that enables companies to streamline all purchasing into one view and business process by offering visibility deep into the supply chain. It does this by aggregating operations such as managing reporting and queries, alerting for exceptions, critical path management, best practice modeling, workflow, and collaboration. The TradeStone Unified Order Management module tracks finished goods, raw materials, blanket orders, and aggregations by customer, channel, or store type, enabling quality assurance, vendor and channel management, and planning. It also supports the creation of smaller, more frequent orders, giving retailers the ability to respond to sales data and changing market conditions. Pacific Alliance plans to use TradeStone to improve its work-in-process visibility at the factory level, especially in the quality assurance and quality control areas. The ultimate goal is to improve order delivery as its designers and global manufacturing plants work closely with key retail customers, including J.C. Penney and Kohl's department stores.

Furthermore, even outside the high-tech sector, acquirers are looking to buy and integrate the technology of today and— through innovations in research and development (R&D)—that of tomorrow. Technology and innovation have always driven a good portion of mergers. Cisco, Lucent, and Nortel, for example, have all used M&A to enhance their networking capabilities. Yet because technology is constantly changing, every technology-based acquisition runs some risk of failure. In the high-tech market, product life cycles are measured in months, in contrast to the years contemplated by industries such as auto, pharmaceuticals, or steel.

This chapter will not focus on technology that enables merger transactions or integration.[5] Rather, it will take a broad look at how two companies merge all their technology and R&D. After an overview, this chapter will offer guidance on integration issues in four realms, from general to specific: knowledge management (how data become information, and how information becomes knowledge) information technology (specific IT systems), research and development (laboratory operations), and intellectual property (patents and trademarks). The chapter ends with a few observations on international issues.

POSTACQUISITION KNOWLEDGE MANAGEMENT

If two companies have different information technology, how can these be integrated?

- A more complete way of posing this question would be to ask: If two companies each have *systems* and/or *technologies* for managing their *data, information,* and/or *knowledge,* how can these be integrated? Some of these terms are used interchangeably (although they really should not be). Therefore, some definitions are in order: *Systems.* Systems are repeatable ways of doing things. A system may be documented, or merely followed without benefit of documentations. The term "operating system" means, most generally, a way of operating. In the parlance of information technology, it often refers to a kind of technology that enables the operations of a computer, such as Windows.
- *Technology* refers to the hardware and software/programs that can automate a system through the use of non-human forces, such as electronics. The term technology encompasses any particular *application* (set of program files that make up a particular software).
- *Data* are discrete observable facts. For example, here are two data points: "(1) This equipment malfunctions during the life cycle of 2 percent of all purchases. (2) The company's quality standards tolerate an error rate of 1.5 percent."
- *Information* is data in a context that is meaningful and can be acted on. For example, "The 2 percent malfunction rate of this equipment falls outside the scope of our quality standards, so management recommends recalling this product."
- *Knowledge* is the reception of of information; the term focuses on the person or entity that is gathering, storing, and acting on the information. For example, "Our sales force doesn't know anything about this new product; to increase their knowledge, we need to train them in it."[6]

Knowledge can be explicit (written down or spoken) or tacit (not articulated).

- *Integration of data and/or information* means combining or linking places where data and/or information are stored and processed. Examples: purging duplicate data, renaming data fields for consistency, matching time spans for data collection, changing formulas for interpreting data and/or information, modernizing technology for gathering and delivering data and/or information, and merging two libraries or Web sites (and their databases) into one.

- *Integration of knowledge management* means combining *management systems* for generating, transmitting, and receiving data and information. Examples: combining training programs and appointing a chief knowledge officer to oversee the quality, accessibility, and usefulness of data and information in combining organizations. Research shows that knowledge management can increase postmerger efficiency.[7]

In a 2005 study called "Know How: Managing Knowledge for Competitive Advantage," the *Economist* surveyed 122 senior information technology managers and asked them about their greatest challenges.[8] Here is a short paraphrase of the study's main findings, as they might apply to a merger.

Knowledge Management Checklist

Appoint a *knowledge management leader* to ensure the right collaborative environment.

Identify *business needs* in the newly combined organization and what information is needed to fulfill them, and then invest in tools and processes—not the other way around. (Technology should not dictate knowledge management.)

Identify *who knows what* in the new organization and in its larger network of contacts; gather and convey contact information from these knowledge sources.

Adapt knowledge management tools to the areas and depth of knowledge needed by the individuals in the new organization.

Update data and information regularly; markets, customers, technology, and competition are continually changing.

Track what information is being acted on, and how effectively.

Align the metrics of the two organizations.

Learn from experience (good and bad), and share that learning when a similar situation occurs. Don't repeat the same mistakes or reinvent the wheel.

Provide forums, tools, and opportunities for informal networking to encourage employees to share data, information, and knowledge actively. For example, use bulletin boards/message boards and listservs.

When choosing technology, also consider the culture and behavior in the new organization. If the company is centralized, using a single enterprise resource planning approach will be easier than it will be in a more decentralized organization. In short, make sure technology is usable.

It is possible to "institutionalize" usability, according to engineer Eric Schaffer.[9] To ensure usability of information:

- Educate your organization about the importance of usability.
- Hire and coordinate usability staff and/or consultants.
- Plan the standards, design, and implementation phases.
- Retrofit a method that has added user-centered activities.
- Recruit participants for usability interviews and testing.

Can you give an example of a company that has used "knowledge management" to manage their acquisitions?

A good example is Schlumberger, a leading oilfield services provider that has made numerous acquisitions over time.

Schlumberger's business segments were spending a great amount of time gathering client information and preparing job files. Information traveled slowly and inefficiently up a hierarchy, one step at a time through manual reports. To counteract this pattern, Schlumberger identified and used tools and processes that were common among its many and dispersed technology centers, and developed and promoted common standards. It wanted to capture the lessons learned during service delivery, retrieve/store frequently needed data and information, and ensure that operations sites retained past knowledge of operations. More specifically, the company aimed for:

- *Answer delivery vs. data delivery.* In the answer delivery approach, engineers receive a text message on their cell phones disclosing that their wells have reached total depth and asking for a yes or no answer on a sidetrack. In the data delivery approach, they sit in an office or at a wellsite monitoring raw data to make the same decision. Answer delivery means that they receive workflow intelligence, not simply data.
- *Integration of workflow processes* that require input from and output to a large number of discrete data sources (i.e., client relationship management, HSE, technical data, operations).
- *Compression of data* to help transmit large amounts of information.
- *Standardization of databases* by using common identifiers, enabling quick access to data from any database around the world.
- *Investment in technology (or buying new technology)* to support workflow.
- *Development of competencies and training.* This avoids problems related to the "big crew change."

Along these lines, the company started a program called InTouch service to provide operational and technical support to field staff 24 hours a day, seven days a week.

"InTouch is an enterprisewide internal service providing timely technical support to field operations covering all products and services for Schlumberger. InTouch acts as a bridge between the company's technology centers and the field, with a mandate to accurately capture and store knowledge, and disseminate it to the field as quickly as possible. The goal of this mandate is to improve service delivery to clients and achieve faster deployment of new, more robust technology through improved technical support and comprehensive solutions."[10]

Schlumberger has reported $200 million in savings per year, as well as improvement of response time by 95 percent for technical queries and 75 percent for making engineering modifications.[11]

INTEGRATING TECHNOLOGIES: THE BIG PICTURE

When two companies want to combine their capacities for creating and sustaining new technologies, why would they merge? Wouldn't a strategic alliance be easier?

Companies that wish to expand their technological base can start out with alliances rather than mergers. In general, alliances are better than mergers for the expansion of technical knowledge.[12] But strategic alliances face many of the same integration challenges as outright mergers, and have a shorter life span in which to work them out.[13] For major, long-term technology bets, acquisitions can be superior to alliances.

What guidance do you have for the integration of information technology?

Since a significant portion of all capital spending in corporate America goes for information technology,[14] it is worthy of senior management attention, not only in the IT industry itself, but also in industries that are being driven by a need to consolidate their IT— for example, the health insurance industry. Technical success in this area depends greatly on managerial practices, which means that it should be monitored by general managers, not technical staff.

A recent Boston Consulting Group study on bank mergers[15] found that certain management practices in information technology can improve the chances of postmerger success. Here are the six tips offered by BCG.

1. *Choose from existing systems landscapes; do not build a third.* Having at least one organization use a familiar system minimizes the amount of new training required.

FIGURE 9-1

A Matrix for Integrating Information Technology by Cluster

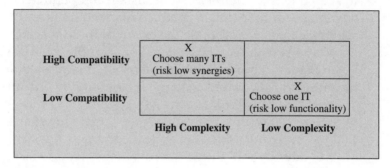

Source: Based on a paper by Boston Consulting Group, July 2004.

2. *Identify clusters of applications within a system.* Newly acquired companies or divisions usually want to keep their own IT applications. Acquirers need a method for choosing which systems to keep and which to jettison. BCG suggests creating a matrix that plots where a technology falls. The vertical axis indicates compatibility (potential for business alignment), and the horizontal axis shows the complexity of the IT. Managers take different actions depending on where the technology falls on the matrix. (See Figure 9-1.) IT managers can get involved in identifying the clusters on a purely technical basis. A typical large organization may identify up to 70 clusters that fall in various spots along the matrix.

3. *Follow a rigorous selection process.* After each merger partner has divided its IT structure into clusters, the IT groups make a technical evaluation of each cluster. Criteria include functionality (which operations does the cluster support); the quality, durability, and flexibility of each cluster's technological architecture; potential savings; feasibility (migration costs and major risks); and speed of implementation (avoid choosing clusters that will take too much time to integrate). The team then selects "nuggets" as described in the next step.

4. *Look for nuggets.* Identify isolated applications that are most critical to success—for example, those that are needed to keep offering core services, to sustain competitive advantage, or to maintain productivity. Acquirers and acquirees may overestimate the extent of these specific applications within an IT system. For example, says BCG, when Bank Austria bought Creditanstalt, it requested that the target make 2,000 IT changes. By identifying only the "nuggets" within Bank Austria's IT system, BCG was able to reduce that wish list by half. Of the target IT systems, 1,000 were permitted to stay as is; the acquirer's systems did not offer critically superior advantages (and in fact were inferior, BCG suggests).

5. *Disclose your criteria and reasonable timelines for selection.* Having a transparent process for selecting applications and building a system should not be rushed. But it also enables deadlines for making choices. The selection of IT applications typically takes three to six months.

6. *Monitor implementation closely.* Once the applications have been selected and the system created, implementing the system can take more than a year, warns BCG. It is advisable to set up a tracking mechanism to mark milestones. During BCG's work on the BNP-Paribas merger, the banks set up 20 programs involving 1,000 projects, with 12,000 progress milestones.

The moral is that managers may need to reorganize tasks and redesign jobs following the switch to a new or augmented information system—particularly if management is using a new "management tool," such as Six Sigma.[16] (For more on this point, see the discussion of the ISO 9001 standards in Chapter 7, "Integrating Management Systems.")

How can procurement departments help in the integration of IT?

Procurement departments can create a unified plan for IT purchases. This can help larger organizations, which may have more than one purchasing department involved with IT. In some cases, it may be advisable to integrate all the purchasing departments.[17]

How can an integration team make sure it is doing a good job on the managerial side of IT integration?

One helpful benchmark is "Internal Control—Integrated Framework," issued by the Committee on Sponsoring Organizations of the Treadway Commission (COSO), cited in Chapter 7. This report urges managers overseeing IT changes to ask the following questions:

- *Is content appropriate?* Is the needed information there?
- *Is information timely?* Is it there when it is required?
- *Is information current?* Is the latest information available?
- *Is information accurate?* Is it based on observable data and sound interpretation of the data?
- *Is information accessible?* Can it be obtained easily by appropriate parties?

COSO says that information and internal control are interrelated. Having the right information, on time, at the right place is essential to effecting control. In turn, information systems must be controlled: the quality of information can depend on the quality of the control system that generates it.

Another benchmark that is useful when linking information to the practicalities of design, production, and distribution is the new global ISO 9001 standards. (For more about these standards, see Chapter 7.)

If two companies merge, and one is using a new information technology while the other is using an older one, should the old system be upgraded to the new one?

Despite the challenges of keeping up with the revolution in information technology, it is a mistake to assume that newer technology provides better control just because they are new. In fact, the opposite may be true. Older (so-called legacy) technology may have been tried and tested through their use and provide what is required. The process is such that an organization's technology often evolves to suit that organization's requirements and become an amalgam of many technologies.[18]

What are the biggest challenges for information integration?

There are two: the integration of information itself and the communication between managers about IT.

Information integration   Data processing managers and computer programmers work with many hard realities. In terms of data, files with different bit-level software (16, 32, 64) cannot be merged directly; in terms of software, programs running on one technical platform cannot run on another. To be sure, there are new "cross-platform" programming languages, such as Sun Microsystems' Java and Lucent Technologies' Inferno. Also, software engineers in companies large and small are developing new technology for gateways, bridging, routing, and switching. But when it comes to postmerger integration, every situation is unique; there are few off-the-shelf solutions. Some technical programs require nothing short of genius from programmers.

Solutions are especially difficult in light of recent shifts from mainframe computer systems to client-server networks to network computers. When two companies merge, it is likely that at least one of them will be in the process of moving forward somewhere along this technological timeline.

Also, the new practice of warehousing data for mining has encouraged some companies to store too much so-called information—really just clusters of combined data that have not risen to the level of usable information. After buying such a company, the acquirer may have to spend days deleting tens of thousands of files containing useless information—for example, details on accounts that have been dormant for over five years.

Communication about IT   One challenge in integrating information technology is linguistic. IT terminology has become so specialized that many senior managers from a more general or different background may not understand it. IT managers need to talk "apples and oranges," not "bits and bytes."

For example, companies in the grocery industry or in other industries that use product identification codes, bar codes, and electronic data interchange support an organization called the Uniform Code Council in Dayton, Ohio, which offers courses in various technical aspects of distribution technology. A past two-page educational flyer produced by the UCC contained 10 acronyms, only half of them translated into English. What is DEX-UCS? Only product coding specialists know. But postmerger integration teams should not be afraid to ask.

In the telecommunications field, a similar cluster of acronyms has developed. Consider one past educational calendar for the Data-Tech Institute of Clifton, New Jersey. The DTI's course description for "Fundamentals of Telecommunications" featured 58 acronyms, with only 17 translated into English.

In all fairness to the "techies" (that is, technical managers), though, some words have become fairly common buzzwords that every manager should know. A list of these words appears in Appendix 9-A. Appendixes 9-B and 9-C use common terms.

What is cybersecurity, and how can merging companies attain it?

Cybersecurity is assurance of the availability, confidentiality, integrity, and privacy of data and information. To protect it, companies need to recognize and track metrics for information security. The most broadly used standard is ISO 17799. For an assessment tool developed by private sector advisors, see Appendix 9-D.

What are some examples of mergers that faced technological challenges?

Two recent telecommunications mergers faced technology differences:

- In the merger between Cingular Wireless and AT&T Wireless, Cingular's network was largely GSM (Global System for Mobile Communications), while AT&T's was mostly TDMA (Time-Division Multiple Access). Phones that worked on one system would not work on the other. There were also frequency differences. Some AT&T Wireless customers had to be on both networks for several months, seeing "AT&T" on their phone screens at some times and "Cingular" at others. This was because Cingular allowed "home-on-home" roaming as the two networks were reconfigured.

■ The Nextel-Sprint merger in late 2005 faces a challenge—namely, that their networks are incompatible. Nextel primarily uses a technology called iDen, while Sprint favors QUALCOMM-produced CDMA. Resolving this technological hurdle is likely to be high on the agenda for the companies.

Suppose a company decides to sell a unit. How should the IT for that unit be handled?

In general, preserving the status quo is the best option. The following case is instructive:

> "[Our] requirement was to dis-integrate the division from the corporate parent to prepare it for acquisition. This meant establishing localized business functions, such as financial and payroll functions, procurement, and even electronic data interchange (EDI), that had been managed by the corporate parent. Once the necessary business functions were identified, the systems to support them had to be implemented. Often legacy systems may still be required by the division being sold until the divestiture is completed. In this scenario, service level agreements (SLA) for use of these systems for one year with options to renew may be crafted to provide critical legacy systems access. This may be true for IT infrastructure and software licenses as well. Access to data centers, use of mainframes, servers, and networks, and use of software covered under corporate licensing arrangements must all be considered in order to set up a division for acquisition.
>
> Another consideration during this process was whether to continue with various ebusiness initiatives that were underway. In this case, the client had already implemented a B2B (business-to-business) trading exchange including forecast collaboration with key suppliers and customers. The question that arose was, "Should we continue the rollout of these ebusiness initiatives or postpone them until we know who is buying us?" The recommendation was to continue the rollouts for two reasons: 1) The migration of these business functions to the Internet is a requirement, not an option, so delaying the rollouts would have deleterious affects on the firm; and 2) having a solid ebusiness strategy with processes and infrastructure in place will enhance, not diminish, the value of the division to an acquiring firm."[19]

INTEGRATING SYSTEMS FOR RESEARCH
AND DEVELOPMENT (R&D)

Can you give an example of a firm that continued R&D collaboration after a merger?

The 2005 Gillette–Procter & Gamble merger strengthened the work of the two firms in an "RFID" project they had been piloting for Kraft Foods, Johnson & Johnson, Unilever, and Wal-Mart. RFID means radio frequency identification, a method of storing and remotely retrieving data using devices called RFID tags or transponders. An RFID tag is a small object that can be attached to or incorporated into a product, animal, or person. The companies plan to pool their research programs to reorganize their warehouse operations around RFID technology.

How can newly combined companies manage their ongoing and future R&D projects?

As with any area to be integrated, it is a good idea to have one person in charge of ensuring that R&D integration stays on track. This person will manage the process of R&D integration by scheduling meetings to define future areas of R&D collaboration, helping managers set priorities for senior management approval, reporting back to senior management on progress and obstacles, and scheduling meetings to revisit the goals and strategies of the collaboration. This individual should not be responsible for the results of the collaboration, only for ensuring that it stays on track.

What are the main barriers to success in merging R&D efforts?

One challenge, mentioned in Chapter 4, is *retention of human capital*. Hundreds of employees left the networking firm 3Com after it merged with modem maker U.S. Robotics in a $6.6 billion deal in 1997, damaging product development. One of the reasons that 3Com bought U.S. Robotics was to get Palm. But the creator of this handheld technology, Jeff Hawkins, and his marketing director, Donna Dubinsky, left to start rival Handspring in 1998.[20]

Another challenge is differing R&D *cultures*. The AT&T–NCR merger is widely cited as an unsuccessful deal.[21] AT&T bought the computer maker in 1991 to bring together telecommunications and computing services. The NCR employees who were retained could not fit into AT&T's highly structured system after years of working in a "fluid" entrepreneurial workplace. A similar IT culture clash occurred when IBM acquired Rolm, a Silicon Valley–based maker of computerized phone systems, in 1984. Analyst Rob Enderle, who was an internal auditor at Rolm at the time, recalls a difference in decision-making style: "At Rolm, you made decisions from the hip. At IBM, decisions were made by committee." IBM sold Rolm to Siemens for $333 million in 1998. It is easier to integrate smaller acquisitions, culturally speaking. The acquirer simply makes its culture stick, much like the Romans. Cisco, IBM, and Microsoft have acquired many smaller high-tech companies and integrated them well by most reports.

Customer drain can be acute for high-tech deals. When Hewlett-Packard acquired workstation maker Apollo Computer for $476 million in 1989, it got mired in integration challenges and reportedly lost $750 million in business. Similarly, when Compaq was integrating Digital Equipment Corporation, its rivals gained many former Compaq customers.[22]

An additional challenge is *differing time frames* (or what some call "culture"). Here is a typical (composite) scenario. A pharmaceutical company decides to combine its expertise in antibiotics with a medical device company's skill in manufacturing various types of implants. The pharmaceutical company is staffed with scientists who have advanced degrees and a background in pure (as opposed to applied) research, whereas the medical device company has a staff of engineers with no more than bachelor's degrees. Result: the scientists have a 10- or even 30-year time frame (particularly if they have received "patient" capital from university or government sources), while the engineers are looking for results in five years or less.

Turf conflicts also can cause problems. Not everyone stands to gain from collaboration. Some individuals or groups may lose prestige, titles, and power as the new order unfolds. Members of one R&D team may resist working with representatives of a second company. To preserve their place in the sun, they may refuse to share knowledge and resources.

Finally, there can be *differing corporate-level strategies* for R&D. Top management may have different ideas about the level of funding for different research projects, the markets they hope to serve, the returns they expect to achieve, and the link between those returns and the rewards paid to executives. They might position R&D differently within the company.

What do you mean, they might "position" R&D differently?

One firm might link research to development by bringing in marketing very early in the research process. The other firm might keep research and development separate.

The urge to mainstream research has been reported at Bell Labs and at Battelle, two legacy names in scientific research. Merck reportedly separates the two. Beecham also follows this downstream approach.

So what is the right answer? Clearly, the choice between the mainstream and the downstream approach will depend in part on the type of innovation sought.[23]

Could you give an example of merging companies that resolved a difference in R&D strategies?

Years ago, *Across the Board* asked Lockheed Martin CEO Norman Augustine if it was fair to characterize Lockheed as having a "long-term" culture and Martin Marietta as having a "short-term" culture."[24] Augustine said no, disputing the importance of cultural differences. In his view, they are merely an excuse for postmerger failure. The aerospace leader also discounted the importance of politics at his company. He said that because Lockheed Martin has senior executives from several companies (both merger partners had been active acquirers), "we're all a minority."

In Augustine's view, the key challenge to postmerger integration of R&D efforts lay not in culture or politics, but in planning and cost estimating:

> Some companies have a tradition of doing their long-range planning on a probabilistic basis where they assign a probability to each program, while other companies plan on a quantum basis where they say, either we'll win this program or we'll lose it. We've come up with a melded way of planning that is stronger than either of these approaches.

The two companies also blended their differing methods of cost estimation—one detailed, the other big-picture.

Aside from combining planning methods, in what other ways can merging companies bridge the gap between their R&D styles?

One way to go through this process is to have the teams make presentations to each other (in person and via videoconference); to meet with each other, sometimes in off-site locations and with the help of a facilitator (for more on the role of a facilitator in postmerger integration, see Chapter 3); and to work side by side. Another way to bridge the gap is to make sure that pay systems motivate and reward collaboration.

Teams can also create a *balanced scorecard* for resource allocation. The columns on the card are key constituencies (customers, shareholders, and so on), and the rows are key measures (quality, stock price appreciation, and so on). Projects get graded from these multiple perspectives—many of them nonfinancial.

If all else fails, it may be necessary to seek the resignation of project team members who are unwilling to work collegially. Senior management should not hesitate to intervene from time to time to force solutions for the good of the company.

In *Built to Last: Successful Habits of Visionary Companies*, recently reissued in paperback, James C. (Jim) Collins and Jerry I. Porras expose the myths of the "great idea" and the "charismatic leader." Companies with vision have "an enduring core ideology plus envisioned progress for the future." They do not begin with cutting-edge concepts, but rather with the desire to build a lasting company.[25]

How can a newly merged company be creative and visionary with respect to technology and innovation?

There are two loaded terms in this question. Let's take them one by one.

There is a wealth of literature on this important question of how to encourage creativity. *Across the Board*, a publication of the Conference Board in New York, recently published 22 "how-to" techniques, derived from a review of *four thousand* articles on the topic.

Significantly, several of the techniques centered around teamwork. This is certainly helpful in our quest. To integrate innovation, one must integrate the innovators. So Step 1 is to gather key R&D staff from both companies in the same peaceful setting. Step 2 is to have someone lead these people in an exercise for creativity, for example:

- *Brainstorming.* Hold a technical "rap" session in which one idea leads to another through a freewheeling exchange. Encourage quantity of ideas at first. Quality will follow.
- *Brainwriting.* Get a small group together with a sheet of paper. Ask the first person to write down a research or development idea and pass the paper to the next person, who will add some thoughts and pass the paper on.
- *Crawford blue-slip writing.* Present participants with a question in "how-to" form, such as, "How can we find more ways that businesses can use our technology?" Ask everyone to write as many answers as possible within five minutes, putting each answer on a separate, anonymous blue slip. Collect the slips and have the group evaluate the ideas.
- *Left-brain, right-brain alternatives.* Have participants list solutions to problems. Collect the answers and describe them as either left-brain (analytical) or right-brain (intuitive). Find compatible answer pairs, one from each side of the brain.
- *Wildest ideas.* Ask participants for wild ideas. Pick one and have the group discuss it. If the discussion doesn't lead to practical ideas, pick another wild idea.

Vision represents a broader challenge. To meet it, we will turn to Collins and Porras, applying their findings to the postmerger context:

- *Build clocks, not time tellers.* Create efficient technology processes, avoiding the star system.
- *Think* and, *not* or. Try to use the best technological resources and processes from both companies, not just one.

- *Strive for value, not just profits.* Go beyond financial projections for projects; ask what they mean for the company as a whole.
- *Determine and stick to core values.* Determine and articulate what the core values for the emerging company will be.
- *Persist.* Don't let failure in a newly combined R&D project set you back. Learn from it.
- *Keep and promote good people.* In selecting leaders for the merging companies, put first priority on insiders.
- *Pursue continual progress.* Let the best achievements of the combined companies' past set a new bar for their joint achievement in the future.
- *Align values with practice.* Don't just say you will value technological contributions in the newly combined company; show it through decisions and reward structures.
- *Dream big.* Don't limit technology and research efforts to the sure bets of the past. Use cooperative research efforts to move toward the future. In addition to protecting and using the intellectual property of yesterday, generate the property of tomorrow.

Finally, to encourage creativity and vision, invest in conferences for your key people after the acquisition. Many leading think tanks hold meetings at least once a year to encourage innovation. Give one a try.

VALUING AND COMBINING PATENTS AND TRADE SECRETS

In many high-tech acquisitions, a high percentage of the value comes from patents. What is the official definition of a *patent*?

Black's Law Dictionary defines a patent as "a grant of some privilege, property, or authority, made by government, or sovereign of a country to one or more individuals." In the normal business context, a patent is "a grant [by the government] to exclude others from making, using, or selling one's invention and includes the right to license others to make, use, or sell it."

In the United States, a patent is a right granted to an inventor by the U.S. government by an action of the U.S. Patent and

Trademark Office. A *design patent* covers a unique appearance or design in an article of manufacture. A *pioneer patent* covers a function never before performed and marking a distinct step in the progress of an art, as distinct from a mere improvement.

Why are patents valuable?

Some acquisitions are motivated primarily or even solely by a desire to buy the seller's patent rights. This may be in order to avoid patent infringement charges, to build a patent "portfolio," or to exploit synergies between the technology of the acquirer and that of the acquired company.

How are patents valued at the time of an acquisition?

Patent valuation is typically based on a measure of the future economic income that is expected to result from the use or licensing of the patent.[26] (Historical development cost approaches are generally not very reliable for patent valuation purposes, but they may be used in the absence of a predictable future income stream.)

Prior to closing, the buyer and seller may negotiate an explicit price for the patent or may set a price to license or sell the patent to a third party. When the invention underlying the patent is being fully exploited through license agreements with third parties, the valuation will be based on the expected future royalties to be received from licensing the patent over its remaining life. The expected future royalties should be reduced for applicable corporate income taxes and then discounted to present value.

This sounds good for newly developed, untested patents, but what happens if the patents are linked to existing products or services?

It depends on whether the patents will be used internally or externally.

When a patent is used internally to help produce a product, it may be valued according to the *relief-from-royalty* (or *avoided cost*) method. This approach begins with applying market royalty rates to the expected future stream of revenue from the products. The imputed royalty revenues are then reduced for corporate income taxes and discounted to present value. An alternative means of estimating the royalty is to estimate the after-tax cost savings as a percentage of revenues or the excess economic income as a percentage of revenues associated with the use of the patent.

When a patent is used externally to help sell a product, it may be valued according to the *income method*. This method attributes to the patent all or a share of the economic income from the expected future sales of relevant products and services (that is, the income realized above a fair return on all financial, tangible, and other intangible assets required to produce the products and services).

What happens to the value of a patent after its protection expires?

The income attributable to a given patent may extend well beyond its legal life. This value arises because the existence of a patent creates a business opportunity and advantage that does not cease with the loss of patent protection. Although the income stream from the patent may decline if competitors copy it, nonetheless additional patents may follow from and relate to the original product, thus extending the original life of an invention far beyond its origins.

How can patent license agreements be valued over time? Suppose an acquired invention turns out to be more valuable than anticipated prior to the merger?

Patent license agreements can be valued as though the holder of the license agreement owned the patent, less any payments made under the license agreement. Often, a corporation receives an exclusive right to an invention in return for helping the inventor perfect the invention, agreeing to develop products from the invention, and agreeing to compensate the inventor through lump-sum payments or through a modest royalty on future sales.

When, in retrospect, the invention turns out to be substantially more valuable than expected, the holder of the license agreement should recognize it as a valuable intangible asset (similar to a leaseholder asset).

Overall, patent valuation is rarely easy—either before the merger or after it. Patent portfolios, interrelationships among patent rights, and cross-licensing agreements can make patent valuation an intractable exercise. It is often impossible to identify the specific set of products and services arising from each individual patent right or group of patent rights, or to determine the percentage of economic income to allocate to each patent right. The simplest approach in such complex cases may be to group the entire set of patent rights and proprietary technology together and value it collectively, based on a single royalty rate applied to a declining percentage of a company's future revenue.

How are two companies' patents usually combined on a consolidated balance sheet?

The expenses associated with patents developed internally are generally not capitalized and, therefore, do not appear on the balance sheets prior to an acquisition or merger. Acquired patents do get capitalized. (For more on this general topic, see Chapter 5, "Integrating Financial and Tangible Resources.")

What happens if the buyer and seller had a license or cross-license agreement prior to the acquisition?

The acquisition consolidation will eliminate the intercompany royalty income and royalty expenses resulting from these agreements and may give rise to patent-related intangible assets on the balance sheet to the extent that the acquired firm was the licenser.

In the absence of a patent for a developing product, isn't secrecy important? In this regard, what is the official definition of *trade secret*, and to what extent are trade secrets protected by law?

The Uniform Trade Secrets Act, which has been adopted by a majority of states, defines trade secrets as:

> Information, including a formula, pattern, compilation, program, device, method, technique, or process, that: i. derives independent economic value, actual or potential, from not being generally known to, and not being readily ascertainable by proper means by, other persons who can obtain economic value from its disclosure or use, and ii. is the subject of efforts that are reasonable under the circumstances to maintain its secrecy.[27]

Trade secrets can include any confidential information, such as a company's business methods, future plans, or confidential customer information, but the secrets that are of most concern to high-technology companies are those that are related to scientific and technical information. These include technical know-how and experience, designs (including drawings), and the results of tests and studies. This definition of trade secrets was developed before the advent of "knowledge management" as a business process. As mentioned, knowledge management refers to management systems used for generating, transmitting, and receiving data and information.

How are trade secrets valued?

Trade secrets is a broad term for a variety of production-related intangible assets. (For a discussion of these, see Chapter 6, "Integrating Reputational and Other Intangible Resources.") Trade secrets never appear on a balance sheet and, although valuable, often are not explicitly valued for purchase price allocation purposes. Trade secrets can be valued, however.

Each type of trade secret should be identified and valued in a manner consistent with its nature. Thus, each specified technology (or combination of technologies) that is included in a specific product or service should be separately identified and valued, if possible. Trade secrets should be valued like patents, with slowly declining usefulness or with uncertain lives. Declining usefulness can be forecast as decreasing royalty rates and/or revenues over time. Uncertain lives can be forecast as cumulative probabilities of those rates and/or revenues.

Some trade secrets can be valued only by measuring the value of avoided R&D costs. This cost approach requires a careful analysis of how much money was invested to develop the technology and when it was invested—with downward adjustments for the accumulated costs of dead-end initiatives and for lower-than-expected demand.

How are two companies' trade secrets combined on a consolidated balance sheet?

The principles and practices are consistent with the previous discussion with regard to combining patents.

INTERNATIONAL CONSIDERATIONS

When integrating the technical aspects of management systems, how global should a company try to be?

For most companies, it makes sense to be entirely global in some respects and regional in others. For example, some companies may have an entirely global system for some aspects of logistics—with single, global pipelines for material-coding schemes, databases, real-time tracking, and/or internal control—but remain regionally based in other respects.

Tyco Toys Inc. tried for many years to run the logistics aspects of its European divisions from its Mount Laurel, New Jersey, headquarters. The growth of European sales (and the growth of logistical problems in Europe) finally convinced the company to centralize its management—and its logistics. At first, Tyco Toys attempted to use the same distribution software in Europe as it used in the United States, but this caused problems. Shipping from Tyco Toys' central distribution facility in Sint-Niklass, Belgium, took up to 45 days. The warehouse used computer software designed to handle orders from a few huge U.S. retailers rather than from thousands of smaller European shops, and the results were disastrous. Problems subsided after Tyco took a regional approach to the problem.

Could you cite some examples of multinational acquirers that have tried to install a single electronic network to link global operations?

Aluminum Company of America (Alcoa), a $23.5 billion multinational based in Pittsburgh, Pennsylvania, is the world's leading producer of primary aluminum, fabricated aluminum, and alumina and is active in all major aspects of the industry. It has 131,000 employees in 43 countries.[28] To help integrate its foreign operations, Alcoa has developed a global system for accounting. The system allows plants to look at one another's books on computer terminals and provides detailed cost benchmarks for specific items.

Another global integrator is Pilkington Plc, the U.K. glassmaker. After a period of diversification, Pilkington wound up with a far-flung research empire, with facilities located not only in the United Kingdom, but also in Germany and Italy. Researchers were devoting most of their time to what management calls "blue sky" research. The company installed a new computer system for centralized mathematical modeling and set up a central research laboratory. After some downsizing and a reorganization, it now has four business innovation groups covering the company's four main product areas (auto glass, building glass and other building products, float glass, and technical glasses). As a result, innovation at Pilkington has sped up over the past decade. As of late 2005, Pilkington is recognized as the world's technological leader in glass and spends £29 million a year on R&D.

APPENDIX 9–A

IT Buzzwords for the Twenty-First Century

Business intelligence is key business information used for critical decisions.

Chief knowledge officer (CKO) is a senior management position responsible for the development, protection, and transfer of a company's *intellectual capital.* Alternative terms are *chief learning officer, director of intellectual capital,* and *director of intellectual asset management.*

Client-server networks are computer networks that have multiple "clients" (computers) and dedicated "servers" (computers that store data and files for other computers).

Data warehousing is storing information in a central place for companywide access.

Data mining is analyzing warehoused data to find patterns. For example, through data mining, retail stores can obtain profiles of customers and their buying patterns, and supermarkets can analyze their sales and the effect of advertising on sales.

Electronic data interchange (EDI) is a type of technology that allows data to move from one system to another. It is used in a variety of industries, including manufacturing, retailing, and transportation.

Explicit knowledge is knowledge, information, or data that is written down and/or codified.

Extranets are intranets of customers and suppliers that are linked through the Internet. (For more on this subject, see Chapter 10, "Fulfilling Commitments to Customers and Suppliers.")

Groupware is software that allows people to access the same information simultaneously.

Integrated software is a single software system that can be used for a variety of functions, including design, production, supply, and financial controls. It contrasts with the "best-of-breed" approach, in which different systems are interfaced or used separately.

Intellectual capital is the full spectrum of a company's intangibles, including, for example, its databases, software, manuals, trademarks, and organizational structure and the expertise and abilities of its employees. In the traditional terms of appraisal, it is closer to the broad concept of "trade name" than to the narrow concept of "intellectual property."

Intranets are internal Web sites. They are linked by *network computers (NCs)*.

Knowledge management is the management of a firm's *intellectual capital*.

Knowledge mining, a step beyond data mining, is the transformation of business information into *business intelligence*.

Local area networks (LANs) are electronic networks at a single location. They can connect to one another via wide-area networks (WANs).

Learning organizations are those that have good *knowledge management*.

Open-market innovation means collaborating with outsiders, including customers, vendors, and even competitors. Companies treat innovations as confidential and proprietary only in their areas of comparative advantage.[29]

Network computers (NCs), also known as *network appliances, thin clients,* or *network terminals,* are a new hybrid with features of the old mainframe systems and the newer *client-server networks.* In a mainframe system, a central processing unit (CPU), a "smart" computer, is linked with many "dumb" computer terminals. In client-server networks, all the linked units are smart. The NC hybrid is like the old mainframe system, but the terminals are not completely dumb. The advantage of the NCs is that the units are less expensive and less complex than in the client-server network.

Open systems (as opposed to "proprietary" systems such as Java, UNIX, and NT) are systems using hardware and software built from published specifications that anyone can copy. Open systems enable companies to choose among multiple IT suppliers.

Platforms are starting points for innovation. A platform is one or more technical elements (for example, a computer chip, a computer, an operating system, and/or a software package) used in creating new products.

RFID means radio frequency identification. This is a new technology used in retailing.

Supercomputers are computers with substantial amounts of physical memory that are composed of multiple central processing units (CPUs).

Tacit knowledge is knowledge that is understood, but not articulated in writing or, in some cases, speech.

Virtual factories are electronic networks that enable several modern manufacturing miracles. Through such networks, multiple factories can operate in unison, as if in a single location; dissimilar computers can exchange information (about inventory levels, for example); different computer-assisted design (CAD) systems can collaborate on designs; and multiple suppliers can bid on jobs using the same parameters. For example, BMW has initiated an international system of linked plants, particularly for easily transportable parts with high "tool" (manufacturing) costs.

Virtual machines are compact pieces of software code. A virtual machine can be written to support a device from any manufacturer. The user downloads a browser that can connect to whatever software, data, and information the user needs. Virtual machines are used in *intranet systems.*

Wide-area networks (WANs) are computer networks that extend beyond a single location or local area network (LAN).

APPENDIX 9 – B
Integration Planning Worksheets

Key Business Process: Network Integration (Data/Voice/Access)						
Primary Integration Activities	Priority	Tasks/Subtasks	Task Owner	Prerequisites	Required Tactical Data	Relevant Strategic Questions
Network element consolidation • Contracts • Equipment	• Day 1 • 100 days • 6 months • Year 1 • Eventually	1.				
		2.				
		3.				
		4.				
		5.				
		6.				
		7.				
		8.				
		9.				
		10.				

(Continued)

Key Business Process: Network Integration (Data/Voice/Access)						
Primary Integration Activities	Priority	Tasks/Subtasks	Task Owner	Prerequisites	Required Tactical Data	Relevant Strategic Questions
Network access consolidation						
• Radio	• Day 1	1.				
• Fiber	• 100 days	2.				
• Leased circuits	• 6 months	3.				
	• 100 days	4.				
	• Eventually	5.				
		6.				
		7.				
		8.				
		9.				
		10.				

(Continued)

Key Business Process: Network Integration (Data/Voice/Access)							
Primary Integration Activities	Priority	Tasks/Subtasks	Task Owner	Prerequisites	Required Tactical Data	Relevant Strategic Questions	
Interconnect consolidation	• Day 1 • 100 days • 6 months • Year 1 • Eventually	1					
		2.					
		3.					
		4.					
		5.					
		6.					
		7.					
		8.					
		9.					
		10.					

(Continued)

Key Business Process: Network Integration (Data/Voice/Access)						
Primary Integration Activities	Priority	Tasks/Subtasks	Task Owner	Prerequisites	Required Tactical Data	Relevant Strategic Questions
Element security	• Day 1 • 100 days • 6 months • Year 1 • Eventually	1				
		2.				
		3.				
		4.				
		5.				
		6.				
		7.				
		8.				
		9.				
		10.				

Source: E-Know, Arlington, Virginia 2005.

Key Business Process: Systems Integration (Applications)						
Primary Integration Activities	Priority	Tasks/Subtasks	Task Owner	Prerequisites	Required Tactical Data	Relevant Strategic Questions
• Network management • Billing • Provisioning	• Day 1 • 100 days • 6 months • Year 1 • Eventually	1.				
		2.				
		3.				
		4.				
		5.				
		6.				
		7.				
		8.				
		9.				
		10.				

(Continued)

Key Business Process: Systems Integration (Applications)

Primary Integration Activities	Priority	Tasks/Subtasks	Task Owner	Prerequisites	Required Tactical Data	Relevant Strategic Questions
		11.				
		12.				
		13.				
		14.				
		15.				
		16.				
		17.				
		18.				
		19.				
		20.				
		21.				
		22.				
		23.				
		24.				
		25.				

(Continued)

Key Business Process: Systems Integration (Applications)						
Primary Integration Activities	Priority	Tasks/Subtasks	Task Owner	Prerequisites	Required Tactical Data	Relevant Strategic Questions
		26.				
		27.				
		28.				
		29.				
		30.				
		31.				
		32.				
		33.				
		34.				
		35.				
		36.				
		37.				
		38.				

Source: E-Know, Arlington, Virginia 2005.

Key Business Process: Network Operations Integration

Primary Integration Activities	Priority	Tasks/Subtasks	Task Owner	Prerequisites	Required Tactical Data	Relevant Strategic Questions
• Field operations	• Day 1	1.				
• NOC	• 100 days	2.				
• TAC	• 6 months	3.				
• Provisioning	• Year 1	4.				
• Technical training	• Eventually	5.				
• NOC certification		6.				
		7.				
		8.				
		9.				
		10.				

(Continued)

Key Business Process: Network Operations Integration						
Primary Integration Activities	Priority	Tasks/Subtasks	Task Owner	Prerequisites	Required Tactical Data	Relevant Strategic Questions
		11.				
		12.				
		13.				
		14.				
		15.				
		16.				
		17.				
		18.				
		19.				
		20.				
		21.				
		22.				
		23.				
		24.				
		25.				

(Continued)

Key Business Process: Network Operations Integration

Primary Integration Activities	Priority	Tasks/Subtasks	Task Owner	Prerequisites	Required Tactical Data	Relevant Strategic Questions
		26.				
		27.				
		28.				
		29.				
		30.				
		31.				
		32.				
		33.				
		34.				
		35.				

Source: E-Know, Arlington, Virginia 2005.

APPENDIX 9 – C

Integration Planning Worksheet for IT

Key Business Process: Enterprise Operations Integration/Information Technology						
Primary Integration Activities	Priority	Tasks/Subtasks	Task Owner	Prerequisites	Required Tactical Data	Relevant Strategic Questions
E-mail	• Day 1 • 100 days • 6 months • Year 1 • Eventually	1.				
		2.				
		3.				
		4.				
		5.				
		6.				
		7.				
		8.				
		9.				
		10.				

(Continued)

Key Business Process: Enterprise Operations Integration/Information Technology						
Primary Integration Activities	Priority	Tasks/Subtasks	Task Owner	Prerequisites	Required Tactical Data	Relevant Strategic Questions
Phone systems	• Day 1	1.				
	• 100 days	2.				
	• 6 months	3.				
	• Year 1	4.				
	• Eventually	5.				
		6.				
		7.				
		8.				
		9.				
		10.				

(Continued)

Key Business Process: Enterprise Operations Integration/Information Technology

Primary Integration Activities	Priority	Tasks/Subtasks	Task Owner	Prerequisites	Required Tactical Data	Relevant Strategic Questions
Voice mail	• Day 1	1.				
	• 100 days	2.				
	• 6 months	3.				
	• Year 1	4.				
	• Eventually	5.				
		6.				
		7.				
		8.				
		9.				
		10.				

(Continued)

336

Key Business Process: Enterprise Operations Integration/Information Technology

Primary Integration Activities	Priority	Tasks/Subtasks	Task Owner	Prerequisites	Required Tactical Data	Relevant Strategic Questions
File severs	• Day 1	1.				
	• 100 days	2.				
	• 6 months	3.				
	• Year 1	4.				
	• Eventually	5.				
		6.				
		7.				
		8.				
		9.				
		10.				

(Continued)

Key Business Process: Enterprise Operations Integration/Information Technology						
Primary Integration Activities	Priority	Tasks/Subtasks	Task Owner	Prerequisites	Required Tactical Data	Relevant Strategic Questions
Desktop applications	• Day 1 • 100 days • 6 months • Year 1 • Eventually	1.				
		2.				
		3.				
		4.				
		5.				
		6.				
		7.				
		8.				
		9.				
		10.				

(Continued)

Key Business Process: Enterprise Operations Integration/Information Technology						
Primary Integration Activities	Priority	Tasks/Subtasks	Task Owner	Prerequisites	Required Tactical Data	Relevant Strategic Questions
PC hardware	• Day 1 • 100 days • 6 months • Year 1 • Eventually	1.				
		2.				
		3.				
		4.				
		5.				
		6.				
		7.				
		8.				
		9.				
		10.				

(Continued)

Key Business Process: Enterprise Operations Integration/Information Technology

Primary Integration Activities	Priority	Tasks/Subtasks	Task Owner	Prerequisites	Required Tactical Data	Relevant Strategic Questions
Domain name	• Day 1	1.				
	• 100 days	2.				
	• 6 months	3.				
	• Year 1	4.				
	• Eventually	5.				
		6.				
		7.				
		8.				
		9.				
		10.				

(Continued)

Key Business Process: Enterprise Operations Integration/Information Technology						
Primary Integration Activities	Priority	Tasks/Subtasks	Task Owner	Prerequisites	Required Tactical Data	Relevant Strategic Questions
User IDs	• Day 1	1.				
	• 100 days	2.				
	• 6 months	3.				
	• Year 1	4.				
	• Eventually	5.				
		6.				
		7.				
		8.				
		9.				
		10.				

(Continued)

Key Business Process: Enterprise Operations Integration/Information Technology

Primary Integration Activities	Priority	Tasks/Subtasks	Task Owner	Prerequisites	Required Tactical Data	Relevant Strategic Questions
Security	• Day 1 • 100 days • 6 months • Year 1 • Eventually	1.				
		2.				
		3.				
		4.				
		5.				
		6.				
		7.				
		8.				
		9.				
		10.				

(Continued)

Key Business Process: Enterprise Operations Integration/Information Technology

Primary Integration Activities	Priority	Tasks/Subtasks	Task Owner	Prerequisites	Required Tactical Data	Relevant Strategic Questions
Network connectivity	• Day 1 • 100 days • 6 months • Year 1 • Eventually	1.				
		2.				
		3.				
		4.				
		5.				
		6.				
		7.				
		8.				
		9.				
		10.				

Source: E-Know, Arlington, Virginia 2005.

Information Security Program Elements

Establishing an effective information security program or merging programs requires attention to the following program elements and the associated metrics. These metrics involve several implicit assumptions about what the board and executive management should do in designing and implementing program, the extent of which will be influenced by the size and complexity of the organization.

- First, explicitly identify information assets and functions that are critical to the success of the organization.
- Second, assess the risks to which this information is potentially exposed, with respect to confidentiality, integrity, availability, and privacy.
- Third, establish acceptable thresholds for those risks.
- Fourth, identify, implement information security strategies, policies, and controls involving people, process, and technology to mitigate known risks and maintain these risks at acceptable levels.

Below is a list of metrics suggested for a company including a small or mid-sized enterprise (SME) to use in connection with its information security responsibilities. The baseline metrics are indicated with a (B). Most metrics in this document are expressed as a percentage where a *higher value is desirable*. The exceptions involve: (1) metrics that are better understood when they are expressed such that a lower percentage value is desirable, and (2) those that are expressed as a number rather than a percentage. For metrics that are an exception a bold, underlined comment appears.

Information elements and supporting metrics for board oversight

1. *Oversee Risk Management and Compliance Programs Pertaining to Information Security (e.g., Sarbanes-Oxley, HIPAA, Gramm-Leach-Bliley, etc.)*
   1.1 (B) Percentage of key information <u>assets</u> for which a comprehensive strategy has been implemented to

> mitigate information security risks as necessary and to maintain these risks within acceptable thresholds

1.2 Percentage of key organizational <u>functions</u> for which a comprehensive strategy has been implemented to mitigate information security risks as necessary and to maintain these risks within acceptable thresholds

2. *(B) Percentage of key external requirements for which the organization has been deemed by objective audit or other means to be in compliance*

3. *Approve and Adopt Broad Information Security Program Principles and Approve Assignment of Key Managers Responsible for Information Security*

   3.1 Percentage of Information Security Program Principles for which approved policies and controls have been implemented by management

   3.2 (B) (SME) Percentage of key information security management roles for which responsibilities, accountabilities, and authority are assigned and required skills identified

4. *Strive to Protect the Interests of all Stakeholders Dependent on Information Security*

   4.1 Percentage of board meetings and/or designated committee meetings for which information security is on the agenda

   4.2 (B) Percentage of security incidents that did not cause damage, compromise, or loss beyond established thresholds to the organization's assets, functions, or stakeholders

   4.3 Estimated damage or loss in dollars resulting from all security incidents

   (A lower value is desirable)

5. *Review Information Security Policies Regarding Strategic Partners and Other Third Parties*

   5.1 (B) Percentage of strategic partner and other third-party relationships for which information security requirements have been implemented in the agreements with these parties

6. *Strive to Ensure Business Continuity*

   6.1 (B) Percentage of organizational units with an established business continuity plan

7. *Review Provisions for Internal and External Audits of the Information Security Program*
   7.1 (B) Percentage of required internal and external audits completed and reviewed by the Board
   7.2 (B) Percentage of audit findings that have been resolved
8. *Collaborate with Management to Specify the Information Security Metrics to be Reported to the Board*

INFORMATION SECURITY PROGRAM ELEMENTS AND SUPPORTING METRICS FOR MANAGEMENT

Below is a list of metrics suggested for management use in connection with its information security responsibilities.

1. *Establish Information Security Management Policies and Controls and Monitor Compliance*
   1.1 (B) Percentage of Information Security Program Elements for which approved policies and controls are currently operational
   1.2 (B) (SME) Percentage of staff assigned responsibilities for information security policies and controls who have acknowledged accountability for their responsibilities in connection with those policies and controls
   1.3 (B) Percentage of information security policy compliance reviews with no violations noted
   1.4 Percentage of business unit heads and senior managers who have implemented operational procedures to ensure compliance with approved information security policies and controls
2. *Assign Information Security Roles, Responsibilities, Required Skills, and Enforce Role-based Information Access Privileges*
   2.1 (B) (SME) Percentage of new employees hired this reporting period who satisfactorily completed security awareness training before being granted network access
   2.2 (B) (SME) Percentage of employees who have satisfactorily completed periodic security awareness refresher training as required by policy

2.3 Percentage of position descriptions that define the information security roles, responsibilities, skills, and certifications for:
   a. Security Managers and Administrators
   b. IT personnel
   c. General staff system users

2.4 Percentage of job performance reviews that include evaluation of information security responsibilities and information security policy compliance

2.5 (B) (SME) Percentage of user roles, systems, and applications that comply with the separation of duties principle

2.6 (B) Percentage of individuals with access to security software who are trained and authorized security administrators

2.7 (B) Percentage of individuals who are able to assign security privileges for systems and applications who are trained and authorized security administrators

2.8 Percentage of individuals whose access privileges have been reviewed this reporting period
   a. (B) (SME) Employees with high-level system and application privileges
   b. (B) (SME) Terminated employees

2.9 Percentage of users who have undergone background checks

3. *Assess Information Risks, Establish Risk Thresholds and Actively Manage Risk Mitigation*

3.1 (B) (SME) Percentage of critical information assets and information-dependent functions for which some form of risk assessment has been performed and documented as required by policy

3.2 Percentage of critical assets and functions for which the cost of compromise (loss, damage, disclosure, disruption in access to) has been quantified

3.3 (B) (SME) Percentage of identified risks that have a defined risk mitigation plan against which status is reported in accordance with policy

4. *Ensure Implementation of Information Security Requirements for Strategic Partners and Other Third Parties*

    4.1   Percentage of known information security risks that are related to third-party relationships

A lower value is desirable.

    4.2   (B) (SME) Percentage of critical information assets or functions for which access by third-party personnel is not allowed

    4.3   (B) (SME) Percentage of third-party personnel with current information access privileges who have been reviewed by designated authority to have continued need for access in accordance with policy

    4.4   (B) (SME) Percentage of systems with critical information assets or functions for which electronic connection by third-party systems is not allowed

    4.5   Percentage of security incidents that involved third-party personnel

A lower value is desirable.

    4.6   Percentage of third-party agreements that include/demonstrate external verification of policies and procedures

    4.7   (B) (SME) Percentage of third-party relationships that have been reviewed for compliance with information security requirements

    4.8   Percentage of out-of-compliance review findings that have been corrected since the last review

5. *Identify and Classify Information Assets*

    5.1   (B) (SME) Percentage of information assets that have been reviewed and classified by the designated owner in accordance with the classification scheme established by policy

    5.2   Percentage of information assets with defined access privileges that have been assigned based on role and in accordance with policy

    5.3   Percentage of scheduled asset inventories that occurred on time according to policy

6. *Implement and Test Business Continuity Plans*
   6.1 (B) Percentage of organizational units with a documented business continuity plan for which specific responsibilities have been assigned
   6.2 (B) Percentage of business continuity plans that have been reviewed, exercised/tested, and updated in accordance with policy
7. *Approve Information Systems Architecture during Acquisition, Development, Operations, and Maintenance*
   7.1 Percentage of information security risks related to systems architecture identified in the most recent risk assessment that have been adequately mitigated
   7.2 (B) Percentage of system architecture changes (additions, modifications, or deletions) that were reviewed for security impacts, approved by appropriate authority, and documented via change request forms
   7.3 Percentage of critical information assets or functions residing on systems that are currently in compliance with the approved systems architecture
8. *Protect the Physical Environment*
   8.1 (B) (SME) Percentage of critical organizational information assets and functions that have been reviewed from the perspective of physical risks such as controlling physical access and physical protection of backup media
   8.2 Percentage of critical organizational information assets and functions exposed to physical risks for which risk mitigation actions have been implemented
   8.3 (B) (SME) Percentage of critical assets that have been reviewed from the perspective of environmental risks such as temperature, fire, flooding, etc.
   8.4 Percentage of servers in locations with controlled physical access
9. *Ensure Regular Internal and External Audits of the Information Security Program with Timely Follow-up*
   9.1 (B) Percentage of information security requirements from applicable laws and regulations that are included in the internal/external audit program and schedule

9.2 (B) Percentage of information security audits
     conducted in compliance with the approved
     internal/external audit program and schedule

9.3 (B) Percentage of management actions in response
     to audit findings/recommendations that were
     implemented as agreed as to timeliness and
     completeness

10. *Collaborate with Security Staff to Specify the Information
     Security Metrics to be Reported to Management*

Note: A carefully chosen set of information security metrics for
reports to management of information security status will clarify to
operational units what management considers important and the
topics on which management wishes to be informed. Management
can choose its set of information security metrics from those defined
above and/or create others considered appropriate for the organization. For large enterprises, it is assumed the metrics will be calculated
by various units of the organization and aggregated at various levels
up to the entire enterprise. Each metric is reported for the current and
last n reporting periods so trends and changes are visible (such as
$n = 3$ if quarterly reports are generated, to provide an annual perspective). For percentage metrics, the numerator and denominator as well
as the resulting percentage should be reported. Management should
specify reporting frequency and target values for the chosen metrics.

For more guidance on information security in general, see:

Julia H. Allen, Governing for Enterprise Security
     (Carnegie-Mellon, 2005), http://www.sei.cmu.edu/
     publications/documents/05.reports/05tn023.html.
Lawrence A. Gordon, Martin P. Loeb, and Tashfeen Sohail,
     "A Framework for Using Insurance for Cyber-Risk
     Management," *Communications of the ACM*, Vol. 46,
     No. 3, March 2003.
"Change and Patch Management Controls: Critical for
     Organizational Success," Institute of Internal Auditors,
     2005.

Source: Corporate Information Security Working Group,
"Report of the Best Practices and Metrics Teams," presented to the
Subcommittee on Technology, Information Policy, Intergovernmental
Relations, and the Census, Government Reform Committee, Nov. 17, 2004.

N O T E S

1 Jon Swartz and Michelle Kessler, "History Not on Side of Tech Titans' Merger," *USA Today*, Mar. 19, 2002.

2 When Compaq CEO Michael Capella left HP-Compaq to lead WorldCom (renamed MCI, after a previous acquisition target), people said that he went "out of the frying pan into the fire." Now, in late 2005, after trials by fire in technology integration, MCI may well be acquired as part of a large-scale consolidation in the network service provider industry. Jay E. Pultz, "The AT&T and MCI Acquisitions Will Shape the Future of the U.S. Network Services Market," *USA Today*, Apr. 28, 2005.

3 Oracle paid $24 per share, which was 60 percent higher than the closing price of PeopleSoft the day before Oracle began bidding. (As is typical during protracted tender offers, the price of PeopleSoft shares dropped as the bid wore on.)

4 This list is based on one provided by WashingtonTechmology.com, vol. 20, no. 15, Aug. 1, 2005.

5 The author serves on the advisory board of E-Know, Inc., Arlington, Virginia (eknow.com). E-Know has a technology that can be used for integrating companies following a merger. Other companies offering merger-focused technology include Alchemy (alchemy.com) and TSX (tsx.com).

6 The hierarchy of data, information, and knowledge appears in many academic papers on the subject. The one most commonly cited is M. H. Zach, "Managing Codified Knowledge," *Sloan Management Review*, Summer 1999.

7 See, for example, Caroline Sagis Roussel, "An Analysis of KM in a Merger," IESEC School of Management, Lille, France, Mar. 18, 2004.

8 Cited in "Companies Turn to Knowledge Management to Solve Information Overload," *TMC Net News*, July 13, 2005, http://eb.eiu.com.

9 This list is from Eric Schaffer, *Institutionalization of Usability: A Step-by-Step Guide* (New York: Addison-Wesley, 2004).

10 Jeff Spath and Arnis Judzis, "Promoting R&D in Management and Information," JPT Online, February 2005.

11 According to Stephen H. Kan, *Metrics and Moles in Software Quality Engineering*, 2d ed. (New York: Addison-Wesley, 2002), the fix response time metric is usually calculated as mean time of all problems from open to closed. If there are data points with extreme values, medians should be used instead of means. Such cases could occur when there are less severe problems for which customers may

have been satisfied with the circumvention and didn't demand a fix. Therefore, the problem may have remained open for a long time in the tracking report. The authors note that there is a difference between fix responsiveness and short fix response time. From the customer's perspective, the use of averages may mask individual differences. The important elements of fix responsiveness are customer expectations, the agreed-to fix time, and the ability to meet one's commitment to the customer. The metric for IBM Rochester's fix responsiveness is operationalized as percentage of delivered fixes meeting committed dates to customers. Another metric is percent of delinquent fixes. A percentage improvement in response time indicates the percentage (down to zero) by which response time decreased.

12 See Douglas Reid, David Boussiere, and Kathleen Greenaway, "Alliance Foundation Issues for Knowledge-Based Enterprises," Queens University at Kingston, April 2000.

13 See Kathryn R. Harrigan, "Joint Ventures, Alliances, and Corporate Strategies" (Frederick, Maryland: Beard Books, 2003). This reprint of a classic study analyzed 492 specific joint ventures and 392 other cooperative arrangements in 1985 and concluded that arrangements are relatively unstable and temporary.

14 According to the 2005/2006 *IS Spending and Technology Trends* 2005/2006 study from Computer Economics, Inc. (www. computereconomics.com), the percentages of IT spending in relation to revenue range between about 1 to 3 percent. Figures in 2005 were 0.9 percent at the 25th quartile, 1.7 percent at the median, and 3.2 percent at the 75th percentile.

15 Christopher Duthoit, Ralf Dreischmeier, Antoine Gourevitch, and Mathieu Mnegaux, "Clusters and Nuggets: Mastering Postmerger IT Integration," Boston Consulting Group, July 1, 2004 (white paper).

16 In 2005, the consulting firm Bain & Company published a list of the most popular "management tools." Some of the tools are purely philosophical. Some, however, are linked to technology and/or systems. Therefore, it is relevant to list them here, putting asterisks by the tools with the closest association with information technology. The tools are: activity-based management*, balanced scorecard, benchmarking, business process reengineering, change management, core competencies, customer relationship management*, customer segmentation, economic value-added analysis, growth strategies, knowledge management*, loyalty management, mass customization, mission and vision statement, offshoring, open-market innovation*, outsourcing, price optimization models*, radio frequency identification (RFID)*, scenario and contingency planning, Six Sigma*, strategic alliances, strategic planning, supply chain management*, and total quality management*.

17   In August 2005, the Department of Homeland Security announced that it would begin consolidating $6 billion worth of information technology acquisitions into two programs with the purpose of creating a departmentwide IT infrastructure. Addressing industry representatives in Washington, DHS Chief Procurement Officer Greg Rothwell said that the consolidation will create a support services program known as EAGLE and a commodities initiative called FirstSource. The programs will bring the eight procurement shops in DHS under one roof.

18   This discussion is based on a paper found at http://wp.bitpipe.com/resource/org.

19   Eric Marks, "Mergers and Acquisitions: Assessing the Role of Technology," October 20, 2000. Mr. Marks is President and CEO of AgilePath Corporation, a service-oriented architecture (SOA) and Web Services consulting firm based in Newburyport, MA.

20   Swartz and Kessler, "History Not on Side of Tech Titans' Merger."

21   This transaction is cited in Jerry Collins, *Good to Great* (New York: Collins, 2001), a book detailing how only a few good companies have become great, and in Robert Bruner, *Deals from Hell: M&A Lessons That Rise Above the Ashes* (New York: John Wiley & Sons, 2005).

22   Larry Downes, quoted in Swartz and Kessler, "History Not on Side of Tech Titans' Merger."

23   A useful observation appears in Henry W. Chesebrough and David J. Teed, "When Is Virtual Virtuous? Organizing for Innovation," *Harvard Business Review*, January–February 1997, pp. 65ff: "Some innovations are autonomous; they can be pursued independently from other innovations. . . . Some innovations are fundamentally systemic—that is, their benefits can be realized only in conjunction with related, complementary innovations."

24   Norman Augustine, "The Latest Chapter," *Across the Board* (interview), June 1996.

25   Collins and Porras, *Good to Great*, p. 23.

26   Two applicable court cases outlining some of the important factors to consider in patent valuation are *Panduit Corp. v. Stahlin Bros. Fibre Words, Inc.* (1978), 575 F. 2d. 1152 and *Georgia-Pacific Corp. v. U.S. Plywood-Champion Papers, Inc.* (1970), 318 F. Supp. 1120, modified and affirmed (1971) 496 F 2d. 295. See also Miguel Figuera v. The United States, filed in the U.S. Court of Federal Claims No. 01457C, June 2005.

27 Uniform Trade Secrets Act, Section 1ff., 14 U.L.A. 541. The UTSA has been adopted by the majority of states. States that have not adopted the act tend to rely on judicial precedent, which defines a trade secret more narrowly as "any formal pattern, device, or compilation of information which is used in one's business, and which gives one an opportunity to obtain an advantage over competitors who do not know or use it." See *Rector-Phillips-Morse, Inc.* v. *Vroman* (1973), 489 S.W. 2nd 1,3; and *Ashland Management, Inc.* v. *Janien* (1993), 624 N.E.2d at 1013.

28 Alcoa has been a relatively active acquirer since the 1960s, when it used acquisitions to diversify. (The author's father, Stanley Foster Reed, was a consultant to Alcoa in the 1970s during its return to its core industry.)

29 See C.K. Prahalad and Venkat Ramaswamy, *The Future of Competition: Co-Creating Unique Value with Customers* (Boston: Harvard Business School Press, 2004).

Integrating Corporate Responsibilities—Fulfilling Stakeholder Commitments

The remedy for unpredictability, for the chaotic uncertainty of the future, is contained in the faculty to make and keep promises.

Hannah Arendt, *The Human Condition*

INTRODUCTION AND ACKNOWLEDGMENTS

Each company comes to a merger with a unique set of promises. Some of them are in the fine print of contracts made with individuals and groups. Others are in the bolder print of mission statements or advertisements. Some are unwritten yet understood. During a merger, many of these promises are repeated or even fused in the public statements of the merging companies. After a merger, it is time to take stock of all these promises to make sure they are fulfilled—hence this book's final section on integrating corporate responsibilities.

We have now come full circle. In Part 1, we got our bearings, asking what M&A integration is, why integration is important, and how companies can plan and communicate their integration efforts. In Parts 2 and 3, we saw how companies can integrate their various resources and processes.

Here, in Part 4, we return to fundamentals as we look at integration from the perspective of stakeholders, asking what integration can and should mean to customers, suppliers, shareholders, bondholders, lenders, employees, and communities of merged companies. These corporate constituents want and deserve assurance that a company will continue to honor past commitments—from respecting the stipulations of a signed contract to meeting the unspoken expectations of a customary arrangement.

Chapter 10, "Fulfilling Commitments to Customers and Suppliers," guides companies in preserving good relations with their customers and suppliers. Our expert on customer relations was Thomas G. McGonagle, senior vice president, Vistar Corporation. The legal advisor for this chapter was Neil Falis, partner, Kilpatrick Stockton, LLP, Atlanta, Georgia.

For supplier relations expertise, we turned to Jonathan Casher, chairman, RECAP, Inc., a financial management consulting business based in Oak Ridge, New Jersey. This chapter received helpful review from two experts in global business relationships: Hugh Latif, chairman of Hugh Latif & Associates, Toronto, Canada, and Richard Zeif, an international negotiations consultant affiliated with the International Federation of Training and Development Organizations.

Chapter 11, "Fulfilling Commitments to Shareholders, Bondholders, and Lenders," explores the legal and ethical obligations that a company has to its financial stakeholders, particularly long-term shareholders. This chapter drew on the expertise of shareholder activist Nell Minow, founder and editor, *The Corporate Library*, as well as investor relations expert William Mahoney of West Chester, Pennsylvania. Howard Sherman, chief operating officer, Governance Metrics International, New York, was a primary source of wisdom on the international aspects of this chapter.

Chapter 12, "Fulfilling Commitments to Employees and Communities," offers information and advice to companies on maintaining and improving their ties to employees and communities. Frank Sonnenberg, founding member of Sonnenberg, Haviland & Partners, Inc., in Ridgewood, New Jersey, shared insights on trust and related issues. Stephen B. Young, global executive director, Caux Round Table, Minneapolis, Minnesota, provided insights into the use of the Caux principles. George Lumsby, diversity director, New York State Society of Human Resource Managers, reviewed the original draft of this chapter, and provided helpful commentary. Perspectives on change management and investment in human capital came from James Hatch, a principal with PricewaterhouseCoopers in Saratoga, New York.

Fulfilling Commitments to Customers and Suppliers

If we don't take care of our customers, someone else will.

Unknown

INTRODUCTION

"Under new management." Whether they are printed in a billion-dollar merger press release or scrawled on a dollar-store door, these words raise more fears than hopes in most customers and suppliers. So how can a new company make sure that its "new management" will be good news from the start?

We provide some answers here. The first part of this chapter shows managers how to be good "suppliers" to their customers, and the second part shows them how to be good "customers" to their suppliers. Both sections will explore the "three Cs"—commitment, communications, and continuity—with close attention to post-merger pricing, quality, and outsourcing. In closing, this chapter will take a brief look at emerging technological and global issues for customer-supplier relations "under new management."

COMMITMENTS TO CUSTOMERS

What commitments to customers will a company typically inherit after a merger?

As mentioned earlier, every company comes to a merger with a unique set of promises that it has made to various individuals and groups, including customers. Some of these promises are written, some unwritten. Some are contractual (enforceable by law), some "covenantal" in nature.[1] As companies merge, they must merge these promises, and the first step is to define what they are.

To fulfill commitments to wholesalers and distributors (who buy directly and in bulk), a first step for the integration team will be to look over all the legal agreements the company has inherited along with these customers. For each product or service, the company will need to know *how much* each of the merging companies has promised to provide to *what customers* at *what price* for *what period of time* and *under what conditions* (delivery, servicing, and so forth). It will also want to know about any *exemptions* or *waivers* that may apply to those conditions.

To fulfill commitments to retail customers (who buy indirectly and in small quantities), the integration team should note all promises the company has published to the general public, such as slogans used in space ads—and recommend ways to fulfill them, so that there is no inconsistency between the company's words and actions. If a company's words and actions do not match, one or the other needs to change. More generally, managers might consider a list that appears in the "Stakeholders" section of the Caux Round Table's *Principles for Business*. This document is the consensus of leading business executives from the United States, Europe, and Japan, who meet regularly to discuss global business ethics. Here below is the "Customers" section of the stakeholder list (with our postmerger "checkpoints" added in italics).

CUSTOMERS

We believe in treating all customers with dignity, irrespective of whether they purchase our products and services directly from us or otherwise acquire them in the market. We therefore have a responsibility to:

- provide our customers with the highest quality products and services consistent with their requirements;
   Checkpoints: What quality programs does each merging company have in place? Should these programs be merged? If so, who will do this, how, and by when?

- treat our customers fairly in all aspects of our business transactions, including a high level of service and remedies for their dissatisfaction;

> *Checkpoints: What standards of fairness does each company have with regard to customers? Will these standards be reconciled? If so, who will do this how and by when?*

- make every effort to ensure that the health and safety of our customers, as well as the quality of their environment, will be sustained or enhanced by our products and service.

  Checkpoints: What product health and safety standards does each of the merging companies have? Will these standards be reconciled? If so, who will do this, how, and by when?

- ensure respect for human dignity in products offered, marketing, and advertising, and respect the integrity of the culture of our customers.

  Checkpoints: Is human dignity a distinct value in both of the merging companies? How can managers work to ensure that it will be? What are the cultures of the customers in the newly combined company? How can managers show respect for them?

  Overall: How does the compensation of managers and employees reward behavior that accomplishes all the goals listed here? For example, do incentives for salespeople reward customer retention and satisfaction?

Why is it so important to fulfill commitments to existing customers after a merger?

First of all, there is the ethical dimension. Promise keeping is one of the oldest and most basic moral principles known to humankind. Also, there is the legal dimension: keeping promises is a good way to prevent lawsuits. Last, but not least, there is also the economic dimension. Customers are a key driver of a company's economic value, and current customers are worth more than future ones.

Why do you say that existing customers are more valuable than new ones?

It is usually easier and less expensive to maintain an existing relationship than to attract a new one. Business appraisers acknowledge this fact when allocating the purchase price to various financial, tangible, and intangible assets. When allocating a portion of the price to intangibles, they allocate it to present and future customers differently. As stated in Chapter 6, GAAP allocates a portion of the purchase price to an *acquired customer list,* but treats *potential future customers* as part of goodwill. Statement 142 gives this example:

a direct mail company acquired a customer list and expects that it will be able to derive benefit from the information on the acquired customer list for at least one year but no more than three years.

- The customer list is amortized over management's best estimate of its useful life.
- By contrast, the expectation of *future* customer relationships becomes part of goodwill.

And more generally (beyond postmerger price allocation), values assigned to present relationships are much higher than those assigned to future relationships. This is true whether the values are derived using an income approach or a replacement cost approach. Appraisers use an income approach to value customer relationships when they can identify income directly attributable to customers, and a replacement cost approach when they cannot. For replacement cost, they assume that the amount of money a business is willing to spend to attract a new customer equals the value of an existing customer. Similarly, in allocating marketing and selling expenses, the income and/or replacement cost attributable to present relationships is often higher than that attributable to future ones.

Take, for example, the classic rule of diminishing costs used in the periodicals publishing industry, which says that for every marketing dollar it takes to get a new subscriber, it takes only 50 cents to get that same subscriber to renew in Year 2, 25 cents in Year 3, 12.5 cents in Year 4, and so forth, assuming a continuing match between publication content and customer interest. This simple algorithm would suggest that the value of an existing customer is at least double that of a future customer.

What percentage of customers usually leave after a merger, and what can a company do to stem this exodus?

It depends on how much competition there is for the customer's business. The old rule of thumb was a 5 to 10 percent loss, but that is a very low loss for industries with many players.

Yankee Group research indicates that a sizable portion of PeopleSoft customers may stop using PeopleSoft following its merger with Oracle—particularly those who use customer relationship management (CRM) products from PeopleSoft. Out of 162 PeopleSoft customers surveyed after the announcement of the deal, 46 percent reported an intention to switch from their current applications, with another 30 percent remaining undecided.

The issue was not product functionality; survey respondents reported above-average levels of satisfaction with that. The issue was service-level agreements (SLAs).[2]

To keep customer drain to a minimum, companies need to strive for *positive continuity*—maintaining or improving service levels for all customers after the merger, irrespective of the amount of business these customers represent.[3]

What benefits can mergers bring to existing customers, and how can these be communicated?

Merger announcements often claim that the merger will benefit customers by increasing product range and/or by reducing prices through economies of scale and technology.

Examples of product range abound; any merger that diversifies into new product areas can easily deliver on that promise.

Price savings do not materialize as often as they are promised, but they do occur. For example, following its merger with Compaq in 2002, Hewlett-Packard was reportedly able to lower its component costs and thus its prices. As a concrete example, before the merger, its prices ran about 15 percent higher than its competitor, Dell. Nine months later, they were in line.[4]

LEGAL ASPECTS OF CUSTOMER RELATIONS

How common are customer lawsuits, what are they usually about, and how much do they usually cost companies?

According to the 2004 Tillinghast–Towers Perrin survey of director's and officer's liability claims, 8 percent of those responding reported claims against officers and directors in 2004. The most common issues alleged were

- Antitrust law violation
- Contract disputes
- Cost or quality of products or services

- Debt collection
- Deceptive trade practice
- Dishonesty/fraud
- Extension/refusal of credit
- Lender liability

The average payment that insurers paid in response to lawsuits from customers in 2004 was $12,771,460—higher than in past years because of fraud lawsuits by financial services customers.[5] This total does not include payments that insurers made to regulators in response to claims from customers. That average was nearly $6 million.[6]

Why do regulators often try to block mergers?

The main issue is antitrust—the idea that a merger will lessen competition for a particular product or service in a particular market. This stands to reason. After all, basic economics (and common sense) will tell you that the presence of a competitor will give any business a stronger drive to provide consumers with the highest possible quality at the lowest possible price. If a business has a monopoly on a market, that incentive is weakened. Of course, a strong sense of right and wrong can provide that drive, but not all business decision makers have that. If they did, many of our business laws would not be necessary.

What agencies monitor "anticompetitiveness" in mergers, and how do they define it?

As mentioned in Chapter 3, "Integration Planning and Communication," both the Federal Trade Commission (FTC) and the Antitrust Division of the Department of Justice (DOJ) examine mergers to see if they are anticompetitive, or in violation of "antitrust" laws (a *trust* in this sense is a monopolistic combination). Certain other federal agencies, such as the Department of Transportation, also have regulators who are in charge of merger watching. States also have antitrust enforcers that concentrate on certain regulated industries, such as utilities or insurance.

The main federal antitrust law is the Hart-Scott-Rodino Act of 1974, which prohibits transactions that might "substantially ..."

lessen competition, or tend to create a monopoly" in any line of commerce in any part of the country.[7]

Generally speaking, only proposed mergers of fairly large size get scrutinized for this effect. Under amendments to the Hart-Scott-Rodino Act through mid-2005, reporting is triggered in a change of control (as defined in the act) involving a company with $106.2 million in gross assets or (for manufacturers) sales and a company with at least $10.7 million in assets or sales. There are other thresholds relating to transaction size and asset holdings value.

The acid test here is the Herfindahl-Hirschman formula (H-H Index) in the merger guidelines jointly developed by the FTC and the DOJ.[8] Acquisition planners need to write all documents—internal and external—with great care to avoid giving the impression that the merger will put any present or future customers at any disadvantage.

Regulators also look at the general effect that the merger might have on the companies' customers, in terms of supply, quality, and pricing.

- If the merging companies have been dominant distributors of a particular product, or might dominate a point of distribution, they may be subject to special antitrust scrutiny.
- Quality is another sensitive point. If a merger is likely to cause a decline in product or service quality, regulators or courts may disallow or prevent the merger.
- Finally, regulators look at pricing when considering a merger. In some industries, such as utilities, U.S. state regulators can require that a certain percentage (for example, 50 percent) of the merger savings be passed on to customers. In banking, pricing may refer not only to deposits, but also to loans. If conditions could become less favorable for borrowers after a merger, regulators may step in.[9]

If postmerger pricing will be lower, will regulators consider giving a merger an antitrust break?

Yes. Federal regulators today see pricing, not just market share, as a key indicator of competitiveness in a market. Fortunately for deal makers, this signal can be a green light as well as a red one. The FTC has stated that increased efficiencies from a merger of competitors can offset the negative effects of reduced competition. These postmerger efficiencies—if recognized by both parties prior to the merger and corroborated by third parties—can keep regulators from even targeting a merger that they might otherwise try to ban.

Do customers ever sue to block mergers?

This is rare, but it does happen—usually as a private class-action lawsuit that shadows a government lawsuit. Government lawyers do most of the litigation work, and then plaintiff's attorneys shadow the effort. This occurred in the case of *In re First DataBank Antitrust Litigation* (Jan. 2, 2002). The FTC had opposed a merger as anticompetitive and, as part of the settlement, got First DataBank to agree to refund $16 million to consumers. Later, private class-action counsel negotiated a settlement that added $8 million to the fund, for a total of $24 million. Attorneys for the class-action suit wanted 30 percent of the entire $24 million as a fee. But the FTC pointed out that this would give the attorneys 90 percent of the value added by their efforts—with customers receiving only 10 percent. The court lowered the amounts payable to private counsel to 30 percent of the $8 million value added.

POSTMERGER PRICING

Pricing is clearly an important factor for customers, but how important is it compared to quality?

The relative importance of price in relation to quality varies greatly, and depends on a great variety of factors. A limited list of those factors includes

- The competitive landscape of the industry
- Demographics (for individual accounts)
- Industry (for business accounts)
- Strength of the economy
- Frequency of purchase (daily? every 10 years?)
- Point of purchase (wholesale/retail/catalogue)
- Uniqueness of the product

- Quality of sales and marketing effort
- Quality of services supporting the product
- Availability and value of financing

Who in a company is generally responsible for pricing?

In smaller companies, the CEO may determine the prices. As companies grow, the CEO may delegate this authority to another senior executive or, in the case of larger firms, a company department or division.

If a company is organized by function, then pricing power might go to the marketing, sales, or finance department, or even to a dedicated pricing department. If a company is organized by product, then the power to price would go to brand managers. Hybrid, matrix, or cluster-type organizations will use a team approach to pricing.

Who in a company is generally responsible for quality?

Again, the authority begins (and ultimately ends) with the CEO, but he or she may delegate it to an individual or, in larger companies, an entire department. In the United States, these individuals and departments often have the word quality in their titles.

(For more on quality, see the next section of this chapter, and see Chapter 7.)

Prices for any given product or service may go down, up, or stay the same after a merger. How typical is each of these pricing effects, and why?

Pricing strategies are based on a myriad of factors, as just mentioned. In the short term following a merger, however, pricing changes generally come because cost and/or demand has changed (see Figure10-1).

If a merger changes the cost of making a product or changes the elasticity of demand for a product, the company will adjust its prices accordingly, to the extent that its prices are based on these

FIGURE 10-1

Postmerger Pricing Grid

		Elasticity of demand		
	Higher	+	+	=
Merger effects on costs	**Same**	+	=	−
	Lower	=	−	−
		Low	**Neutral**	**High**

Key: − Lower prices   = Preserve prices   + Raise prices

Postmerger pricing is primarily a function of cost and demand.

two factors. Elasticity of demand is the extent to which demand will change in response to a change in prices.

Suppose that the top pricing executives of two merging companies have different views on pricing. How can they resolve their differences?

There is no rule that says that a firm can't have more than one pricing strategy. In a merger between a commodity business and a premium-brand business, senior executives are bound to have different pricing approaches—and both may be right.

Ideally, a merger should not change the company's pricing strategy for any significant group of customers, unless it is to *improve* quality and/or *lower* price, giving customers a net positive result. Even then, a message of change should be communicated with care. Customers can become literally *accustomed* (pun intended) to a company's pricing strategy. If this strategy changes, and the change does not sit right with the customer, the company could jeopardize that relationship.

Given the importance and complexity of pricing, a constructive argument about pricing can be beneficial to the firm. But if the merger is between companies that sell essentially the *same product* using *different pricing strategies* (for example "rock bottom" pricing versus merely "low" pricing), there will not be room for two approaches. The argument must be resolved as quickly as possible, so that management will have time to explain the change to the sales and marketing force. In turn, these people can explain the change to customers and address concerns other than price—such as quality, another customer concern.

POSTMERGER QUALITY MANAGEMENT

Quality is obviously important, but how important are programs such as "total quality management"? What impact do they have on performance?

Total quality management (TQM) is a management system that focuses on product and service quality. It revolutionized manufacturing in the latter half the last century, and has now become ingrained in corporate culture. Not every company has a "total quality" program, but many companies refer to "quality" for their products and services. A key concept in quality management is *process improvement* (also known as the *continuous improvement process*). This approach seeks improvements by identifying and correcting root sources of defects. In some cases, these may be subtle factors with small but cumulative effects. To achieve process improvement, organizations can analyze process value, measure process cycle time, and simplify processes. As a measure of process improvement, companies may lower their tolerance level for defects down to a very tiny standard deviation ("sigma") from perfection. *Supplier certification*, discussed later in this chapter, is another practice associated with the quality movement, as are various types of programs for *improved communications* with various stakeholders, especially customers.

Other key concepts are *benchmarking* (comparisons to the competition) and *empowerment* (greater employee involvement). Empowerment is often achieved through *quality circles*—teams that may include workers, supervisors, managers, and engineers, often from different functions or departments, that meet to discuss ideas for making improvements in manufacturing or other processes. For more on quality systems (ISO 9001), see Chapter 7.

CONTINUITY FOR CUSTOMERS

What concerns might a customer have beyond price?

It depends on the nature of the customer's relationship with the company. All customers will be concerned about quality, but wholesale buyers or distributors—who buy in bulk directly from the company, as previously mentioned—will also be concerned about their relationship with the company.

How can a merger change the dynamics of a company's relationship with its direct customers?

Wholesale customers and distributors will naturally be apprehensive when their supplier undergoes a merger. They may have spent years building a strong relationship with a company before a merger, only to see that relationship erode after the merger has closed. The change in the relationship may come about because, after the merger, the customer's business may represent, in percentage terms, less sales and profit to the combined supplier firm than before the merger.

And so it begins: The customer may not receive the same frequency of visits as it did before the merger, and it may not get its calls returned as quickly as before. When the customer asks for a benefit from the relationship, such as a reduction in price or an increase in quality, it may have a harder time getting it—or may not get it at all. In such a case, the customer may take its business elsewhere.

To combat this cause of attrition, companies should try to guarantee positive continuity for all their customers following a merger—that is, the same or better quality of service and products for the same or a lower price.

How can a company's Web site help provide positive continuity to customers?

Many companies today put Frequently Asked Question (FAQ) sections on their Web sites following a merger to address the concerns of various constituencies. (For an example from Sprint Nextel, a merger announced in December 2004, see Box 10-1.)

B O X   1 0 – 1

Frequently Asked Questions—An Example from
Sprint Nextel (September 2005)

What is the combined company name?
What is the new Sprint Nextel and why did the two companies
seek to merge?
When did the combined company's brand enter the marketplace?
What are the plans for Sprint's local telephone division?
What is the combined company's branding?
Why did you select Sprint as the lead go-to-market brand name?
Where will customers see the Nextel brand name?
What is the combined company logo?
What happens to NASCAR NEXTEL Cup Series™ sponsorship?
What is the new ticker symbol for Sprint Nextel?
How does the merger benefit customers?
How will the transition process be managed to ensure no
disruption to services, customers, innovation, or necessary
continued product enhancements?
Will coverage for Sprint Nextel customers "improve" now that the
merger is complete? In other words, will they have more coverage
than before and will this be included in their current agreements?
Will you close retail stores? If so, how many and where?
Will you be re-branding the stores and if so when?
What is the future of iDEN?
Will the combined company continue to support and invest in
both networks?
Will Sprint Nextel offer a walkie-talkie solution?
How soon will you come to market with new products and
services under the name?

**Positive continuity sounds good, but suppose a
newly merged company can't afford to offer positive
continuity to all its customers?**

This may be a sign that the merger was overpriced and/or over-
leveraged. Although regrettable, if this is the reality, then it must be
faced. Managers will need to concentrate not so much on positive

continuity as on *profitable continuity*. Rather than seeking to retain all customers, they should seek to retain only the profitable accounts, letting the unprofitable ones go. For everything there is a season, and sometimes it is the season of profitability, not market share.

Managers operating in a profitability-focused environment need to make a special effort to honor all customer commitments. Although keeping promises to unprofitable customers may seem like a waste of resources in the short term, it might well be a wise move for the future. Moreover, senior managers in a profit-focused environment must be very careful not to preach goodness and light while paying people to slash and burn. It is unfair to ask managers to keep all their customers, at no matter what cost, while cutting their bonuses and profit sharing for doing so.

If positive continuity is a core value, then workloads and compensation should be adjusted to encourage it. For example, the company can award incentive pay to managers who keep old customers while maintaining or improving their level of satisfaction during the postmerger period. This is particularly challenging in a merger that blends diverse customer bases, and it should be recognized and rewarded.

Could you give an example of a merger that combined two very different customer bases?

Consider the merger of Morgan Stanley and Dean Witter, Discover & Company (now called Morgan Stanley), which blended an investment banking firm with a stock brokerage and credit card company. The much-vaunted "cultural differences" in this $8.8 billion 1997 deal were really differences in customer base. Morgan Stanley's customers were generally large institutional investors buying company securities in million-dollar chunks. Dean Witter's customers were generally individuals buying mutual funds in hundred-dollar increments or using the Discover credit card. The firm did not do as well as hoped in the retail market. The original architect of the merger, Philip Purcell, left the firm in 2005, replaced by new CEO John Mack. One of the first things Mack did in his new position was to cut 1,000 retail broker jobs. Time will tell whether Morgan Stanley will ever successfully secure a retail brokerage client base and train the sales force needed to serve it.

COMMITMENTS TO SUPPLIERS

What commitments does a company typically have to fulfill for its suppliers after a merger?

Again, the Caux *Principles for Business* are instructive. Here is the supplier section of the document, along with expert checkpoints.

Suppliers

Our relationship with suppliers and subcontractors must be based on a mutual respect. We therefore have a responsibility to:

- seek fairness and truthfulness in all our activities, including pricing, licensing, and rights to sell;

  Checkpoints: What policies for pricing, licensing, and subcontracting do the two merging companies have in place? What plans are there to merge these policies?

- ensure that our business activities are free from coercion and unnecessary litigation;

  Checkpoints: During the due diligence process, did each company check out the other one for pending litigation from or against suppliers? If such litigation is pending, how can it be resolved with honor?

- foster long-term stability in the supplier relationship in return for value, quality, competitiveness, and reliability;

  Checkpoints: Do the merging companies have supplier certification programs? How can these programs be merged?

- share information with suppliers and integrate them into our planning processes;

  Checkpoints: What are the current channels of communication with suppliers? How good is each company's linking technology? How can this technology be merged?

- pay suppliers on time and in accordance with agreed terms of trade; and

  Checkpoints: What is the billing cycle for each company? If the cycles are different, can this difference be reconciled for a net benefit to suppliers? If some suppliers must be paid later than before, how will this news be communicated, and by whom?

- seek, encourage, and prefer suppliers and subcontractors whose employment practices respect human dignity.

  Checkpoints: During the due diligence phase, did someone check out supplier ethics for each of the merging companies? If problems surfaced, how will these be resolved?

Why is it so important to fulfill commitments to existing suppliers after a merger?

As mentioned earlier, it is a matter of ethics, economics, and law. A company's word should be its bond—and if it is not, a company can expect attrition and litigation. Some companies have long-term contracts with suppliers that cannot be broken with impunity. Also, some companies have programs to ensure diversity of suppliers—for example, a certain percentage of suppliers must be small businesses or businesses owned by minorities and/or women. Finally, and most generally, just as a current customer is worth more than a future one, so a current supplier (given a positive history) is worth more than a future one.

Why do you say that existing suppliers are more valuable than new ones?

Any relationship with a history (if that history is positive) is better than one without a history. Companies, like people, gain knowledge and confidence from experience. While extremely close supplier relationships may signal fraud (and you should check these out), it is not wise to rule suppliers out on these tentative grounds. Long-term, multiproduct suppliers often get to know parts of your business better than you do. A supplier that works with several parts of a company often sees opportunities for improvement that insiders fail to see. Why lose a supplier like this in favor of an unknown one?

There is also the buyer's market mentioned earlier, which offers a distinct "leverage" factor. That is, an existing supplier may be more willing to give you a better deal than a new one is, simply to keep your business. (Unlike customers, who may use the merger as an excuse to switch suppliers, suppliers are usually very anxious to please, for fear of losing business to a known competitor.)

How can a company take advantage of the leverage it has with its suppliers, and what are the limits of this leverage?

There is a very delicate balance here. On the one hand, since it is a buyer's market after a merger, a newly combined company can and should take advantage of its strong position to obtain better contract terms, quality, pricing, and service, to the extent that these are possible. On the other hand, the newly combined company should treat its existing suppliers with respect, honoring all commitments and refraining from unreasonable demands.

Managers of newly merged companies would be wise to think of suppliers as partners, rather than as adversaries. If a supplier knows a customer's needs, it can help meet them—even bailing out a customer with an unforeseen problem. Newly merged companies with high leverage should resist any temptation to use it to the disadvantage of current suppliers, or to force the hand of potential new suppliers.

Hard-nosed negotiation can get top quality at low prices for a while, but in most cases, the bargain will not last. If the prices companies pay are not high enough to sustain a supplier over time, quality will suffer, prices will rise, or the supplier will fail. Instead, companies can and should use their leverage in a positive way, to bring mutual benefits through increased efficiency over the long term—not just cost savings in the short term.

What is the first step in merging suppliers?

As soon as this is practical, both parties to the merger need to identify their most critical suppliers. It's best to do this as part of pre-merger due diligence, but better late than never. Typically, each company should list its most important suppliers, limiting this list to no more than 100 (even if the company uses thousands of suppliers). Taking the joint list of 200 or fewer suppliers, the integration team can create lists based on types of products or services, amount of money spent, frequency of purchase, lead time needed for orders, and similar elements.

Doing this will give the newly combined company much of the information it needs in order to approach suppliers for improvements in terms and quality, if needed. The company can also work on consolidating its accounts with shared suppliers and eliminating redundant suppliers, or "streamlining."

What guidelines should a company follow in streamlining suppliers?

Four principles are politics, moderation, convenience, and selectivity.

- By *politics*, we mean that if a supplier is also a customer, think twice. "Cut not lest ye be cut," so to speak, unless you are willing to lose the supplier's business.
- By *moderation*, we mean that a company should not cut to the bone. Some overlap in suppliers is desirable to avoid dependence on a single supplier for any one item.
- By *convenience*, we mean that companies should avoid consolidating for the sake of consolidating. If equal value is being received from two different vendors for the same service, it makes little sense to force a choice.
- By *selectivity*, we mean that in streamlining suppliers, a company should be sure to select the highest quality and the lowest price. As mentioned in our earlier discussion on quality, supplier certification can be very helpful to companies seeking improvements in performance (including postmerger performance).

Could you give examples of merged companies that merged their supplier development programs?

With respect to supplier diversity, a good example is the merger of GTE and Bell Atlantic, which merged to form Verizon.[10] Both companies had a supplier diversity programs, and they merged the two. The new Verizon decided to approach supplier diversity by focusing on three areas: outreach, access, and coaching.

- *Outreach.* This may be as informal as having a cup of coffee. More formally, Verizon "sends teams to trade shows—50 or so per year, ranging from local and regional to national events." Verizon also supports organizations like the U.S. Hispanic and the U.S. Pan-Asian-American chambers of commerce.
- *Access.* Verizon helps suppliers gain access not only as contractors, but also as subcontractors. If Verizon chooses Lucent or IBM for a major IT project, it may

provide a reference for a subcontracting opportunity to a minority-owned or woman-owned supplier.
- *Coaching.* In the coaching process, Verizon advises suppliers not to become overly dependent on the company as a source of income, or on a single skill set.

To encourage the use of diverse suppliers, Verizon sets goals for expenditures on diverse suppliers and includes this goal as one of the factors considered in senior management compensation.

More generally, a good example of a merged company with a strong supplier relations program would be Boeing. Boeing Company, McDonnell-Douglas Corporation, and North American Rockwell all had successful supplier development programs prior to their merging. After the merger of these companies into Boeing, the new company established an "integrated supplier training program," incorporating best practices from each former company.

Specific steps listed on Boeing's Web site include

- Holding supplier focus groups to promote communication and feedback
- Involving suppliers early in new business acquisitions
- Working with suppliers in assessing their processes to achieve leanness
- Supporting supplier development by offering courses, including Lean Enterprise Overview, Lean Production System Simulation for Suppliers, Value Stream Mapping, Statistical Process Control, Accelerated Improvement Workshops, and Preferred Supplier Certification

What exactly are supplier certification programs, and how common are they?

Supplier certification programs are simply formal programs that a company uses to approve particular suppliers. Purchasers require a high level of past quality performance for certification (with ISO 9001 being used as a common standard for quality management processes) and give certified contractors more future business as an incentive for participation.

In addition, some companies like to see external supplier certification. Verizon, profiled earlier as a diversity-oriented procurer, looks for certification by one of the minority supplier organizations, such as the National Minority Supplier Development Council (NMSDC) or the Women's Business Enterprise National Council (WBENC).

What are the chief benefits to suppliers from a merger, and how can these be communicated?

After a successful merger, just as customers can hope for a broader range of products, so suppliers can hope for a broader range of purchases from the newly combined companies. The newly merged company should let its suppliers know that as long as they provide value, they have a good chance of being retained after the merger. In this way, the company can avoid losing good suppliers unnecessarily.

As mentioned in Chapter 3, suppliers should be included in the communications loop from the beginning. If one or both of the merging companies has product development teams that include suppliers, these teams would be a good place to do the communicating face to face.

LEGAL ASPECTS OF SUPPLIER RELATIONS

How often do suppliers sue companies, what do they sue over, and for how much?

It is relatively rare for suppliers to sue companies. In 2004, consistent with previous years, only 5 percent of major public companies (those with more than 500 shareholders) reported lawsuits from suppliers, contractors, or competitors. This was only about 120 of 2,409 companies surveyed by Tillinghast–Towers Perrin. For smaller companies (those with fewer than 500 shareholders, the level was 10 percent.) Issues included business interference, contract disputes, deceptive trade practices, antitrust violations, and copyright or patent infringement.[11] The average payment from claimants in this group is about $1 million.[12]

Among repeat participants (survey participants who filled out the survey two years in a row), claim frequency increased by 11 percent from 2003 to 2004, and claim susceptibility increased by

6 percent. Average severity for repeat participants increased in three out of five claim classes, including employees, competitors/ suppliers, and shareholders. This figure does not include suits filed by regulators on behalf of suppliers, which are relatively rare.

Why are lawsuits filed by and for suppliers so rare?

Although suppliers are generally considered to be a corporate "constituency" like any other (customers, shareholders, employees, and so forth), they have very few legal protections in relation to their customers beyond the common law of contracts. Most regulatory and legal protections are directed toward customers, not suppliers. This differential is reflected in the much higher incidence of customer than of supplier lawsuits. This is not so much because customers are more litigious than suppliers, but rather because the law protects buyers rather than sellers.

Supplier vulnerability does not justify callous treatment, however. The ethics and economics of good supplier relations can and should prevail in the absence of legal incentives.

Could you give an example of a postmerger contract dispute with a supplier?

Shortly after its May 1991 acquisition of American Original Corp., a clams product business based in Seaford, Delaware, Borden Inc. (now called Borden Foods) stopped buying clams from Sons of Thunder, a small fishing operation in Cape May, New Jersey. In early 1997, the Supreme Court of New Jersey upheld a $738,000 jury award against Borden Inc., finding that the company had urged the company to buy a boat and take on debt, and then failed to fulfill its commitment to buy clams. The decision affirmed the judgment of the trial court for breach of Uniform Commercial Code Section 1-203, which imposes the obligation of good faith in the performance of a contract.[13]

Do regulators ever try to stop mergers based on their possible effects on suppliers?

Yes. The Antitrust Division of the Department of Justice tries to thwart "monopsony" as well as monopoly. Monopsony is market power exercised by a buyer against sellers of a particular good or service. Concerns with increased monopsony power featured prominently in regulatory reviews of the Anthem-WellPoint merger in 2004, as well as in reviews of Aetna's acquisition of Prudential's health insurance assets and Cargill's acquisition of Continental's grain trading division five years earlier.[14]

Do suppliers ever try to prevent mergers?

It is rare. However, in the case of a company that has filed for bankruptcy, suppliers may have leverage to stop a merger. In August 2005, large suppliers said that they would oppose Super Sol's acquisition of Clubmarket (in Israel) because they did not want to reduce their level of recovery.[15]

KEY SUPPLIER ISSUE: POSTMERGER OUTSOURCING

What is "outsourcing," and what are its chief benefits and drawbacks?

Outsourcing is a company's use of an external, independently owned supplier to provide goods or services that were formerly provided by employees of the company or a unit of the company. If the supplier takes over only part of the function, sharing it with company employees, this is called "cosourcing."

Outsourcing and cosourcing are part of a larger trend toward corporate downsizing in favor of the "virtual corporation." Almost any function that can be performed inside a company can be performed outside the company. A manufacturer may use an outside firm to store and distribute parts. A labor-intensive company may outsource its human resource paperwork to an HR consulting firm. A branch of government may outsource specific communications, planning, or research functions to a think tank. Examples are endlessly varied. In the extreme case, a company can be entirely "outsourced," with no employees—only contractual relations with suppliers. In this model, a company is all "head" (headquarters) and no "body" (divisions).

Opponents argue that outsourcing is expensive and can lower quality. Generally speaking outsourcing costs are higher per hour, but they may not have a high total cost, if the work can be requested and delivered on a "just in time" basis. As for quality, it can suffer but to counteract this effect, the company merely needs to teach suppliers about company standards, and offer incentives for meeting them.

CONTINUITY FOR SUPPLIERS

How can a company create positive continuity for its suppliers, and what are the challenges here?

Let's look at Figure 10-2, going clockwise from the lower right.

Different products/same suppliers. This situation offers low leverage and high continuity.

Different products/different suppliers. This situation offers low leverage with little guarantee of high continuity (for simplicity's sake, low continuity).

Same products/different suppliers. This situation offers high leverage and low continuity.

Same products/same suppliers. This situation offers the double benefit of high leverage and high continuity. The merging companies will be able to compare and contrast their treatment, obtaining better terms and quality, while at the same time continuing their commitment to the existing suppliers.

High leverage and high continuity are most likely to occur when merging companies are buying the same products from the same suppliers.

If the merging companies use different suppliers for the same good or service, how can the newly merged company choose between suppliers?

In such a situation, the new company can compare the sources for *each* product, and can choose both of the suppliers, one of the suppliers, or a new supplier altogether. Each of these three options has advantages and drawbacks, depending on the company's situation.

Choosing only *one* supplier for each product is more compatible with two new trends in supplier relations. The first is the *systems* (or *subsystems*) approach, in which companies buy integrated, assembly-ready "subsystems" rather than mere components. The other, often simultaneous approach is supplier *streamlining*, in which a buyer reduces the total number of suppliers.

FIGURE 10-2

The Leverage Continuity Grid

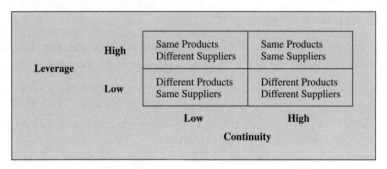

By continuing to use *both* suppliers, the new firm can gain a margin of safety, hedging against the possibility of a supplier crisis, such as a strike or a plant fire. Also, using both firms may serve to keep quality and service levels from each supplier high, as each knows that the other is a potential competitor for the business. Competition may also put competitive pricing pressures on suppliers. There is also a chance that using two suppliers will allow a company to gain some synergy, buying each one's best products. Finally, using suppliers from different parts of the world provides global diversity—an important attribute in some industries.

Finding an entirely *new* supplier for the item is the least attractive alternative, and should be pursued only when both suppliers have poor quality.

In the end, of course, the choice will depend on the goals of the new company and on the cost, quality, reliability, and flexibility of each supplier.

TECHNOLOGICAL CONSIDERATIONS FOR CUSTOMERS AND SUPPLIERS

When companies merge their operations, what are some of the technological challenges they face in "merging" their suppliers?

Many times, the merger partners have incompatible systems. Even when two companies share common customers or suppliers, the ways in which the two companies' systems "talk" to their trading partners may be quite different. Replacing custom software with standard electronic data interchange (EDI) can mitigate this problem. (For more on technology integration, see Chapter 9.)

Thanks to the new technologies that are available, a growing number of companies are forming technological partnerships with their customers and suppliers to focus the supply chain around customer demand. These new alliances all require systems that enable a continuous flow of demand and supply information between enterprises. This requires both intranets and extranets—linking internal company systems together, and linking those systems with both the company's customers and its suppliers. In general, building informational links along the customer-company-supplier chain requires knowing line speeds, changeover times, activity rates, and productivity levels.

Multisourced products pose technological challenges at the planning stage. If a product is made from a variety of components, each from a different supplier, this requires special attention. Purchases need to make a list of the components needed, along with calculations of when each component will be needed. This is one reason that many buyers are using the systems approach to purchasing mentioned earlier.

What IT challenges do companies face in merging their suppliers, and how can they solve these problems?

On the supplier side, there are questions of sheer volume. Some large organizations can literally lose track of who their suppliers are, leading to overpayment.

Therefore, one of the first steps is to count up how many suppliers each company has for each of its products, then to work together to choose which suppliers to keep and which to drop.

Many companies today use computers not only to process bids and payments, but also to link customers with suppliers. In larger organizations, this can lead to considerable complexity. Major companies often make over 500,000 vendor payments per year. A merger creates a danger zone for vendor payments, including overpayments, duplicate payments, and payments to the wrong vendor.[16]

Could you give an example of a company that had too many suppliers after a merger, and tell how it used IT to streamline them?

Sure. One major bank,[17] after a series of acquisitions, wound up doing business with over 160,000 vendors. Over the years, it had acquired several banks of similar size. Each time it acquired another bank, the new bank's vendors were added to a common vendor file with a prefix so that the same vendor number would not be used for two different vendors.

Although this numbering system seemed to make sense, it created huge unseen redundancies. The computer system could check for duplicate payments to the same vendor number, but it could not check for duplicate payments to the same vendor if payments were made to different vendor numbers. More generally, it was extremely difficult to determine how much business was being done with a vendor because there could be many different vendor numbers for a single vendor, and even the vendor's name might be inconsistent. Prior to a supplier analysis, this major bank knew that it did a lot of business with AT&T and IBM, but it did not realize how much. Analysis revealed that AT&T was in the file over 2,000 times, and IBM appeared over 1,500 times!

When the same vendor is paid under different names and numbers, overpayments are bound to occur. That was the situation at this bank. Both just before and just after each merger, different people were approving invoices and sending them to the company's accounts payable department.

The bank hired a vendor management consulting firm to analyze its situation. The firm discovered that the bank had made over $1 million in overpayments within the past year, and was able to recover most of that amount. The firm also helped the bank cut down its number of suppliers to 30,000.

Could you give an example of technological problems in postmerger customer relations and tell how they were resolved?

Consistent with the previous chapter (Chapter 9) there are basically four choices after a merger:

- Keep IT systems separate.
- Pick one system over another.

- Use a third, new system and convert the two into that one.
- Blend IT systems.

Consultants from Boston Consulting Group and McKinsey have recommended a blended approach.[18]

The McKinsey study cites an example from the banking sector. This is a good example, because IT underlies every process a bank performs. Also, banks tend to have complex operational structures, often with many brands, branches, and product sets. The McKinsey consultants worked with one acquiring bank that had accumulated more than 700 branches, nearly 400 product sets, and about 300 IT systems—and was set to buy a competitor with almost as many branches, about 250 product sets, and close to 200 IT systems. The McKinsey advisors recommended a hybrid approach that "taps synergies, serves customers at least as well as they were served before, and achieves suitable trade-offs among internal parties."

History teaches lessons. When Smith Barney (now a unit of Travelers Group) merged with Shearson in 1993, keeping Shearson's back-office system, it changed all the Smith Barney customers' account numbers without telling them. As a result, duplicate confirmations of the same purchase showed different prices, and client transfer forms got wiped out of the system. Over time, these problems were resolved one at a time through trial and error. Early consultation with information management specialists might have prevented some if not all of these problems.

INTERNATIONAL CONSIDERATIONS

What are some key challenges in customer and supplier relationships in cross-border mergers?

It depends on the degree of integration expected of the two companies. As mentioned in Chapter 7, some international mergers decide to remain binational, maintaining separate headquarters. Under such an arrangement, customer and supplier relationships pose no new challenges and offer no new rewards. In an integrated company, by contrast, the challenges are enormous, as are the rewards. One leading source of challenges is *global antitrust*.

What is global antitrust, and how can it affect postmerger integration?

Global antitrust is the emerging principle in international trade law that says countries can prosecute any corporate conduct that injures their citizens as consumers. This theory has been used to justify applying the Sherman Act, the U.S. antimonopoly law discussed in Chapter 3, in international civil cases. Justified by this theory and legal precedent, the U.S. Department of Justice and Federal Trade Commission have tried to block cross-border deals that don't even involve U.S.-based companies—and to set conditions for those companies' postmerger life together.[19]

N O T E S

1 For more on a company's covenantal commitments, see Robert K. Mueller, *Enforcing the Unenforceable: Anchoring Points for Corporate Directors* (New York: Quorum Books, 1997).

2 Lisa Vaas, "Study: Many PeopleSoft Users Inclined to Ditch Software Post-Merger," *E-Week.com*, Mar. 4, 2005.

3 In April 2005, the author interviewed an account representative who had been working for AT&T and survived the transition to Cingular. A change in territory, combined with problems of technical integration, doubled his workload. "I get 100 e-mails a day," he lamented. And even though gas prices were rising, he continued to make onsite calls. Cingular wisely decided to retain this employee, and to provide him with an assistant.

4 John G. Spooner, "HP Aims to Match Dell on Price," *CNET News.com*, Feb. 13, 2003.

5 *2005 Directors and Officers Liabiilty Survey.* Tillinghast-Towers Perrin, 2005.

6 Ibid.

7 The Hart-Scott-Rodino Act, Section 7 of the Clayton Act, is 15 U.S. Code, Section 18a. Year 2000 amendments, calling for annual adjustments of the threshold, were enacted as Pub. L. No. 106-553, 114 Stat. 2762, http://www.ftc.gov/bc/docs/statute.pdf. For a good overview of the changes and their implication, see Malcolm R. Pfunder, "Indexing Comes to the HSR Act," *The Antitrust Source*, January 2005, www.antitrustsource.com. The Sherman Antitrust Act also seeks to ensure competitive markets. Section 1 prohibits "contracts, combinations, and conspiracies that unreasonably

restrain trade," and Section 2 prohibits "monopolization, attempted monopolization, and conspiracies to monopolize." Government actions under the Sherman Act are relatively rare, as the burden of proof is high.

8 For figures on the H-H Index in the manufacturing sector in 2002, see http://www.census.gov/prod/ec02/ec0231sx1.pdf.

9 Charles Colomiris and Thanavut Pornrojnancool, "Monopoly-Creating Bank Consolidation? The Merger of Fleet and BankBoston," NDER Working Paper No. 11351. This paper found that after the 1999 merger, medium-sized middle-market borrowers experienced a 1 percent increase in the average interest-rate credit spreads, attributable to the merger.

10 "Verizon Picks Pinnacle for High-Level IT Projects," *Diversity Careers in Engineering and Technology*, May/June 2004, DiversityCareers.com.

11 *2005 Directors and Officers Liability Survey* (op. cit., note 5).

12 Ibid.

13 *Sons of Thunder* v. *Borden*, 1997 WestLaw 104592, Supreme Court of New Jersey (1997) or 690 A 2d 575 (Sup. Ct., N. J., 1997).

14 Marius Schwartz, "Buyer Power Concerns and the Aetna-Prudential Merger," Fifth Annual Healthcare Antitrust Forum, October 1999; Andrew G. Simpson, "Feds See No Harm in Anthem-WellPoint Merger," Mar. 11, 2004.

15 Hadas Manor, "Large Suppliers May Oppose Super-Sol-Clubmarket Deal," *Globe Online*, Sept. 4, 2005.

16 For additional guidance on postmerger savings from purchasing consolidation, see Andrew Jones and Michael Knapp, "Maximizing Postmerger Savings from Purchasing," a brochure published by Boston Consulting Group in 2001.

17 Jonathan Casher, the expert providing this answer, declined to name this bank—because it is a valued customer!

18 Scott A. Christofferson, Robert S. McNish, and Diane L. Sias, "Where Mergers Go Wrong," *McKinsey Quarterly*, No. 2, 2004, pp. 92–99. See also the Boston Consulting Group study on "clusters and nuggets" cited in Chapter 9.

19 See, for example, David Laing, "Foreign Nationals Who Break US Antitrust Rules Can Find Themselves in Front of US Courts," *Competition Law*, Vol. 4, No. 9 (May 2005).

Fulfilling Commitments to Shareholders, Bondholders, and Lenders

He who pays the piper calls the tune.

Proverb

INTRODUCTION

When two companies merge, many stakeholders stand to lose or gain from the change. Certainly customers and suppliers have an important stake in the future of the new enterprise, as we have seen in the previous chapter. And obviously employees and communities do also, as shown in the next chapter. But perhaps no group has a more vulnerable interest in a newly merged entity than the one that has put at risk that fragile commodity that we call *cash*.

When a corporation accepts funding from a source, it gives back "paper" and promises. To shareholders, it grants stock certificates conferring partial ownership, along with an implicit pledge to increase the value of that ownership. To bondholders, it gives bonds—pledges to repay the face amount of the bond by a certain date, with interest. To lenders, it offers loan agreements along with a pledge to return the full amount of the borrowed cash with interest.

In this chapter, we will explore some of the postmerger implications of all these promises, with emphasis on the implicit ones made to shareholders. This emphasis is natural. After all, corporate directors owe their primary fiduciary duty to shareholders, and although the interests of shareholders often conflict with those of other constituencies in the short term, they tend to agree with them in the long term.[1] (To paraphrase former General Motors Corporation Chairman Charles E. Wilson, what is good for long-term shareholders is good for all stakeholders, and what is good for all stakeholders is good for long-term shareholders.[2])

COMMITMENTS TO SHAREHOLDERS

What commitments to its shareholders does a company typically have to fulfill after a merger?

All shareholders have stock certificates showing that they have "ownership" in a company. But what does ownership really mean? Without protections, ownership is fragile indeed—especially when shareholders are not managers.

Despite the increasing use of the term *shareowner* by some shareholder groups,[3] the sad reality is that shareholders don't always possess what they "own," much less control it. Depending upon the *liquidity* of a given share of stock—that is, the ease with which it can be bought or sold—an owner may or may not be able to relinquish it in return for cash. In an extreme case, a stock certificate may be worth no more than the paper it is printed on.

This is where corporate promises come in. To give value to the stock certificates it trades for cash, a corporation promises to adhere to certain standards. In privately held companies, these standards are typically expressed in shareholder's agreements. In publicly held companies, standards have their life and force in federal and state securities laws and in stock exchange listing rules.[4] Companies that sell shares to the public must disclose certain information in accordance with certain standards in offering documents prior to selling those shares and listing them on an exchange, and in financial statements after listing them. They also have to grant holders of common stock certain voting rights, often exercised by proxy—hence the term *proxy voting*. And beyond these mandatory and legally enforceable promises are some that corporations may make and keep voluntarily as part of their bylaws or corporate policies.

How exactly can postmerger integration teams make sure that the new company meets these various commitments to shareholders?

In a merger that involves a privately held company, legal counsel (internal or external) should look over all the agreements the company has signed with its owners, asking what rights the company has promised to what owners, under what terms, for what period of time.

In a merger involving a publicly held company, the advisor will need to know where that company stands with respect to the securities laws for its jurisdiction (for example, in the United States, both state and federal securities laws).

For firms that have a general counsel or other inside attorney, the resources of an organization like the Association of Corporate Counsel (ACC) can be helpful. When outside counsel is engaged, a resource such as Martindale Hubbell can guide the selection of a firm with experience in securities law.[5]

Attorneys specializing in securities law keep abreast of these issues and often send out letters to clients (and potential clients) summarizing major trends. Securities regulators, such as the Securities and Exchange Commission (www.sec.gov) in the United States, regularly post new and pending rules.[6]

In addition to compliance with securities law, what are some general ethical considerations that companies must address?

With respect to the ethics of shareholder relations, postmerger integration managers can benefit from consulting a document such as the Caux Round Table *Principles for Business,* mentioned earlier as an excellent checklist for essential corporate commitments.

Here is the "Shareholders" section of the stakeholder list (with our postmerger "checkpoints" added in italics).

OWNERS/INVESTORS

We believe in honoring the trust our investors place in us. We therefore have a responsibility to:

- apply professional and diligent management in order to secure a fair and competitive return on our owners' investment;

> *Checkpoints: Do the managers of the new company think like owners? Are they owners? How do they define return on owners' investment (ROI)? How will they benchmark it against the competition?*

- disclose relevant information to owners/investors subject to legal requirements and competitive constraints;

  Checkpoints: In disclosing their postmerger plans, have the managements of both companies met the disclosure requirements of federal and state regulators? Have they stayed within the "safe harbor for forward-looking statements"?[7]

- conserve, protect, and increase the owners/investors' assets; and

  Checkpoints: Has the financing of the deal had a negative impact on share value? If one or both companies experienced a decline in value after announcement of the merger, what plans has management made and communicated to restore that value? How realistic are these plans? Who will monitor their achievement?

- respect owners/investors' requests, suggestions, complaints, and formal resolutions.

  Checkpoints: Have the two merging companies encouraged communications from their shareholders about the merger? What kinds of communications have shareholders made? What kind of responses did they get?

Another important manifesto for shareholder rights is the landmark Principles of Corporate Governance, published by the Organization for Economic Cooperation and Development in 1999 and updated in June 2004. All member nations of the OECD agreed to this document, discussed at the end of this chapter.

Adhering to codes such as Caux or the OECD guidelines can ensure retention of shareholders after a merger.

Why is it so important to retain existing stockholders after a merger? Why not just let them take the "Wall Street walk" by selling, and court new shareholders to replace them?

Beyond the obvious ethical and legal advantages of keeping explicit and implicit promises to existing shareholders, there are economic advantages to retaining shareholders—at least three of them.

> First, it is less expensive to retain old shareholders than to court new ones.

Second, companies that honor their promises to shareholders tend to attract the most desirable kind of shareholders— long-term rather than short-term.

Third, stable ownership can reduce share price volatility and thus contribute to a higher "shareholder value."

On your first point, why is it less expensive to retain existing shareholders than to court new ones?

In any competitive market, as seen in the previous chapter with respect to customers and vendors, it is usually easier and less expensive to maintain an existing relationship than to attract a new one.

Certainly the market for equity shares is competitive. A company's stock is only one of many investment vehicles available at any time—including investments in the company's peers. That is one reason why investor relations (IR) professionals devote a large part of their energies after a merger (and in fact in any strategic season) to retaining the shareholders that their company already has attracted, rather than merely attempting to court new ones.[8]

On your second point, could you say more about "long-term" versus "trader" investors?

Yes. The spectrum of shareholders has two ends.

At one end, there are long-term shareholders, who invest for a relatively long period of time and who base their buy-sell decision on fundamentals of performance, both financial and nonfinancial. At this end of the spectrum, we find individuals and some institutions, notably pension funds for public-sector and private-sector employees.

At the other end of the spectrum, there are short-term holders who base their trades on technical minutiae, such as differences between analysts' projections of earnings and published earnings reports. This kind of trading is most common among money managers, mutual funds, and banks.

Although neither state nor federal law makes a distinction between these two types of shareholders, many court opinions support the notion that companies should not be operated for the benefit of short-term shareholders, but rather for the benefit of long-term shareholders and other long-term constituencies. Leading corporate executives and investors support this notion.

Typical long-term owners—for example, the pension funds that belong to the activist Council of Institutional Investors—cannot easily sell a large position. Instead, such holders prefer to engage in activism through such vehicles as shareholder resolutions to change a company's policies. Although activism can be beneficial over time, it can be embarrassing to the company and its management in the short term.

And on your third point, why are current holders more likely to stabilize share prices than potential future shareholders, and why does this matter?

Shareholders whose ownership predates a merger are by definition owners who have some level of confidence in the merger. Confident shareholders are less likely than tomorrow's buyer to drive the stock price down by selling out in hard times. This means less volatility in stock price, an important consideration. Some investors consider high volatility, or high "beta," to be a negative factor when calculating a company's value to them. This is one of the basic principles of the "shareholder value" approach to company valuation.

What is the "shareholder value" approach to company valuation?

The shareholder value approach to company valuation says that the total economic value of a company, or its corporate value, equals the value of its debt plus the value of its equity or "shareholder value."[9] This sounds as easy as a balance sheet (just subtract debt from equity), but it is not. In this approach, the values of debt and equity are not computed separately. Rather, they are seen as having a dynamic interrelationship.

Under this approach, corporate value is defined as the present value of cash flows from operations during a forecast period, plus the present value of business attributable to a period beyond the forecast period (or "residual value"), plus marketable securities. In calculating present value, companies have to figure out their cost of capital—on both the debt and the equity side. This is where beta comes in, by the way: stock volatility is considered part of a company's cost of equity capital.

Should postmerger financial reports include non-GAAP financial information? Why or why not?

Postmerger reports should include a range of information that shareholders will find useful. Some of it will conform to GAAP, but some will not. (Consider the shareholder value calculation just discussed.)

Non-GAAP numbers are desirable to shareholders because accounting numbers can be constrained by accounting conventions that may fail to make economic sense over time. A favorite culprit is the "book value" (historical price) of an asset—obviously a number that has little value years later as the true value of the asset grows or declines. Fortunately, there is a constant evolution of accounting standards to keep pace with economic value. For example, GAAP standards make many allowances now for "fair value" in reporting. In fact, the accounting profession has long recognized the importance of nonaccounting measures, and has always encouraged accountants to note them.[10] Whenever non-GAAP measures enable abuses—for example, the "off-balance-sheet entities" that enabled Enron's fraud—they eventually come under GAAP. And to cover all bases, securities law requires a disclaimer for non-GAAP disclosures, so that investors can take them or leave them, as they wish.

Most major companies today take an eclectic approach to valuation and reporting. Many include discounted cash flow statements in their annual reports alongside the required accounting-based financial statements. In addition, major business publications such as *BusinessWeek* use a mix of measures to judge financial performance. The lesson is simple: give shareholders a variety of performance measures to consider.

BUILDING SHAREHOLDER VALUE

From a general, strategic point of view, how can managers increase shareholder value after a merger?

There are a number of general strategies that appear to build the value of a company's shares, no matter how that value is measured. Here are three to consider.

Aim for continued, profitable growth. When it comes to shareholder value, as stated in Chapter 2, profitable growth is superior to cost cutting, and unprofitable growth is superior to downsizing. Companies that grow profitably have a disproportionately higher rate of stock appreciation than do companies that only cut costs: a dollar earned through growth is worth more to shareholders than the same dollar earned through cost cutting. (Of course, in some cases, cost cutting and downsizing may be the best option.)

Alternate external and internal growth. In pursuing growth, a company can either buy or build. Obviously, by the time a company has reached the integration stage, it has already chosen to buy rather than build in at least one case. But after every major acquisition, a company starts back at square one with the same question: should we continue to buy rather than build, or should we spend time building instead? Most companies alternate the two strategies, going from periods of acquisition to periods of internal growth, just as farmers rotate crops. These companies take time to integrate major acquisitions before embarking on new ones. (Again, there is no single correct choice. Some companies may be suited to growth that is entirely internal, others to a steady flow of acquisitions.)

Develop and disclose good corporate governance practices. Corporate boards that practice "good governance" are likely to have the independence and expertise necessary to oversee financial performance after a merger.

Good governance practices include, but are not limited to, independence of the board and its key committees (such as the audit committee), development and disclosure of processes for senior executive evaluation and compensation, and lack of undue restrictions on shareholder voting. Although individual companies lacking some or all of these practices may be successful for long periods of time, these practices tend to be associated with positive share price performance, and many business catastrophes can be traced in part to the absence of one or more of them."[11]

Companies have followed these governance practices on a voluntary basis for years, in part thanks to urging from shareholders. Until recently, however, these practices were not required. The bankruptcies of Enron and WorldCom changed that. In response to these financial disasters, Congress passed the Sarbanes-Oxley Act of 2002. This new law focused mainly on strengthening the audit committee, internal controls, and whistle-blowing. But Sarbanes-Oxley also triggered new stock listing rules pertaining to governance. In late 2003, after consulting with shareholder groups and others for their best practice recommendations, the New York Stock Exchange, the Nasdaq Stock Market, and the AMEX Stock Market all announced new governance standards. These governance standards have caused more board and shareholder involvement in areas that were previously considered management turf.[12]

Are there any model governance guidelines that a merging company could consider adopting?

The most comprehensive and stringent governance standards today are the ones required of New York Stock Exchange companies, namely Section 303A: Corporate Governance Rules, most recently amended in November 2004.

With a few exceptions,[13] these rules could be beneficial to most companies. In addition, companies can study national or international surveys of director and shareholder views[14] or study national and global proxy voting trends. Peer company examples can also be helpful. Most public companies today disclose their governance guidelines on their Web sites.

What postmerger financial indicators are most important to shareholders?

Shareholders look at sales growth and earnings growth, as well as several key ratios based on numbers from the balance sheet, the income statement, and/or stock prices.

In debt-financed acquisitions, shareholders may focus on ratios involving debt, namely:

Current ratio (current assets/current liabilities)
Debt ratio (total liabilities/total assets)
Debt/equity ratio (total liabilities/total equity)
Net working capital (current assets minus current liabilities)

If the merger was financed through equity capital, then shareholders may focus on ratios involving equity:

Earnings per share [(net income – preferred
    dividends)/common shares outstanding][15]
Price/earnings (market price per common share/earnings
    per share)
Equity ratio (total stockholders' equity/total assets)
Return on common stockholders' equity [(net income –
    preferred dividends)/average common stockholders'
    equity]

If a company issues more shares to pay for a merger, this may dilute the value of the existing shares. How can a company mitigate concerns about this?

First, be straightforward about the dilution. Shareholders will notice it, so you might as well point it out and explain it. If future earnings prospects are good, say so—and explain how those earning will be achieved.

Are there any rules against dilution?

No, but there are rules that require disclosure and/or approval of potentially dilutive transactions. For example, in the mutual fund area, the SEC requires the board of any mutual fund that merges with a trust fund or account that is not registered with the SEC to make sure that the interests of the fund's shareholders will not be diluted as a result of the merger. As part of this determination, the fund's board has to approve procedures for the valuation of the securities (or other assets) that the unregistered entity will convey to the fund. The records of the merger must include a report by an independent evaluator on the fair market value of any assets not quoted on a market.[16]

Could you give an example of a successful postmerger communication about dilution?

Here are excerpts from a recent postmerger press release:

INCOME FROM CONTINUING OPERATIONS UP NINE PERCENT; SALES UP 23 PERCENT; COMPANY CONFIRMS ITS FISCAL YEAR 2006 OUTLOOK

ORRVILLE, Ohio, Aug. 22 /PRNewswire-FirstCall/—The J. M. Smucker Company (NYSE: SJM - News) today announced results for the first quarter ended July 31, 2005, of its 2006 fiscal year. . . .

Income from continuing operations was $29.9 million, an increase of nine percent over $27.5 million in last year's first quarter. Sales growth was mostly offset by increased marketing costs in support of the brands, costs associated with establishing the Company's new distribution network, an increase in net interest expense, and compensation expense related to the Company's new restricted stock program. Earnings per diluted share from continuing operations for the first quarter of 2006 were $0.51, compared to $0.50 last year, *impacted by the additional shares issued as part of the Multifoods transaction.*

Income from continuing operations for the first quarter of 2006 included pretax merger and integration costs of $2.9 million, *or $0.03 per diluted* share, and restructuring charges of $1.6 million, or $0.02 *per diluted share*. Income from continuing operations for the first quarter of 2005 included pretax merger and integration costs of $2.8 million, or $0.03 *per diluted share*, and restructuring charges of $3.0 million, or $0.04 *per diluted share*. Excluding these costs in both years, the Company's income from continuing operations was up six percent. *Due to the additional shares issued as part of the Multifoods transaction, earnings per diluted share were $0.56 and $0.57,* in the first quarters of 2006 and 2005, respectively.

For financial strategies to minimize the impact of dilution, see Chapter 5.

One cause of dilution is the use of equity to finance a deal. Could you comment on the use of equity versus debt?

Sure. There are four common ways to finance a merger, as mentioned earlier in this book. In order of frequency, companies use cash, stock, a combination of cash and stock, and a combination of notes and cash and/or stock. Each of these payment strategies will have a different impact on the value of a company's equity.[17]

- *Equity impact of an all-cash deal.* This can vary, depending on whether the acquirer used its own cash or borrowed the cash that it used. Overall, when compared to share-financed deals, cash-financed deals have a more positive impact on share prices over a long (five-year) term. Acquirers should avoid taking on too much debt, though. As explained in Chapter 8, a debt-financed transaction that causes the acquirer to have a debt/equity ratio of 0.75 or more is considered to be a heavily leveraged transaction (HLT). Such transactions often have a negative impact on share values.
- *Equity impact of an all-stock deal.* The impact of this type of deal also varies depending on the source (in this case, the source of the stock). In exchanging its stock for the seller's stock, the acquirer can either issue new shares or convince existing shareholders to exchange their shares with the seller's shareholders.

  The first scenario (using new shares) may cause dilution.

  The second scenario (using existing shares) can signal that the acquirer knows that its stock is priced high.

Both of these possibilities can explain why share values do not do as well overall following stock deals as following cash deals.

- Equity impact after a cash-and-stock deal. If the acquirer combines cash and stock in the payment, the impact on postmerger compensation may be positive or negative, depending on the sources of these instruments, as explained earlier.
- Equity impact of a contingency deal. Sometimes acquirers offer the seller notes promising additional payments or "earn-outs" based on meeting certain financial goals. Obviously, from the shareholders' perspective, this mode of financing, although rare, is ideal. If the goals are not met, the company (and its shareholders) pays nothing. If the goals are met, then the company (and the value of its equity) is bound to improve. This is especially true if the performance goals relate to share price or to ratios that relate to share price.

In summary, an acquisition may have a negative or a positive effect on the acquirer's share price, and this effect depends in part on how the deal was financed. It is up to postdeal managers to do what they can to ensure the most positive outcome for shareholders, and to admit, explain, and work to correct any negative result to existing shareholders, rather than hoping for a new generation of owners to come along.

As mentioned, many companies today put Frequently Asked Question (FAQ) sections on their Web sites following a merger to address the concerns of various constituencies. In Chapter 10, "Fulfilling Commitments to Customers and Suppliers," we saw an example from Sprint Nextel, a merger announced in December 2004. The example in Box 11-1, from JPMorgan Chase, includes questions shareholders might ask.

POSTMERGER RETURNS

What kind of returns can shareholders expect following a merger?

Researchers in universities and consulting firms have produced scores of studies on postmerger financial returns over the past few decades. Summarizing more than 100 studies, Robert Bruner, dean of the Darden School of Business,[18] found that in general,

> The shareholders of *selling firms* earn *large* returns.
> The shareholders of *buyers and sellers combined* earn *significant* returns.
> The shareholders of *buyers* usually earn the *required rate of return*.

This summary may surprise those who are used to reading in consultants' PowerPoint presentations, "80 percent of all mergers fail." Although such findings do appear in some credible studies, they do not represent an average. Consulting firms are not necessarily skewing the data in their own research; however, in reporting research findings from themselves and others, they may gravitate toward negative results, since they are geared to providing solutions to problems.

B O X   1 1 – 1

Frequently Asked Questions from Shareholders—An
Example from JPMorgan Chase (September 2005)

Merger FAQ for stockholders

- What happens to my JPMorgan Chase stock?
- What happens to my Bank One stock?
- What should I do with my Bank One stock certificates?
- Is the exchange of Bank One stock certificates mandatory?
- What if I cannot locate all of my Bank One certificates or if I
  have any questions about lost, misplaced, or stolen shares?
- Will I receive a physical certificate from the exchange of my
  Bank One common stock certificates?
- How long will it take the exchange agent, Mellon Investor
  Services, to exchange my Bank One certificates?
- How should I send my Bank One stock to the exchange agent,
  Mellon Investor Services?
- Does JPMorgan Chase pay a dividend on its common stock?
- How will I get paid for dividends going forward?
- Does JPMorgan Chase have a dividend reinvestment plan?
- What are the tax consequences of the merger?
- What is the tax basis of my new JPMorgan Chase stock?
- What is JPMorgan Chase's ticker symbol?
- Who can I contact if I have additional questions?

LEGAL ASPECTS OF SHAREHOLDER RELATIONS

How often do shareholders sue companies, what are their main issues, and how much do they sue for?

In 2004, 57 percent of all director's and officer's liability insurance
claims were filed by shareholders of large companies. (Such claims
represented 31 percent of lawsuits filed by shareholders of private
companies.) The average payment made to shareholders in 2004
was $11,443,250.

Could you give an example of a recent shareholder lawsuit over a merger?

In August 2005, Time Warner reached a $2.4 billion settlement with a shareholder group (or class) that had filed a class-action lawsuit against the company for poor financial performance after its merger with AOL.[19] Under the settlement, Time Warner agreed to pay $2.4 billion into a settlement fund for the plaintiffs in a class-action suit that alleged fraud at America Online. The reserve covers only the primary securities class action. Remaining litigation threats include shareholder derivative actions and securities actions brought by individual shareholders.

Time Warner established an additional reserve of $600 million for those unresolved complaints. The shareholder class named in the suit as plaintiffs was the subset of owners who had purchased shares in AOL or Time Warner between Jan. 27, 1999, and Aug. 27, 2002. Three years later (August 2005), the company's shares were still trading at 75 percent lower than premerger levels.[20]

How can shareholders sue over strategic decisions such as mergers or sell-offs? Doesn't the "business judgment rule" protect directors and officers against these kinds of lawsuits?

Yes, the business judgment rule—a judicial doctrine used in state courts—does offer some legal protection. The rule says that directors cannot be sued for making any particular decision (even one with bad results) as long as they made the decision on an informed basis, in good faith, and in the honest belief that the action taken was in the best interest of the company. The burden is on litigants to prove that directors failed to meet these standards. However, the legal meaning of these standards has evolved over time in response to changing aspirational standards—as noted by Chancellor William Allen in the August 2005 decision concerning excessive compensation to a departing CEO at the Walt Disney Company.

So how can companies avoid getting sued because of mergers and other strategic decisions?

In making decisions, companies should not only follow the spirit of the business judgment rule, but keep a paper trail to prove it. Also, before, during, and after any major corporate decision, companies should seek the views of shareholders (particularly major, long-term shareholders) to ensure their support.

You mentioned earlier that a corporate board of directors owes its primary fiduciary duty to shareholders "in most cases." When can the interests of other stakeholders take primacy?

In U.S. law, there are two well-defined circumstances in which directors can place a priority on nonstockholder interests. The first is a merger or other special transaction, and the second is insolvency.

The first circumstance arose from backlash against the hostile takeovers of the 1980s. A majority of states have passed laws that allow directors to look beyond short-term shareholder returns in making decisions on corporate transactions, including mergers. These laws go under a variety of names (*stakeholder laws, other constituency laws, directors' duties laws, nonmonetary considerations laws,* and *nonstockholder considerations laws*), but they all mean the same thing: directors need not automatically and always put shareholder interests first, but may consider the effects of a transaction on other groups, including customers, suppliers, bondholders, lenders, employees, and communities. So, for example, directors may refuse to accept a hostile takeover bid that pay a premium to shareholders at the price of massive layoffs.

Insolvency can bring nonshareholder interests to the fore, thanks to the "absolute priority" principle under Chapter 11 of the U.S. Bankruptcy Code. This principle says that creditors must be paid before shareholders. Traditionally, this "absolute" has put bondholders, lenders, and other creditors ahead of shareholders in a bankruptcy. Some experts believe that this affirmative duty to creditors can begin well before a formal declaration of insolvency.

COMMITMENTS TO BONDHOLDERS

This brings us to the subject of bondholders. What basic duties does a newly merged company owe them?

Unlike the multiple, complex, and often elusive duties that companies owe to the stakeholders discussed so far (customers, suppliers, and shareholders), a newly merged company has only one basic duty to bondholders, and this is simple and clear: *a company must honor the terms of the bonds it sells.*

Unlike building shareholder value, repaying bonds is fairly straightforward. A typical bond is a promissory note (generally issued in large quantities to multiple buyers) whose issuer promises to repay the principal value of the bond (also known as *par* or *face* value), along with interest at a stated annual rate. Interest on a bond is usually paid twice a year (for example, June 30 and December 31), and the face amount of the bond is typically repaid on a predetermined maturity date. These terms are typically written up in a *bond indenture.*

A regular bond (as opposed to a convertible or hybrid bond) is a debt instrument, as opposed to an equity instrument. The common signs of debt, according to rulings of the U.S. Internal Revenue Service and U.S. courts, are a certain maturity date that is neither unduly remote nor contingent, a reasonable interest rate, and holders' rights upon default. If a so-called bond lacks these traits, it may in fact be an equity security—and should be valued as such. In fact, in some cases, such as when bonds are collateralized through company equity, bond-holders can automatically gain control of the company's stock.

The Caux Round Table's *Principles of Business* does not have a section on bondholders. If it did, this section would probably be very similar to the one on investors. Here is an adaptation of the shareholder section of the Caux statement, along with postmerger checkpoints.

BONDHOLDERS

We believe in honoring the trust our bondholders place in us. We therefore have a responsibility to:

- apply professional and diligent management in order to ensure full repayment of bonds;
  Checkpoints: How much money will the company owe what bondholders when? Can the company afford to pay? How do the interest rates of the bonds compare with current rates? Will it be in the long-term interest of the company to pay bondholders at these rates? If not, does the company plan to repurchase or call the bonds? Are any of the bonds convertible to securities? If so, is the company prepared to honor that commitment?[21]

- disclose relevant information to bondholders subject to legal requirements and competitive constraints;

Checkpoints: In disclosing their postmerger plans, have the managements of both companies addressed the potential concerns of bondholders?

- conserve, protect, and increase as appropriate the amounts in any funds set up for bond repayment;
  Checkpoints: Which bonds are backed by bond sinking funds (funds set up for the purpose of repaying bonds)? What is the state of those funds? Is there a shortfall? What plans are there for making up the shortfall? Is the company keeping the promises it made in its indenture?

- respect bondholders' requests, suggestions, complaints, and formal resolutions.
  Checkpoints: Have the two merging companies encouraged communications from their bondholders about the merger? What kinds of communications have bondholders made? What kind of responses did they get?

In the previous section, we explored shareholder value. What about bondholder value?

If bonds are traded on the open market, their valuation on that market, combined with their rating, indicates their value. If they are not traded on the open market, they can be compared to similar instruments with similar ratings that are traded on the open market.[22]

Bond rating agencies tend not to use the term *value*, but rather to use the term *protection*. To see if a bond is "protected," they look at three key ratios:

Debt/EBITDA (total debt/earnings before interest, taxes, depreciation, and amortization)
Risk-adjusted leverage (EBITDA times an industry risk factor)
EBITDA/cash interest

Could you give an example of how bondholders (or a bond rating agency) might view a specific merger that involves extensive integration?

What are some key bondholder rights?

Bondholder rights are spelled out in the indenture promises, or *covenants*. In these provisions, the company promises to refrain (except under certain stated conditions) from doing anything that would reduce the chances of repayment—such as paying dividends, borrowing money, selling assets, or merging with another company. Achieving waivers on these points (especially the last one!) can be an important part of planning a merger, and can be vital to achieving postmerger integration as well.

Clearly, one important task of managers after a merger will be to study all bond indentures of both the buyer and the seller to ensure continued conformity to the promised conditions. It might be useful to create a master document summarizing all promises.

COMMITMENTS TO LENDERS

What basic duties does a company owe its lenders?

The basic duty is to repay lenders at the terms stated in the loan agreements. Expanding on this core duty, we might once again adapt the Caux document, this time to lenders.

LENDERS

We believe in honoring the trust our lenders place in us. We therefore have a responsibility to:

- apply professional and diligent management in order to ensure full repayment of loans;
  Checkpoints: How much money does the company owe what lenders when? Can the company afford to pay? How do the interest rates on the loans compare with current rates? Will it be in the long-term interest of the company to pay loans at these rates? If not, does the company plan to pay the loans off early?

- disclose relevant information to lenders subject to legal requirements and competitive constraints;
  Checkpoints: In disclosing their postmerger plans, have the managements of both companies addressed the potential concerns of lenders?

- conserve, protect, and increase as appropriate any amounts earmarked for loan repayment; and
  Checkpoints: Have funds been set aside to repay specific loans? Are the amounts adequate?

- respect lenders' requests, suggestions, and complaints.
  Checkpoints: Have the two merging companies encouraged communications from their lenders about the merger? What kinds of communications have lenders made? What kind of responses did they get?

What is the basic "value" of a loan, and what rights do lenders have?

Like bonds, loans are debt instruments. They have a maturity date, an interest rate, and lenders' rights on default. So the value of a loan is basically principal plus interest—unless the company defaults, in which case (as mentioned earlier) lenders join bondholders as the first in line to be repaid.

Lenders' rights are spelled out in the covenants of their loan agreements. These typically include the same proscriptions that appear in bond indentures, plus several others. As mentioned in Chapter 2, one common prohibition is the sale of company units. In a highly leveraged transaction, the borrower is often asked to promise that it will comply with the business plan, provide early warning of economic trouble, protect collateral, and control expenditures. Some loan agreements specify in great detail exactly how the borrower is expected to fulfill these promises.

Our earlier suggestion about creating a master list of bond covenants could be extended to loan covenants. What actions has each of the combining companies promised to perform (or avoid) under its various loan agreements? A master list of these will be a useful checklist for postmerger behavior.

INTERNATIONAL CONSIDERATIONS

What are some key challenges in shareholder relations for cross-border mergers?

The primary challenges are differing shareholder rights and expectations based on different securities laws, stock exchange regulations, and corporate bylaws.

How can a postmerger team help a company meet the challenge of different shareholder rights and expectations?

First, of course, the team will want to determine which laws, regulations, and bylaws apply to its newly expanded shareholder base. So it will need to know where the company is incorporated, where its shares are listed, and who its shareholders are. This might sound easy, but in the case of a multinational holding company, it can be extremely complex. Such a company can have multiple places of incorporation, multiple stock exchange listings, and a highly multinational shareholder base.

Could you give an example of a multinational with a complex ownership structure?

Sure. One that comes to mind is Solvay S.A., a EUR$8 billion multinational headquartered in Ixelles, Belgium, that has continued to evolve through M&A and divestiture.

Most recently, it completed the acquisition, via a public bid (tender offer) to shareholders, of Girindus AG, a specialty chemicals company in Bensberg, Germany. Solvay is the parent company of a worldwide chemical and pharmaceutical group specializing in the pharmaceuticals, chemicals, and plastics areas. It employs 30,000 people in 50 countries. Its shares trade on the Euronext stock market (formed by a merger of the Paris, Amsterdam, Brussels, and Lisbon stock exchanges and that of the United Kingdom), and also sells equity via American Depository Receipts in the United States, where it trades over the counter.

How does Solvay cater to the various nationalities of its shareholders?

Solvay communicates with investors in several languages. The company's 2004 annual report was published in Dutch, English, and French. It conforms to the Lippens Code, the governance code of Belgium, which focuses on shareholder rights.[23]

Speaking of the European Union, what is the regulatory climate for mergers there, and how does it affect postmerger integration?

Each member of the European Union has its own comprehensive merger laws, but these are superseded by E.U. law—just as in the United States, state law is generally superseded by federal law. The European Union has in force a European Directive on Takeovers.

What is the European Directive on Takeovers?

The European Directive on Takeovers, also called the 13th Company
Directive (or, in this chapter, the directive), sets forth five principles
for the conduct of public company acquisitions in the European
Union and requires that each member state set up a supervisory
authority to ensure conformity to these principles.

What are the five guiding principles asserted in the directive?

The directive addresses itself to the responsibilities of both offerors
(those buying shares in a tender offer) and offerees (those selling
their shares in a tender offer), as follows:

1. Offerors must offer the same terms to all offerees in the
   same position.
2. Offerors must give offerees enough time and information
   to make an informed decision on the offer.
3. Board members of the offeree company must act in the
   best interests of the company as a whole.
4. An offer must not create false markets in the securities of
   the offeree company, of the offeror company, or of any
   other company concerned in the offer.
5. The business of an offeree company should not be
   hindered beyond a reasonable time by an offer for its
   securities.

Each country implements the directive through its own laws.
For example, in January 2005, the United Kingdom published
guidance on implementing the directive.[24]

What is the Organization for Economic Cooperation and Development (OECD), and what has it published on the subject of shareholder rights?

The OECD is an organization of 30 countries that wishes to create
voluntary best practices for business. It is similar to the Caux
Round Table in its purpose, but it is much broader in scope. (Caux
focuses exclusively on social responsibility.)

The OECD Principles of Corporate Governance call for

Effective institutional and legal frameworks to support good
   corporate governance practices
Corporate governance frameworks that protect and facilitate
   the exercise of shareholders' rights
Equal treatment of all shareholders, including minority and
   foreign shareholders
A role for stakeholders in corporate governance
Timely, accurate, and transparent disclosure mechanisms
Improved board structures, responsibilities, and procedures

The guidelines say that all shareholders, including institutional investors, must be enabled to exercise ownership rights so as
to influence the companies in which they own shares. As part of
this, the principles advocate that shareholder rights include participating in the nomination and election of board members, as well
as in the removal of board members. Shareholders should be able
to make their views known about executive and board remuneration policy. Any equity component of remuneration should be
subject to their approval. These rights are currently mandated
under securities laws in the United States and certain other countries, but the OECD guidelines aspire to make them a standard for
all 30 OECD member countries. The World Bank has worked to
broaden their application to countries around the world. Thus, any
postmerger integration team charged with shareholder relations
following an international merger would be wise to become familiar with these guidelines.

APPENDIX   1 1 – A

Simple Formulas for Calculating Shareholder Value

Earlier in this chapter, readers encountered a discussion of shareholder value. For the mathematically inclined, here is that same
discussion, with formulas.

The shareholder value approach to company valuation says that the total economic value of a company, or its corporate value, equals the value of its debt plus the value of its equity (shareholder value).[25]

Corporate value = debt + shareholder value

Therefore,

Shareholder value = corporate value − debt

Corporate value in this approach is defined as the present value of cash flows from operations during a forecast period plus the present value of business attributable to a period beyond the forecast period (or *residual value*), plus marketable securities.

Corporate value = present value of cash flows from operations during the forecast period + residual value + marketable securities

The calculation of the *present value of cash flows during a forecast period* begins, of course, with a calculation of cash flows. To get the present value of cash flows, a company must set a discount rate, also called a company's cost of capital. A company's cost of capital is the weighted average of its costs of debt and equity capital. A company's cost of debt is calculated as the cost of new debt (as opposed to previously outstanding debt). Its cost of equity is the risk-free rate of return that the company could get from a low-risk instrument, plus an equity risk premium. A company's risk-free rate of return is the real interest rate paid by the low-risk instrument plus the expected inflation rate. Its equity risk premium, also known as the stock's beta, is the volatility of the return on a company's stock compared to the volatility of returns in the stock market as a whole.

Here are the formulas:

Cash flow from operations is cash inflow minus cash outflow. These are calculated as follows:

Cash flow = cash inflow − cash outflow

Cash inflow = sales in the prior year × (1 + sales growth rate) × operating profit margin × (1 − cash income tax rate)

Cash outflow = incremental fixed capital investment + working capital investment

In calculating the *present value* of cash flow, companies have to figure out a company's *cost of capital*—on both the debt and the equity side.

A company's cost of capital is the weighted average of its costs of debt and equity capital.

A company's *cost of debt* is calculated as the cost of new debt (as opposed to previously outstanding debt). This is the long-term rate or yield to maturity that reflects the rate currently demanded by debtholders.

A company's *cost of equity* is the risk-free rate of return the company could get from a low-risk instrument, plus an equity risk premium.

Cost of equity = risk-free rate + equity risk premium

A company's *risk-free rate of return* is the real interest rate paid by the instrument, plus the expected inflation rate.

Risk-free rate = real interest rate + expected inflation rate.

A company's *equity risk premium*, also known as the stock's *beta*, is the volatility of the return on a company's stock compared to the volatility of returns in the stock market as a whole. Individual stocks tend to be more or less risky than the overall market. The riskiness of a stock, as measured by its beta, is the volatility of its return in relation to that of the market portfolio. The rate of return from dividends and capital appreciation on the market portfolio will, by definition, fluctuate identically with the market, and therefore its beta is equal to 1.0. Stocks with betas greater than 1.0 are more volatile than the market, and thus carry a risk premium greater than the overall market risk premium. For example, if a stock moves up or down 1.5 percent when the market moves up or down 1 percent, the stock would have a beta of 1.5.

Risk premium = beta (expected return on market
− risk-free rate)

Residual value, also called going-concern value, often constitutes the largest portion of the value of a firm. It can be calculated in several ways. One common way is the perpetuity method. This method assumes that a company that is able to generate returns above the cost of capital (i.e., excess returns) will eventually attract competitors, whose entry into the business will drive down returns to the minimum acceptable or cost of capital rate. Thus, the perpetuity method assumes that after the forecast period, the business will earn, on average, the cost of capital on new investments. Therefore, future flows can be treated as if they were a perpetuity, or an infinite stream of identical cash flows. The residual value is the perpetuity cash flow divided by the cost of capital.

Present value of a perpetuity = annual cash flow/rate of return

Residual value = perpetuity cash flow/cost of capital

Marketable securities is the current value of any investments that can be converted to cash and are not essential to operating the business.

Note: This shareholder value approach, pioneered by Dr. Rappaport, is one of several established approaches to corporate value. Others include *economic value added,* or EVA, pioneered by Joel Stern of Stern Stuart, New York, and *cash flow return on investment,* created by Bart Madden of HOLT Value Associates, Chicago. All three of these approaches have been in use for over two decades. In addition, there are many newer approaches that show promise. A notable example is the brand-new formula used for the "BusinessWeek 50. This book emphasizes the shareholder value approach because it has the longest M&A applications history.

N O T E S

1 This is the philosophy of most shareholder activists, for example, Robert A. G. Monks and Nell Minow, *Corporate Governance,* 3d ed. (Oxford, U.K.: Blackwell Business Publishers, 2003).

2 Charles Erwin Wilson, former CEO and chairman of General Motors, told the Senate Armed Forces Committee in 1952 that "What is good for the country is good for General Motors, and what is good for General Motors is good for the country."

3 See, for example, *Board-Shareowner Communications: Report of the CII-NACD Joint Task Force* (Washington, D.C., 2004). This task force was co-chaired by Peter M. Gilbert, chief investment officer, Pennsylvania State Employees' Retirement System, and board member of the Council of Institutional Investors (CII); and Warren L. Batts, corporate director and a board member, National Association of Corporate Directors (NACD). See also *Boardroom Briefing* (Philadephia PA: Director & Boards, Fall 2005).

4 In the United States, federal securities laws are embodied in the Securities Act of 1933 and the Securities Exchange Act of 1934; state laws are modeled (more or less) on the Model Business Corporation Act, compiled and periodically updated by the American Bar Association–American Law Institute. The three main U.S. stock exchanges are the New York Stock Exchange, the Nasdaq, and the AMEX.

5 The Web site for the ACC, which used to be called the American Corporate Counsel Association, is acca.com. The Web site for Martindale Hubbell is http://www.martindale.com.

6 It is beyond the scope of this chapter to review securities law pertaining to mergers. For an overview of this area of securities law, see Alexandra R. Lajoux and Charles M. Elson, *The Art of M&A Due Diligence: Navigating Critical Steps and Uncovering Crucial Data* (New York: McGraw-Hill, 2000), and Alexandra R. Lajoux and H. Peter Nesvold, *The Art of M&A Structuring: Techniques for Mitigating Financial, Tax, and Legal Risk* (New York: McGraw-Hill, 2004).

7 For more on the safe harbor for forward-looking statements, see Chapter 3.

8 This is not to deny the importance of courting new shareholders. For guidance, see Benjamin Mark Cole, *The New Investor Relations: Expert Perspectives on the State of the Art* (New York: Bloomberg, 2003). Also, see anything published by the National Investor Relations Institute (NIRI), at www.niri.org.

9 This answer summarizes Alfred Rappaport's *Creating Shareholder Value* (New York: The Free Press, 1997), still the undisputed bible on the topic since its original publication in 1986.

10 For a discussion of "enhanced business reporting," see Chapter 5.

11 For recent studies linking governance and performance Paul
MacAvoy and Ira M. Millstein, *The Recurrent Crisis in Corporate
Governance* (Stanford, California: Stanford University Press, 2004);
and Sang Woo Nam and Il Chong Nam, "Linkage between the
Quality of Corporate Governance and Firm Performance," Asian
Development Bank Institute, February 2005, http://www.adbi.org.

12 For a recent survey, see David W. Anderson, Stewart J. Melanson,
and Jiri Maly, "An Emerging Governance Model," working paper,
Aug. 14, 2005. The Toronto-based authors are affiliated, respectively,
with HRI Corporation; Rotman School of Management, University
of Toronto; and McKinsey & Company.

13 The NYSE guidelines state that audit committees must have charters
detailing their duties, and set forth a minimum list of duties that
may not be delegated to any other committee. One of the duties is
oversight of legal compliance. Many directors and their counsel
believe that it would be better to have a separate independent
committee to oversee legal compliance, as financial risk oversight is
already a very broad task for the audit committee.

14 For a recent survey, see Anderson, Melanson, and Maly, "An
Emerging Governance Model." See also the *2005 Public Company
Governance Survey* (Washington, D.C.: National Association of
Corporate Directors, 2005).

15 Companies that have issued instruments (bonds and/or preferred
stock) that are convertible into common stock require more complex
calculations.

16 This was part of an SEC rule relaxing restrictions on mergers
between affiliated funds. See "Investment Company Mergers,"
Securities and Exchange Commission, Final Rule, 17 CFR
Part 270, Release No. IC-25666; File No. S7-21-01, RIN 3235-AH81,
July 26, 2002.

17 The value of equity can be measured in various ways. In this
discussion, we are assuming a simple valuation—stock price
appreciation or decline over a defined postmerger period.

18 Robert F. Bruner, "Does M&A Pay," *Applied Mergers & Acquisitions*
(New York: McGraw-Hill, 2004), pp. 30–66.

19 "Time Warner Sets Settlement of Suit over AOL Merger: Media
Conglomerate Sets Share Buyback, Swings to $321 Million Loss for
Quarter," *Wall Street Journal Online*, Aug. 3, 2005.

20 As of Sept. 6, 2005, the settlement had not yet been approved.

21 Some bonds are *callable* under the indenture. If a bond is callable,
the company can retire the entire issue early, paying whatever call

premium is promised under the indenture. If a bond is not callable, a company can try to buy back the bonds in the open market.

22 For a step-by-step procedure for bond valuation, with special instructions on complex hybrid instruments, see Tim Koller, Mark Goedhart, and David Wessels, *Valuation: Measuring and Managing the Value of Companies* (New York: McKinsey and Company, 2005). The original edition (1990) of this classic was authored by Tom Copeland, Tim Koller, and Jack Murrin.

23 The Belgian Governance Code, Dec. 9, 2004. The group writing this code was chaired by Maurice Lippens.

24 See http://www.dti.gov.uk/consultations/files/publication-1439. pdf, published January 2005.

25 The author acknowledges the contributions of Alfred Rappaport to this section.

Fulfilling Commitments to Employees and Communities

Man is not the sum of what he has but the totality of what he does not yet have, of what he might have.

Jean Paul Sartre, *Situations*

INTRODUCTION

During the critical months that follow the closing of a deal, managers must strive to create a climate of trust. To do this, they must honor any and all commitments that the merging companies have already made to their stakeholders. So what are these promises when it comes to employees and communities?

Once again, the Caux Round Table's *Principles for Business* offers a useful introduction to our inquiry. This important document urges companies to create and preserve jobs, build positive working conditions, communicate and negotiate openly and honestly with employees, grant equal opportunity, accommodate differences in ability, foster safety and wellness, provide training, and help employees find opportunities when and if they leave the company. In this closing chapter, we will touch on all these values as they affect postmerger integration, with advice on how to build trust in a changing environment. Next, this chapter gives tips on how to fulfill commitments to local communities, affirming Robert Bruner's opening observation, "All M&A is local." Our closing pages describe how mergers can affect multiple locations, with comments on employee and community issues in cross-border deals.

COMMITMENTS TO EMPLOYEES

What commitments to employees does a company typically have to fulfill after a merger?

Once again—as with customers, suppliers, stockholders, bondholders, and lenders—managers should review all outstanding contractual commitments with employees. Ideally, this will be a second review, benefiting from good due diligence. (See Appendix A to this book.)

For a general overview, the Caux Round Table's *Principles for Business* again proves useful. Here is the "Employees" section of the stakeholder list, with our postmerger *checkpoints*.

Employees

We believe in the dignity of every employee and in taking employee interests seriously. We therefore have a responsibility to:

- provide jobs and compensation that improve workers' living conditions;

    Checkpoints: Are there plans to eliminate locations and/or jobs as a result of this merger? Are these plans ironclad, or can the company consider alternatives such as divisional sales? If layoffs are unavoidable, has the company given the affected employees adequate notice and compensation? For those who stay, will work and pay improve? Can workers who are to be laid off be used as part of the team that closes operations? (See Chapter 3.)

- provide working conditions that respect each employee's health and dignity;

    Checkpoints: How do the two merging companies compare with respect to working conditions? Does either company have a history of violations of the Occupational Safety and Health Act (OSHA) or other labor laws? If one company's policies are clearly superior to the other's, will its policies take precedence?

- be honest in communications with employees and open in sharing information, limited only by legal and competitive concerns;

Checkpoints: What is the communication style of the leading postmerger management team? What about the rest of the company? What can be done to improve the postmerger communication environment?

- listen to and, where possible, act on employee suggestions, ideas, requests, and complaints;

  Checkpoints: Does the company have an employee hotline for whistleblowers? Does it have a whistleblower policy, and is this policy included in a larger code of conduct?

- engage in good faith negotiations when conflict arises;

  Checkpoints: What potential conflicts concern the management of the newly merged concern? Who should address these, when, and how? What procedures will the new company have for resolving grievances?

- avoid discriminatory practices and guarantee equal treatment and opportunity in areas such as gender, age, race, and religion;

  Checkpoints: Does the newly merged company have a clear, consistent plan for equal opportunity? What is the level of diversity/"proversity"[1] in each of the two merging companies? Is there a plan to improve these?

- promote in the business itself the employment of differently abled people in places of work where they can be genuinely useful;

  Checkpoints: With respect to the differently abled, do the hiring, training, and promotion practices and policies of the newly merged company engage and reward the best in people, making reasonable accommodations for their differences?

- protect employees from avoidable injury and illness in the workplace;

  Checkpoints: What safety and health policies does each of the merging companies have? How will these be combined?

- encourage and assist employees in developing relevant and transferable skills and knowledge;

  Checkpoints: What training and retraining will the combination require? To what extent will the new company consider these as alternatives to replacement of employees?

- be sensitive to the serious unemployment problems frequently associated with business decisions, and work with governments, employee groups, other agencies, and each other in addressing these dislocations.

  Checkpoints: Is the management of the newly merged company engaged in a dialogue with various stakeholders about the long-term employment outlook? What hope can this dialogue offer? What outplacement programs does the new company offer?

Of all the Caux lists, this one is the longest, presenting positive values in nine distinct areas: job creation, working conditions, communications, negotiations, equal opportunity, accommodation of differences, safety/wellness, training/retraining, and outplacement. If the merging companies have made commitments in these areas, the new company must honor them. If the new company has not made commitments in these areas, it should consider doing so, for reasons discussed throughout the rest of this chapter.

Why is it important to make and keep commitments to employees?

Once again, as we have seen in considering other stakeholders, the answer involves ethics, law, and economics. Breaking a promise not only is wrong (and sometimes illegal), but may have negative economic consequences. For example, key employees may leave because they lose trust in the new organization.

If employees leave, can't the new company just hire new people to replace them, or outsource their work?

Yes, but each of these alternatives can be costly. Existing employees have already been recruited and trained. Replacing them with equally qualified employees is not economically neutral, because it usually means that a company must pay for recruitment and training a *second time* for the same positions.

In addition, there are the negative "multiplier" effects of employee departures, whether voluntary or involuntary. For example, the employees who remain may feel guilt with respect to the employees who lost their jobs—either managerial guilt because they were the ones who planned and/or communicated the job cuts, or survivor guilt because their own jobs were spared.

As for outsourcing, it is not a magic bullet. It takes a lot of management time communicating with a vendor about expectations for quality. Also, vendors have their own overhead to cover, and the hourly rate of their employees or contractors reflects that charge.

When firms eliminate large numbers of jobs, the negative impact shows up in their number of disability claims (salary-replacement benefits paid to employees). Research has shown a correlation between corporate changes such as downsizing and a rise in claims for disability payments.[2]

Aside from the issue of disability claims, though, don't job cuts usually lead to savings?

The short answer is yes, but so what? Job cuts reduce the outflow of compensation payments to employees over the long term (after all the first-year hits costs of severance pay, outplacement costs, and the like). But job reductions can also reduce the inflow of revenue over the long term, and they may lead to a decrease in shareholder value (defined in the preceding chapter). And remember, savings from job cuts count only if they are net savings, after payment of termination benefits. These payments often lead to large one-time charges immediately after a merger, depressing financial performance in the very short term (a single quarter).

Most investors recognize this charge as an accounting phenomenon and do not penalize companies for it per se; instead, they focus on savings one or two years out. So stock prices may rise temporarily on downsizing announcements. In the longer run, however, as mentioned in Chapter 2, investors gain more from profitable growth companies than from cost-cutting downsizers.

This is why some companies involve human resources staff as early as possible in a transaction, and keep them engaged.

When do human resources personnel typically get involved in a merger?

Traditionally, the human resources department (HR) was frozen out until the actual moment of integration. In recent years, this has changed. A 2005 survey by Mercer Human Resource Consulting indicates that only 36 percent of merging companies wait that long. Most companies now involve HR *before* integration: 40 percent begin in the transaction phase (due diligence); and 24 percent begin even earlier getting involved during the strategy phase (planning).[3]

Reasons for earlier involvement of HR involvement in merger integration include:

- General recognition of the value of human capital, as promoted by professional service firms consulting in this area (for example, Arthur Andersen LLP employed more than 80 professionals in its "human capital" practice before the firm's untimely demise in 2002).

- Growth in the professionalism of the HR function through organizations such as the Society for Human Resource Management in Alexandria, Virginia (shrm.org).
- Increase in the use of employee stock option plans.

What are employee stock ownership plans, and how common are they?

Employee stock ownership plans (ESOPs) are plans that enable employees to own the stock of their employer.

- There are approximately 11,000 ESOPs in place in the United States, covering 10 million employees (10 percent of the private-sector workforce).
- These employees draw in excess of 3 percent of their total compensation from ESOP contributions.
- The growth of ESOP formation has been influenced by federal legislation. While the rapid increase in new ESOPs in the late 1980s subsided after Congress removed certain tax incentives in 1989, the overall number has remained steady, with new plans replacing terminated ESOPs. The approximate chronology is as follows:

1974	200 companies with ESOPs
1981	1,500
1984	2,500
1987	5,000
1990	10,000
1996	10,000
1997	10,000
2000	11,500
2002	11,500
2003	11,500
2004	11,000
2005	11,000

- About 800 ESOPs (7 percent) are in publicly traded companies. However, these companies employ just under 50 percent of the nation's 10 million employee owners.
- In an estimated 6,000 of the 11,000 companies with ESOPs, the ESOPs are large enough to be a major factor in the corporation's strategy and culture.

- Approximately 3,500 ESOP companies are majority-owned by the ESOP.
- Approximately 2,000 ESOP companies are 100 percent owned by the ESOP.
- About 4 percent of ESOP companies are unionized.
- While ESOPs are found in all industries, more than 25 percent of them are in the manufacturing sector, followed closely by construction and distributing.
- At least 75 percent of ESOP companies are or were leveraged, meaning that they used borrowed funds to acquire the employer securities held by the ESOP trustee.
- A majority of ESOP companies have other retirement plans, such as defined-benefit pension plans or 401(k) plans, to supplement their ESOP.
- Of the 11,000 employee-owned companies nationwide, fewer than 3 percent were financially distressed when they established their ESOP.
- Total assets owned by U.S. ESOPs are estimated to be $600 billion at the end of 2004.[4]

What effect does employee ownership have on shareholder value?

In general, it has a positive effect, since it links employee and shareholder interests. The precise effect depends on whether the employees have voting rights. When they do, they often vote for initiatives that are in their own short-term interests rather than the interests of the corporation as a whole—for example, they might oppose a merger on the grounds that it might lead to job cuts, irrespective of its benefits for the corporation as a whole. Do pension funds take the same attitude as ESOP owners? Since pension funds represent workers, don't they usually consider job security when voting for or against mergers?

Pension funds are not supposed to cast their proxy votes for the interests of current employees; they are supposed to vote for the interests of retirees. Explaining this point requires some historical background. Under the Employee Retirement Income Security Act of 1974, which covers private (nongovernment) companies, fund fiduciaries have an affirmative duty to vote in the interests of beneficiaries. For many years, most funds ignored this duty and voted with management instead.

In 1988, however, the Department of Labor (DoL) wrote a letter to the Avon Company pension fund that articulated this duty. The letter was widely influential. Many fiduciaries interpreted it to mean that, in most cases, they should vote for a high-premium bidder, even if it was a known liquidator that would lay off union members.

In subsequent communications, the DoL has clarified this "Avon letter duty," letting pension funds consider long-term returns to beneficiaries. Fund fiduciaries can vote against a tender offer with a high premium, said the DoL, if they have reason to believe that resisting the takeover would bring larger gains to beneficiaries in the future.

In recent years, many large companies have carried out massive layoffs. What are some examples, and what connection did they have, if any, to mergers?

The largest layoffs in this decade have *not* been associated with mergers. In both 2004 and 2005, for example, more than one million individuals filed for unemployment insurance due to "mass lay-offs"—10,773 in 2004 and 9,815 in 2005. (The Department of Labor, which tracks these statistics, defines such a layoff as one involving 50 or more uninsurance claims against a single company in a period of more than five weeks.)

Judging from the industries cited, many of these layoffs were unrelated to merger activity. For example, transportation equipment manufacturing and motion picture and sound recording, cited as two industries with rising layoffs in 2005, were not particularly active in M&A in 2005. Furthermore, the U.S., while it has a more active environment for M&A than other countries, has a relatively low rate of layoffs compared to China, Japan, and Brazil.[5] Nonetheless, it is fair to say that large-scale layoffs do often result from mergers, especially large mergers of equals. According to a mid-2005 survey by the executive recruiting firm Challenger, Gray & Christmas, merger activity accounted for the elimination of almost 77,000 jobs in the first quarter of 2005, or 27 percent of the total cuts that were announced. Merger-related cuts in the first quarter of

2005 were 17 percent higher than they were in all of 2004. Industries registering the largest job losses so far this year are telecommunications, defense, and consumer goods.[6]

Media accounts tend to tar all layoffs with the same brush, but aren't some worse than others?

Yes. Media accounts tend to make all layoffs look bad. (Remember *Newsweek*'s "Corporate Killers" cover a decade ago, back in 1996?[7]) But it is not just a question of *how many* people are affected—that is, the number of employees and the percentage of a company's work force. It's also a question of *why* and *how*. By communicating legitimate *reasons* for the layoffs, and by offering humane *policies* for notice, compensation, and outplacement, managers can reduce the personal trauma of the event. Marty Sikora, longtime editor of *Mergers & Acquisitions* magazine, recently speaks of a "merger syndrome" in which employees distrust acquirers even if the acquirers treat them well.[8]

Employees can some of the negative consequences of mergers by avoiding extremes of pessimism and optimism. Rather than assuming that all will go poorly or well, they can maintain a proactive, yet realistic attitude.[9]

How often do employees sue companies, what do they sue for, and how much do they sue for?

In 2004, 23 percent of all claims filed with director's and officer's liability insurers were from employees. Over half of these suits were for wrongful termination. Other issues, in order of frequency, were discrimination, breach of employment contract (not termination), harassment or humiliation, employee benefits, defamation, and workplace safety.[10] Claim costs for employee lawsuits (for judgment or settlement amounts alone, excluding legal defense costs) have been averaging a half a million ($506,226) per claim, based on the most recent 10 Years.[11] This total does not include suits filed on behalf of employees by regulators, who have sued over worker health, safety, and working conditions, among other issues. The average insurer payout from a regulatory lawsuit is $5 million ($5,577,500)—about 10 times the size of an employee lawsuit.

What are some recent legal and regulatory developments highlighting these commonly litigated employee issues?

Wrongful termination   Employees fired (or claiming to be fired) because they tried to stop an illegal practice can file suits under Sarbanes-Oxley Section 806, which protects "whistleblowers." In one recent case, a former executive at TXU Energy accepted a settlement in the suit he brought against TXU, seeking whistleblower protections under Section 806. The executive's decision to settle came after a judge ruled that he was not entitled to punitive damages or a jury trial. The executive alleges that he was let go after raising objections about questionable financial practices at TXU. TXU claims that the employee was let go as a result of a company restructuring. Whistleblower laws let workers sue if they are fired for reporting illegal acts by their companies. The Family and Medical Leave Act of 1993 lets workers sue if they are fired for taking up to 12 weeks of unpaid time off to care for a sick family member. An amendment to the Fair Credit Reporting Act means companies can be sued if they fire someone due to a criminal record turning up in a background check if they don't give the worker an opportunity to refute it. Courts are still sorting out the 1992 Americans With Disabilities Act. Some have ruled that workers can sue for being fired because of drug addiction or not doing a job properly due to stress.

Discrimination   Employees can allege employer discrimination if they are in any group protected by federal laws, which protect against discrimination based on:

- Age (under the Age Discrimination in Employment Act of 1967). In *Reeves v. Sanderson Plumbing, Inc.*, the U.S. (99-536) 530 U.S. 133 (2000) 197 F.3d 688, reversed, the court stated that the "ultimate question in every employment discrimination case involving a claim of disparate treatment is whether the plaintiff was the victim of intentional discrimination," and found that in this case intent was proved. The U.S. Supreme Court ruled in 2005 to allow current or former employees to sue for age discrimination even if *no* evidence of intentional discrimination exists. The case, *Smith v. City of Jackson*,

No. 03-1160 (March 30, 2005), involved a group of city police officers over age 40, who alleged that they were adversely affected by the city's adoption of a pay plan to grant raises to its police officers.

- Disability (Americans with Disabilities Act of 1990). In *Toyota Motor Manufacturing, Kentucky, Inc. v. Williams,* — U.S.—, S.Ct.—, 2002 WL 15402 (January 8, 2002) the United States Supreme Court ruled that for a worker to be deemed "substantially limited" in performing manual tasks, that person must have a permanent or long-term impairment "that prevents or severely restricts the individual from doing activities that are of central importance to most people's daily lives." This involved the claims of an assembly line worker with carpal tunnel syndrome who was unable to perform some of the tasks associated with certain types of manual labor within her job description.

- Race (Title VII of the Civil Rights Act of 1964, as amended, prohibits discrimination based on *race, color, religion, sex, and national origin*). The Civil Rights Restoration Act of 1991 strengthened the 1964 law by letting plaintiffs recover not only back wages but also legal fees and punitive damages (up to $300,000).

Breach of employment contract (not termination)
In *Garcetti v. Ceballos,* pending before the U.S. Supreme Court in late 2005 (Docket Number: 04-473) the question is whether the First Amendment of the U.S. Constitution (protecting free speech) ever protects the job-required speech of public employees. The decision in a lower court (Ninth Circuit) said that it did not.

Harassment or humiliation   (Title VII of the Civil Rights Act of 1964). In the U.S. Supreme Court case of *Pennsylvania State Police v. Suders,* (03-95) 542 US 129 (2004) 325 F.3d 432, showed the importance of having a policy for preventing and reporting sexual harassment. The court found that if a company has a nonharassment policy, and the employee never uses it to seek recourse for alleged harassment, that this may bar a claim that the employee was forced to resign because of intolerable sexual harassment.

Employee defamation   Three recent cases show that an employer's explanations for why an employee was dismissed can be used to support defamation claims.

- In *Moore v. Cox*, 341 F.Supp.2d 570, 572 (M.D. N.C. 2004), a North Carolina federal court judge allowed a terminated employee to pursue a defamation claim against his former employer. The employee alleged that a manager falsely reported to other company personnel that the employee used profanity and made a derogatory statement against management.
- In *Popko v. Continental Casualty Co*, 2005 Ill. App. LEXIS 28 (Ill. Ct. App. January 21, 2005), the Illinois Court of Appeals upheld a $300,000 jury verdict in favor of an employee who sued his former employer based on statements made in an internal company memo distributed to a manager.
- In *Gambardella v. Apple Health Care, Inc.*, 863 A.2d. 735 (2005), the Connecticut Court of Appeals held that a nursing home employee could pursue a defamation claim based on a statement in an internal disciplinary report. The court held that simply distributing the memo to the employee's supervisors and putting it in her personnel file satisfied the publication requirement of a defamation claim.

Workplace safety   In the United States, regulators traditionally focused on filing cases, criminal as well as civil, on behalf of employees. Federal cases—including some that have resulted in jail sentences—have been filed by the Occupational Safety and Health Administration (OSHA), which has 1,200 employees monitoring more than seven million workplaces. Since 1998, OSHA has emphasized prevention. Almost 800,000 employees and over 13,000 employers have participated in the OSHA Strategic Partnership Program, which aims to reduce fatalities, injuries, and illnesses. Working jointly, employers and OSHA set and implement meaningful safety and health management systems and by tackling occupational hazards such as lead and silica exposure, falls, electrocution, and muscular-skeletal disorders. The program, says OSHA, "moves away from traditional enforcement methods and embraces collaborative agreements." [12]

What other legal and regulatory issues should managers look out for after a merger?

Pensions

Retirement issues continue to be important in the United States, where companies have special duties to present and past employees as administrators of their employee pension plans under the Employee Retirement Security Act of 1974. Now, after more than 30 years, this law is receiving renewed attention from all three branches of the U.S. government. Here are developments as of late 2005:

- The Supreme Court offered an expansive interpretation of fiduciary duties in the merger setting in *Varity Corp. v. Howe et al.* (94-1471), 516 U.S. 489 (1996). The court said that Varity breached its ERISA duties when it convinced the participants and beneficiaries of a pension plan to transfer their employment and plan coverage to a new, money-losing subsidiary. Following this case, there was an increase in postmerger pension litigation by employees.
- In 2002, as part of the Sarbanes-Oxley Act, the U.S. Congress made it illegal to have pension fund blackouts that would prevent employees from selling employers' shares unless officers were also frozen out.
- The Financial Accounting Standards Board (FASB), a standard setter for the accounting profession, has expanded pension disclosure requirements under Financial Accounting Statements No. 87, 88, 106, and Statement No. 132 (revised 2003).

Collective bargaining agreements

Obviously, these are a major source of obligations for new management when it comes to working conditions, including hours, safety, and staffing. Also, some agreements stipulate that companies must consult with employees in a change of control. In such cases, the leverage that employees have prior to deal closing may help them preserve or improve their working conditions. All agreements negotiated by labor organizations in the United States receive strong enforcement from the National Labor Relations Board (NLRB).

In May 2005, when US Airways and America West announced plans to merge, labor issues posed a challenge to the potential merger partners. Although the pilots and flight attendants from the two companies belonged to the same unions, the mechanics belonged to two different unions—the International Brotherhood of Teamsters at America West, and the International Association of Machinists and Aerospace Workers at US Airways—raising questions of seniority and assignments. By the time the companies merged in September 2005, these issues had been resolved through negotiations.[13]

Can a group of nonunion employees negotiate with management over working conditions?

No, not under current labor laws. Under the National Labor Relations Act, only "labor organizations"—unions that are independent of management—may do so.

What role can job training and development play in the postmerger phase?

Training programs are the fastest way to reassure the employees of both the acquired and the acquiring company that their jobs are secure. These training programs should have two aspects.

First, the management of the newly combined companies can start by educating all employees in the values, vision, and mission of the newly combined companies. As mentioned in Chapter 3, these elements should reflect the histories of both companies, even if their framework is derived largely from the acquirer.

What are some relocation issues that newly combined companies should consider?

Five questions will arise concerning the relocation of a company's headquarters, plant, or branch. In order of importance, these are: *Why* is it relocating? *Where* is it going? *Who* will be asked to relocate? *How* will the acquirer handle relocation? *What* support will be provided? Also, facts and figures about the new locations should be disseminated. Comparative information can lessen the shock and trauma of relocation—and may even make it appealing. At the very least, it will enable employees to make good decisions.

Several companies provide such information. One established company, Economic Research Institute of Redmond, Washington (erieri.com), provides cost of living comparisons among 10,000 locations, with unlimited numbers of printed reports. These are used to assist employees considering a relocation offer or temporary assignment.

In any event, the acquirer should establish a detailed relocation policy that includes adequate reimbursement of relocation expenses and job security following the move.

What is "outplacement," and why is it important for companies that are cutting jobs?

According to the Association of Career Consulting Firms International (aocfi.org), the outplacement industry is composed of "firms and professionals who help organizations to *plan, implement, and follow-up* individual terminations and group layoffs" (emphasis ours). Outplacement services, whether provided by outside consultants or by inside human resources managers, can help companies and individual employees to make the best of a bad situation. Proper planning can keep job losses to a strategic minimum, proper implementation can preserve corporate and personal dignity, and proper follow-up can foster goodwill among departing employees. With good outplacement, layoffs can preserve the trust that is essential to corporate life.

THE CONTEXT FOR COMMITMENTS

What exactly is trust, why is it important, and how can managers build it after a merger?

Trust is faith that is based on an expectation of integrity—the belief that a person or people are who they say they are and will do what they say they will do.[14] Trust is also confidence based on the experience of integrity—repeated proof that one's faith is well founded. Finally, and most importantly, trust is a bond between or among people based on these values of honest communication and responsible action.

In the postmerger context, trust has great value. High levels of trust reduce friction among employees, bond people together, increase productivity, and stimulate growth. Conversely, low levels of trust aggravate friction, alienate people from one another, depress productivity, and hamper growth.

Trust is built ring by ring, as a tree grows. It starts with an act that inspires trust, and it grows with each continued act until faith becomes sure confidence. To build trust after a merger, managers must show that they are worthy of it. They can do this by making and fulfilling unwavering commitments in changing circumstances. Trust is an integral component of *change management*.

What is change management, and why is it important after a merger?

Change management is the art of managing change in an organization. In a complex organization, change management is often associated with facilitating a major change initiative, such as a pay-for-performance plan or a total quality management system. But change management can also be useful in facilitating day-to-day changes that have no special name. For example, a change in computer software may change a key operational process, which in turn triggers changes in job descriptions, compensation systems, and so forth. Change can come from any direction and can go in any direction at any level, sparking responses that can range from enthusiasm to resistance.

Every manager should know how to be a "change manager"— someone who is able to track change and understand the repercussions of change. This is particularly important after a merger because *unanticipated changes* are often seen as *broken promises*. Change management therefore begins with early, continued, and honest communication about the changes ahead, and actions consistent with the promised changes.

No one can predict every aspect of postmerger change, but in a climate of trust, even the unpredictable can become a part of postmerger success.

How can managers make and keep promises in a changing environment?

First, they must themselves recognize, admit, and accept the fact of change. After a merger, change is inevitable. It is even more prevalent than loss. Obviously, mergers are only the cause of employee turnover.[15]

Second, managers need to be, and to encourage others to become, a part of the change themselves. This goes beyond traditional "change management," in which senior management initiated organization-wide change, middle managers communicated the change, and employees either accepted the change or left. Postmerger change is for everyone in an organization. Senior management must set and communicate the new postmerger direction, but that direction must be rooted in corporate reality. It must emerge with the active participation of the employees who will make it operational.

COMMITMENTS TO COMMUNITIES

What kinds of promises do companies make to communities?

Companies can commit themselves to fostering a better quality of life in their communities. As in previous chapters of this book, the Caux Round Table offers a useful list.

Communities

We believe that as global corporate citizens we can contribute to such forces of reform and human rights as are at work in the communities in which we operate. We therefore have responsibility in those communities to:

- respect human rights and democratic institutions, and promote them wherever practicable;
- recognize government's legitimate obligation to the society at large and support public policies and practices that promote human development through harmonious relations between business and other segments of society;
- collaborate with those forces in the community dedicated to raising standards of health, education, workplace safety, and economic well-being;
- promote and stimulate sustainable development and play a leading role in preserving and enhancing the physical environment and conserving the earth's resources;
- support peace, security, diversity and social integration;

- respect the integrity of local cultures; and
- be a good corporate citizen through charitable donations, educational and cultural contributions, and employee participation in community and civic affairs.

Beyond these promises, a company's most important contribution to a community is the "promise" of its presence. When a company locates in their jurisdiction, states, counties, and municipalities hope for jobs and tax dollars. Sometimes regulatory approval of the merger is dependent on pledges to the community. For example, the public utility code of the state of California requires that economic impact on the local community be considered when the merger is reviewed by state utilities regulators. Sometimes communities try to get this guarantee in writing, offering incentives in return for jobs. These pledges are often enforceable by law. For example, a company that pledges jobs to a city and receives incentives in return may be required to pay the city back the amount (or even some multiple of the amount) if it breaks its pledge.[16]

What kind of incentives do communities offer companies, and what do companies promise in return?

The most common incentives offered are property tax or sales tax rebates and income tax credits. Others include job training, preferred financing, employment or payroll tax credits, and utility rebates. In return, companies promise to build or keep plants, stores, or office buildings in the community, and say or imply that they will hire local people and pay local taxes. Sometimes these promises and implications are in writing, and sometimes they are taken on faith alone.

Can a community sue a company for breaking the promises it makes in return for incentives?

Yes. A community can sue a company for breaking an agreement, citing either general principles of contract law or specific "claw-backs" in the contracts. *Claw-backs* are provisions in a contract between a community and a company that specify penalties for breaking the promises made in the contract. These appear in most contracts, and most states have made such provisions mandatory.[17]

Suppose a company does not promise to stay in a location, and then leaves. Can it still be sued?

Yes. Some localities have local ordinances that force companies to pay for demolition and, if necessary, cleanup of abandoned sites.

Could you give an example of a company that made a special effort to accommodate communities after a merger?

A good example would be Sentara Healthcare's acquisition of Obici Health System, a community hospital. Obici had fallen into debt, and Sentara agreed to assume it. In a joint press release dated September 26, 2005, and summarizing information already delivered to "Obici employees, physicians, and community leaders," the companies **emphasized their commitment to their community.** "We chose to affiliate with Sentara because of the high quality healthcare they provide and they are locally-based," said J. Samuel Glasscock, Chairman of the Board of Obici Health System. "Sentara's leadership understands where we came from and the importance of community-based care." "The current economics of health care make it difficult for independent community hospitals like Obici to survive," Glasscock stated. "A large, integrated system like Sentara offers services, technology, and financial strength that we simply cannot achieve as an independent hospital."

In the same press release, Sentara CEO David L. Bernd is quoted as saying that "Sentara respects the legacy of Amedeo and Louise Obici, whose generosity helped start this great community hospital. We'll maintain that historic link with the name Sentara Obici Hospital. This merger will ensure that quality health care will be a part of the Suffolk and western Tidewater area for generations to come as the Obicis had intended. Sentara Home Care already serves many patients in the Suffolk area and more than 400 Sentara employees call Suffolk home. We look forward to being a greater part of the community." Sentara left the Obici Foundation independent and donated it a "substantial sum" of money to be used for programs to improve community health, including care and medicine for the indigent, diabetes control, hypertension management, reduction in teen pregnancy, and drug treatment.

If an acquirer has plants that are not performing well, what alternatives to selling them does it have?

As mentioned in Chapter 7, the acquirer can improve its manufacturing processes, or it can sell the plants to a competitor who can do so. A study by Alliance Capital found that increased capital investment often determines whether a manufacturing plant will survive (not close). Surviving plants are 31 percent more "capital intensive" than plants that exit an industry, and 3.3 percent more productive than the plants that fail.[18]

What is the current state of U.S. law with regard to notice of plant closings or other large-scale layoffs?

Under the Worker Adjustment and Retraining Notification (WARN) Act of 1988, a company must give 60 days' notice before shutting a plant or laying off large numbers of employees. For each day that a company is late in making this deadline, it can owe each employee one day of back pay. So, for example, if a company gives only 30 days' notice, each affected employee may sue it for 30 days of back pay. The employees can sue collectively even if they were not all fired at the same time. Also, unions can sue on behalf of employees.

The following details are cited directly from the Department of Labor.

Who is Covered.   The Worker Adjustment and Retraining Notification Act (WARN) generally covers employers with 100 or more employees, not counting those who have worked less than six months in the last 12 months and those who work an average of less than 20 hours a week. Regular federal, state, and local government entities that provide public services are not covered. Employees entitled to notice under WARN include managers and supervisors as well as hourly and salaried workers.

Basic Provisions/Requirements.   WARN protects workers, their families, and communities by requiring employers to provide notification 60 calendar days in advance of plant closings and mass layoffs. Advance notice gives workers and their families some transition time to adjust to the prospective loss of employment, to seek and obtain other jobs and, if necessary, to enter skill training or retraining that will allow these workers to compete successfully in the job market. WARN also provides for notice to state dislocated worker units so that they can promptly offer dislocated worker assistance.

A covered plant closing occurs when a facility or operating unit is shut down for more than six months, or when 50 or more employees lose their jobs during any 30-day period at a single site of employment. A covered mass layoff occurs when a layoff of six months or longer affects either 500 or more workers or at least 33 percent of the employer's workforce when the layoff affects between 50 and 499 workers. The number of affected workers is the total number laid off during a 30-day (or in some cases 90-day) period.

WARN does not apply to closure of temporary facilities, or the completion of an activity when the workers were hired only for the duration of that activity. WARN also provides for less than 60 days notice when the layoffs resulted from closure of a faltering company, unforeseeable business circumstances, or a natural disaster.

Employee Rights.   Workers or their representatives, and units of local government may bring individual or class action suits. U.S. district courts enforce WARN requirements. The Court may allow reasonable attorney's fees as part of any final judgment.

Compliance Assistance Available.   For general information about WARN, an employer's guide (PDF) is available from the Employment and Training Administration's Web site (doleta.gov).

Penalties/Sanctions.   An employer who violates the WARN provisions is liable to each employee for an amount equal to back pay and benefits for the period of the violation, up to 60 days. This may be reduced by the period of any notice that was given, and any voluntary payments that the employer made to the employee.

An employer who fails to provide the required notice to the unit of local government is subject to a civil penalty not to exceed $500 for each day of violation. The employer may avoid this penalty by satisfying the liability to each employee within three weeks after the closing or layoff.

Relation to State, Local, and Other Federal Laws. WARN does not preempt any other federal, state, or local law, or any employer/employee agreement that requires other notification or benefit. Rather, the rights provided by WARN supplement those provided by other federal, state, or local laws.

Aren't there some restrictions on union suits on behalf of employees?

Yes. There is a legal principle that says that individual members of a group must sue on their own behalf when damages have to be calculated individually. That theory was weakened in May 1996, however, with the U.S. Supreme Court case of *United Food & Commercial Workers Union v. Brown Group, Inc.* This case involved a series of layoffs at Brown Shoe Co., a unit of Brown Group, Inc., that occurred over several months in 1992. The UFCW claimed that Brown Shoe had violated the WARN Act and owed 277 union members 60 days of back wages. Lower courts said that the union did not have standing to sue, but the Supreme Court said that it did.

INTERNATIONAL CONSIDERATIONS

What are some key challenges to employee and community relations in cross-border mergers?

Differences in local culture and law can make postmerger life difficult in a cross-border merger. The Caux Round Table's *Principles for Business* urges companies to "respect the integrity of local cultures," an attitude that can require action: acquirers can and should adapt company policies and practices to local cultures.

What standards are operative in the European Union with respect to these issues?

In May 2005 the European Parliament published the provisional text of a new directive on cross-border mergers. An important focus of the directive was participation of employees in mergers across Europe. (See Box 12-1.)

BOX 12-1

Statement by Charlie McCREEVY, European Commissioner for Internal Market and Services, on the adoption of the European Parliament opinion on the Cross-Border Mergers Directive

Brussels, 10 May 2005

Commissioner Charlie McCreevy welcomes today's vote in the European Parliament on the proposed 10th Company Law Directive on cross-border mergers of limited liability companies. He said: "The cross-border Directive opens new ground. It is a major step in favour of EU businesses, which have been calling for the adoption of this text for many years. This is true, in particular, of those mid-sized businesses which are active in more than one Member State, yet too small to form European companies. With this Directive, European companies will be able to organise themselves and develop efficiencies on a cross-border basis, and further reap the benefits of the Single Market."

This key measure will allow cross-border mergers of limited liability companies in the European Union. The Directive sets up a simple legal framework avoiding the winding up of the acquired company.

The directive covers all limited liability companies, with the exception of undertakings for collective investment in transferable securities (UCITS). The text contains special provisions as regards cooperative societies. Given the very diverse types of cooperatives in the EU, Member States have the possibility to exclude them from taking part of cross-border mergers for a limited period of five years and under the control of the European Commission.

Employee participation was a key issue in the negotiations, given the widely diverging systems in force in the Member States. This raises the question of how to deal with cross-border mergers implying a loss or a reduction of employee participation. The Parliament agreed that employee participation schemes should apply to cross-border mergers where at least one of the merging companies is operating under an employee participation system. Employee participation in the newly created company will be subject to negotiations based on the model of the European Company Statute.

NOTES

1 "Proversity" is a term coined by R. Roosevelt Thomas, who wrote about it in *Beyond Race and Gender: Unleashing the Power of Your Total Work Force by Managing Diversity* (New York: Amacom, 1992).

2 "Downsizing—rightsizing—reorganization—whatever we call it, there is an impact on disability. . . . We need to develop stronger links among programs that improve productivity while integrating medical and disability, and implement programs that focus on disease management, stress prevention, and stress management," said Mark Marsters, Cigna, Feb. 2, 2004, press release from Cigna Group Insurance, Mar. 29, 2004. Previous Cigna research (a 1996 study of 292 companies with 100 or more employees) showed that after a downsizing, employees—whether they go or stay—file more disability claims for longer periods of time.

3 *Personnel Today,* Aug. 11, 2005.

4 ESOP Association, www.esopassociation.org, September 2005.

5 Daniel Drezner, "The Outsourcing Bogeyman," *Foreign Affairs,* May/June 2004.

6 Cited in Gretchen Morgenson, "What Are Mergers Good For?" *New York Times,* June 5, 2005.

7 The cover of Newsweek's February 26, 1996, issue showed mug shots of CEOs who had accepted higher salaries while laying off workers, and featured cover story called "Corporate Killers."

8 "The Latest Mergers: Why Some Will Fly, And Others Won't," an online article from whartonknowledge.com dated March 30, 2005. A good example appears in Lee Smith, "How to Survive a Corporate Merger," usnews.com/August 15, 2005. Roy Howe, a truck driver

who rose to become general manager of a Lucky Stores distribution center, says that he was "treated well" when Lucky was taken over by Albertson's, a national chain, in 1998, but left eventually anyway. In September 2005, Albertson's put itself up for sale by auction. Bids so far would put its final purchase price in the neighborhood of $10 billion.

9   Lee Smith, in "How to Survive a Corporate Merger," cited in note 8, organizes his advice into four sections: "Learn the new culture. . . Embrace change. . . Promote yourself. . . and Know when to quit.

10   Source: *2004 Director and Officer Liability: Understanding the Unexpected*, Towers Perrin Tillinghast, 2004.

11   Regulators have collected insurance payments over not only employee matters but also antitrust, consumer protection, environment, securities, and taxes. Source: *2004 Director and Officer Liability: Understanding the Unexpected*, Towers Perrin Tillinghast, 2004.

12   From http://www.osha.gov/dcsp/partnerships/.

13   Micheline Maynard, "US Airways and America West Plan to Merge," *New York Times*, May 20, 2005. For subsequent news, see the company's website, Americawest.com.

14   This answer is provided by Frank K. Sonnenberg, author of *Managing with a Conscience: How to Improve Performance through Integrity, Trust, and Commitment* (New York: McGraw-Hill, 1993).

15   "The Path to Employee Disengagement" *Optimize*, Sept. 2005, Issue 47 (optimizemag.com), lists 24 common causes of employee turnover.

16   See Tim Reason, "Stingers: The 2004 State Tax Survey," *CFO Magazine*, February 3, 2004, cfo.com.

17   Ibid.

18   Alan Christman, "CAD/CAM Outlook : Some Conundrums In Worldwide Manufacturing, Modern Machine Shop Online" (mmsonline), April 2004.

Acquisition Process Overview:
Objectives, Activities, and Inputs/Outputs for the Three Phases of the Acquisition Process

* = key input and output documents

The acquisition process is composed of three primary phases, each of which contains multiple stages or subphases, as follows:

PHASE 1: STRATEGY

Subphases
Planning
Search
Valuation
Selection

PHASE 2: TRANSACTION

Subphases (These start during the Strategy phase and extend through the Transaction phase.)
Due Diligence
Financing
Negotiation
Structuring (Tax, legal, accounting treatment of transaction)
Closing

PHASE 3: INTEGRATION

Subphases (These start during the Transaction phase and extend through the Integration phase.)
Integration Planning
Integration Communication
Integration Implementation

For *each phase* and for *each subphase*, acquirers need to know:

Objectives

Activities (= subphases)
Inputs and outputs

PHASE 1: STRATEGY PHASE

Strategy Objectives
To build value, acquisition planning, search, valuation, and selection should seek to

Increase value in multiple dimensions (e.g., earnings in the short term, return on shareholder equity in the medium term, number of patents in the long term).

Supplement the increase in value through *increase in size and/or strength* (revenues and/or market share).

Increase in value and size by *building on the company's core business* (for example, value-added chemical processing).

Grow in value and size by building on a core business, *supplementing strengths and complementing weaknesses.*

Supplement strengths and/or complement weaknesses through *considering all types of acquisitions*—i.e., horizontal (industry competitor), vertical (industry supplier or customer), and diagonal (outside industry).

Strategy Activities (Subphases)
Planning
Search
Valuation
Selection

Inputs and Outputs in Strategy Phase
See subphases.

Planning

Planning Objectives
Multiple, authoritative views on measurable value goals.
Multiple, authoritative views on measurable growth goals.

Multiple, authoritative views on core businesses.

Multiple, authoritative views on strengths and weaknesses in core businesses and hence acquisition fields (size, location, industry, and so on, of potential acquirees).

Nominations for acquisition strategy subphase teams (planning team, valuation team, search team, and selection team—teams may be combined).

Planning Activities

Meetings of corporate development team or equivalent to write acquisition portion of strategic plan.

Obtain approval of board of directors to proceed.

Inputs to Planning Activities

Vision and mission statements.

Internal factors: descriptions of core competencies, core assets, and culture.

External factors: descriptions of business environment, customers, competitors, and suppliers.

Analysis of strengths, weaknesses, opportunities, and threats (SWOT).

Outputs from Planning

Strategic plan—usually captured in formal *"strategic plan" document(s) for the company and, if the company has multiple units, its units.

Acquisition plan—usually described as a section of the strategic plan, with additional memos on criteria.

Search

Search Objectives

An effective search requires companies

To seek companies that will increase the acquirer's *value*.

To seek companies that will increase the acquirer's *size and/or strength*.

To seek companies that will supplement or complement the *acquirer's core business*.

To seek companies that will meet the criteria set forth in the
  acquirer's list of chosen *traits.*
To operate effectively as an acquisition search team.
To *transfer key outputs to the due diligence team.*

Search Activities
In conducting an acquisition search, acquirers should

Rank acquisition candidates by *value.*
Rank acquisition candidates by *size* (revenues, market share,
  and/or employees).
List acquisition candidates by *fit with core business.*
Rank and list acquisition candidates according to chosen traits.
Contact candidates and begin signaling interest; note any
  discrepancies between goals and acquiree traits, and
  convey goals and discrepancies to the due diligence team.

Inputs to Search Activities
During the acquisition search, managers should collect

Data on the financial *performance of candidates* (key ratios).
Data on the *size of candidates.*
Data on *fit with core business.*
Data on *relevant traits.*
*Internal reports summarizing these data and recommendations for
  pursuit, including contact information.*

Outputs from Search Activities (Based on Inputs)
During an acquisition search, managers should report

Ranking of candidates by *value* (key ratios).
Ranking of candidates by *size.*
Ranking of candidates by fit with *core business.*
Master weighted ranking of candidates *by all these criteria.*
Records of conversations and meetings with candidate
  companies, if any, with comments on input summary
  as well *copies of all key public documents,* if any. (Create
  **search records form.*)

Valuation

Valuation Objective
To assess the value of acquisition targets in financial terms.

Valuation Activities
Analysis of discounted cash flow trends and of key ratios for entity.

Inputs to Valuation Activities
Reports on key ratios.

Output from Valuation Activities
Suggested price range for offer to seller.

Selection

Selection Objective
To select acquisition targets that will meet the criteria of the acquisition plan.

Selection Activities
Study the following inputs to produce the listed outputs.

Inputs to Selection Activities
Reports on targets, highlighting conformity to acquisition plan criteria.

Outputs from Selection Activities
Short list of acquiree targets.
Final choice of acquiree(s).
Profile of acquiree(s).
Deal objectives memorandum.

PHASE 2: THE TRANSACTION PHASE

Transaction Objectives:
During the transaction phase, companies need to ensure that what they are buying is

Free from undue risks (Due Diligence subphase).

Paid for via financing from the appropriate source of capital (Financing subphase).

Transferred with the appropriate contractual understandings, including representations and warranties (Negotiation subphase).

Transferred in a transaction that has the best tax results for each party (Tax Structuring subphase).

Closed in a thorough yet timely manner (Closing subphase).

Transaction Activities (Subphases)

Due Diligence
Financing
Negotiation
Tax Structuring
Closing

Inputs and Outputs

See subphases.

Due Diligence

Due Diligence Objectives

Companies conduct acquisition due diligence in order to improve the overall value of the successor company, and in particular to

Avoid overpaying for a company (thus contributing to the Valuation, Financing, and Structuring subphases[1] of the total acquisition process).

Anticipate and mitigate the financial risks associated with owning and operating a company (thus contributing to the Valuation and Integration phases of the total acquisition process).

Anticipate and mitigate operational risks associated with owning and operating a company (thus contributing to the Integration phase of the total acquisition process).

Anticipate and mitigate legal risks associated with owning and operating a company, (thus contributing to the Integration phase of the total acquisition process).

Anticipate and mitigate transactional risks associated with buying a company (thus contributing to the Financing, Tax Structuring, and Negotiation phases of the total acquisition process).

Due Diligence Activities

During the acquisition Due Diligence process, acquirers should appoint representatives to study public documents (if any) and/or conduct interviews with the acquiree (if possible) to

Identify potential threats to the value criteria identified during the Strategy subphase (use *checklist for due diligence*).

Ascertain the accuracy of the outputs from the Search subphase, especially representations made about the candidate company's value, size, fit with core business, and related criteria.

Produce documents relating to the *financial, operational, transactional, and legal risks* of the company as a key output of this Due Diligence subphase.

Provide key negotiating points for the Negotiation subphase.

Provide key process points for the Integration phase.

Inputs to Due Diligence

During due diligence, the acquirer's managers and advisors should ascertain the

Match of data against the output from the Strategy phase.

Nature and probability of significant financial risks associated with owning and operating a company (thus contributing to the Integration phase of the total acquisition process).

Nature and probability of significant operational risks associated with owning and operating a company (thus contributing to the Integration phase of the total acquisition process).

Nature and probability of significant legal risks associated with owning and operating a company (thus contributing to the Integration phase of the total acquisition process).

Nature and probability of significant transactional risks associated with buying a company (thus contributing to the Financing, Structuring, and Negotiation subphases of the Transaction phase).

Output from Due Diligence

During due diligence, the acquirer's managers and advisors should report data on the

> Financial, operational, transactional, and legal risks.
> Implication of these risks for integration planning.
> Implication of these risks for integration of acquiree activities
> and assets—use *checklist for acquisition due diligence* and
> for culture, link to negotiation via *acquisition terms set
> forth in acquisition agreements.*

Other due diligence outputs include document request list and due diligence checklist.

Financing

Financing Objectives

To decide whether to use internal or external capital to finance the acquisition, and to decide what instruments and sources to use.

Financing Activities

Contact sources of financing and obtain financing.

Inputs to Financing Activities

> *Acquisition plan*
> *Basic financial documents* from acquirer and potential acquiree(s).

Outputs from Financing

> *Financing agreements* (for debt and/or equity capital).

Negotiation

Negotiation Objective

To buy the company for the least amount of money on the most favorable terms.

Negotiation Activities

Hold meetings with the acquiree and its advisors to negotiate the provisions of the acquisition agreement.

Inputs to Negotiation Activities
Financial statements of acquiree, plus all outputs from previous phases and subphases.

Output from Negotiation Activities
Drafts of the *acquisition agreement*, including provisions describing *acquisition terms.*

Deal summary (derived from acquisition agreement).

Shareholder approval of transaction (if it involves a public company)—filings of proxy materials under Section 14 of the Securities Exchange Act of 1934, as relevant:

PRE 14A: A preliminary proxy statement providing official notification to designated classes of shareholders of matters to be brought to a vote at a shareholders meeting.

PREC14A: A preliminary proxy statement containing contested solicitations.

PREC14C: A preliminary information statement containing contested solicitations.

PREN14A: Nonmanagement preliminary proxy statements not involving contested solicitations.

PREM14A: A preliminary proxy statement relating to a merger or acquisition.

PREM14C: A preliminary information statement relating to a merger or acquisition.

PRES14A: A preliminary proxy statement giving notice regarding a special meeting.

PRES14C: A preliminary information statement relating to a special meeting.

PRE 14C: A preliminary proxy statement containing all other information.

PRER14A: Proxy soliciting materials. Revised preliminary material.

PRER14C: Information statements. Revised preliminary material.

PRE13E3: Initial statement—preliminary form.

PRE13E3/A: Amendment to a previously filed PRE13E3.

PRRN14A: Nonmanagement revised preliminary proxy soliciting materials for both contested solicitations and other situations. Revised preliminary material.

PX14A6G: Notice of exempt solicitation. Definitive material.

DEF 14A: Official notification to designated classes of shareholders of matters to be brought to a vote at a shareholders meeting. This form is commonly referred to as a "proxy."

DEFM14A: Official notification to designated classes of shareholders of matters relating to a merger or acquisition.

DEFM14C: A definitive information statement relating to a merger or an acquisition.

DEFS14A: A definitive proxy statement giving notice regarding a special meeting.

DEFS14C: A definitive information statement regarding a special meeting.

DEFC14A: A definitive proxy statement in connection with contested solicitations.

DEFC14C: A definitive information statement indicating contested solicitations.

DEFA14A: Additional proxy soliciting materials—definitive.

DEFN14A: A definitive proxy statement filed by nonmanagement not in connection with contested solicitations.

DFRN14A: A revised definitive proxy statement filed by nonmanagement.

DFAN14A: Additional proxy soliciting materials filed by nonmanagement.

DEF13E3: Schedule filed as definitive materials.

DEF13E3/A: Amendment to a previously filed DEF13E3.

DEFA14C: Additional information statement materials—definitive.

DEFR14C: Revised information statement materials—definitive.

DEFR14A: Revised proxy soliciting materials—definitive.

Tax Structuring

Tax Structuring Objectives
To structure the transaction in the way most favorable to buyer and seller.

Tax Structuring Activities
Working with attorneys and accountants to structure the transaction.

Inputs to Tax Structuring
Financial statements and tax returns for both entities.

Outputs from Tax Structuring
> Decision on structure of the transaction (merger or nonmerger? taxable or nontaxable? net operating loss carryforwards?)
> Captured in structural provisions within *acquisition agreement* and *financing agreement.*
> Evident in first *pro forma financial statement* for the combined entity.

Closing

Closing Objectives
To transfer legal ownership of the entity from the old owner to the new owner.

Closing Activities
> Create closing checklist.
> Gather closing documents.

Inputs to Closing Activities
> *Closing documents.*
> *Closing checklist.*

Outputs from Closing Activities
> *Final cosigned and notarized acquisition agreement.*
> Key regulatory filings with Securities and Exchange Commission (SEC), Department of Justice (DOJ), and Federal Trade Commission (FTC):
> SEC: *Schedule 13-D, 13G, and amendments thereto.*
> DOJ/FDC: *Premerger notification form under Hart-Scott-Rodino Antitrust Improvements Act.*

PHASE 3: INTEGRATION

Integration Objectives
Acquisition integration planning/execution should:

> Support company strategy by adding value.
> Avoid or mitigate risks identified in the Transaction phase.

Take place in the shortest amount of time for the least possible cost.

Use and improve a repeatable process for planning and communication.

Integration Activities (Subphases)
Integration Planning
Integration Communication
Integration Implementation

Inputs and Outputs in Integration
See subphases.

Integration Planning

Integration Planning Objectives
To plan ahead for all phases of integration, in order to fulfill strategic objectives in a timely and cost-effective manner.

Integration Planning Activities[1]
Prepare to plan.
Assess current environment.
Define planning process objectives.
Develop plans and identify resources (turn objectives into action plans by forming teams at corporate and functional levels).
Validate the plan.

Inputs to Integration Planning Activities   Reports from team members on their areas of responsibility.

Outputs from Integration Planning
Acquisition integration plan, including milestones and timelines.[2]

Integration Communication

Integration Communication Objectives   Communicate plans and results to all key stakeholders.

Integration Communication Activities
Create and follow timeline for communication with all key stake-holders, using all key media.

Inputs to and Outputs from Integration Communication
*Milestone memos
*Communication grid.[3]
*Communication timelines.

Integration Implementation

Integration Implementation Objectives
To integrate the two companies in a rapid and cost-effective manner
To capture value identified during the Strategy phase in conformity with constraints and priorities identified in the Transaction phase.

Integration Implementation Activities
Form teams.
Set specific, measurable, integration goals.
Set timelines.
Acquire and use resources to make the plan happen.
Communicate on a regular basis and document all communications.

Inputs to Integration Implementation Activities
Partial list—includes only key summary documents for *core and support activities*; for *key financial, intellectual, human, physical, and relational assets*; and for *culture.*

Proposed acquisition timelines and milestones (value drivers).
Organization charts from the two organizations.
Financial statements from the two organizations.
Intellectual property/knowledge data bank from the two organizations.
Contracts and commitments from the two organizations.
Vision and mission statements from the two organizations.

Outputs from Integration Implementation Activities
Produced from partial list of inputs given here.

* *Reports on success in meeting acquisition timelines and milestones (value drivers).*
* *Organization charts for the combined organization.*
* *Financial statements for the combined organization* (combined income statements and balance sheets).[4]
* *Intellectual property/knowledge data bank for the combined organization.*
* *Contracts and commitments for the combined organization.*[5]
* *Vision and mission statements for the combined organization.*[6]

NOTES

1 The source of this appendix is E-Know, Arlington, Virginia. The author developed this entire tool in consultation with the cofounders of E-Know, Manuel Sanches and Larry Dell.

2 For a sample timeline, see Appendix 3-A.

3 For a communication matrix, see Appendix 3-B.

4 See the discussion of financial statement combinations in Chapter 5.

5 See the discussion of contracts in Chapter 12.

6 See the sample vision statement in Chapter 3.

Sample "Assets" Checklist of Resources, Processes, and Responsibilities[1]

Every corporation is composed of valuable resources, processes, and responsibilities. Following the acquisition of a company, it is important to make sure that management does not neglect any of these "assets" (using the term broadly). Every company will have its own list of assets, but this checklist may be helpful.

PHYSICAL ASSETS

Equipment*[2] (including computer hardware and software)
  Office equipment
  Plant equipment
Inventory*
  Finished
  Work-in-process
Land*
Materials
Mines
  Production, reserves, locations, development
  Maps
Real estate
  Branch buildings*
  Factory buildings*
  Construction in progress
Real estate—other*

FINANCIAL ASSETS

From Balance Sheet

Financial Assets*
  Cash
  Investment securities

Accounts receivable
Prepaid income taxes
Other prepaid expenses
Deferred charges
Other financial assets
    Goodwill
    Long-term receivables
    Investments in affiliates
    Goodwill from previous acquisitions
    For banks, debt owed to bank via outstanding loans

For other common balance sheet assets, such as Property, Plant, and Equipment, see "Physical Assets."

Financial Liabilities and Equity*
    Financial Liabilities
        Accounts payable
        Debt
        For banks, cash deposits held by bank and
            owed by bank to customers
    Financial Equity*
        Common stock outstanding
        Preferred stock outstanding
        Retained earnings

From Income Statement

Gross revenues
    Growth trend
Net revenues
    Growth trend

INTELLECTUAL ASSETS

Contracts (if favorable—otherwise, a liability)
    Employment agreements
    Franchise agreements
    No compete agreements

Culture
  Reporting relationships (real versus formal)
  Policies and procedures
  Any other cultural factor not covered elsewhere
    in this taxonomy
Marketing intangibles
  Company name recognition
  Brand name recognition
  Service mark (right to use company signage)
  Trademark (right to use company name)
Production intangibles
  Copyrights
  Favorable supplier contracts
  Patents
  Product design
  Product quality
  Production costs
  Production speed
  Productions standards
  Software
  Trade secrets

HUMAN ASSETS (PEOPLE)

Knowledge, experience, competencies, and leadership and/or
  teamwork ability of each of the following individuals:
  Directors (including chairman if separate)
  CEO/COO/president
  Other senior managers
  Sales force
  Other employees

See also "HR function" under "Organizational Assets."

ORGANIZATIONAL ASSETS (ACTIVITIES)

Quality of the "infrastructure" described here
  Contracts and commitments
    Relating to all human capital and also to external relations

*If a contract is unfavorable and/or broken, it can
turn from an asset into a liability.*

Primary Functions

Management systems
  Processes for design, production, and supply
  Channels for distribution
Inbound logistics (for manufacturing; see also "Purchasing"
  under "Support Functions")
  Receiving
  Storing
  Material handling
  Warehousing
  Inventory control
Outbound logistics
  Distribution
Manufacturing function
Quality control policies applied to production R&D function
  Laboratory notebooks
  Invention disclosure forms
Sales function
  Established territories

Support Functions

Accounting function
  Bookkeeping
  Treasury
  Internal auditing
Communications/marketing function(s)
  Marketing
  Public relations
Corporate administrative function
  Headquarters administration
Facilities function
  Facilities management
Finance function
  Financing (issuing equity, borrowing debt)

Management of funds (opening/closing deposits; lock box)
HR function
    Rewarding and giving incentives for performance)
        Base pay
        Bonus pay
        Pensions
        Benefits
        Special pay arrangements
        Recognition programs (awards and honors)
    Retention (retaining key qualities: relevant knowledge, experience, competencies)
    Recruitment (seeking relevant knowledge, experience, competencies)
    Termination/retirement (see also Compensation)
    Performance management
    Career development
    Succession planning
    Training
IT function
    Hardware, software, and systems for internal communications
        E-mail
        Telephones (LAN, WAN, routers, switches)
Legal function
    Compliance programs, including internal code of conduct (see also "Regulatory relations" in "External Relations")
    Purchasing function
    ——Policies pertaining to vendor relations.
    Internal Financial Controls (see COSO)
Control environment *
    Appropriateness of the entity's organizational structure and its ability to provide the necessary information to manage its activities
    Adequacy of definition of key managers' responsibilities and their understanding of these responsibilities
    Adequacy of knowledge and experience of key managers in light of their responsibilities
    Appropriateness of reporting relationships

Extent to which modifications to the structure are made in
light of changed conditions
Sufficiency of numbers of employees, particularly in man-
agement and supervisory capacity
Risk assessment
Control activities
Information/communication re finances
Monitoring

Mission, Vision, and Strategy

Mission statement
Vision statement
Strategic plan document

EXTERNAL RELATIONSHIP ASSETS

If any of these has a corresponding function, see that function
under Organizational Assets.

Customer relations
  Reputation of brands
  Reputation of service
  Major customers (required under SAS131)
  Major geographic areas (SAS131)
Shareholder relations
  Reputation for increasing market share/paying dividends
  Stability of holdings by shareholders
Bondholder relations
  Reputation for repaying debt instruments
  Bond rating
Lender relations
  Rate of interest charged by lenders
  Credit rating
Supplier relations
  Favorable contracts (see also "Production intangibles")
Community relations
  Community programs
Public relations

Reputation of company name re public issues—see also "Company name recognition" under "Intellectual Assets"

Regulatory Relations Lobbying (if any)—see also "Legal function" under "Support Functions"

History of fulfilling contracts and commitments

NOTES

1 This list can be used as column D of a spreadsheet with these columns:

Column A—**Phase 1: Strategy**
Subphases:
  Planning
  Search
  Valuation
  Selection

Column B—**Phase 2: Transaction**
Subphases (these start during the Strategy phase and extend through the Transaction phase)
  Due Diligence
  Financing
  Negotiation
  Tax Structuring
  Closing

Column C—**Phase 3: Integration**
Subphases (these start during the Transaction phase and extend through the Integration phase)
  Integration Planning
  Integration Communication
  Integration Implementation

Column D—**Assets to Track during All Phases**
For more on this subject, see Chapter 1 and Appendix A.

2 Items with an asterisk appear on the balance sheet. Items without an asterisk do not appear on the balance sheet or any other traditional financial statement. However, they are usually discussed in the Management Discussion and Analysis section of the 10-K report, along with balance sheet items, especially if they are at risk.

Pairwise Comparison

During integration, it is important to prioritize actions. One way to do this is to consider proposed actions in a series of pairs, picking the most important one pair by pair, and in that way creating a ranking. The following primer on "pairwise comparison" (using a stepladder as an example) can be useful.

INTRODUCTION

Pairwise comparison is a kind of divide-and-conquer problem-solving method. It allows one to determine the relative order (ranking) of a group of items. This is often used as part of a process of assigning weights to criteria in design concept development.

Consider the evaluation of a stepladder. In that problem, the following criteria were deemed pertinent:

- Functionality
- Durability
- Quality
- Affordability
- Fabricability
- Usability
- Maintainability
- Safety
- Marketability

In order to weigh these criteria, we could simply tackle the problem all at once and, for example, discuss what weight should be assigned to each criterion. This can be very difficult; it can become an insurmountable task in more complex problems where there may be dozens of criteria. An alternative is to divide the problem of assigning weights into two parts:

Determine *qualitatively* which criteria are more important—i.e., establish a ranking of the criteria.

Assign each criterion a quantitative weight so that the qualitative ranking is satisfied.

Pairwise comparison can be used for Step 1. Here's how it would work.

STEP 1: IDENTIFY THE CRITERIA TO BE RANKED

This has already been done. Typically, the criteria can be derived from the *functional requirements* and *product characteristics* determined during the development of a Product Design Specification. Assuming that you keep the PDS very handy while you evaluate concepts, you can just use the main PCs as the criteria—as we've done here.

STEP 2: ARRANGE THE CRITERIA IN AN *N* × *N* MATRIX

For the ladder design problem, the matrix would look like Table C-1.

Obviously, we need only one triangle of the matrix. That is, since the rows and columns contain exactly the same things in the same order, one triangle of the matrix will contain exactly the same cells as the other triangle.

Furthermore, the diagonal itself does not matter—it simply doesn't make sense to consider how important one criterion is with respect to itself! So now we have Table C-2.

STEP 3: COMPARE PAIRS OF ITEMS

For each row, consider the first item in the row with respect to each item in the rest of the row. In the example, we begin with functionality versus durability. Which is more important?

In the corresponding cell of the matrix, we put the letter of the item that we consider more important in each pairwise comparison. If we really, really think that the two criteria are equally important, we put both letters in the cell. There are, of course, other ways

TABLE C–1

Setting up the Pairwise Comparison Matrix

		A	B	C	D	E	F	G	H	
Functionality	A									
Durability	B									
Quality	C									
Affordability	D									
Fabricability	E									
Usability	F									
Maintainability	G									
Safety	H									
Marketability	I									

TABLE C−2

Identifying the Useful Part of the Matrix

		A	B	C	D	E	F	G	H	I
Functionality	A	—								
Durability	B	—	—							
Quality	C	—	—	—						
Affordability	D	—	—	—	—					
Fabricability	E	—	—	—	—	—				
Usability	F	—	—	—	—	—	—			
Maintainability	G	—	—	—	—	—	—	—		
Safety	H	—	—	—	—	—	—	—	—	
Marketability	I	—	—	—	—	—	—	—	—	—

to fill the cells. The point is that whatever way is chosen, it must indicate which of the items is more important.

Note that the comparison is *pairwise*—we completely ignore all the other criteria.

Say we determine that functionality is more important than durability. We would put an *A* in cell (2,4) of the matrix. We continue doing this until all the first row is complete. We then proceed to the second row and repeat until the upper triangle of the matrix is filled. We could end up with Table C-3.

Note the double letters. We have used this convention to indicate that there is no difference in importance between the items being compared.

STEP 4: CREATE THE RANKING OF ITEMS

Now we simply create an ordered list of the items, ranked by the number of cells containing their flag letter. This leads to:

1. Safety (7)
2. Usability (6)
3. Affordability (6)
4. Quality (5)
5. Marketability (5)
6. Functionality (4)
7. Durability (4)
8. Fabricability (2)
9. Maintainability (0)

CONCLUSION

We now have a ranked list of the relative importance of the various criteria. Given this, we can begin considering the actual weights we wish to attach. This is the extent of the pairwise comparison technique, but we can take this particular problem one step further and consider how we could assign the actual weights.

Consider the constraints on the problem of assigning weights.

TABLE C-3

Filling the Useful Part of the Matrix

	A	B	C	D	E	F	G	H	I
Functionality A	—	A	C	D	A	F	A	AH	—
Durability B	—	—	C	D	B	B	B	H	BI
Quality C	—	—	—	D	C	F	C	H	C
Affordability D	—	—	—	—	D	F	D	D	—
Fabricability E	—	—	—	—	—	F	E	H	E
Usability F	—	—	—	—	—	—	F	FH	—
Maintainability G	—	—	—	—	—	—	—	H	—
Safety H	—	—	—	—	—	—	—	—	H
Marketability I	—	—	—	—	—	—	—	—	—

470

1. The total of all the weights must be 100 percent.
2. The weights must obey the qualitative ranking given in Step 4.

We can begin to wrestle with the problem in a strictly ad-hoc manner, or we can try to structure our solution. It's inevitable that some iteration will be required, so there's no point in looking for a method that will give us actual weights in one pass.

However, we can try to set up an initial set of values that satisfies the constraints, and then tweak the values until they are satisfactory to all stakeholders.

One very easy way to get that initial set of values is to assume a linear proportion between all the weights and solve the following equation:

$$100 = 7x + 6x + 6x + 5x + 5x + 4x + 4x + 2x + 0x$$

Therefore,

$$x = 2.56 \text{ (approx)}$$

where the coefficients are the number of occurrences of each criterion in the matrix. This leads to

- Safety: $7x = 18$
- Usability and affordability: $6x = 15$
- Quality and marketability: $5x = 13$
- Functionality and durability: $4x = 10$
- Fabricability: $2x = 5$
- Maintainability: $0x = 1$

Note: The "1" for maintainability arose by gathering all the round-off errors from the other calculations.

There are obviously problems with this. For example, the lowest-ranked item in a pairwise comparison will, strictly speaking *always* end up with zero importance. This means that we cannot assume that zero importance implies that we can omit the item altogether. If, for example, we omit maintainability because it ranked zero and redo the pairwise comparison, we will then find that fabricability will now rank zero. This would quickly lead to a set of *no* criteria at all.

Still, there is now a baseline from which meaningful discussion can ensue. It is noted that we can get the actual weights shown in the concept evaluation matrix by taking a few points away from each criterion and giving them to the handling criterion. This may be enough.

Whatever is done, however, it is *essential* that all stakeholders in the project agree to the actual weights.

Source: Provided by Professor Filippo A. Salustri
(salustri@ryerson.ca), Assistant Professor, Mechanical
Engineering, Ryerson University, Toronto, Canada.

Sample Integration Planning Process (as shown in Table 3-1)

prepare to plan	assess current environment	define integration plan objectives	develop plans and identify resources	validate plan
define core operating model	identify key areas for "as is" analysis	define critical integration areas and objectives	develop action plans for each integration area	validate integration area action plans against integration area objectives
determine governance structure & exec. leadership	identify and collect data required for "as is" analysis	define scope of integration for each integration area	develop preliminary consolidated integration plan	validate consolidated integration plan against acquisition objectives
define integration scope, objectives, and critical success factors	plan/schedule and conduct site visits and interviews	define integration priorities	define resource requirements for integration projects	review plan with executive leadership for approval
develop high-level integration plan	document results		quantify costs and benefits for integration projects	launch integration plan
develop integration timeline			finalize consolidated integration plan and timeline	
define provisions for integration and assemble transition teams				
develop communications strategy				

Source: E-Know, Arlington, Virginia © 2005.

Prepare to plan

activity	task	desired outcome
develop core operating model	• determine core business activities – firm model	– firm model
determine governance structure and executive leadership	• define key leadership positions for new organization ■ i.e. board, CEO, senior management, other • define organization chart for new entity	– leadership team – organization chart

define integration scope, objectives and critical success factors (csf's)	• review corporate/business unit strategy and the core competency needs of the combined company
	 • review acquisition strategy and acquisition criteria
	 • review target profile
	 • review terms of the deal
	 • review the results of the due diligence analysis and assess the implications of integration
	   ■ strategic
	   ■ operational
	   ■ legal
	   ■ environmental
	   ■ cultural
	 • review value drivers for the combined company
	 • define critical areas for integration
	 • define requirements for the transition phase
	 • define integration priorities and required scope of integration
	 • define critical success factors
	 • determine key value drivers
		– deal summary worksheet
		 – acquiree profile
		 – critical success factors
		 – value drivers

develop high-level integration plan	• develop high-level integration plan based on masterplan template	– high-level integration plan
develop integration timeline	• identify key milestones and check points • develop program management meeting schedule	– timeline – checkpoints

(Continued)

| define provisions for integration and organize transition team | • determine operating guidelines
• levels of participation for acquirer/acquiree
• formation of task forces
• planning phases
• leadership roles
• organize transaction team | – transition team
– roles and responsibilities |
| develop communications strategy | • determine communication's who, what, when, and how | – communications strategy |

Assess current environment

activity	task	desired outcome

identify key areas for "as is" analysis	• identify target areas:
	  ■ primary activities
	  ■ support activities
	  ■ corporate responsibilities
	  ■ intangible assets and intellectual property
	  ■ corporate culture
		– list of focus areas

identify and collect data required for "as is" analysis	• determine data required for each area • determine who has responsibility for each area • collect data	– data for as is analysis
plan/schedule and conduct site visits and interviews	• determine data needed from interviews • plan/schedule interviews and site visits • conduct interviews	– site visit and interview results

document results	• document:
	  ■ observations regarding assumptions, synergies, opportunities, and challenges
	  ■ potential synergies
	  ■ integration risk
	  ■ opportunities
	  ■ high-level organizational structure and staffing requirements
	  ■ infrastructure needs
	  ■ information systems requirements
		– AS IS analysis

Define integration plan objectives

activity	task	desired outcome
define critical integration areas and objectives	• connect objectives to integration csf's • conduct integration inventory to define workstreams • identify key stakeholders	– inventory of activities – detailed integration objectives by workstream
determine scope of integration for each area	• determine whether/how to integrate each workstream • determine when to integrate • determine level of integration	– commitments to integrate – communications requirements – cultural integration requirements
define integration priorities	• prioritize based on integration objectives	– refined high-level integration timeline

Develop plans and identify resources

activity	task	desired outcome

develop action plans for each integration area	• for each workstream, define
	   ■ objectives
	   ■ action items
	   ■ action item and plan dependencies
	   ■ timeframes
	   ■ resourace requirements
	   ■ deliverables
	   ■ "area" communications plans
	   ■ performance measures
	   ■ costs/benefits
	 • develop detailed cultural integration plan
	 • develop detailed communications plan
	 • connect action items to value drivers
		– preliminary workstream plans

develop preliminary consolidated plan	• consolidate each workstream plan • validate completeness to masterplan • identify plan dependencies and constraints	– preliminary consolidated integration plan – integration priorities and dependencies
define resource requirements	• define resource requirements for the consolidated plan • update consolidated plan with resource requirements	– preliminary consolidated integration plan with resource requirements
quantify costs and benefits of integration	• determine costs and benefits of preliminary plan	– cost/benefit analysis
finalize consolidated plan and timeline	• summarize resource requirements • develop integration calendar • finalize preliminary consolidated plan • determine action plan items that can be enabled by communications and planning technology	– finalized preliminary consolidated plan

Validate plan

activity	task	desired outcome
validate integration area plans against integration area objectives	• consensus meetings to review plan draft • review plan against value drivers and overall integration objectives • revise plan as necessary • follow-up meeting if necessary	– updated plan draft
validate consolidated integration plan against acquisition objectives	• consensus meetings to review plan draft • review plan against value drivers and overall integration objectives • revise plan as necessary • follow-up meeting if necessary	– updated plan draft
review plan with executive leadership for approval	• consensus meetings to review plan draft • review plan against value drivers and overall integration objectives • revise plan as necessary • follow-up meeting if necessary	– updated plan draft
launch integration plan	• revise plan as necessary	– a living integration plan

Sample Press Releases
Generic models based on recent, real examples, highlighting passages pertaining to postmerger integration

Joint premerger press release—high-tech

Joint postmerger press release—high-tech

Joint premerger press release—industrial

Joint postmerger press release—industrial

Premerger press release from target in hostile takeover—high tech

Postmerger press release from acquirer in hostile takeover—high tech postmerger press release from acquirer—retailer

1. JOINT PREMERGER PRESS RELEASE—HIGH TECH

Software industry leaders Company A and Company B to merge

Combination reduces complexity of securing and managing information

CITY, STATE and CITY, STATE (Date)—Company A and Company B today announced that the companies have entered into a definitive agreement to merge in an all-stock transaction. Based on Company B's stock price of $XX.XX at market close on (date), the transaction is valued at approximately $XX.X billion/million.

The new company will provide leading communications technology for the _____ industry, offering customers with new ways to manage their information and to protect it from risk. *The combined company will have a unique ability to deliver information solutions and security across all platforms drawing on extensive service providing solutions to private sector companies as well as state and federal government agencies overseeing the industry.*

Under the agreement, which has been unanimously approved by both boards of directors, Company B's stock will be converted into Company A's stock at a fixed exchange ratio of X. XXXX shares of Company A common stock for each outstanding share of Company A common stock. Upon closing, Company A shareholders will own approximately 60 percent and Company B shareholders approximately 40 percent of the combined company. The transaction is expected to be tax-free to shareholders of both companies for U.S. federal income tax purposes.

The combined company will operate under the Company A name. _____, Chairman and Chief Executive Officer of Company A, will continue as Chairman and CEO of the combined company. _____, Chairman, President, and Chief Executive Officer of Company B, will be Vice-Chairman and President of the combined company. The board of directors of the combined company will include 6 members of Company A's current board and 4 from Company B's current board, for a total of 10 members.

*"As our industry evolves, customers are looking for new ways to communicate their important management information," said*_____ *Chairman and CEO, Company A. "The new Company A will help customers achieve this goal."*

"Our customers deserve the best solutions, and we can deliver them," said _____, Chairman, President and CEO of Company B. "This merger will enable our company to combine our core products in ways that can help our customers work more efficiently." By merging with Company B, Company A will gain more financial resources to invest in future research and development. The aggregate revenue of the combined company is expected to be approximately $X billion/million for fiscal year 200X, which begins in April 200X and ends in March 200X. Approximately 75 percent of the revenue of the combined company is expected to come from our business to business work, and 25 percent from our work with regulatory agencies.

The combination will create significant benefits for the customers and partners of both companies, including:

- *Product variety—A broad range of leading communications and data storage solutions at every tier of the enterprise—end point, gateway, and application—across all platforms from a single vendor;*

- *Technological strength—Leading-edge technology combined with expertise in designing and managing communications, storage, and IT infrastructures; and*
- *Distribution power—Worldwide sales, service, and channel partner organizations supporting millions of consumers, and small, medium, and large enterprise customers.*

The transaction is expected to close in the second calendar quarter of 200X and is subject to customary closing conditions, including approval by the shareholders of both companies and regulatory approvals. Non-GAAP earnings per share for this transaction, which exclude the amortization of deal-related intangibles, the write-down of Company B's deferred revenue, restructuring charges, amortization of deferred compensation, and any one-time costs associated with the merger, will be accretive in the first combined year of operations.

The companies will be holding a joint Webcast for press and interested investors from 9 A.M. to 10 A.M. Eastern Standard Time. To join the Webcast, go to the CompanyA.com home page, and click on the "Webcast" link.

Forward-Looking Statements. This press release contains forward-looking statements, including forecasts of future revenue and earnings per share, expected industry patterns, and other financial and business results that involve known and unknown risks, uncertainties and other factors that may cause our actual results, levels of activity, and performance or achievements to differ materially from results expressed or implied by this press release. Such risk factors include, among others: . . . *ability to integrate acquired companies and technology; ability to retain key employees; ability to successfully combine product offerings and customer acceptance of the combined company's product.*

2. JOINT POSTMERGER PRESS RELEASE—HIGH TECH

Company A and Company B Complete Merger

CITY, STATE (Date)—Company A (Nasdaq: XXXX) and Company B today announced the completion of their merger following approvals by both companies' stockholders. The transaction was finalized on (date). As a result of the merger, shares of Company B stock were converted into the right to receive shares of Company A stock, and Company B shares will no longer be traded.

By merging leaders in communications software and storage software, Company A will provide its business and government customers with a more effective way to manage their most valuable asset, their information. Company A can now deliver information communications and storage solutions across all platforms and to customers of all sizes.

About Company A

Company A is a leader in providing solutions to help individuals and enterprises communicate and store information. Headquartered in (City), Company A has operations in more than 40 countries. More information is available at www.companya.com.

3. JOINT PREMERGER PRESS RELEASE–INDUSTRIAL

Materials Processor and Manufacturer Announce Definitive Merger Agreement

Merger Creates Vertically Integrated Processor and Manufacturer with Leading Market Positions and $X Billion/Million in Annual Revenues–Management Team to Lead Merged Company Brings Deep Experience and Strong Track Record of Generating Shareholder Value

CITY, STATE and CITY, STATE (Date)—Company C (Ticker: CCC) and Company D (Ticker: DDD) announced today that they have signed a definitive merger agreement creating a vertically integrated materials processor and manufacturer. The strategic combination will have approximately $X billion in annual revenues (based on last twelve months), X,XXX employees, XX facilities worldwide, a leading global position in the _____ processing industry, a leading position in North American _____ manufacturing industry, and a leading U.S. position in _____ recycling.

Under the terms of the merger agreement, which was unanimously approved by the Boards of Directors of both companies, Company D stockholders will receive 0.XXX Company C shares in exchange for each of their Company D shares. Upon the completion of the transaction, Company C stockholders will own approximately 54 percent and Company D stockholders approximately 46 percent of the merged entity, based on the number of shares outstanding as of June 16, 200X. As of the close of trading on Wednesday, June 16, 200X, the combined equity market capitalization of Company C and Company D was about $XXX million. The merger transaction is expected to be tax-free to the stockholders of both companies and is expected to close in the fourth quarter of 200X, subject to the approval of the stockholders of both companies, approval under the Hart Scott Rodino Act, refinancing of indebtedness and other customary closing conditions.

Upon completion of the transaction, _____, who has served as a Company D President and Chief Executive Officer (CEO) since (date), will be Chairman and CEO of the combined company, _____. _____, President and CEO of Company D, will serve as President of the company's Materials Processing Division. The current Chairman and CEO of Company C has announced his retirement, effective June 200X. The Board of Directors of the combined company will include four directors from each company, plus the new Chairman and CEO. The combined company is expected to be named and its headquarters selected prior to the closing of the transaction.

Commenting on the planned merger, Chairman and CEO _____ said, *"This strategic combination creates a new vertically integrated company that can be a strong competitor in the _____ processing and production industries. The merged company will benefit from significant procurement savings and cost synergies, an enhanced competitive position, increased scope and scale, greater technological capabilities, as well as improved access to capital. We plan to dedicate these combined benefits to create customer value through enhanced service and product offerings, and to increase the growth of this business over the long-term."*

_____, retiring Chairman of Company C, said, *"This merger of equals integrates one of the world's largest processors of _____ with the U.S.'s leading manufacturer of _____. In addition to the compelling competitive advantages, the merged company will benefit from significant operational and technology synergies that will drive productivity, as well as cost savings. We expect the new company will deliver significant value to stockholders."*

The Company expects to achieve an annual cost synergy run rate of approximately $XX million in the 18 to 24 months after the close of the merger from *procurement savings, the integration of complementary operations, selling, general and administrative cost reductions, and the application of best practices at plant operations.*

The companies will be holding a joint teleconference call for press and interested investors from 9 A.M. to 10 A.M. Eastern Standard Time. To join the call, go to the companyc.com home page, and click on the "conference call" link.

Forward-Looking Statements. Certain statements set forth above may constitute forward-looking statements within the meaning of the Private Securities Litigation Reform Act of 1995. *All statements regarding the consummation of the closing of the definitive merger agreement and the companies' expected future financial position, results of operations, cash flows, funds from operations, dividends, financing plans, business strategy, budgets, projected costs, capital expenditures, anticipated synergies, competitive position, technical capabilities, access to capital and growth opportunities are forward-looking statements.* Such forward-looking statements are based on management's current expectations and include known and unknown risks, uncertainties and other factors [that] may include, without limitation, *the ability to complete the merger while obtaining the approval of the regulatory agencies and shareholders, the ability to successful integrate and achieve cost savings and revenue enhancements in connection with the transaction,* the *success of the implementation of the information system across both companies,* the effect of global economic conditions, the ability to achieve the level of *cost savings or productivity improvements anticipated by management,* the effect (including possible increases in the cost of doing business) resulting from war or terrorist activities or political uncertainties, the ability to successfully implement *new marketing and sales strategies, . . . , the success of the companies in implementing their respective business strategies,* and other risks as detailed in the companies' various filings with the SEC.

4. JOINT POSTMERGER PRESS RELEASE—INDUSTRIAL

Company C, Company D Merger Finalized

Company C and Company D today finalize their merger and begin business under the name Company CD International, Inc. The merger has resulted in the retirement of a number of top Company C executives. This strategic combination created a vertically integrated _____ processor and manufacturer. Company CD has more than $X billion in annual net sales (based on last 12 months), X, XXX employees and XX production facilities worldwide.

Company CD is one of the world's largest processors of _____ and one of North America's leading manufacturers of _____. The company has XX U.S. production plants and five international facilities located in (countries).

As a result of the merger, _____, outgoing chief executive officer of Company A, announced the retirement of _____ [Insert career accomplishments of retiring executives.]

In his statement, _____ said Company D expresses great appreciation to these four individuals for their contributions to the growth of the company and wishes them well in future endeavors.

5. PREMERGER PRESS RELEASE FROM TARGET IN HOSTILE TAKEOVER—HIGH TECH

Company Y Agrees to Definitive Merger Agreement with Company X at $XX.XX Per Share in Cash; Total Transaction Value Approximately $X Billion

CITY (date). Company Y (YYYY) today announced that following discussions throughout the weekend, the Board of Directors, based upon the recommendation of the Transaction Committee of independent directors, has approved a definitive merger agreement under which a subsidiary of Company X (XXXX) will acquire all Company X shares for $XX.XX per share in cash. The total value of the transaction is approximately $X.X billion.

Under terms of the agreement, Company X will revise its tender offer by this Wednesday, December XXth, and it will remain open through December XXth, unless extended in accordance with the merger agreement. The Board recommends that Company Y stockholders tender their shares into Company Y's offer. Following the completion of the tender offer, Company Y intends to complete a merger in which all remaining Company X shares will be acquired for $XX.XX per share.

_____, Chairman of Company X's Transaction Committee, a board committee composed of independent directors, said, "After careful consideration, we believe this revised offer provides good value for Company Y stockholders and represents a substantial increase in value from the previous bid. Company Y is a strong and vibrant company. Our fourth quarter numbers have been running ahead of plan. Our ability to deliver this shareholder value would not have been possible without the relentless efforts of our employees. This has been a long, emotional struggle, and our employees have consistently performed well under the most challenging of circumstances. The Board salutes our employees for their outstanding dedication to Company Y and is grateful to our customers who have continued to buy our products and stand by us during these uncertain times."

Company X and Company Y will each stay all pending litigation and will dismiss such litigation permanently following the consummation of the offer.

The offer is subject to at least a majority of the fully diluted outstanding shares being validly tendered into the offer and to a limited number of other customary conditions.

Forward-Looking Statements. This press release may contain forward-looking statements that state Company Y's intentions, beliefs, expectations, or predictions for the future. . . . Forward-looking statements are subject to a number of risks, assumptions, and uncertainties that could cause actual results to differ materially from those projected in such forward-looking statements. These risks, assumptions, and uncertainties include, but are not limited to: *the costs and disruption to Company Y's business arising from the Company X tender offer and related litigation; the Company's ability to successfully complete the integration of a previous acquisitions into Company Y and to achieve anticipated synergies.*

[The press release concludes with additional information about filings and contact information.]

6. POSTMERGER PRESS RELEASE FROM ACQUIRER IN HOSTILE TAKEOVER—LARGE

Company Y Announces Combined Workforce

CITY (Date)—Company Y today announced that its *integration plan is proceeding on schedule and that it will be reducing the size of its combined workforce to XX,XXX, a reduction of approximately 10 percent.*

Notifications at Company Y and Company X began today and a majority will be completed over the next ten days.

Company X plans to retain over 90 percent of Company Y product development and product support staff. The Company Y development team will finish the development and deployment of Company Y Key Product Version, and then begin development of the next upgrade to this version. The Company Y support teams, with the assistance of the Company X support organization, will continue to support Company Y customers around the world.

"By retaining the vast majority of Company Y technical staff, Company X will have the resources to deliver on the development and support commitments we have made to Company Y customers over the last 18 months," said Company X CEO _____.

Detailed information about Company X's applications organization, product plans, and go-to-market strategies will be presented to customers and partners next week at the launch of the combined applications business.

Company X completed its acquisition of Company Y on (date), following the completion of a tender offer in which more than XX percent of Company Y shareholders tendered their stock.

7. POSTMERGER PRESS RELEASE FROM ACQUIRER – LARGE RETAILER

R1 Holding Corporation and R2 Agree to Merger

Combination Creates U.S. Retailer With $X Billion in Annual Revenues; Will Have Broader Retail Presence and Improved Scale and Operational Efficiency

CITY (Date)

R1 Holding Corporation (R1R1) and R2 (R2R2) announced today they have signed a definitive merger agreement that will *combine R2 and R1 into a major new retail company named R2 Holdings Corporation.* R2 Holdings will be the nation's third largest retailer, with approximately $X billion in annual revenues, XXX full-line and off-mall stores, and XXX specialty retail stores.

Both R2 and R1 have made significant strides in transforming their organizations, and the merger will further accelerate this process for both companies. R2 Holdings will be headquartered in (city) and R1 will continue to have a significant presence in (city). *The combined business will have a broader retail presence and improved scale through a national footprint of nearly XXX retail stores. The combined company will also benefit from improved operational efficiency in areas such as procurement, marketing, information technology and supply chain management.*

Under the terms of the agreement, which was unanimously approved by both companies' boards of directors, R1 shareholders will receive one share of new R2 Holdings common stock for each R1 share. R2, shareholders will have the right to elect $50.00 in cash or 0.5 shares of R2 Holdings (valued at $50.61 based on yesterday's closing price of R1 shares) for each R2 share. Shareholder elections will be prorated to ensure that in the aggregate 55 percent of R2 shares will be converted into R2 Holdings shares and 45 percent of R2 shares will be converted into cash. The current value of the transaction to R2 shareholders is approximately $11 billion. The transaction is expected to be tax-free to R1 shareholders and tax-free to R2 shareholders to the extent they receive stock.

_____, Chairman of R1, will be the Chairman of R2 Holdings. He will be joined in an Office of the Chairman by _____, current chairman and chief executive officer of R2, and _____, current president and chief executive officer of R1. _____ will be vice chairman and chief executive officer of R2 Holdings; _____ will be president of R2 Holdings and chief executive officer of R1 and R2 Retail._____, currently executive vice president and chief financial officer of R2, will be executive vice president and chief financial officer of R2 Holdings._____, currently senior vice president - finance of R1 and a R1 Board member, will be executive vice president, finance and integration of R2 Holdings.

These officers will join a ten-member R2 Holdings board of directors, which will include a total of seven members of the current R1 board and three members of the current R2, Roebuck board. R2 Holdings will act as the holding company for the R2 and R1 businesses, which will continue to operate separately under their respective brand names.

Chairman _____ *said, "The combination of R1 and R2 is extremely compelling for our customers, associates and shareholders as it will create a powerful leader in the retail industry, with greatly expanded points of distribution, leading proprietary brands and significant opportunities for improved scale and operating efficiencies. The merger will enable us to manage the businesses of R2 and R1 to produce a higher return than either company could achieve on its own."*

Vice-Chairman _____ said, *"The combination will greatly strengthen both the R2 and R1 franchises by accelerating the R2 off-mall growth strategy and enhancing the brand portfolio of both companies. This will clearly be a win for both companies' customers while significantly enhancing value for all shareholders. We will have a total combined store base of nearly XXX stores and the leading service organization in the industry capable of a major expansion to serve the needs of existing R1 and R2 customers."*

_____ said, *"R1 has made great progress over the past 18 months to strengthen the organization in terms of profitability and product offerings. We believe the combination of R1 and R2 will create a true leader in the retail industry—both as a key part of local communities and as a national presence. Together, we will further enhance our capabilities to better serve customers by improving in-store execution and ultimately transforming the customer's in-store experience."*

R2 Holdings will feature a powerful _____ franchise as well as strong positions in _____. Key proprietary brands include _____, _____, and _____. The company will have a broad apparel offering, including such well-known labels as _____, _____, and _____. R1 specialty retail stores will continue to carry their current lineup in proprietary home and fashion lines including _____, _____, _____, and _____. *The combination of the two companies is conservatively estimated to generate $XX million of annualized cost and revenue synergies to be fully realized by the end of the third year after closing. The transaction, after giving effect to estimated synergies, is expected to be significantly accretive to earnings per share in the first year before one-time restructuring costs.*

The companies expect to realize approximately $XX million in incremental gross margin from revenue synergies by capitalizing on cross-selling opportunities between R1 and R2' proprietary brands and by converting a substantial number of R1 stores to the R2 nameplate in addition to the XX R1 stores R2 acquired earlier this year.

The company expects to achieve annual cost savings of over $XX million principally through improved merchandising and non-merchandising purchasing scale as well as improved supply chain, *administrative and other operational efficiencies. In addition, the combined company will complete a full store asset review as part of a plan to monetize non-strategic real estate assets as appropriate.*

The Chairman and Vice-Chairman will jointly lead an integration team of key operating executives from both companies to drive planning and execution of the integration of the companies' operations.

The merger, which is expected to close by the end of (date), is subject to approval by R1 and R2 shareholders, regulatory approvals, and customary closing conditions.

The companies will be holding a series of joint Webcasts for press and interested investors from 9 A.M. to 10 A.M. Eastern Standard Time. To join the Webcast, go to the R2.com home page, and click on the "Webcast" link.

Forward-Looking Statements. This press release contains forward-looking statements within the meaning of the Private Securities Litigation Reform Act of 1995. *Such statements include, but are not limited to, statements about the benefits of the business combination transaction involving R1 and R2, including future financial and operating results, the new company's plans, objectives, expectations and intentions and other statements that are not historical facts. Such statements are based upon the current beliefs and expectations of R1's and R2's management and are subject to significant risks and uncertainties. Actual results may differ from those set forth in the forward-looking statements.*

The following factors, among others, could cause actual results to differ from those set forth in the forward-looking statements: *the ability to obtain governmental approvals of the transaction on the proposed terms and schedule; the failure of R1 and R2 stockholders to approve the transaction; the risk that the businesses will not be integrated successfully; the risk that the cost savings and any other synergies from the transaction may not be fully realized or may take longer to realize than expected; disruption from the transaction making it more difficult to maintain relationships with customers, employees, or suppliers; competition and its effect on pricing, spending, third-party relationships, and revenues.*

Screen Shots from an M&A Integration "Cockpit"

The S3 Cockpit is an M&A integration management system developed by M&A Partners in Dallas, Texas. The tool manages work flow and offers complete "drill-down" capabilities to provide management with transparency for merger-related actions, issues, documents, and metrics. The system features work flow at the individual, team, and enterprise levels. Collaboration between all users, with document management with version control and search capabilities, is incorporated. The system leverages "point-to-point" meetings that enable users to connect through the Internet with audio, video, and desktop sharing. Also, iMemos allow for the creation of mass e-mail for surveys, announcements, and so on.

FIGURE F-1

Log-in page. All users are given various levels of access to view or interact within the Cockpit.

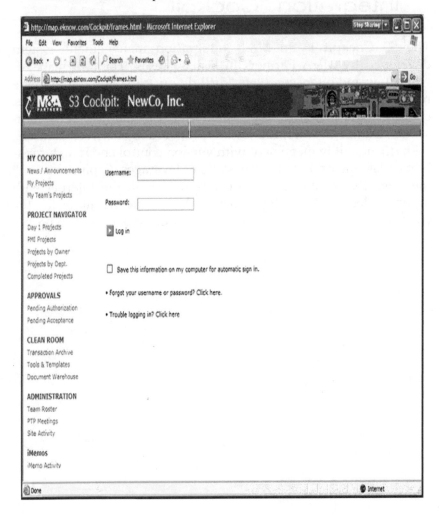

FIGURE F – 2

Clean Room

Housed within the exclusive clean room are areas of the highest security. Prior to transaction close, these should be accessed only by authorized third parties or others who can conform to Department of Justice requirements in the event that the transaction does not close. The Transaction Archive (collapsed and expanded) is the area where all of the documents and historic activities leading up to the announcement are kept for access by authorized users prior to and after close.

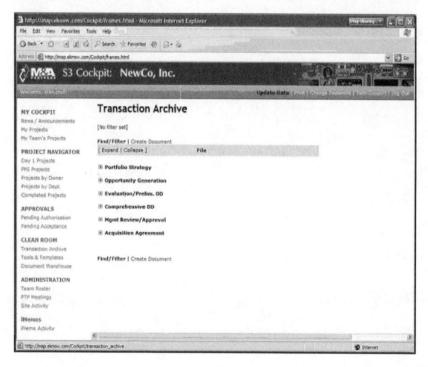

FIGURE F-3

Tools and Templates library (collapsed)

Diagnostic and other tools and standard templates are housed in the library for easy access by topic and can be issued to or requested by integration team members for training, assessing actions, planning, implementing, or measuring.

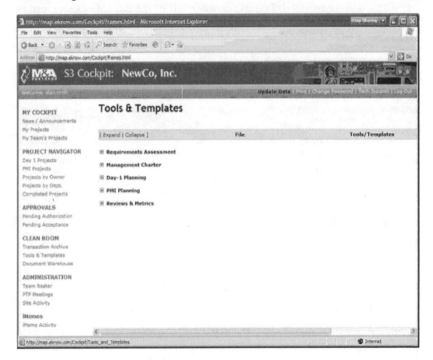

FIGURE F-4

Tools and Templates library (expanded).

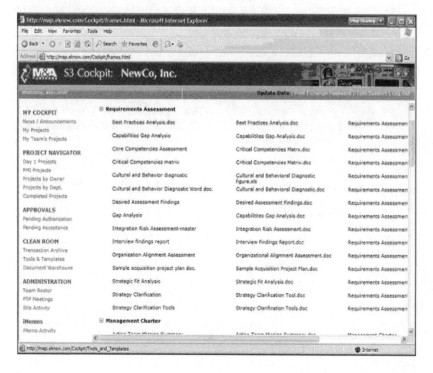

FIGURE F – 5

Document Warehouse

This is the secure area where the most sensitive documents from the merging companies are housed for analysis.

FIGURE F-6

Project form

Each assignment (project) begins by filling out a simple form with drop-down menus for selecting personnel, departments, authorizers, approvers, and so on. Once the form is saved, it generates notifications to the assignee, manager, and/or approver, as determined by the author. This simple form contains descriptions, related documents, financial values, due dates, history, and continual status of the project.

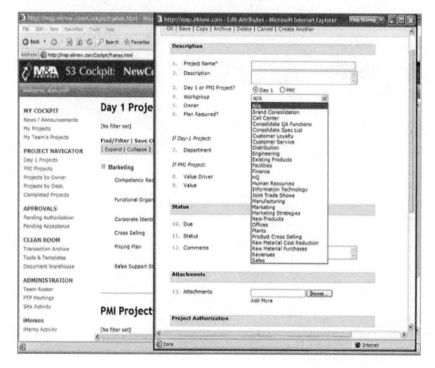

FIGURE F-7

My Cockpit

Each user is assigned a personal cockpit that he or she enters upon sign-in. The cockpits are divided into two areas—Day 1 Projects and Postmerger Integration (PMI) Projects. When each area is expanded, the user is given an "at a glance" view displaying all projects, descriptions, due date, status light, and comments regarding the status. By clicking on the project name, the user is taken to the project form, which is prepopulated with all the information.

FIGURE F-8

My Cockpit (Expanded)

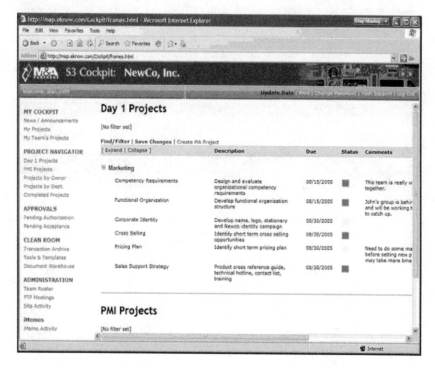

FIGURE F-9

Team Leader Cockpit

Each team leader can observe and manage from a Team Leader Cockpit that displays all actions for the team by Day 1 departmentally or PMI by value driver (collapsed and expanded view). Value driver projects will most often be assigned a dollar value when synergy actions are planned. As synergy actions are completed, the dollar values of the actions are rolled up and totaled upon electronic approval.

FIGURE F-10

Report Views

Based on user security level, management may access and view a number of reports, including All Day 1 Projects, All PMI Projects, Projects by Owner, Projects by Department, Completed Projects, and others.

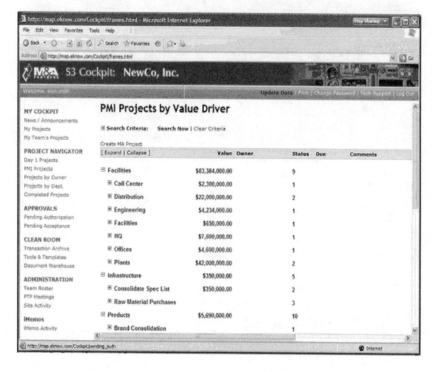

FIGURE F-11

Directory

Cockpits maintain a directory for communications as well as to schedule point-to-point meetings.

FIGURE F-12

iMemos

iMemos are used for mass messaging and surveys. This technology allows for the tracking of messages from management, administering employee and customer surveys, and so on.

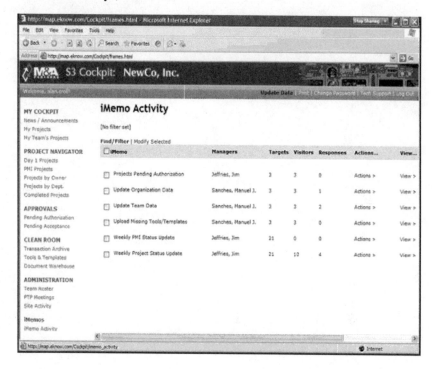

Baldrige Self-Analysis Worksheet for Quality Assessment (optional)

For confidential company use. Not to be submitted with the application for the Baldrige Award.

While insights gained from external examiners or reviewers are always helpful, you know your organization better than they will. You are currently in an excellent position to identify your organization's key strengths and key opportunities for improvement (OFIs).

Use this optional worksheet to list your key strengths and key OFIs. Start by identifying one or two strengths and one or two OFIs for each criteria category. For those of high importance, establish a goal and a plan of action.

Criteria Category	Importance High, Medium, Low	Stretch (Strength) or Improvement (OFI) Goal	For High-Importance Areas		Who Is Responsible?
			What Action Is Planned?	By When?	

Category 1—Leadership

Strength
1.
2.
OFI
1.
2.

Category 2—Strategic Planning

Strength
1.
2.
OFI
1.
2.

Category 3—Customer and Market Focus

Strength
1.
2.
OFI
1.
2.

Category 4—Measurement, Analysis, and Knowledge Management

Strength
1.
2.

(Continued)

Criteria Category	Importance High, Medium, Low	Stretch (Strength) or Improvement (OFI) Goal	For High-Importance Areas		
			What Action Is Planned?	By When?	Who Is Responsible?
		Category 5—Human Resource Focus			
OFI					
1.					
2.					
Strength					
1.					
2.					
OFI					
1.					
2.					
		Category 6—Process Management			
Strength					
1.					
2.					
OFI					
1.					
2.					
		Category 7—Business Results			
Strength					
1.					
2.					
OFI					
1.					
2.					

Source: Baldrige National Quality Program 2005, http://www.quality.nist.gov/Criteria.htm.

INDEX

Alexandra Reed Lajoux, M.B.A., Ph.D., is chief knowledge officer of the National Association of Corporate Directors (NACD). She has written extensively on corporate governance, mergers and acquisitions, international trade, and corporate finance. Coauthor of the bestselling *Art of M&A* (with her father Stanley Foster Reed), she is lead coauthor of McGraw-Hill's "Art of M&A" series, recruiting and writing with a variety of specialists on M&A topics including due diligence, financing, and structuring. Dr. Lajoux is past editor of *Mergers & Acquisitions*, *Directors & Boards*, *Export Today*, and NACD's *Director's Monthly*.